THE SOCIAL MEDIA BUSINESS EQUATION: USING ONLINE CONNECTIONS TO GROW YOUR BOTTOM LINE

Eve Mayer Orsburn

Course Technology PTR

A part of Cengage Learning

COURSE TECHNOLOGY
CENGAGE Learning™

Australia, Brazil, Japan, Korea, Mexico, Singapore, Spain, United Kingdom, United States

COURSE TECHNOLOGY
CENGAGE Learning™

The Social Media Business Equation: Using Online Connections to Grow Your Bottom Line
Eve Mayer Orsburn

Publisher and General Manager, Course Technology PTR:
Stacy L. Hiquet

Associate Director of Marketing:
Sarah Panella

Manager of Editorial Services:
Heather Talbot

Marketing Manager:
Mark Hughes

Senior Acquisitions Editor:
Mitzi Koontz

Project Editor:
Kate Shoup

Copy Editor:
Kate Shoup

Interior Layout Tech:
William Hartman

Cover Designer:
Jamie Nanquil

Indexer:
Valerie Haynes Perry

Proofreader: Sandi Wilson

Course Technology, a part of Cengage Learning
20 Channel Center Street
Boston, MA 02210
USA

For product information and technology assistance, contact us at **Cengage Learning Customer & Sales Support, 1-800-354-9706.**

For permission to use material from this text or product, submit all requests online at **cengage.com/permissions**. Further permissions questions can be e-mailed to **permissionrequest@cengage.com**.

All trademarks are the property of their respective owners.

All images © Cengage Learning unless otherwise noted.

Library of Congress Control Number: 2011924482

ISBN-13: 978-1-4354-5986-1

ISBN-10: 1-4354-5986-5

Cengage Learning is a leading provider of customized learning solutions with office locations around the globe, including Singapore, the United Kingdom, Australia, Mexico, Brazil, and Japan. Locate your local office at: **international.cengage.com/region**.

Cengage Learning products are represented in Canada by Nelson Education, Ltd.

For your lifelong learning solutions, visit **courseptr.com**.

Visit our corporate website at **cengage.com**.

Printed in the United States of America
2 3 4 5 6 7 13 12 11

This book is dedicated to my family

Guy and Regina Mayer, my parents,
who started it

Rob Orsburn, my husband,
who supported it

Mia Mayer Orsburn, my daughter,
who makes it all worth it

This book would not have been possible or made
sense without my online connections and friends,
many of whom are listed at the end of this book.
Thank you.

About the Author

Photo by David McGhee
(http://davidmcgheephotography.net)
Hair by Robert Wilson of Live Hair Group

Eve Mayer Orsburn is the CEO of Social Media Delivered, one of the fastest growing social media–optimization companies serving clients in the USA, Canada, and Europe. Eve is one of the most sought-after speakers worldwide on the subject of social media for corporations and nonprofits and is one of the leading consultants on leveraging LinkedIn to strengthen bottom line growth in B2B organizations. She has been ranked by *Fast Company Magazine* as one of the "100 Most Influential People Online" and has been featured by CNN Radio, CIO.com, and Dallas Morning News. Eve hosts the weekly radio show *Social Media for the CEO*. She shares social media knowledge that people can actually understand with an online network of more than 60,000 fans, followers, and connections every day.

You can follow or connect with Eve at the following links:

- http://www.LinkedIn.com/in/EveMayerOrsburn
- http://www.Twitter.com/LinkedinQueen
- http://www.SocialMediaDelivered.com

Press, interview, and speaker requests should be submitted to Orsburn's agent at press@socialmediadelivered.com.

Contents

Introduction: Everything You Ever
Wanted to Know About Social Media
But Were Too Embarrassed to Ask ix

Chapter 1

Why You Need Social Media 1

What Is Social Media? 3

Why Is Social Media Growing So Rapidly? 4

How Strong Is Social Media? 5

Are All Traditional Forms of Media Going to Wither and
    Die Because of Social Media? 6

Is Social Media Going to Change the World So Humans
    Don't Know How to Communicate in Person Anymore? 7

What Social Media Delivers 8

Why You Can't Live Without Social Media 10

Chapter 2

Shut Up and Listen! 11

Listen to What People Are Saying About Your Industry 13

Listen to What People Are Saying About Your Organization ... 14

Listen to What People Are Saying About Your Products
    (or Services) 15

Why Go to All This Trouble? 16

The Risk of Not Being at the Party 17

Case Studies 18

Case Study #1: Mayo Clinic 18

Case Study #2: James Wood Motors 23

Case Study #3: Anheuser-Busch 27

Case Study #4: Bodycology............................ 31

Case Study #5: Eve Mayer Orsburn and Social
    Media Delivered 35

Case Study #6: Lane Bryant........................... 40

Chapter 3

Opposites Attract..**45**

Pick the Right Room!.................................. 47

Why Opposites Attract................................ 48

Case Studies 50

Case Study #7: 21st Century Dental..................... 50

Case Study #8: Cable & Wireless Worldwide 54

Case Study #9: Beauty Cakes Cupcakes 57

Case Study #10: Starwood Hotels and Resorts
    Worldwide, Inc.................................... 61

Case Study #11: The Women's Museum.................. 67

Case Study #12: In The Know 71

Chapter 4

You Need More Than One Ball to Juggle...............**77**

Leveraging Social Media for Customer Service.............. 79

Using Social Media for Marketing 80

Harnessing Social Media for Company Goal Fulfillment 81

Case Studies 84

Case Study #13: The Adolphus Hotel..................... 84

Case Study #14: Stand Up To Cancer (SU2C) and
    Virgin America 88

Case Study #15: General Motors 93

Case Study #16: The Fresh Diet........................ 99

Case Study #17: Pink Elephant 104

Case Study #18: Sears Blue Blogger Group 108

Chapter 5

The Social Media Business Equation **115**

The Social Media Business Equation: 100-Percent Effective . . . 117

Informing: 20 Percent 119

Entertaining: 20 Percent 121

Interacting: 40 Percent 123

Converting to Business: 20 Percent 128

Chapter 6

The ROI of Social Media **131**

The Two Keys for Measuring ROI in Social Media. 133

Measuring ROI: An Example 134

Less Really Is More 136

Parting Words About the ROI of Social Media 137

Conclusion 138

Acknowledgments **139**

Index **189**

Introduction:
Everything You Ever
Wanted to Know
About Social Media
But Were Too
Embarrassed to Ask

My journey down the social media road began years ago, and many people have praised me for my foresight and brilliance. They are very kind, but the truth is, what really took me down this road was *desperation*. A few years ago—perhaps you remember—the economy took a heck of a dip. On its way down, it punched me in the gut. All of a sudden, the things I had done well for my entire career, the areas in which I had been a shining executive, no longer applied. Like any professional who had a substantial amount of experience and success under her belt, I began to fight. I did all the things that had always worked in the past— but this time, nothing worked. Prospects were not calling back. No one was returning e-mails. I couldn't get a deal done to save my life.

Then, one day, I went on LinkedIn, the largest professional social media networking site. I had been a member of

LinkedIn for a long time. I can't remember why I logged in that day; perhaps it was because people immediately think of LinkedIn when they are thinking about finding a new job. I spent the next few days on LinkedIn discovering connections, industry information, and industry events. Best of all, I found prospects and leads. That's when it hit me: Prospects and leads were right there, as plain as day. All I had to do was look in the right place!

And so my social media obsession began.

I spent the next few years trying to figure out this beast people called "social media," which I had dismissed for so long. Hearing the word "Twitter" simply made me giggle. It really didn't make sense to me why people would join Twitter and listen to people they didn't know talk about their cats. I thought, in the words of the great Betty White, speaking about Facebook in her *Saturday Night Live* appearance (which was itself prompted by people on Facebook begging for her to host), "It sounds like a huge waste of time."

But then it clicked for me. Millions of people are on social media. And if millions of people are there, then there is an audience to which a business could get exposure! And the best part? They can get exposure to these millions of people for *free*. I've always liked free things. I like to try the samples at Whole Foods, and I make sure to bring home the shampoo from the hotel even if I have plenty at home just because it's free. As a marketing professional who is familiar with the cost of print ads, radio time, and television spots, the idea of free "air time" was certainly intriguing.

Imagine you met a television executive today, and because he was in a fabulous mood, he decided to give you a national 60-second spot during prime time—free! What would you do with 60 seconds? Would you have your child go on live TV and talk about your company, or ask someone in the office to put together a few things to say real fast? Hopefully not! Instead, you would most likely hire a marketing company or use your own marketing team and put together a smashing concept with a fully produced commercial that entertained and informed the audience enough that they would want to buy your product.

Apparently, the "free-ness" of social media has intrigued many a business person, so they dive in right away, totally unprepared. Just because the vehicle of delivery is free doesn't mean there should be no preparation in embracing the fastest-growing media in the history of the world, social media.

With this book, in just a few hours, you'll take a journey that took me years to walk. You'll understand the how, the why, and the ROI of social media through real-life case studies from companies of all sizes. Yes, we can learn from the large companies showcased in this book, but there are also small- and medium-sized companies with very important and very real stories to share as well.

In this book, I'll reveal the down-to-earth truth about social media—not with complicated graphs, charts, or schedules, but with a very simple system in everyday language you can actually understand. Here's a run-down of each chapter:

- **Chapter 1, "Why You Need Social Media"**
  I want you to understand not just how to get the most out of social media, but something equally important: why you need social media in the first place. That's what this chapter is about.

- **Chapter 2, "Shut Up and Listen!"**
  Questions and answers—that's really all there is to social media. Your prospects and customers have questions. How do I garden without hurting my knees? How do I get a word-processing program without buying the rest of the package? How do I get from point A to point B quicker, smarter, shorter, etc.? If you're broadcasting all the time, sending out nothing more than digital billboards, how will you ever hear their questions?

- **Chapter 3, "Opposites Attract"**
  If you do all the right things, but you do them in the
  wrong place, social media will not grow your business.
  Many people go into social media looking to put "like
  with like." In other words, they join networks filled
  with counterparts and competitors. Don't do that! You
  need to go where your prospects and customers are.
  Opposites attract!

- **Chapter 4, "You Need More Than
  One Ball to Juggle"**
  Have you ever watched a juggler engage a crowd by
  throwing around one ball? No. Of course you haven't.
  And yet, in the game of social media, many companies
  try just that. Unfortunately, when it comes to social
  media most people only think of one thing at a time,
  when in fact you need to juggle several.

- **Chapter 5, "The Social Media Business Equation"**
  Believe it or not, there is an equation you can use to
  make sure your social media efforts *convert into business*.
  This chapter not only tells you what the equation is, but
  walks you through it step by step.

- **Chapter 6, "The ROI of Social Media"**
  Measuring social media results can be a challenge, but
  it's not impossible. In fact, when you have two
  things—a specific goal in mind and a way to track your
  progress through clearly delineated checkpoints—you
  actually *can* determine the return on your social media
  investment.

That's it: six simple chapters to total social media domination!
Okay, okay, maybe not *total* domination, but at least a proven
and effective way to make sure your social media efforts will
lead to business growth.

1

Why You Need Social Media

The other day, I was sitting outside Starbucks, fostering my caffeine addiction with a few friends. It wasn't too long after we'd all gotten comfortable that a young man raced out, ear to his cell phone, on what was obviously a Very Important Call.

It was hard not to eavesdrop. Besides, I always like to hear how people speak on the phone because, after all, I'm in the communication business. I like to hear how people make their business case, how they sell, and how they close the deal.

He was good, I'll give him that—at least, good at using plenty of the latest industry buzz words. I heard "bandwidth" quite a few times, and "we need to close the loop," and a few others I'm sure were in the same vein.

Shortly, the call was over. As soon as the young man removed his phone from his ear, he did a quick little pivot from the parking lot to face the coffeehouse patio.

"How is everybody doing?" he asked our cozy little crowd. Before we could mumble our surprised response, he launched into what I can only call a soliloquy. In the five minutes he spoke to us, we learned his name (Richard), how old he was (31), how long he'd been in town (nine months), what he did for a living (software sales consultant), who he was here with (his date, but it was "nothing serious"), her name (Camille), and what she was having (white mocha).

It wasn't what he said during this minutes-long oration that caught my attention. Rather, it was what he said when he'd had his fill and was ready to go. He shook each of our hands, looked us in the eye, and said—without a trace of irony—

"It was really great talking with you!" Then he disappeared, as quickly as he'd arrived.

We immediately resumed whatever chat he had interrupted, but his comment stuck with me all through my latte: "It was really great talking with you!"

What bothered me about the man's statement was this: He wasn't talking *with* us, he was talking *at* us.

At its heart, that is the frailty—and the power—of social media. There are many things that social media is not, but one thing it *is*, is a conversation. And like a conversation, every time you use social media, you have a choice: You can either talk *with* people, or you can talk *at* people.

My job is to help you talk *with* people. It's called a conversation, and it's what social media is all about. But don't take my word for it! Let's get into our discussion of what social media is (and isn't) right away.

What Is Social Media?

What, exactly, *is* social media? According to Wikipedia.com social media is "media designed to be disseminated through social interaction, created using highly accessible and scalable publishing techniques." (Of

> Social media is simply people communicating online.

course, that's just the definition on Wikipedia as it stands today. Odds are, it will be different by the time you read this book because it gets tweaked fairly often these days.)

Hmmm, sounds pretty challenging. Fortunately for you, my definition is a lot simpler: Social media is simply people communicating online.

Not bad, huh? I mean, how hard can *that* be?

Well, the problem is, most of us don't know how to communicate offline, let alone *online*! Take that snazzy young salesman in the great suit with the sleek phone who thought he was talking *with* us when, really, he was just talking *at* us.

How many conversations do you have like that per day? And not just with salesmen, but with bosses, clients, colleagues, neighbors…even friends? We're so used to talking *at* people, it's rare when we get the chance to finally talk *with* people.

Well, here's your chance. Social media is an open dialogue—in real time with real people. Social media professionals are really just communication professionals who leverage the power of social media so they can talk with thousands of people at a time instead of only one person at a time.

Why Is Social Media Growing So Rapidly?

Social media is the fastest growing type of media in the history of the world. How fast is it growing? Too fast for me to feasibly include the latest statistics in these pages; they'll be outdated long before the book goes to press. For the very latest numbers, I suggest you visit Mashable.com, the Bible of all things social media.

Why is social media growing so rapidly? In my experience, the answer to this question is fairly simple: People are eager for this one-on-one conversation, particularly with CEOs, entrepreneurs, business owners, and industry leaders with knowledge that has rarely been so easily accessible in the past. People want juicy, easily digestible morsels of bite-sized (*byte-sized?*) information served up on a silver platter.

For so long, companies, businesspeople, advertisers, and the media have talked *at* us. Now we have a chance to talk *with* them. Historically, advertising was a one-way dialogue. Whether it was an engaging TV commercial, a 30-second radio spot, a full-page magazine spread, a direct mailer, or a bench sign, marketing and PR specialized in "billboards." Suddenly, the floodgates have opened up to make a two-way dialogue possible, and people—your customers—are responding with attention verging on obsession.

Imagine a world in which the second you put your ad for toothpaste on TV, you had the ability to hear from Susie, a housewife in Scranton, in her own words: "I love your mint toothpaste. My family has used

> You now have the ability to get real-time data from your actual customers, in their own words.

it for years! But your cinnamon toothpaste is too hot—and it leaves little red bumps all over my sink." Could you imagine? Forget focus groups and test markets and tastings and surveys. You now have the ability to get real-time data from your actual customers, in their own words. It's not science fiction; it's social media. The best part? This kind of open-ended dialogue happens in real time, every day, all over the web. If you're not mastering social media, you're missing out on this essential form of modern communication.

How Strong Is Social Media?

How strong is social media? Let me put it this way: If Facebook were a country, it would be the third most populated country on the planet. Here are some other staggering facts:

- Social media is the number-one activity on the web now—overtaking pornography.

- It took radio 38 years to reach 50-million users.

- It took television 13 years to reach 50-million users.

- It took the Internet four years to reach 50-million users.

- It took Facebook nine months to reach 100-million users.

> If Facebook were a country, it would be the third most populated country on the planet.

To help these amazing statistics (plus plenty more) sink in, go to YouTube.com and search for "Socialnomics." These videos, by Erik Qualman, will get the point across!

Are All Traditional Forms of Media Going to Wither and Die Because of Social Media?

My background is with media, marketing, and ROI, so people naturally ask me if my passion for social media leads me to believe that traditional forms of media are no longer viable. Of course not! Things are simply changing at a rate we have never seen before. And you need to be part of that change.

I still believe in the power of television, radio, print, and other traditional forms of media. But I think those traditional forms must work in conjunction with social media. For example, I believe that companies can get more mileage out of their television commercials, which they have paid big money to produce, by sharing them on a social media vehicle like YouTube.

You should take whatever messages you are proud of in any format you have and recycle them. Squeeze every bit of juice out of them that you can. Someone who may have missed that hilarious print ad that perfectly positions your product might come across it on your Facebook page. Great content is great content, wherever it's found. It's up to you to put that great content out there as often as you can, in front of as many of the right prospects as possible.

Is Social Media Going to Change the World So Humans Don't Know How to Communicate in Person Anymore?

Yes and no.

Social media is going to change the world. Trust me, you can't stop it. It's too fast and you're too late. And yes, it is changing the way we communicate. Younger generations may well have a tougher time with social skills in person because they will have less practice. But humans are crafty. We'll adjust.

Many people are concerned about the "evil downsides" of social media. The tool is certainly powerful, but like any tool, it can be used for good or evil. In fact, the potential social media has to do good for the world astounds me. I am overwhelmed by the possibilities of the rampant spread of needed medical information, rapid warning abilities when inclement weather approaches an area, virtual mentorships to enable one person to help another with emotional support from across the world are just a few of the thoughts going through my head.

The truth is, social media won't change the world as much as it will put the world on display for everyone to see at every minute. It will amplify and magnify the good, the bad, and the ugly.

What Social Media Delivers

I talk with CEOs all the time. When I mention a social media site like Facebook or Twitter, they inevitably say, "Yes, my [wife/husband/child/mom/friend] wastes all kinds of time on that site. But what does it have to do with my business?"

Great answer! Why? Simply, the client has already begun to argue my case for me. For any effective marketing and communication process to work, you have to get people there. Guess what? When it comes to social media, they are already there—and the rest of the world is running there quickly to catch up.

I also tell clients with small or medium-size companies to pay attention to the last five seconds of nearly every ad on TV, look at the bottom of every article on Inc.com or in *Newsweek*, and check out the corner of every magazine ad. You'll see one consistent message: "Find us on Twitter and Facebook."

Do you know how much it costs per second to be on national TV? Or how valuable space is in a print or online ad? The last time I checked, it cost a whole lot of money. So why in the world would Tide or Coca-Cola or John Deere or Target waste valuable TV or ad copy time asking you to join them on Twitter and Facebook? The answer: They value your communication—or, at least, the chance to communicate with you.

But enough about communication. Let's talk about delivery. In other words, what can social media do for you? How can it deliver value for your time, energy, and constant maintenance? What, in the end, is your ROI going to be? I'll keep the answer(s) simple and direct. Here are the three things social media delivers:

- Customer service
- Communication
- Marketing

8

Most people in social media are doing one or maybe two of these fundamentals, but not all three. But social media has the potential to deliver all three things, not just one or the other.

If you're only talking about using social media for customer service, that's great, but you're missing a huge opportunity when it comes to marketing and communication. Likewise, if you only market your product through social media, you're only getting a third of the way down the road. And if you focus only on communicating, you lose out on opportunities to serve your customers and promote your offerings.

When you combine these three deliverables, they are exponentially more effective. Why? For the same reason it works to take a holistic approach to running your business and growing your company. It comes together.

> Social media is simply a tool. If you use this tool to increase customer service, marketing, and communication, you'll start seeing business results at an exponential rate.

Imagine organizing a strategy meeting to move your company forward and inviting only one or two divisions. Such a lopsided effort would, frankly, be bound to fail. Most CEOs understand the power that each department adds to the foundation and the possibilities of synergy when they all move in the same direction. The same applies for social media. Social media is simply a tool. If you use this tool to increase customer service, marketing, and communication, you'll start seeing business results at an exponential rate.

Why You Can't Live Without Social Media

Why can't you live without social media?

Imagine living without...the Internet.

Imagine living without...e-mail.

Imagine living without...television, airplanes, a microwave, or the radio.

Once upon a time, all these things, from TVs to microwave ovens to the Internet, were thought of as "fads" that wouldn't stand the test of time—kind of how some people describe social media today. But the fact is, the social media conversation has already begun. It's going on *right now*. Your prospects are already there, and so are your competitors.

Of course, you *can* survive without social media. But you can probably also survive with your company making a lot less money. The question is, why would you want to? Take a look down the road two years from now. Can you really afford to miss out on a competitive edge for two long years? Imagine not having a website for the next two years, or not allowing customers to shop online, or blocking e-mails. Not having a social media presence for another two years can and will have a similarly detrimental effect on your business.

Social media is a conversation. People are using it to talk about you *now*, with or without you. You want to be part of the conversation—sooner rather than later. This book will help you share your message, loud and clear.

2

SHUT UP AND LISTEN!

Remember the old philosophical riddle, "If a tree falls in the forest and no one is there, does it really make a sound?" Many executives treat their organization's online reputation like this. They stay out of the forest, thinking that if they don't hear the tree, then it won't matter. The problem is, the forest of social media is already populated with millions of people. When a sound is made, they hear it—whether you're there or not.

"So," you're thinking. "I need to get into the forest and start talking." After all, that's what everybody else seems to be doing, right? Using social media to talk about their industries, their companies, and their products and services? Wrong. Now is not the time to start talking. Now is the time, to put it bluntly, to shut up and listen.

Right now, somewhere—probably in a lot of places—people are talking about you, your brand, your organization, your cause, your product, your service, and

> **The very first step to effective social media is simply to listen.**

your competitors. This conversation is already taking place; you are powerless to prevent it from happening. The only way to stay relevant to the conversation—and potentially influence it—is to show up and hear what everybody is already saying. The very first step to effective social media is simply to listen.

How? How can you possibly "listen in" on the thousands of conversations that are taking place about your industry, your company, and your products every day? Simple. You can leverage many free and paid technologies to hear what people are saying about you. These tools, some of which are discussed in upcoming sections, are used every day, and they are always changing.

The most important thing you can do before you begin listening is to understand the climate of three critical areas:

- Your industry
- Your products (or services)
- Your organization

Listen to What People Are Saying About Your Industry

Begin by listening to what people are saying about your industry in general. Whether you work in heavy machinery, fashion, publishing, greeting cards, scented markers, holiday socks, or cosmetics, your industry is a world unto its own. Every industry has a lingo, a feel, a mode, a tone, an arc, and new trends.

Join industry groups on social media sites like LinkedIn and Facebook. Follow the popular industry blogs. Devote a fraction of every day simply honing in on your industry. What is the general tone? What are the hot topics—the things that matter, that people are passionate about? What are the more controversial developments?

> Keeping your finger on the pulse of the industry in general lets you know where you stand in comparison with others.

You may be wondering why you should listen to what others in your industry have to say about your industry. Why should you care what your competitors think about this trend or that technology? Many times, what we think is important to the industry is, in fact, considered rather insignificant by others in the industry—let alone our customers. Keeping your finger on the pulse of the industry in general lets you know where you stand in comparison with others.

Listen to What People Are Saying About Your Organization

Next, drill down deeper to hear what people are saying specifically about your organization. Google yourself! Bing yourself! (It's not as dirty as it sounds!) You can also search for your organization on Facebook, Twitter, YouTube, and LinkedIn to find out what people are saying. Whatever method you choose, this is a great way to find out what folks are really saying about your organization...and not just the folks you pay to say things about your organization. Remember, you're not here to post your own rants or comment on users' comments; you're here simply to listen to what the mood is toward your organization at this moment in time.

> You're not here to post your own rants or comment on users' comments; you're here simply to listen to what the mood is toward your organization at this moment in time.

In nearly every organization, there is the perception of how others feel about the organization and what folks really feel about the organization. Case in point: When the Sci-Fi Channel switched to SyFy, I read a profile about the company's head honchos and the spin within—and perhaps even by—corporate headquarters. Walking away from the article, I truly felt like the name change was a great decision. Then I Googled "SyFy" and learned what people *outside* the company felt. The perceptions couldn't have been more different if they were night and day. Fans were irate, industry insiders were doubtful, TV and cable columnists considered it "wasteful."

It's important to remember that the things you, your department heads, your managers, and even your employees consider clever, unique, different, and valuable can be seen quite differently not only by others in your industry and your competitors, but by potential customers as well. In fact, even the opinions and carefully crafted ads you've sent out may or may not match the reality of the mindset of your customers. How will you ever know if you don't listen?

Listen to What People Are Saying About Your Products (or Services)

The last step is to take a deep, long, careful look at what people are saying about your products, and to compare that to what they are saying about your competitors' products. Read the comments on your company website. Follow your products in the local and national media. Check out your reviews of your products on Amazon.com. (While you're there, you should probably write a great review about this book!) Don't just read the rave reviews; read the jeers at least as often.

I liken this step to going to counseling, where someone who is an objective party sits you down and tells you your faults and weaknesses, sharing an opinion

> Don't just read the rave reviews; read the jeers at least as often.

that isn't designed to protect—or hurt—your feelings, but instead to tell you the unvarnished truth. It's not always pretty and it's not very fun, but the knowledge you gain can change the way you go to market forever.

It's important to remember the reason social media is the most powerful and fastest-growing media in the history of the world. It's not just that the technology has enabled free and

15

instant delivery; it's about the human need to communicate. And as anyone who is a communication expert will tell you, the best and most effective communication comes from listening first.

Why Go to All This Trouble?

The reason for all this listening and gathering of information is for you to get a clear picture of where you stand before getting started. This is a foundation from which you can create a valid and authentic social media presence in the real world, as opposed to the presence you *thought* you had. Listening will help you bridge that gap between perception and reality.

It's a little like buying a new outfit, trying it on, and asking your grandmother what she thinks about it. Perhaps your grandmother—a sweet, elderly, gray-haired woman who loves you and would never, ever want to hurt your feelings—tells you it's

> It's important to celebrate the positive feedback you get, but it's even more important to listen to the criticism.

"gorgeous, simply gorgeous." Or maybe your grandmother is more like my grandmother, Honies, who was a beauty queen in the 1930s and possesses an impeccable sense of fashion (which, somehow, skipped over me). These kinds of grandmothers love you just as much as the other ones, but don't want to see you looking like a fool, so they offer you a much more realistic (and perhaps unpleasant) opinion. Like it or not, you need people like this—people who will tell it like it is. Then, you have to have the guts to consider making the change.

In other words, it's important to celebrate the positive feedback you get, but it's even more important to listen to the criticism. When you know what people are *really* saying about you, you're in a better position to craft a social media campaign that is credible because it is rooted in reality, and that will actually have a shot at breaking through.

The Risk of Not Being at the Party

Here's how I like to describe social media to my clients. Let's say there's a great big party happening and everybody is going. All your clients, your prospects, and even your competitors will be there.

You're going, right?

What's that?

You're *not* going?

You're staying home instead?

Hmmm, that's not such a great idea. After all, this "party" is social media. Everybody will be talking; what will you lose by not listening? What will you miss when your customers say things you should know about your product or service, but aren't there to hear? Why would you let your competitors be privy to that information while you stay at home and put up your feet? They may very well be listening.

The folks who get to this party early get a better spot, while those who don't show up get left in the dust. That is social media, and that's why listening is such an important part of social media.

Case Studies

The following case studies are designed to help you see how the concepts discussed in this book can be put into action in the real world.

Case Study #1: Mayo Clinic

Organization

Mayo Clinic (http://www.mayoclinic.org)

Background

Mayo Clinic is a not-for-profit medical practice dedicated to the diagnosis and treatment of virtually every type of complex illness.

Business Need

To leverage Mayo Clinic's established reputation in direct promotion rather than relying only on third-party media representation. In short, "Don't just pitch the media, *be* the media."

Social Media Solution

A custom YouTube channel to serve as a platform to distribute syndicated press-package videos created for traditional TV news and information to the media parties interested in featuring Mayo Clinic.

Business Result

Very large numbers of viewers (currently more than 3,000,000) means a lot of exposure. Thanks to low

Mayo Clinic YouTube channel.

production costs on many of the clips, any return on investment is significant. This channel has become a destination within itself and a way for Mayo Clinic to leverage its reputation without having to always use a third party. Furthermore, the YouTube channel has become a place for amateur and casual videos.

What Actually Happened

Lee Aase, Manager, Syndication and Social Media at Mayo Clinic notes that for more than 100 years, Mayo Clinic has relied almost completely on word of mouth and third-party media to spread its reputation. Because social media is the new word of mouth, the various platforms available fit in perfectly with the clinic's traditional means of promotion. Plus, it affords Mayo Clinic the opportunity to use its own reputation to its advantage.

As Mr. Aase has stated, "Don't just pitch the media, *be* the media," meaning Mayo Clinic has a very strong reputation and does not have to rely solely on third-party media representation to establish credibility. They already have a lot of credibility in their field, and can use that as a way to appeal to a wider audience.

In addition, because the clinic is a not-for-profit organization, there is less pressure to see an immediate return on investment and more opportunity to use social media in a purely altruistic sense. Of course, this also brings greater social media success, because social media is often about sharing valuable information.

The implementation of a YouTube channel provides the clinic with another platform to utilize the 90-second to two-minute syndicated press-package videos created for traditional TV news and information to the media parties interested in featuring Mayo Clinic. It also creates a platform to pitch to traditional media, as well as reinforces the clinic's established reputation by providing information and advice to patient communities, speeding up the dissemination of medical information on rare or specialized illnesses to people across the world at a rate never experienced before. Although there is not as strong a focus on ROI as there might be in a corporation, Mr. Aase explains that the clinic still sees new patients coming in because of content they viewed on Mayo Clinic's YouTube channel.

A perfect example is the 10½-minute video of Mayo Clinic's Dr. Mesa discussing myelofibrosis, a rare form of blood cancer, which was shot with a simple $150 Flip camera. This video has been viewed more than 6,000 times, and more than 50 out-of-state patients who chose Mayo Clinic because they saw this video have contacted Dr. Mesa. Not only does this video provide necessary information to potential patients, the clinic's ROI from making that information widely available through YouTube is substantial.

One key element in the clinic's social media strategy is the inter-connectedness across platforms. Mayo Clinic maintains a Twitter feed, a Facebook page, a YouTube channel, and several blogs. Mr. Aase says these different channels are all crucial to a successful social media campaign.

In July 2010, Mayo Clinic increased its commitment to using social media by creating Mayo Clinic Center for Social Media. The center's purpose is to go beyond the public relations and marketing uses of social media, and to use variations of these tools throughout the organization. Through the center, Mayo aims to accelerate adoption of

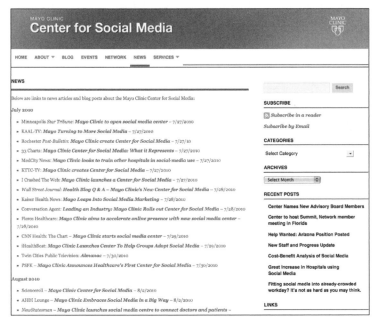

Mayo Clinic Center for Social Media.

social media in clinical practice, education, research, and administration.

The center's focus is not only internal to Mayo Clinic, however. The center also will be a resource for other hospitals and health-related organizations looking for guidance in applying social media. "Many staff in healthcare organizations who are interested in using social media have pointed to our Mayo Clinic example to help make their case to leadership," Mr. Aase explains. "Through the center, we have a way for them to join a formal network, and to get access to materials and resources to support their venture into social media."

Mr. Aase says the network will not be limited to medical providers. It will also include non-profit health-related organizations and associations. "We want to be a resource to any organization looking for ways to apply social media to improve health," he says. "Our fundamental goal is to help patients through social media, whether that means giving them increased access to scientific information or helping them to get together and learn from each other, becoming active partners with their healthcare providers. We also want to help medical professionals in research and education connect with each other, and are eager to play a role in spreading the use of these powerful communication tools throughout the health system."

For more information about Mayo Clinic Center for Social Media, visit http://socialmedia.mayoclinic.org.

Case Study #2:
James Wood Motors

Organization

James Wood Motors (http://www.jameswood.com)

Background

James Wood Motors consists of several car dealerships with numerous brands located in Denton and Decatur, Texas, close to the Dallas area.

Business Need

To build more relationships with prospects who prefer to shop virtually.

Social Media Solution

A Twitter campaign to be used as an information resource for potential customers.

Business Result

James Wood Motors experienced increased sales as a direct result from Twitter interactions and grew its online reputation thanks to customers who shared positive reviews on Yelp, which describes itself as a "fun and easy way to find and talk about great (and not so great) local businesses." In other words, it's a review site.

What Actually Happened

In early 2009, the management at James Wood Motors hypothesized that using one or several social media vehicles might aid them in connecting with potential customers and helping them to make car-purchasing decisions.

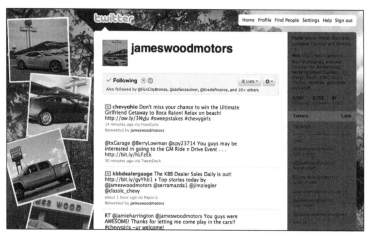

The James Wood Motors Twitter page.

They decided to provide a wealth of information through Twitter at Twitter.com/JamesWoodMotors. "We communicate different things with Twitter," says Amanda Williams, Internet Director at James Wood Motors. "From up-to-the-minute new vehicle arrivals to community involvement projects, inside views of operations, behind the scenes, even interaction with moms test-driving our vehicles." Additionally, social media allows James Wood Motors to bridge the gap that exists between their geographic location and their customer base, which works and resides all over the Dallas–Fort Worth–Denton area.

Williams notes, "We use Twitter to communicate with our customers who use it as a way to maintain distance while shopping for vehicles. Not everyone is comfortable shopping for vehicles, we know that. In today's times, people are more at ease keeping their distance and using a site like Twitter. We send pictures, exchange info via direct message, video, etc. The customers obtain the info they need."

By sharing information about their dealership and relevant product information via Twitter, James Wood Motors caught the attention of Mr. Colin Burns, a marketing professional looking to purchase a new car. Burns was so moved after pleasantly interacting with James Wood Motors throughout the buying process, he felt compelled to submit a Yelp review praising the experience he had at the dealership, with its staff, and with the car itself:

> Amanda from @jameswoodmotors was a HUGE help. It was nice to have someone quickly respond to my questions on Twitter with pictures, information about the car, if they worked with my bank, etc.... I was able to do all my homework on the back end to figure out that I was getting a good deal and left the entire

Reviews of James Wood Motors on Yelp.

process 100-percent comfortable with the car I had picked and the price I was paying. If I could do it all over again, I'd do it the same way—shop on Twitter, see it in real life, make the purchase.

In addition to social media, James Wood Motors continues to use traditional methods of advertising such as billboards, radio, and television. Social media has offered them a less expensive and surprisingly effective addition to the marketing mix. Owner James Wood commented, "Our business has always been about building relationships and if social media can speed that up for us, then it is definitely a smart business decision."

Case Study #3: Anheuser-Busch

Organization

Anheuser-Busch Companies, Inc.
(http://www.anheuser-busch.com)

Background

Anheuser-Busch is a global brewer that produces the world's highest-selling beers, Budweiser and Bud Light.

Business Need

To create more community with sports fans.

Social Media Solution

A news story–style video of sports fans on YouTube.

Anheuser-Busch's YouTube video.

Business Result

Anheuser-Busch's efforts resulted in an Emmy-award–winning program for 2010 that yielded massive fan audience and interaction.

What Actually Happened

Bud Light wanted to build participation and interaction with passionate sports fans. They turned to Chris Yates and Jim Knox at Huddle Productions, who understood that the habits of television viewers had changed. Nowadays, fans want to watch video whenever they want, and as soon as possible. However, viewers not only want a story—they wanted to be *part* of the story.

With this approach, Huddle Productions created "GameDay Rivals," an interactive social media campaign focused on filming football fans and their unique traditions and quirky rituals. Tailgaters from all over the U.S. competed during football season to be crowned Bud Light's Ultimate Tailgate Fan.

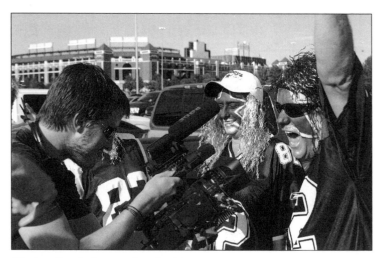

Filming the Anheuser-Busch video.

Interviewing fans for the Anheuser-Busch video.

Huddle Productions filmed fans at stadiums, and then shared the videos on social sites like YouTube, Facebook, and Twitter. Fans voted, commented, created content, and engaged one another, fostering a conversation frenzy all season long. This was the kind of unique marketing and direct interaction with their fans that Anheuser-Busch wanted.

Consequently, the GameDay Rivals program won the 2010 Emmy Award for the "Best Sport Program of the Year." Their concept of engaging fans and the use of video in social media generated the following results:

Stats Increase Year 1 to Year 2

750,000 votes	+1200 percent
417,087 website video views	+522 percent
1,600 Facebook fans	+144 percent
113,900 YouTube views	+60 percent

"GameDay Rivals in search of Bud Light's Ultimate Tailgater was one of the most successful local marketing campaigns. It was creative and effective," said Jay Black, the Director of Marketing at Anheuser-Busch InBev. "We are always looking at trying new and innovative ways to market and Huddle Productions did that with this concept."

Case Study #4: Bodycology

Organization

Bodycology with Advanced Beauty Systems (http://www.bodycology.com)

Background

Bodycology is a product line developed by Dallas-based Advanced Beauty Systems. Their beauty products are designed to be "spa-quality" and are intended for women who want "beauty on a budget."

Business Need

To create an online interactive experience for Bodycology users.

Social Media Solution

Use interactive banners to create a strong call to action (CTA).

Business Result

Bodycology developed a massive consumer e-mail database, which was subsequently used to create My|Bodycology, an interactive health and beauty portal containing blogs, quizzes, and product resources.

What Actually Happened

In 2009, Bodycology launched an offline campaign centered around a simple question: "What's Your Bodycology?" Bodycology's interactive agency, Boxcar Creative, saw this as a promising online opportunity, and defined a strategy to leverage the offline campaign into a

Bodycology's CTA.

strong online interactive campaign with their potential consumers.

This strategy had two key features:

- Incorporate a strong CTA to generate data for their consumer database, with particular emphasis on the collection of contact information.

- Actively respond to user behavior by creating an interactive resource for consumers.

A clear CTA is vital to any marketing campaign. The online initiative began with a banner campaign composed of both standard (non-interactive) and interactive banner types. Both the standard and the interactive banner types had a clear, simple CTA: "Take quiz." Once prompted by the CTA, the interactive units provided the user with the ability to take the quiz within the banner as well as submit an e-mail address, while the standard banners drove users to a landing page with the same quiz/e-mail-capture functionality.

The "What's Your Bodycology?" banner campaign netted nearly 40,000 e-mail addresses in less than eight weeks. The interaction rate was 24.29 percent, far surpassing the industry-standard interaction rate of 7.64 percent. The conversion rate from visits to e-mail signups was 6 percent—the high end of the industry rate, which is between 1 percent and 6 percent.

Having 40,000 unexpected e-mail addresses inspired the next steps, which would ultimately be used to create My|Bodycology. A challenge was extended to the e-mail database, wherein e-mails were blasted out to users, encouraging women to vote on their top areas of interest.

The potential areas of content included the following:

- Fitness
- Beauty tips
- Celebrities
- Health/wellness
- Fashion
- Value
- Parenting
- Household tips
- Horoscopes
- Nutrition
- Finances
- Success stories
- Editorial

The voting was a fun, interactive way to connect the brand with its users.

Presently, Bodycology has their top six areas as generated by their users:

- Nutrition
- Finance
- Fitness
- Value
- Entertainment
- Household tips

The first phase of My|Bodycology launched in summer 2010. It included blogs from various women on the aforementioned topics as well as quizzes and product information. My|Bodycology is a result of Bodycology's active response to users' behavior, and will serve as the online arena to be controlled by the user. An agenda can't be forced in the process of developing such an arena. All a company can do for its consumers is give them a clear CTA and be sure to respond accordingly.

Case Study #5:
Eve Mayer Orsburn and
Social Media Delivered

Organization

Social Media Delivered
(http://www.socialmediadelivered.com)

Background

Eve Mayer Orsburn is an executive who decided to use social media to create a business doing social media for other organizations.

Business Need

To brand herself on social media first, then build business through social media before reaching out to clients and doing the same for them.

Social Media Solution

Create an optimized profile for Eve Mayer Orsburn at LinkedIn (http://www.linkedin.com/in/evemayerorsburn) and use the largest professional network to create and grow a new business, then build an entire company and fulfill almost every need through social media.

Business Result

Eve reasoned that if she could create an enormous social media presence for herself first, she could point to her own success as a great example of what she could do for clients. Eve's company, Social Media Delivered, became one of the largest social media optimization companies worldwide with a thriving client list garnered through social media in the U.S., Canada, and Europe.

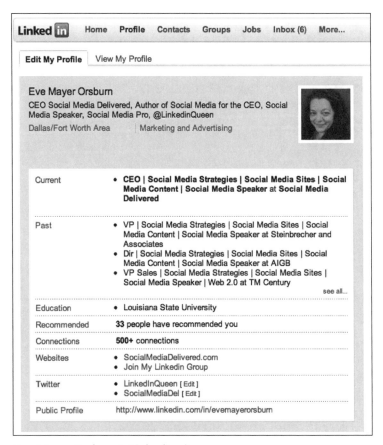

Eve Mayer Orsburn's LinkedIn site.

What Actually Happened

As a "solopreneur," Eve Mayer Orsburn began to build a presence on LinkedIn that would showcase her ability to find clients on the largest professional networking site. At first, her clients were B2B companies needing help specifically on LinkedIn. These consisted primarily of engineers, lawyers, speakers, coaches, non-profit organizations, medical-device companies, and training companies. These companies saw results as Eve trained their executive and sales teams on using LinkedIn. Once she achieved results, she asked these clients to spread the word with recommendations of her services on LinkedIn, then reached out to new prospects via LinkedIn groups.

Eve wanted to share her social media tips on a daily basis, so she started using the address Twitter.com/LinkedInQueen, where she could share social media tips several times a day. These tips were designed to do the following:

- Ignite a passion for social media in individuals who wanted to "do it themselves."

- Promote her services to individuals who would rather hire someone else to perform social media duties for them instead.

As her client list grew, Eve used Craigslist and LinkedIn to hire her first employees. Suddenly, Eve was no longer a solopreneur, but a company, now known as Social Media Delivered—which meant she needed a CPA, a mentor, representatives, and companies to partner with, all of whom she found through Twitter and LinkedIn.

More companies were coming to Social Media Delivered (SMD) and asking for help—and for the first time, they were not all B2B companies. Restaurants, hotels, hospitals, dentists, weight-loss organizations, and retail companies were all B2C companies wanting to understand tools like Twitter, Facebook, YouTube, blogs, and more. To spread the word to executives in a way that was non-technical but focused on business, SMD began posting blogs on social media for business on its own website, http://www.socialmediadelivered.com, and sharing its own social media tidbits at Twitter.com/SocialMediaDel and Facebook.com/SocialMediaDel.

Marketing companies and ad agencies noticed the talents of Social Media Delivered and began to reach out to ask for help with their own clients. Then came an online radio show, "Social Media for the CEO" (SM4CEO.com), where companies of all sizes told their stories of growing business through social media. As the company grew, more employees were brought on through social media, and more clients in the U.S., Canada, and Europe searched out Social Media Delivered for their services.

In your hands now, you hold a book that is a product of this journey. The people, companies, stories, printing, and publishing were all brought together purely through the power of social media and the connections made through that journey. The journey will continue, and you are

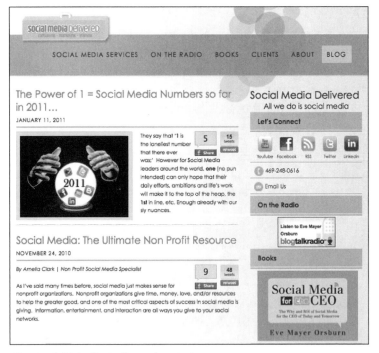

The Social Media Delivered website.

a part of it. So are the 36,000 names appearing at the end of this book, all of which came from Twitter.com/ LinkedInQueen. Readers will post reviews about this book on Amazon.com and tweet questions and feedback. So continues the social media trail that started with just one person, and then found its way to you.

Anyone can achieve this for any organization. Social media levels the playing field. How? Simply give more often than you take, offer value, and then ask for help. It will work. This case study proves it.

Case Study #6:
Lane Bryant

Organization

Lane Bryant, Inc. (http://www.lanebryant.com)

Background

Lane Bryant is one of the most significant women's retail clothing store chains in America, focusing on plus-size clothing. Headquartered in Columbus, Ohio, it was founded in 1901 by Lena Himmelstein Bryant Malsin.

Business Need

To create a place where plus-size women could connect with each other and share their passions, and to connect those passions with the Lane Bryant brand.

Social Media Solution

Inside Curve, a network on LaneBryant.com that is solely dedicated to and designed for the Lane Bryant customer. Within this network, a registered member can shop, read the latest Lane Bryant buzz, and connect with other members over their love for Lane Bryant and fashion.

Business Result

Inside Curve served as a platform to address the Lane Bryant customer and inform them of an apparent double standard being applied to Lane Bryant's TV spot by ABC and FOX TV networks. This started the wildfire that turned into controversy online, on television, and in print, which equaled huge PR gains for Lane Bryant.

What Actually Happened

When Lane Bryant VP of Marketing Jay Dunn began working with the company, he immediately identified that the customer base Lane Bryant was trying to reach was being neglected by mainstream American advertising. Because typical U.S. retail ads didn't feature curvier women, instead highlighting waif-like models, more voluptuous women had a fairly narrow menu of places where they could shop.

Lane Bryant's Inside Curve network.

With this knowledge and observation, Dunn began planning a platform to engage the Lane Bryant customer and foster a conversation between customer and brand that focused on what many customers were already talking about: the under-representation of plus-size women in America. In 2008, Dunn and his marketing team conceived, built, and incorporated into the marketing strategy a fully interactive online community network called "Inside Curve," which is solely dedicated to and designed for the Lane Bryant customer. Within this network, a registered member can shop, read the latest Lane Bryant buzz, and connect with other members over their love for Lane Bryant and fashion.

On April 20, 2010, Lane Bryant's marketing staff published a 377-word blog post on Inside Curve, which by then had approximately 30,000 devotees. The title of the post read as follows: "The Lingerie Commercial FOX and ABC Didn't Want Its Viewers to See." The post then discussed a recent problem the brand had faced when presenting a TV commercial announcing the rollout of its new intimates line, Cacique, to FOX and ABC.

By that evening, with 198 Love Its, 54 comments, and a reporter from *AdWeek* now covering the story, a media war had started. At the end of the blog post, readers faced a "retail line in the sand," and Lane Bryant was encouraging them to pick a side: "Team Cacique or Team Network. Tell us how you feel and pass this along to everyone who shares the view that beauty is in the eye of the beholder not the hands of a television network."

The Battle of Lingerie had begun....

On Wednesday the story continued to gain momentum, showing no signs of stopping as the headline swept through Twitter, the blogosphere, and across the radio.

Reporters, Jay Leno, and loyal Lane Bryant fans all wanted an answer to the same question: "If Victoria's Secret and Playtex can run ads at any time [on any network] during the 9pm to 10pm hour…Why is Lane Bryant restricted only to the final 10 minutes?" And on Thursday, April 22, when the *New York Post* ran an article featuring the story and exposing the "visual" in question, two things became abundantly clear: Team Cacique had scored *major* support points across the nation and, more importantly, in the new era of social media networking, a mere 377 words could create quite an impact.

By raising awareness about the issue among a smaller but dedicated audience of 30,000 within the Inside Curve community, Lane Bryant put in place the means for those members to share that information across their personal and

The New York Post *weighs in on the maelstrom.*

public social networks, causing it to go viral. Lane Bryant's social media use in this instance truly highlights how, when a brand creates an authentic and engaging social media personality and then reaches out to listen to their customer base, momentous things can be accomplished.

By addressing criticism targeting a particular TV spot within Lane Bryant's online community, the reaction from brand loyalists, reporters, and the public defending and supporting Lane Bryant generated unprecedented press/media coverage across both traditional and non-traditional outlets, including TV, radio, newspaper, and online/social media platforms.

As Michael Learmonth, *AdAge* Editor for Digital Media has said, "The upshot is that it was a fantastically orchestrated PR campaign," and Omnicon called it "Possibly the biggest publicity campaign ever for a retailer."

"The Lingerie Commercial FOX and ABC Didn't Want Its Viewers to See" achieved the following:

- More than $40M in earned media on a $5M spend

- Ad shown on more than 300 TV shows and more than 3,000 blogs and websites, including *The Tonight Show with Jay Leno*, CNN, People.com, *The Today Show*, *The O'Reilly Factor*, *The Huffington Post*, etc.

- Effectively relaunched the Lane Bryant brand and introduced Cacique to the country, bringing in thousands of new customers

- 2,000,000 video views in three days

- Named the "Most Watched Ad in the World" by *AdAge* for two weeks in a row

- Appeared in *AdAge's* "Top Ten Most Watched Ads in the World" list for three weeks after that

3

Opposites Attract

Meet Jacob.

Jacob is a man who wants to date a great woman.

Jacob has a very clear goal in his mind: to get a great woman to agree to go out with him. Jacob is an intelligent man and understands that a great woman won't magically appear in his living room anytime soon; he must get out there and meet people to find her.

Jacob heads out for a night on the town to find *exactly* what he is looking for. Jacob walks to the area where the nice establishments are known to be and is surprised to see two doors clearly marked. One doors says, "Enter here to find a room full of great men." The other door says, "Enter here to find a room full of great women." Based on his stated goal, Jacob's choice should be pretty easy. But inexplicably, Jacob enters the "great men" door and spends the evening talking to men just like himself. At the end of the night, he goes home without achieving his goal of meeting a great woman. Naturally, he feels frustrated.

What? Wait a minute—how did this go wrong? Jacob's goal was so clear! How could he mess that up? If you were a man looking for a great woman, which room would *you* enter? "Surely," you say, "the answer is obvious: You enter the room marked 'full of great women.'" But when people engage in social media, they often enter the wrong room, interacting with online groups full of people just like them.

Why do so many of us do this—use social media to interact with people just like us, rather than in groups where very few or none of our prospects are likely to be? I know why I did it: It was less scary. I was familiar with the groups and the people. It was just plain easier to walk in and feel comfortable there—virtually speaking, of course. Besides, when you're first getting into social media, it's a great way to start. You can see what your peers and counterparts are saying and become educated on your industry. It's almost exactly like how you likely use social media in your personal life.

> When people engage in social media, they often enter the wrong room, interacting with online groups full of people just like them.

But we're not talking about your personal life here; we're talking about growing your business. Using social media for personal reasons and using it for your business are two very, very different things. I'm pretty sure you'd have a tough time exponentially growing your business by only selling to people you already know. To build a successful business, you must introduce your brand and product to the world.

Of course, spreading your brand to the world using only traditional media can cost a lot of money. That's why, especially for a small business, social media is a more effective way to reach the masses. And to do that, you have to get in front of people who don't know you. This is why you must join groups that are full of your prospects—that is, the opposite of you.

Pick the Right Room!

Let me explain this concept a little more fully by using a real-life example. Here at SMD, we work with several executive coaches, consulting with them on how to use social media to reach more prospects and gain more clients. Typically, the executive coaches would join lots of groups on Facebook and

LinkedIn labeled with terms like "executive coaching group" or "professional group for coaching." Seems logical, right? After all, this enables them to keep up with what their competition is doing as well as stay current with evolving trends in the coaching industry. However, after spending hours discussing, debating, or posting in these groups, they find no effect on their bottom line or build-up of their business. Why? Because they entered the room full of great men when they were looking for a great woman. In other words, they went into a room full of people just like them, looking to do the exact same thing, instead of going into a room full of the people they wanted to attract—i.e., potential customers.

Why Opposites Attract

When you are leveraging social media, it's important to remember that opposites attract. Although it's okay to join a few groups to keep up with your industry, make like-minded connections, and follow trends, you must make sure the majority of your groups are composed of your prospects.

> Make sure the majority of your groups are composed of your prospects.

- If you're an executive coach, join groups full of executives.

- If your company sells gardening tools, join groups full of gardeners.

- If you're a person who sells health insurance to HR departments, join groups full of HR directors.

- If your company sells sports drinks, join groups full of athletes.

You get the picture. Yes, it seems logical to join groups full of folks who make sports drinks, but do you really think those people ever going to *buy* your sports drink? You have to go where the sports-drink guzzlers are, not the sports-drink makers! The point is, while it's important to use social media to keep in touch with those in your industry, there are only so many hours in the day and only so many resources you can throw at social media. Don't you want the time you *do* spend to count? That way, you'll be the one great guy in a room full of eligible women. Now your chances are much better of attracting what you want. Why? Because you entered the right room!

So, what happens when you enter the right room? Getting back to our real-life example, when the executive coaches began to join large numbers of groups with executives in them, they started to post case studies showing how executive coaching was able to move an executive forward. These were small, short, informal "success stories"—and they worked! Because our executive coaches were the minority in a select group discussing what could help the majority, the result was immediate, and led to a dramatic and marked increase in business and profits.

Case Studies

The following case studies are designed to help you see how the concepts discussed in this book can be put into action in the real world.

Case Study #7: 21st Century Dental

Organization

21st Century Dental
(http://www.21stcenturydental.com)

Background

21st Century Dental is a dental practice and medical spa.

Business Need

To build relationships with their clients and soon-to-be clients.

Social Media Solution

Keep clients updated on Facebook by showing them new services and revealing the hard-working, fun-loving staff; and reach prospects on Twitter with rare facts and lots of interaction.

Business Result

Messages spread quickly about new services such as the med spa and sleep treatments. Clients became more aware of services and expanded their purchasing power.

What Actually Happened

21st Century Dental decided that Facebook and Twitter would be the best social media tools for their business needs. 21st Century Dental ensured that only select Facebook features were used in order to avoid presenting an overwhelming amount of information to their target

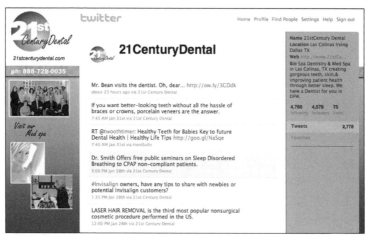

The 21st Century Dental Twitter page.

21st Century Dental's Facebook page.

audience. Clear, simple, and uncluttered information enabled them to reach out proactively and increase their fan base. In particular, they opted to include the following Facebook features on Facebook.com/21stCenturyDental:

- **Video:** This would enable 21st Century Dental to display product demonstrations, real-time customer testimonials, and other engaging content.

- **Photo Albums:** With photo albums, 21st Century Dental could display a variety of perspectives about its brand through pictures.

- **Active Wall:** This provided 21st Century Dental with a forum where the brand could consistently follow up with a target audience and address comments and customer feedback.

Also, the crew at 21st Century Dental is a hard-working but fun-loving group. They showed this by having "Name That Tune" video contests on Facebook, with a patient humming tunes while her teeth were whitened.

Facebook was only one element of the 21st Century Dental social media campaign. In order to reach their target audience quickly, the company opted to use Twitter as a catalyst for conversing with current and future patients as well as within the medical industry. Because Twitter offers various messaging options, 21st Century Dental could interact in different ways on Twitter.com/21CenturyDental:

- The background design was revamped to showcase an attractive design scheme using bold colors, with contact information being critical to recruiting followers.

- The company emphasized consistent replies on their Twitter feed.

They understand that interaction, not just broadcasting, is the key. That's why 21st Century Dental is one of Twitter's top-20 most-followed dentists in the world.

Case Study #8:
Cable & Wireless Worldwide

Organization

Cable & Wireless Worldwide (http://www.cw.com)

Background

Cable & Wireless Worldwide is one of the world's lead-ing international communication companies, specializing in providing critical communication network and services in the UK and globally.

Business Need

To persuade their clients' executives to buy into using social media to improve customer service.

Social Media Solution

A three-pronged approach across Facebook, Twitter, and dedicated websites as customer-service channels.

Business Result

Cable & Wireless Worldwide achieved a measurable ROI both in terms of customer service and reduction in oper-ational costs.

What Actually Happened

In early 2009, a few clients of Cable & Wireless Worldwide (CWW) raised the subject of social media. CWW wanted to understand how the marketing and communication activities they already had in place could be used to handle these requests. As CWW dug deeper into the questions these customers were raising regarding social media, they determined that it would be beneficial

SOCIAL MEDIA
HOW WILL YOUR CONTACT CENTRE BE AFFECTED?

Cable&Wireless
Worldwide

WHEN AND WHERE

Date: Thursday 13th May 2010

Time: 5:00 PM – 6:30 PM BST

REGISTRATION

To register all you need to do is click on the link below – it only takes a couple of minutes.

>> REGISTER NOW <<

AGENDA

Join us for this complimentary webinar and listen to respected international industry speakers who have embraced a social media response strategy talk about:

• What worked, what did not work?

• If they did it again, how they would do it differently?

• What did their customers have to say about it?

• Did social media increase or reduce customer service costs?

• Can social media generate new revenue?

SOCIAL MEDIA – HOW WILL YOUR CONTACT CENTRE BE AFFECTED?

If you ask for one of the biggest buzz words or phrases heard today you are likely to hear a resounding chorus – "SOCIAL MEDIA!"

Brands are about reputation and response. However, social media has created an environment where companies no longer control their own brand.

Everyone is talking about it, but let me share with you four pressing questions:

1. What is driving customer response to social media?

2. Do Contact Centres represent a viable channel to drive a response to social media?

Some companies have actively embraced monitoring of their brand across social media; however many have not implemented a customer response and strategy to proactively engage social media circles...

3. What needs to happen next?

If you think your customer response will not be affected, think again. Social media has opened a whole new paradigm to customer behaviour and how that affects your brand and your company's customer response reputation.

4. Is your contact centre ready?

WHO'S INVITED

The webinar is designed to be a "do not miss" for all companies embracing social media response. We are welcoming a large international audience who will be joining our speakers from England, the United States and Canada.

Cable & Wireless Worldwide's social media information page.

to explore using social media as a full-blown customer-service tool.

There's a wealth of information readily available via social media that enables companies to gain real insight into their customers and improve the services they offer. For example, when customers were asked how likely they were to recommend the brand after resolving their customer-service issues using social media, there was a 70 percent improvement compared to the same customer group being serviced via the telephone.

"Whenever the subject of social media is brought up, you will inevitably have objections," says Craig Palmer, Head of Customer Access and Contact Centres at CWW. "The key to overcoming those objections is by having a model that demonstrates tangible benefits." Palmer's team found that persuading their clients' executives to buy into social media was a formidable challenge. However, says Palmer, "Once we were able to prove that there is an ROI on a social media–based customer-service model, this became a much easier conversation." This was the first lesson CWW's team learned, and one that is a common concern across all the businesses with whom CWW consults.

CWW's solution: defining a model that enables its clients to effectively implement social media as a customer-service channel and measure the benefits. The model has three key tenets:

- **Use a reactive listening approach:** Understand what your customers are saying and put rules in place to define how and when you intervene.

- **Be a resource:** Monitor and act on trends. Post relevant, useful information that your customers will value, so that you will be regarded as a resource that the customer can trust.

- **Combine proactive selling and customer service:** This area offers real long-term benefits to business.

By understanding these three areas and measuring the resulting improvements, Cable & Wireless Worldwide has modeled the ROI both in terms of customer service and reduced costs. Although CWW isn't likely to suggest turning off call-center phones and using social media as a replacement, social media is redefining the business model of many organizations for the better and will continue to do so in the future.

Case Study #9:
Beauty Cakes Cupcakes

Organization

Beauty Cakes Cupcakes (http://www.beautycakes.fr)

Background

Established in 2008, Beauty Cakes is an independently owned, made-to-order cupcakery for parties, weddings, baby showers, art openings, and events in Paris, France.

Business Need

To expand a burgeoning cupcake-delivery business into a full-service boutique and tea salon in Paris. Other goals included educating the local market about cupcakes, raising awareness, showcasing the bakery's expertise, and generating enough buzz to be able to run a viable business in a market where cupcakes are generally either unknown or misunderstood.

Social Media Solution

Use Twitter and Facebook to assemble a vibrant online community of cupcake fans to discuss all things cupcake, while simultaneously gaining exposure for and interest around Beauty Cakes cupcakes.

Business Result

Solid business growth led to the opening of Beauty Cakes Boutique and Tea Salon in Paris' trendy 17th arrondissement in December 2010. More than just cupcakes, the boutique is also serves lunch and brunch on the weekends.

The Beauty Cakes Twitter page.

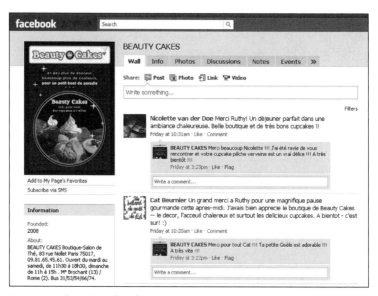

Beauty Cakes' Facebook page.

What Actually Happened

Once upon a time, having just left the world of show business in Paris, Ruthy Avayou was ready for a new kind of adventure. Avayou discovered cupcakes years ago while living abroad in the U.S., and began baking them in her spare time. She started sharing her treats with friends and family, who were unfamiliar with them. Whilst *les brownies* and *les cookies* had begun to appear in French pastry shops in recent years and were enjoying mild success, American-style desserts were generally thought to be too sweet for the local palate. What's more, cupcakes were assumed to be filled with preservatives and artificial ingredients and topped with *crème au beurre* (buttercream), which the French typically dislike.

In addition to the challenges of educating people about cupcakes, Avayou faced tough competition in the form of the popular traditional national dessert, the *macaron*, not to mention countless other mainstays such as the fruit tarts, cakes, Madeleines, and financiers sold on just about every street corner in the French capital.

Avayou's recipes were developed for the French palate, using only fresh and natural ingredients, and no buttercream. She loved the reactions of surprise and delight when people tasted her beautiful, delicious cupcakes. Before long, she was making cupcakes regularly under the name Beauty Cakes. They became a huge hit at birthdays, weddings, fashion shows, baby showers, housewarmings, art openings, and galas around Paris. She wanted to continue to build on her success and dreamed of opening a boutique.

Avayou began working with Social Media Delivered in early 2010 to help her get closer to her goals. Two new pages, http://www.twitter.com/beautycakesfr and http://www.facebook.com/beautycakes were established, and the Social Media Business Equation, discussed later in this book, was put into action immediately. Avayou was able to attract many followers, build relationships with community members, and establish her credibility by sharing valuable content and discussing innovative cupcake recipes, baking tips, and events, such as Paris' first Cupcake Camp, which took place in July 2010. She also successfully gained business by inviting prospects to take advantage of Twitter-only and Facebook-exclusive discounts on cupcakes, provide feedback on products, and give referrals.

On Twitter, @BeautyCakesFR has gained a prominent following. Via these relationships, Avayou has solicited ideas and names for new cupcake flavors, and invited fans to attend exclusive events like the boutique opening. Additionally, Avayou has connected with wedding planners and event planners via social media to create partnerships and provide cupcake wedding cakes and other special orders, an unexpected additional revenue stream.

The explosive growth of Beauty Cakes in 2010 led to the opening of The Beauty Cakes Boutique and Tea Salon in Paris' trendy 17th district. Cupcakes are becoming more understood, and have actually become quite fashionable in the French capital. The boutique continues to grow and is now offering weekly lunches and brunch on Sundays. Next time you are in Paris, be sure to stop into the boutique for a cupcake (or two!).

Case Study #10:
Starwood Hotels and Resorts
Worldwide, Inc.

Organization

Starwood Hotels and Resorts Worldwide, Inc.
(http://www.starwoodhotels.com)

Background

With 1,025 properties in 100 countries and territories and
145,000 employees, Starwood Hotels and Resorts
Worldwide, Inc. (Starwood Hotels) is one of the leading
hotel and leisure companies in the world. Starwood
Hotels is a fully integrated owner, operator, and franchisor
of hotels, resorts, and residences, with internationally
renowned brands such as St. Regis, The Luxury
Collection, W, Westin, Le Méridien, Sheraton, Four
Points by Sheraton, and the recently launched Aloft and
Element. Starwood Hotels also owns Starwood Vacation
Ownership, Inc., one of the premier developers and oper-
ators of high-quality vacation interval-ownership resorts.

Business Need

To address social media's impact on peer-to-peer influence
to drive incremental business and engender loyalty, and to
transform guest relationships by providing engagements
based on honesty and transparency 365 days a year, not
just during their stays.

Social Media Solution

A true global engagement platform leveraging more than
1,000 hotel Facebook pages with consistent brand content
and messaging, localization capabilities for market-specific

The Facebook page for W Barcelona.

W San Diego's Facebook page.

executions, and an integrated social-monitoring platform to ensure maximum communication and engagement.

Business Result

Starwood Hotels saw an increase in overall positive sentiment around each brand, an improvement in operational efficiencies on properties, and the ability to initiate specific customer-service improvements based on customer interactions.

What Actually Happened

Starwood Hotels has managed the unthinkable: launching 1,000+ Facebook pages for individual properties, while maintaining consistent brand image and messaging through content and interaction. Where do you even start with such a huge undertaking? How is it possible to unify the social media presence of nine brands and 1,000+ hotels spread across the world? How can you possibly determine the effect of such a broad initiative?

Starwood Hotels began with the most critical aspects of developing a social media strategy: Start by listening to what is being said about you already, establish the business need, and get everyone on board. The next step, of course, is identifying the appropriate social media channels to utilize. Starwood Hotels wanted to engage their guests 365 days a year, while creating a genuine sense of honesty and transparency in order to build relationship equity and loyalty. A major challenge was the need for brand consistency across diverse global markets, while still maintaining local relevance for individual properties. Facebook became the solution.

Each Starwood property has an individual Facebook page, primarily managed by the team at that location.

Incorporated into each page is a tab for the larger brand of that hotel. For example, each of the W hotels has a Facebook page with a tab for the W brand that communicates the overall brand experience consistently but customized with local content from the hotel. A key to success in this formula is that the Starwood team did not attempt to do everything centrally. Instead, they engaged the owners and property representatives, educated them, and gave them the necessary guidelines and tools to establish, monitor, and maintain their own platforms.

Widespread training across the company involved a plan in and of itself. Starwood Hotels created a global training team and started by training key personnel at each property on social media. All global divisions needed to be aware of what platforms are out there, and everyone needed to be educated in the importance of social media in connecting with their customers.

One tool Starwood Hotels implemented for education was a third-party system that monitored sentiment and mentions of the individual properties in social media. The stakeholders at each property could see for themselves that discussions were happening all the time in the digital sphere. From there, Starwood Hotels laid out basic guidelines for online interactions, and then progressed to training on how to approach overall strategy and content.

Starwood Hotels maintained the necessary balance between brand consistency and flexibility for individual properties in a number of ways. The first step was creating a mix of interactive modules on the branded tabs that enabled brand messaging to co-exist with local content managed by each property, but they also made sure that the guidelines for interaction and content production were broad enough to accommodate market needs. After all, guests in each geographic area and within each brand want different types of information and respond differently to promotions and specials. For example, some properties host more events, and some need to offer more travel promotions for value-conscious demographics.

In addition, each property and brand is able to gather valuable customer feedback from social media interactions and sentiment analysis. For example, they could discover that check-ins are consistently slow at a particular location and use it as an opportunity to increase customer service and satisfaction.

These technologies also create for customers the ability to speak publicly and broadly about their experiences. People are very passionate about travel experiences, both positive and negative, and now they can broadcast those experiences to a very wide network very quickly. A decade ago, travelers sent postcards about their adventures to a few people; today, they share where they have been, what they have seen, and how the hotel staff treated them with their entire network though Facebook, Twitter, Foursquare, and other social media services. Because one person can effortlessly relate their experience to hundreds of others, it becomes critical for brands to find and respond to guests who have had bad experiences before they lose not just that customer, but countless others as well.

The emergence of social media platforms and their widespread use means a fundamental shift in guest relations. For Starwood Hotels, this heralded an increased capability to broaden relationships and engage with guests 365 days a year, not just during their stay with the hotel. There is also an opportunity from customer-service and marketing perspectives to leverage social media to benefit the company as well as the guest. Starwood Hotels has profited in many ways from engagement in the social media space. Because they are directly interacting with guests, they can reinforce good experiences and effectively resolve bad ones. As a result, Starwood Hotels has been able to measure an overall increase in positive sentiment across all nine brands and the Starwood Preferred Guest loyalty program.

Case Study #11:
The Women's Museum

Organization

The Women's Museum
(http://www.thewomensmuseum.org)

Background

A Smithsonian affiliate, The Women's Museum makes visible the unique, textured, and diverse stories of American women. Using the latest technology and interactive media, the museum's exhibits and programs expand our understanding of women's participation in shaping our nation's history and create a lively environment for dialogue and discovery. Thousands of stories recount public and private triumphs and the struggles of those who would be denied their freedoms in all its forms: political, social, and spiritual.

Business Need

To maximize national exposure with a minimal budget, being a non-profit organization.

Social Media Solution

A Twitter page to help promote the museum, http://www.twitter.com/thewomensmuseum.

Business Result

The Women's Museum has experienced a rapidly growing national and international brand awareness.

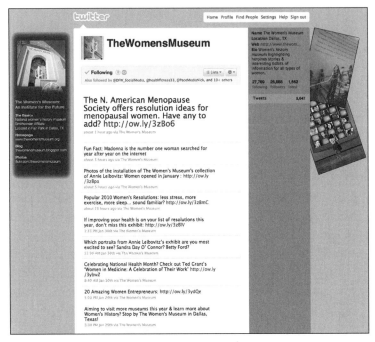

The following text appears within the Twitter page image:

Home Profile Find People Settings Help Sign out

TheWomensMuseum

✓ Following
Also followed by @DFW_SocialMedia, @healthfitness33, @PaceMediaNick, and 10+ others

Name The Women's Museum
Location Dallas, TX
Web http://www.thewom...
Bio Women's history museum highlighting heroines stories & interesting tidbits of information for all types of women.

27,789   26,888   1,862
following   followers   listed

Tweets   8,647

The N. American Menopause Society offers resolution ideas for menopausal women. Have any to add? http://ow.ly/3zBo6
about 1 hour ago via The Women's Museum

Fun Fact: Madonna is the number one woman searched for year after year on the internet
about 3 hours ago via The Women's Museum

Photos of the installation of The Women's Museum's collection of Annie Leibovitz: Women opened in January : http://ow.ly/3zBpa
about 5 hours ago via The Women's Museum

Popular 2010 Women's Resolutions: less stress, more exercise, more sleep... sound familiar? http://ow.ly/3zBmC
about 23 hours ago via The Women's Museum

If improving your health is on your list of resolutions this year, don't miss this exhibit: http://ow.ly/3zBlV
1:35 PM Jan 30th via The Women's Museum

Which portraits from Annie Leibovitz's exhibit are you most excited to see? Sandra Day O' Connor? Betty Ford?
11:30 AM Jan 30th via The Women's Museum

Celebrating National Health Month? Check out Ted Grant's 'Women in Medicine: A Celebration of Their Work' http://ow.ly/3ybwZ
8:40 AM Jan 30th via The Women's Museum

20 Amazing Women Entrepreneurs: http://ow.ly/3ydQe
5:00 PM Jan 29th via The Women's Museum

Aiming to visit more museums this year & learn more about Women's History? Stop by The Women's Museum in Dallas, Texas!
3:00 PM Jan 29th via The Women's Museum

The Women's Museum's Twitter page.

What Actually Happened

Even before you walk into The Women's Museum in Dallas, Texas, the indomitable beauty of its elegant Art Deco façade immediately overwhelms you. When you enter the blissfully cool lobby and walk up the grand stairway, you pass the larger-than-life Wall of Words, which presents a dozen quotes from some of the most inspiring women in history: Susan B. Anthony, Eleanor Roosevelt, Mary McLeod Bethune. Further exploration of the museum yields many stories of women that take place throughout U.S. history from 1500 to now, all presented in an awe-inducing venue that harnesses the power of interactive media. As but two examples, users can watch videos of *The Carol Burnett Show* and listen to audio recordings of Aretha Franklin's four-octave voice. Visitors can also open drawers to discover hundreds of pop-culture images in the Icons of Womanhood section, or peruse the dynamic It's Amazing section. This colorful, brightly lit glass labyrinth explores facts and fiction of past and present dealing with stereotypes and images.

For such a highly interactive and intricate multimedia experience to not garner a national audience would be a waste. And yet, prior to 2008, that was precisely the situation facing the nine-year-old institution. "Here we were," says Lyn Scott, COO at The Women's Museum, "the only museum in the nation dedicated to American women's history, and yet we had no means of speaking to a national audience."

The mission of The Women's Museum was to "bring to life the voices, talents, achievements, aspirations, and stories of the past, present, and future" to be appreciated on a national level. However, it faced the problems common to most non-profits. Limited resources meant limited staff, especially for the marketing department, which consisted of one person. And like most non-profits, marketing had to make do with a slim advertising budget of virtually zero dollars. "We were only able to justify buying ad space in smaller, regional magazines focusing on local tourism and rental events," says Haley Curry, Marketing Manager of The Women's Museum. Not surprisingly, this kind of geographically narrow focus provided limited exposure.

Prior to the advent of social media, the museum's website was its only means of reaching a wider audience, yet it was still limited in its reach. Then, along came Twitter. With Twitter, the museum could reach a wide audience and engage with fans from all over the U.S. and the world.

Needless to say, the museum quickly realized the potential of this new platform. "Twitter allowed us to make huge strides on a limited budget," says Curry.

Using only the highest-quality content—a blend of both entertainment and information—the museum was able to build a strong community of Twitter followers. Within the first year, The Women's Museum's social media outreach campaign was a huge success, attaining an impressive 12,000+ Twitter followers. Furthermore, @thewomensmuseum is ranked among the Top Museums on Twitter, along with the Tate in London, New York's MoMa, and the Brooklyn Museum (http://www.museummarketing.co.uk/2009/06/09/top-museums-on-twitter/), as well as being on the list of 20 of the top non-profits to follow on Twitter.

The most critical result of their efforts: About 60 percent of The Women's Museum's followers are located outside the Dallas/Fort Worth area, with 1 percent located internationally. The Women's Museum has achieved a strong presence and awareness, which continues to grow not just nationally but internationally as well.

"Twitter also allows us to connect with our most enthusiastic fans and participate in a conversation that is constructive to our mission: create conversation and develop understanding of American women's history," says Curry. That connection is critical for a museum with interactive media exhibits that bridge the gap between location and thought. "Not everyone can visit The Women's Museum the building, but they can experience who we are daily at @thewomensmuseum."

Case Study #12:
In The Know

Organization

In The Know (http://www.execsintheknow.com)

Background

In The Know is a division of M.E.R. (McDaniel Executive Recruiters). They have built brand, trust, and relationships over the last 10 years, specializing in the managed services, outsourcing, BPO, CRM, and contact-center industries. The community consists of professionals and executives across all corporate brands who have responsibility for the "voice of the customer" or implementation of customer-response/service strategies.

Business Need

To create leading customer-response events and the Executive Think Tank series to serve as a conduit for bringing like-for-like professionals together and for sharing common areas of interest through digital platforms and in-person events.

Social Media Solution

A LinkedIn group, Worldwide Contact Center Professionals, which is the largest contact-center community on LinkedIn.

Business Result

In The Know has increased its reputation, has developed a strong niche community to tap into in order to host successful events like the Customer Response Summit, and has translated a strong network of professionals into an independent managed community, which has created both new sources of revenue and increased revenue as a whole.

What Actually Happened

In The Know is the evolution of years of growth and development for McDaniel Executive Recruiters. M.E.R. has been building successful communities over the past 10

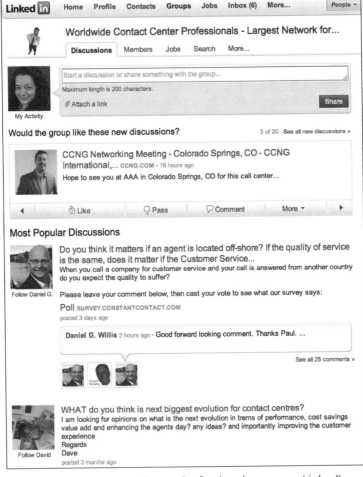

The Worldwide Contact Center Professionals page on LinkedIn.

years, even before the emergence of what we know of today as formal communities and social media. M.E.R. was able to establish a strong LinkedIn group as a focal point for their community, which then provided a niche source of individuals that could be pulled to industry events that provide relevant content and conversation. In The Know is now in the process of expanding and managing the independent platform specifically created for Worldwide Contact Center Professionals, In The Know Across the Globe.

The contact-center industry has always lent itself to community development, as community is a crucial element to solving problems and the generation of customer-response strategy. In the past, these communities have flourished in various forums and digital arenas, but there was no cohesive central community for "voice of the customer" professionals and customer-response experts to ask questions, collaborate, and solve problems.

In their first 10 years, McDaniel Executive Recruiters built a large network of contact-center professionals worldwide. They began cultivating this group through more conventional means, such as e-mail. With the emergence of social media platforms, they recognized the need and the opportunity for a single, powerfully managed community targeted specifically to contact-center professionals.

LinkedIn provided the much-needed platform for developing this type of relationship environment. Because LinkedIn is a networking site for business professionals, it was the logical starting place for building a community of professionals within the business of contact centers. M.E.R. established Worldwide Contact Center Professionals in 2008, which had grown to more than 19,000 members by 2011.

Chad McDaniel, President of M.E.R. and In The Know, sums it up: "Social media has made reaching out to this community much more efficient. Moreover, we've also been able to offer a 'return' for those involved by answering their questions and inquiries with a relatively instant response and sharing of information." Not only does the LinkedIn group provide a forum for "worldwide industry experts in customer-contact strategies including CRM, BPO, direct marketing, managed services, and call-center industries," but it allows In The Know to establish a strong reputation with industry insiders and other businesses as a source for solutions. In addition, In The Know has created a community that can be tapped and translated to conference events, which is unlike any other in the customer-response industry.

In The Know hosted the first Customer Response Summit in Arizona in 2010. It focused specifically on the impact of social media on customer-response strategies, bringing together industry leaders from companies such as AT&T, GoDaddy, and Starwood Hotels. As Chad McDaniel points out, "The success of the event was amazing. It is apparent corporate America is struggling with integration of complex multi-channels of customer communication, and when you layer in the new and emerging channels (i.e., social, web 2.0, video, mobile), these complexities become tenfold."

By providing valuable information and useful connections to attendees, In The Know was able to reinforce their growing reputation and strengthen an already-powerful network. And by broadcasting before, during, and after the event through social media channels, they were able to merge the powerful success of the event with their extensive online network.

The next step for In The Know is to convert its community-management experience, stellar reputation as an industry thought leader, and extensive network into an independent, exclusive community.

A new site, http://www.execsintheknow.com, provides an exclusive, managed environment for Worldwide Contact Center Professionals to gather online, socialize, and share knowledge and success stories. In The Know is an exclusive community of more than 140,000 contact-center professionals and experts worldwide, focused on customer-response strategies and communication within the industry.

4

You Need More Than One Ball to Juggle

Have you ever watched a juggler engage a crowd by throwing around one ball? No. Of course you haven't. And yet, with social media, many companies try just that. Unfortunately, when it comes to social media, most people only think of one thing at a time.

Many companies think the best way to handle social media is with their customer-service department, either internally or outsourced. Other companies believe the right place for social media is the marketing department, where promotions and specials can be highlighted by a team of dedicated experts in their fields.

> Social media is a ridiculously powerful tool—one you must leverage for all parts of your company.

Right about now, you're probably wondering which of these I'm going to say is the "right" answer. Well, guess what? Both are correct. You need to actively engage marketing and customer-service departments to be successful with social media. However, that is just the tip of the iceberg. Social media is a ridiculously powerful tool—one you must leverage for all parts of your company. Fortunately, that's just what this chapter is about.

What should you be using social media for? Here are a few areas of your company that can start leveraging social media today:

- Customer service
- Marketing
- Company goal fulfillment

Leveraging Social Media for Customer Service

By definition, social media is based on frequent interaction with important people, and the most important people in the life of your company are always your customers. They pay the bills and keep you fed. Nearly every comment or bit of feedback is a kernel of information to be exploited and explored, *if* you treat it as such.

Make sure your customer-service department is on the lookout for the following kernels of information:

- Specific complaints about a new or existing product or service that need to be rectified immediately

- General grumblings that should be looked into further

- Rave reviews about a new product or service

- Trends that need to be tracked

> Nearly every comment or bit of feedback is a kernel of information to be exploited and explored, *if* you treat it as such.

Many companies are getting better and better by speeding up response times and reducing costs for customer-service departments through the use of social media vehicles such as Twitter or Facebook. Some companies use social media to share solutions to common product or service problems that their customers experience so they can disseminate the information to large numbers of people quickly. Contact centers are also beginning to leverage the power of social media. Over the coming years, I predict you'll continue to see a rapid shift in the way contact centers and customer-service centers leverage social media to solve complaints more rapidly and in the public eye.

When a company uses social media and works to solve issues openly and honestly, they often develop "crusading customers"—customers who step in on behalf of a company via social media, even before the company can respond. Crusading customers—who answer questions, right wrongs, and defend you till the end because they've seen your company earnestly try to do the same—are a very powerful weapon in your arsenal.

Using Social Media for Marketing

Social media is a great place to serve up customer service, but if it is the only thing a company does with social media, they are missing the boat. What else should be included? So glad you asked. I mentioned that your customers are the most important part of your organization. To continue growing, however, you'll naturally need *more* customers. That's why it's important you use social media in conjunction with marketing: to make sure you are growing.

> It's important you use social media in conjunction with marketing to make sure you are growing.

Note that I'm using the term "marketing" to encompass many things:

- Advertising
- Branding
- Public relations
- Specials
- Promotions
- Sales

It confuses me when companies choose a PR house to handle their social media. I believe a good PR company is worth its weight in gold, but PR is only one aspect of social media.

So yes, you can find a good PR company to spread your message through social media, but don't ask that PR firm to manage the advertising, customer service, or other facets of your company that you should be addressing through social media. Instead, have your marketing department coordinate with your PR team to bring their ads, visuals, and writing to life.

For instance, if the marketing campaign is for a new line of skateboard designs, get with PR to see how they can translate your print, audio, and video ads into flesh and blood. Perhaps they can get some great press by having local skaters try out the boards live at the local skate park (with the popular media in attendance, of course). Then pump all the content from marketing and PR through social media and take it further to real, every-day people. Sticking with the new-skateboard-design example, wouldn't it make sense to post videos of actual kids using the skateboard on YouTube.com to gauge the reaction?

This is a great way to have a two-sided conversation. By posting demonstration videos, you're saying, "Here's our new product. What do you think?" And by providing valuable feedback with their responses and comments, kids who view the videos are saying, "Well, let me tell you...."

Harnessing Social Media for Company Goal Fulfillment

You've taken care of customer service (keeping current customers) and marketing (getting new customers). Now what? Now it's time to harness social media to take care of everything else—or, more specifically, company goal fulfillment. This includes those items your company is working on that don't fall directly under marketing or customer service, such as the following:

- Recruitment
- Research and development
- Geographic or demographic areas of focus
- Business-partnership development
- Acquisitions and mergers
- Company funding
- Competitive research
- Social causes
- Employee recognition

> Social media can provide you with ways to do business more efficiently and less expensively than ever before.

Many companies have no idea that social media can be used to assist them in performing inexpensive, targeted research before the development of a new product or to promote the non-profit causes they support. Similarly, many small businesses don't realize that one of the best keys to finding investors for first- or second-wave funding is through social media. It's a brave new world, my friends, and social media can provide you with ways to do business more efficiently and less expensively than ever before.

I recognize that it can be challenging to think of something as supposedly simple as social media as having so many possibilities, but doesn't everything in business touch on everything else? Doesn't a slow-down in production affect shipping, delivery, and customer service? Doesn't a breakdown in hiring affect management and leadership? Why should social media be any different?

The main thing to remember is that you shouldn't just say to each department, "Here, handle your social media and get back to me." Social media works best when it all works in tandem. Bring your department heads together to discuss their goals and how they will use social media to achieve those goals.

Although this is changing, I still hear some companies say they'll just hire a few interns to take care of social media. After all, this technology is familiar to the younger crowd, so it makes sense to have a young person in charge of it, right? Wrong. This is a common misconception. Although a younger person is more likely to be familiar with the technology and the tools involved, it is doubtful that the average intern would bring the level of experience in marketing, customer service, and communications necessary to represent the reputation of a company. Putting an inexperienced person in charge of social media is like putting the phone-repair guy in charge of your customer-service calls. Just because he knows the technology doesn't mean he can oversee the goals of a strategic social media campaign. Interns are valuable for their knowledge of the technology, but they should be led by a team that you would want representing your company in front of the press, in person, or on the phone. After all, social media puts your company on display in front of the world.

Social media is where customer service, marketing, and everything else your company wants to accomplish should converge. It's one very public place for you to build relationships to get these things done.

Case Studies

The following case studies are designed to help you see how the concepts discussed in this book can be put into action in the real world.

Case Study #13: The Adolphus Hotel

Organization

The Adolphus Hotel and its signature restaurant, The French Room (http://www.hoteladolphus.com)

Background

The Adolphus Hotel is an award-winning luxury hotel. Located in Dallas, Texas, it boasts a golden reputation and is steeped in tradition. Its premier signature restaurant, The French Room, is a four-diamond restaurant, known for offering one of the world's top dining experiences.

Business Need

To connect with devoted guests while exposing younger generations who are unaware of the hotel's hip luxury to the unique personality of The Adolphus Hotel and The French Room.

Social Media Solution

Creation of a heightened online presence using Facebook and Twitter to broadcast diverse and interactive content focused on art, cuisine, travel, local history, pop culture, and other finer things in life that appeal to the target audiences.

The Adolphus Hotel's Facebook page.

Business Result

A passionate following of long-time guests and people experiencing the property for the first time began connecting through shared discussion. The Adolphus Hotel became one of the most followed hotels on Twitter in the world. For the first time in years, The Adolphus Hotel saw a marked increase in new guests gracing both the rooms of the hotel and the restaurant.

What Actually Happened

David Davis, Director of Public Relations for The Adolphus Hotel for more than 27 years, pours all his talents into what is one of the most luxurious and beloved hotels in the nation. When David approached Craig Scott, Managing Director, with his interest in leveraging social media for the hotel, concerns arose. Both The Adolphus Hotel and The French Room enjoy a highly respected, prominent reputation going back almost 100 years. Scott wanted to avoid alienating the hotel's discerning, international client base and risk sacrificing its solid reputation. Could this luxury brand maintain a refined image if it were present on social media platforms like Twitter and Facebook, which are typically associated with everyday wares, services, and brands?

The answer is a resounding yes!

With the help of Social Media Delivered, David Davis and Craig Scott took The Adolphus down a path that few hotels—much less luxury properties—had ever traveled before. Scott understood that in order to build relationships with new prospects, he would need to provide not just information but also a mix of entertaining and engaging content. The hotel's Twitter page (http://www. twitter.com/theadolphus) serves as a platform to spread information not only about hotel happenings, but also for events happening around Dallas, allowing followers to be "in the know."

Thanks to Davis' long and rich tenure at the property, he enjoys relationships with incredible authors, artists, celebrities, and executives, both nationally and internationally. He wanted to be able to reach out to these contacts consistently in a light-hearted and entertaining way. The hotel's Facebook page (http://www.facebook.com/ theadolphushotel) enables him to do just that. It's like an online lifestyle magazine full of bite-sized tidbits of entertaining, historical, informative content. This social media vehicle also enables The Adolphus Hotel to highlight the unique beauty of the property via photos and videos, allowing for immediate, direct interaction from its many fans.

The Adolphus Hotel Facebook page also provides a unique business solution to an ongoing challenge: how to be competitive in a tough wedding market. For years, The Adolphus Hotel has hosted weddings of all sizes and all styles, but modern brides, spoiled by choices, had begun overlooking The Adolphus Hotel. A Facebook initiative changed all that, however. Each month, The Adolphus Hotel showcases a different wedding, displaying wedding photos for all to see and providing the newlyweds a bit of celebrity fame. The modern, sometimes edgy dresses juxtaposed against the hotel's historic beauty provide striking and unforgettable images. This initiative has helped position The Adolphus Hotel as a modern and hip locale for Dallas weddings.

The return on risk has been astronomical. The Adolphus Hotel's Twitter presence, representing the hotel and The French Room restaurant, has increased brand recognition for a whole new, younger audience. With more than 10,000 followers, The Adolphus Hotel is currently the number-one–ranking hotel or restaurant in Dallas. It is also one of the most followed hotels in the world. The Adolphus Hotel now enjoys a revitalized reputation and has become one of the most sought-after wedding locations in Dallas, thanks to its social media presence on Facebook.

The Adolphus and The French Room prove that there is a place for luxury in social media—as long as you cater to the needs of the clientele in the way they wish to be engaged. The Adolphus Hotel has already been doing this in the real world since 1912; the transition to social media was only natural.

Case Study #14:
Stand Up To Cancer (SU2C)
and Virgin America

Organization

Stand Up To Cancer (http://www.standup2cancer.org) and Virgin America (http://www.virginamerica.com)

Background

Stand Up To Cancer (SU2C), launched in 2008, is a program of the Entertainment Industry Foundation, a 501(c)3 charitable organization. It raises funds for translational cancer research. Virgin America, a California-based airline established in 2007, is SU2C's official domestic airline partner. In December 2010, Virgin America launched service from Los Angeles and San Francisco to the Dallas–Fort Worth airport, marking the airline's first mid-continent destination in the United States.

Business Needs

To continue to raise funds and awareness in Texas and throughout the country for SU2C, and to successfully launch Virgin America service in a new market where serious competition already existed.

Social Media Solution

A geographically focused Facebook and Twitter campaign aimed at driving traffic to a co-branded microsite hosted by Virgin America. The microsite was a hub for collecting donations to SU2C as well as promoting a Virgin America launch event in Dallas.

The microsite for the Virgin America launch event in Dallas.

Business Result

Both Virgin America and SU2C gained exposure leading up to and following the Dallas launch event. Online contacts were transformed into real-life donors and participants. Additionally, they raised $25,000 in donations through the microsite, the event itself, and a donation match by Virgin America.

What Actually Happened

Virgin America planned a star-studded inaugural flight and party on the ground in Dallas in its signature style. A company known for its social initiatives and innovation, the airline used the Dallas launch activities to promote its relationship with SU2C. For SU2C, Virgin America's Dallas launch provided the opportunity to reach out to its large social media community and to attract more supporters. The promotion produced real-world participation and new multi-level donors.

The Virgin America Dallas launch was a joint marketing effort with SU2C. Traditional media, such as radio spots, was leveraged, while both organizations reached out to their networks via e-blast and social media channels. SU2C already had an engaged, national online community, but they had not yet participated in an event on the ground in Texas. Virgin America had an existing base of dedicated frequent flyers who were largely based on the east and west coasts. Both organizations needed a way to translate a passionate online community into a real-world event while generating new supporters.

Virgin America built a microsite to incentivize and collect donations to SU2C. A minimum $5 donation earned the benefactor a 20-percent discount on a Virgin America flight. Donors could then spread the word through Facebook, Twitter, and e-mail by means of automated message options, encouraging others to follow their example. If a Dallas-based donor recruited 10 friends to donate on his or her behalf, that donor received two tickets to the launch party. The deal was even sweeter (yet more challenging) for donors in San Francisco and Los Angeles: If a single donor could recruit 100 other people to donate $5, that individual and a guest earned a Virgin America flight to Dallas, hotel accommodations, and two tickets to the event. The 20-percent coupon, coupled with the opportunity to attend a once-in-a-lifetime party, helped to spread the promotion virally.

By reaching out through social media in this way, SU2C and Virgin America translated online communities into a huge event. SU2C particularly benefited from this model because it resulted in a high number of multi-level donors—that is, people who not only give money, but become the non-profit equivalent of brand ambassadors, spreading word and awareness of the organization's cause.

SU2C secured additional media coverage by including two Celebrity Ambassadors to highlight the inaugural flight: Maura Tierney and Eric Stonestreet. The actors participated in photo ops and media interviews that highlighted SU2C, the Virgin America Dallas launch, and the overall partnership. Eric Stonestreet also tweeted about the experience.

The launch party itself was on December 1, 2010, at the Winspear Opera House in the Dallas Arts District. The guests turned out in their Urban Cowboy wear, the valet was complimentary, the red carpet was long, the catering was impeccable, the drinks flowed freely, and the celebrities roamed famously. Sir Richard Branson, head of Virgin Group, himself hosted an exclusive pre-party, while Willie Nelson performed in his SU2C t-shirt.

One key to the success of the initiative was the clear call to action and easily translatable message for people to share. Another key was the dialogue that grew organically online and on the ground. For example, the SU2C signing wall at the event gave guests a place to share why they donated, indicate how cancer had touched their lives, or simply show love and support. Not only was the signing wall a physical representation of how people interact in social media channels, it represented a message and a focus for people to share with their own networks. Thus, guests spontaneously pushed social media messages out to their personal Facebook, Twitter, and geolocation app networks, such as Foursquare or Facebook Places, before, during, and after the event.

SU2C and Virgin America successfully teamed up to execute a real-world event by leveraging online networks. Social media provided a way to promote the event and spread buzz for Virgin America and SU2C. As Mary Pomerantz of SU2C states, social media "has the power to encourage action and build a brand. Social media also helps to cultivate a culture around the brand."

Case Study #15: General Motors

Organization

The General Motors Company (http://www.gm.com)

Background

The General Motors Company, also known as GM, is a U.S.-based automaker with its headquarters in Detroit, Michigan. The company manufactures cars and trucks in 31 countries, employs 209,000 people around the world, and sells and services vehicles in some 157 countries.

Business Need

To completely redefine its established brand image following declaration of Chapter 11/363 bankruptcy. The old GM brand appeared to consumers as faceless, nameless, outdated, and impenetrable; the new GM brand structure would require a more accessible and transparent feeling in order to help humanize the brand.

Social Media Solution

Build a diverse social media team, with CEO engagement and support, to handle all logistical/management social media operations to enable the newly defined GM brand mentality of openness and engagement to be clearly communicated and fully accessible to the media, the general public, and, most importantly, customers.

Business Result

GM held market share with four fewer brands, increased awareness and consideration, and gained solid customer loyalty and positive brand awareness.

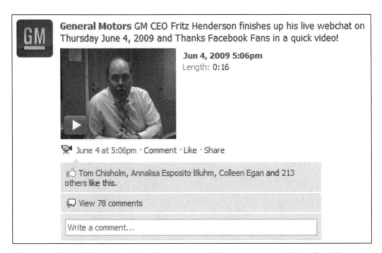

Former GM CEO Fritz Henderson, on the company's Facebook page.

What Actually Happened

GM had weathered many difficult financial climates throughout its long history. In an article for *Business Week*, reporter Ed Wallace notes: "[Even] after the 1910 Financial Panic ended, rising sales proved that GM was viable in any condition." Over the decades since its founding in 1908, the company has persevered through the good times and bad. But more importantly, the GM brand had built a reputation as "a symbol of American industrial might," in the words of the AP. In a word, GM's brand had proven to be resilient.

But as the financial industry collapsed in late 2007, things worsened across all sectors in America, including the automotive industry. A year later, corporate giants and small businesses alike continued to fear the worst was yet to come. For GM, despite countless efforts to prevent the inevitable bankruptcy filings, including putting divisions and parts operations on the block and repeatedly pruning its workforce, problems continued to mount. On June 1,

2009, GM's worst nightmare became a reality: It filed for bankruptcy. Because of this drastic setback, and even with the U.S. government estimated to pledge an additional $30+ billion on top of the $20 billion it had already handed to GM, the future seemed uncertain for one of The Big Three American auto giants.

Consumer confidence in GM's brand plummeted. The company needed a fresh approach to restore faith in its heritage brand. Because of its consistently solid market share and size, GM had a big opportunity to proactively rebound from this destructive period and rebuild a lost relationship with its customers. It did so with social media.

In May 2009, GM assembled an extensive social media team consisting of members with backgrounds in finance, media relations, and marketing. Their task: Implement and oversee a tidal wave of social media touch points to introduce the freshly restructured GM brand mentality with openness and consumers at the center.

First, using platforms like Twitter (http://www.twitter.com/gmblogs) and Facebook (http://www.facebook.com/generalmotors), GM's social media team listened carefully to what was being said about its brand and acted quickly to rectify misconceptions about the company. For example, Mary Henige, Director of Social Media and Digital Communications for GM, saw a comment on Twitter from a customer who wanted GM to stop closing down smaller dealers and instead to "shut down their company-owned dealerships." Within seconds, a member of the team responded to that customer, explaining that at GM, there are no company-owned dealerships. In reality, all dealerships are independent, often family-owned businesses passed down through generations. Although this example illustrates only one customer's incorrect perception, it's highly likely that many others probably thought similarly, which affected GM's brand negatively. But by using Twitter to publicly and positively respond to the misconception, GM was able to correct the negative comment proactively and without distancing the customer.

Social media makes handling this type of communication with a customer more possible now than ever before. Communicating and listening intently to a customer is also one of the most important things a business should be doing at all times. This is just one of many examples of how GM was able to set the record straight by communicating directly with customers and prospects via social media.

Next, GM created an unprecedented program, giving the public direct access to the CEO via social media. GM's CEO at the time, Fritz Henderson, understood the importance and necessity of active listening, being open, and engaging with consumers. Through a series of live web events, customers, the media, and the general public were encouraged to participate in Q&A sessions and press conferences with Henderson. To many, the ability to speak one-on-one with the CEO of a major corporation like GM seemed too good to be true; in fact, some people assumed it was just a PR hoax. But staff used a Flip cam to record Henderson typing his answers during a web chat to prove his active participation and to thank GM supporters. The video coverage was posted on GM's Facebook page as well as on other vehicles, and was quickly disseminated across the social web. GM also created a "Tell Fritz" forum, where customers could exchange ideas and information with the CEO. Within six months, more than 16,500 customer comments and questions were addressed. GM managed not only to wow its customers with this campaign, it set a new standard of engagement.

In this way, GM demonstrated its values of openness and transparency, and built consumer confidence and deepening customer loyalty.

Additionally, GM launched an interactive website, GM Headlines (http://www.gmheadlines.com), inviting visitors to "Take a look at the new GM." The site provides a

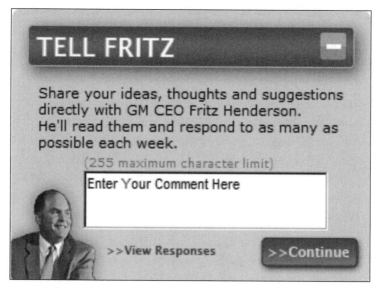

GM's Tell Fritz forum.

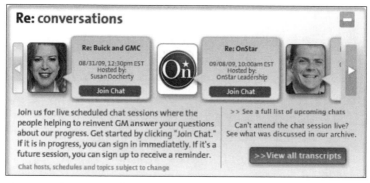

Conversations, one element of the GM Headlines site.

wealth of informative videos about GM and its vehicles, as well as opportunities to chat, get industry news, and get to know members of the organization. Since June 2009, the site has generated an impressive 2.5 million+ unique video views.

By being honest, direct, and real with customers, GM has been able to regain the respect and loyalty it had lost. What's more, a whole new breed of GM "brand ambassadors" has emerged. These enthusiastic customers create buzz around GM products via their social networks, helping GM build its business. Additionally, these brand ambassadors often go to great lengths to defend the brand in the face of negativity or to correct misinformation that may be circulating about GM. These conversations are taking place in real time in the social media space, which means they are reaching an audience of hundreds if not thousands. And the message is that much more powerful and credible coming from a peer rather than from a GM representative.

In this age of social media and in the aftermath of the worst recession since the Great Depression, corporations are held to a higher standard of ethics, professionalism, and transparency than ever before. It's becoming harder to bury flaws because social media serves to magnify them. Instead of running away from social media, General Motors embraced the new technology and seized the opportunity to reinvent its outdated brand.

Thanks to GM's savvy use of social media, results have been steady growth in market share, brand awareness, and customer loyalty. While there's still more work to be done, this iconic American brand sees a bright future as it continues to reinvent itself through the power of social media.

Case Study #16:
The Fresh Diet

Organization

The Fresh Diet (http://www.thefreshdiet.com)

Background

Established in November of 2005, The Fresh Diet was conceived by a Le Cordon Bleu–trained chef. It's based on the 40-percent carbohydrates, 30-percent proteins, and 30-percent fats diet concept. It became the first diet-delivery company in Florida to offer daily meals that are never frozen, freeze-dried, or vacuum packed. Instead, The Fresh Diet hand-delivers three freshly prepared, delicious meals and two snacks directly to your door each day.

Business Need

To connect to customers and potential employees, increase PR, build community, and assist in reducing costs associated with growing a young company.

Social Media Solution

Establish a presence on LinkedIn, and later build robust communities on Facebook and Twitter.

Business Result

Reduced costs of recruiting and PR, expanded branding presence, and 15-percent business growth directly associated with social media.

What Actually Happened

Zalmi Duchman established The Fresh Diet in November of 2005 after a phone call with his friend, Le Cordon

Bleu–trained chef Yosef Schwartz. Schwartz told Duchman about a service that delivered healthy, gourmet meals to clients in the area. Recognizing its appeal and the lack of such a service in the Florida market, Duchman spent a few hundred dollars to set up a website, take out a few ads, and get incorporated. In classic entrepreneurial style, he personally made the first deliveries of fresh, healthy food prepared by him and his wife in their kitchen at home to three clients on the evening of January 1, 2006.

Two months later, with 13 clients, he quit his job and convinced Yosef Schwartz to move east to take over the cooking from Ms. Duchman, who was eight months pregnant at the time. After only five years, The Fresh Diet has accumulated more than 200 employees and an additional 100 independent contract drivers, and serves more than 3,000 people every night. With six kitchens, each capable of delivering to a 300-mile radius, The Fresh Diet is in 12 of the top 20 North American markets, has had national press exposure, and has built large active communities online. And they did it all without a PR company. As Zalmi Duchman says, "Before social media, you had to hire a PR agency for that kind of growth and after social media, you're crazy if you do."

Duchman views social media as a way to assist the business of The Fresh Diet, and has utilized various platforms to build customer relationships, spread good PR, and recruit as the company grows. A key to the amazing success of their social media initiatives is the focus on strategy. As Jim Gilbert, director of marketing, points out, they are always positioning social media with the next step of company growth in mind.

Some of the greatest business returns for Duchman and The Fresh Diet have resulted from LinkedIn, where he spent a significant amount of time developing relationships throughout 2008. One of the main goals of building these relationships was to create exposure for The Fresh Diet in more mainstream media channels. Duchman used LinkedIn to research and send messages to editors in print media, such as *US Weekly*, *People*, *The New York Post*, and other popular publications. A brilliant way to build PR, he created many strong relationships with people involved in these traditional media, and as a result landed a spot in the January 2009 *US Weekly* article, "5 Diets That Work." The Fresh Diet was the only product-based program included in the article and they attribute over $100,000 in revenue directly to the national exposure gained from converting these social media relationships into traditional media exposure.

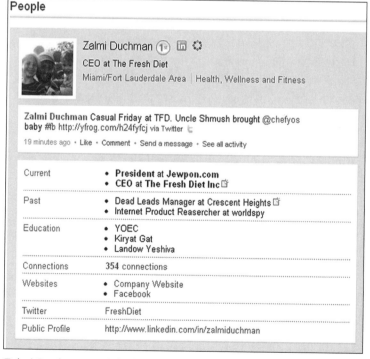

Zalmi Duchman's LinkedIn page.

In addition to direct revenue growth, The Fresh Diet benefited from the recruiting opportunities provided by LinkedIn. Duchman met Jim Gilbert, current director of marketing for The Fresh Diet, through LinkedIn. Because they had built a relationship on the site, Duchman thought of Gilbert when he needed someone to take charge of marketing initiatives for The Fresh Diet. Through that online connection, Duchman knew Gilbert's background in marketing—and even more significantly, that he was an early adopter of social media. After providing consulting services for several months, Gilbert came on full time in November of 2009.

Duchman has also built an amazing community online with Facebook (http://www.facebook.com/thefreshdiet) and Twitter (@freshdiet). Duchman was already on Facebook by the end of 2007, and started tweeting for The Fresh Diet in June of 2008. Duchman credits 10 to 15 percent of their business growth to these social media initiatives' bringing new customers to the door, although he looks at these financial results as simply an added benefit at the end of the day. As Duchman points out, because social media is free, "any dollar it brings is 100 percent ROI."

One of the true benefits of such a strong social media community for The Fresh Diet team is the invaluable customer feedback they gain without spending huge amounts of cash to hire a PR agency, manage focus groups, or implement extensive market research. The community on The Fresh Diet Facebook page is very active, with about 90-percent positive feedback. The team uses the negative 10 percent to make changes and streamline their process.

They rely heavily on the exposure gained through their Facebook and Twitter pages to spread PR. When

Duchman first started the Facebook page, he researched their clients and friended them directly (in the days before Facebook groups). With The Fresh Diet Twitter feed, he started interacting with celebrities to gain exposure in their large networks. By going out and finding customers (instead of waiting for them to show up), The Fresh Diet has managed to build followers and active community members who are not even in any of the markets they currently serve and who have never tasted their food. When they do expand into new markets, they already have a customer base of passionate brand advocates and a platform through which to reach them for promotion.

Duchman and Gilbert believe the huge success of The Fresh Diet's online presence is due to the human element incorporated in their interactions. Duchman still does most of the posting on both platforms with some help from a couple of other members of The Fresh Diet team. Their head chef, Yosef Schwartz, has a very active Facebook page where he promotes The Fresh Diet brand by being himself and building his own reputation. Clients and potential customers can engage directly with the key personalities in the company; those direct interactions on a human level have created a strong sense of community and support. Gilbert states that their goal is always to "not be a nameless, faceless corporate entity but to have a human face and voice." Zalmi Duchman and The Fresh Diet team understand the importance of these relationships in building business success.

Case Study #17:
Pink Elephant

Organization

Pink Elephant (http://www.pinkelephant.com)

Background

Pink Elephant is a privately owned, Toronto-based company established by president David Ratcliffe and CEO Fatima Cabral. Their primary focus is providing information technology infrastructure library (ITIL) consultation and education. Operating through many offices across the globe, the company is the world's number-one supplier of ITIL and IT service management (ITSM) conferences, education, and consulting services. To date, close to 200,000 IT professionals have benefited from Pink Elephant's expertise. Pink Elephant has been championing the growth of ITIL worldwide since its inception in 1989.

Business Need

To build networks and business.

Social Media Solution

Implement multiple company blogs to share information.

Business Result

Increased traffic to blog and increased awareness of the company in almost every country in the world.

What Actually Happened

Pink Elephant has been an industry leader for more than 20 years and can claim 85 of the U.S. *Fortune 100* companies as clients. In the simplest terms, they provide

The Pink Elephant blog.

consulting and guidance to corporate IT departments. In the current state of the IT industry—with its increasing risk, easy access to corporate data, and privacy and security issues heralded by web and mobile technologies—Pink Elephant has distinguished themselves as experts in IT management.

In spite of the stellar company's reputation, President David Ratcliffe recognizes the need to spread awareness and education about their brand and expertise. Particularly in B2B, network building is a vital part of growing business. To help achieve this, Mr. Ratcliffe began personally blogging six years ago. The main purpose of his blogging was to share information and advice. As he points out, "If you can impress in people that you are trustworthy and give them advice and share your experience, they will beat a path to your door for more."

David writes his own blogs, and shares everything from business advice and videos to pictures and insight about what goes on at Pink Elephant and within the industry. He gives away free tips and resources. The blog provides a place for his personality to really shine through and for people to get to know what kind of guy runs the company. Statistics on David's blog show that he now receives visitors from nearly every country in the world.

Other workers within the company are also encouraged to blog and share about their aspect of the business. David recognizes that customers really appreciate insight into the company and the industry, and emphasizes that "people want to buy from people they like." If any Pink Elephant employee gets good attention on their own through blogging or other efforts, then it will reflect well on the company. For these reasons, everyone at the company is encouraged to use their own name and put a personal face to what they do.

Even the company mascot, Pinky the Elephant, was set up with a company blog. Each person who attends a Pink Elephant conference is given a small pink elephant, and the Pinky blog encourages visitors to submit photos of their pink elephants taken in different locations worldwide. This is a fun way to bring awareness and grow participation for the company.

The way David Ratcliffe sees it, "Social media is a godsend, the perfect way for us to interact with our competitors, our customers, and our employees." There has never been any expectation of or focus on ROI for Pink

Elephant's social media endeavors, only relationships and communication. As of early 2011, the company has not even yet created an official social media policy despite communicating in the social space for six years. David simply advises (very strongly) everyone in the company to "Never, never say anything critical, publicly, about our competitors."

Pink Elephant began exploring the possibilities of other social media platforms in late 2009. There was some internal debate between Mr. Ratcliffe and his wife, CEO Fatima Cabral, about why Pink Elephant should launch a social media initiative. At one point David asked Fatima, "When you booked our last vacation, where did you go? What site did you use?"

She replied, "TripAdvisor.com."

"Exactly. You didn't go to the hotel's home page or the airline's main site. You don't want to hear from them how great they are. You want to hear from everyone else how great they are. That's why we need to be on social media."

Case Study #18:
Sears Blue Blogger Group

Organization

Sears Holdings Corporation
(http://www.searsholdings.com)

Background

Celebrating more than 125 years in business, Sears Holdings Corporation is the nation's fourth-largest broadline retailer, with more than 4,000 full-line and specialty retail stores in the United States and Canada. Sears Holdings is the leading home-appliance retailer, as well as a leader in the tools, lawn and garden, consumer-electronics, and automotive repair and maintenance sectors. Sears Holdings Corporation is the nation's largest provider of home services, with more than 11,000,000 service calls made annually. Sears Holdings Corporation operates through its subsidiaries, including Sears, Roebuck and Co. and Kmart Corporation.

Business Need

To identify a way to engage the customer community and offer them considerate, thoughtful resources that would make their consumer-electronics purchasing decision with Sears more informed and enlightened.

Social Media Solution

Recruit well-rounded and knowledgeable bloggers from across the country for the inaugural Sears Blue Blogger Crew initiative. These bloggers would be given the opportunity to engage in events, interact with new resources,

Some Quick Highlights from Day One of 2011 International CES

January 06, 2011 | Electronics | 0 comments

tags: sears electronics, sears blue blogger crew, ces 2011

share this... 🔲 🔲 🔲   🔲 Like

Day One of the 2011 International CES featured some press conferences from some of the biggest electronics manufacturers around.

The big theme we noticed on the first day is that while they talked about the "what" (new products for 2011 and beyond), they're talking about the "how". How do products interact with each other? How does integrating your television, phone and computer (or tablet) *benefit* you?

After seeing only *some* of what CES has to offer, some of these "how" questions are becoming more clear. For instance:

Sony is promoting an all-around approach to 3D, stemming from content production, distribution and display, along with personal content creation ability.

Samsung's big platform for 2011 is "The Smarter Life": smart design, smart experience (e.g. applications) and smart connections (through connectable devices).

What does this mean? Everything from narrower bezels on LED televisions -- we're talking 0.2" wide -- to a 1' wireless connection range for televisions, which will make it simple to hook up laptops, cameras and other devices.

One fun note: to promote the release of Sony Pictures' "The Green Hornet," co-stars Seth Rogen and Jay Chou were present, and they were showing off the famous "Black Beauty car. Enjoy:

Highlights from International CES on the Sears blog.

and enjoy early access to consumer-electronics information, and then relate information to their own social media
communities about the latest technology news.

Business Result

Nearly 18,000,000 media impressions across a variety of
press outlets and social network communities (i.e.,
Mashable and The Next Web Blog) and consumer forums
over a month-long period.

What Actually Happened

To understand the progressive thinking that inspired Sears
to launch the Blue Blogger Crew during the 2011
International Consumer Electronics Show, one must first
travel back a mere three months earlier to October of
2010, when, on a seemingly average day, a smaller more

The Sears Blue Blogger Crew.

intimate event was taking place in Chicago, Illinois at the Sears store located on State Street.

As a foray into experiential blogging events targeted toward consumer-electronics enthusiasts, Sears invited nine local bloggers to attend the first consumer-electronics in-store product demo of Samsung's DualView camera, dubbed the "Sears Megapixel Meetup." Taking the cameras for a spin around town, the troupe strolled about on a photo walk while testing the camera features and capturing life through photography in real time. Commentary from the event was posted on participants' personal blogs and highlighted via Sears' own social media channels, as well as being made shareable for others navigating these online resources. From this point, with such a successful event completed on the micro level, the Sears team dared to think bigger. In conceptualizing ways they could really relate to their customers on an intimate, conversational level, this was only the first step. Blogging was merely the beginning.

Taking inspiration from the October 2010 event and ongoing social media activity and customer engagement, Sears concluded that the 2011 International Consumer Electronics Show (CES) would serve as the perfect platform for a more macro-level initiative through the launch of the Sears Blue Blogger Crew. By selecting a set of enthusiastic, thoughtful, and opinionated bloggers who offered well-rounded feedback via a cross section of interest areas and focuses, Sears set out to provide a "peer-to-peer" perspective from CES while engaging and inspiring the customer community at the world's largest technology trade show.

On January 3, 2011, just three days before CES would kick off around the world, Sears distributed news of its Blue

Blogger Crew activation. Industry competitors, the press, and the consumer masses readjusted their attention and began to watch when Sears announced they would bring a select group of technology bloggers from across the country to report on their experiences after checking out the hottest new items on display at the show. True to its innovative brand history, Sears was ahead of the curve. Accordingly, its engaging strategy stirred major discussion across various world news networks.

Andru Edwards (GearLive.com), Kris Cain (LittleTechGirl.com), Kelly Clay (LockerGnome.com), Jenna Hatfield (stopdropandblog.com), and Barbara Rozgonyi (WiredPRWorks.com) were the five introductory Sears Blue Blogger Crew members charged with a simple mission: Report, Tweet, YouTube, Facebook, blog, and post on everything happening at the CES over a three-day period. Each member was selected based on his or her knowledge in relation to different niches such as photography, technology, and/or small business. More importantly, the chosen bloggers were just normal people who enjoyed writing about the things they were passionate about and sharing their stories online within their personal networks.

When asked how this team was coordinated, Karen Austin, President of Consumer Electronics for Sears Holdings Corporation, shed insight regarding the selection process:

> In researching bloggers for this initiative, we were keen to recruit a well-rounded, diverse set of individuals who displayed a strong track record for producing quality content, and cared about what they generated. With that criteria, we were able to find thoughtful people

who could share their passion for consumer electronics via social communities and thus excite others to be more active online in sharing their own thoughts and opinions on consumer electronics industry news.

Early on in the emerging media revolution, Sears noticed how this "connection synergy" could be positioned to build trust in the customer community. Beyond that, by giving enthusiastic bloggers resources, tools, and access to industry news and events, Sears could offer its customers richer, quality information from the "peer" perspective. When today's consumer spends six months thinking about purchasing a large-screen TV and 70 to 80 percent of consumers trust opinions from people online when faced with a purchasing decision, brands should take a moment to step back and consider the conversations that are currently happening online amongst consumers, in blogging communities, and on social-networking platforms.

For Sears, bringing its Blue Blogger Crew to CES 2011 was only the beginning. Because the Sears Blue Blogger Crew feedback and reporting delivered such well-received and well-earned organic applause from the press and consumers, a broader plan has developed at Sears Holdings Corporation, which includes expanding on potential future opportunities. Shortly after CES concluded at the beginning of January, Kmart's Consumer Electronics gaming business (which falls under the Sears Holding Corporation umbrella) decided take the concept behind the Sears Blue Blogger Crew even further by tapping into its active and passionate online Kmart gaming community for a separate, yet similar, initiative. Kmart Consumer Electronics invited bloggers from its online gaming community to submit themselves for consideration to be among three bloggers to attend and participate in an exclusive Kmart experience at the 2011 Electronic Entertainment Expo (E3), the biggest, international trade show for the computer- and video-games industry.

Both concepts speak to the same long-term goal that Sears Holdings Corporation has always valued and pledged to uphold. As Austin thinks ahead on the months and years to come, she remains optimistic and certain that the established blogging team will hold true to their mission:

> In establishing an orchestrated campaign built upon the four pillars of our brand, which are dedicated to upholding the ideas of sharing voice, trust, insight, and content, Sears and Kmart Consumer Electronics are then able to communicate through blogs and other social media in a different and creative way more than ever before. The more people trust us and talk to us, the more insight we gain into our business and from there we can create the invaluable content which will truly help our customers and community.

With the announcement of the contest via the official KmartGamer.com blog, it's easy to understand why Sears Holdings Corporation is making another move to stir discussion amongst gamers in the blogosphere, as they go on to say, "Why, do you ask, are we extending this invitation? As we've gotten to know many of you, we've discovered that a lot of you are skilled gaming bloggers, podcasters and other media creators and you're darn good at it."

Now that's a brand that genuinely knows, trusts, and listens to its customer community!

5

The Social Media Business Equation

If this book were a hamburger, this chapter would be the beef. If you pay attention to nothing else, remember what's in this chapter, because I'm about to tell you what no one else is willing to spell out: the magic formula for converting social media to business.

Let's say that, in addition to being a great businessperson, you also happen to be a great friend. One of your closest friends is a woman named Julie. You and Julie enjoy spending time together at concerts, at networking events, and with each other's families. You've known Julie for years and the friendship you share is a joy.

One weekend, Julie calls you and asks for your help. She's calling you to see if you can help her move some heavy item—say, a sofa—from one floor to the next early on Sunday morning. You really love Julie, but Sunday is the one morning of the week you sleep late, and you're not terribly "friendly" before your morning cup of coffee. But you set your alarm for 6 a.m., dutifully head over to Julie's house, and carry the heavy sofa up the stairs without complaint.

The question is, why? The reason, in this case, is evident: because Julie is a great friend. In fact, 80 percent of the time you're with Julie, the friendship is rewarding, fulfilling, and fun. So because of the rewarding 80 percent, the 20 percent of the time when Julie asks for help—be it moving the sofa or listening to problems at work—you're always there for her. She's earned that much.

Such is the essence of a personal relationship for most people: As long as the vast majority of it—80 percent—is positively rewarding and affirmative, then the 20 percent of "work" you have to put into it is well worth the time. Of course, there are periods when those numbers may fluctuate, but those would be happy relationship numbers for many of us.

This is how I want you to treat social media for your business. After all, social media is simply enabling you to speed up the rate at which you build relationships. No longer do you have to attend 5,000 networking events to reach 50,000 people (or, in our case at SMD, 100,000 people all over the world). You should still attend those networking events, but you can reach just as many people in a fraction of the time using social media. And relationships, as we all know, will translate into business—that is, profits—when nurtured correctly.

The fact is, if you're asking people to do things for you—visit your restaurant, come to your store, order online, use your service, or buy your product—you need to make it worth their while. At least 80 percent of the time, it has to be rewarding for them to come to your blog, watch your videos on YouTube, or read what you have to say on Facebook or Twitter. If it is, they'll naturally and willingly move your couch—er, buy your stuff—when you ask them.

The Social Media Business Equation: 100-Percent Effective

The problem for most people isn't necessarily presenting a good product or service to the world. The trick is finding the right blend of social media content to help you communicate effectively and have that communication convert to business growth. Not to fear! Through years of serving clients from hospitality to hospitals, I've created what I call the Social Media Business Equation to help you address exactly what you need to do to make your social media efforts more effective. This equation takes the guesswork out by giving you a precise methodology to follow.

Through our work with clients from various countries and industries, we discovered this: Assuming you are using the correct social media vehicle for your business goal, the recipe for success is basically the same. This is not surprising to me. I know through experience that if I am working with a quality product or service, then sales methodologies and customer-service methodologies work the same, regardless of the industry.

So, what *is* the Social Media Business Equation? Simply put, to achieve a positive return on investment (ROI), you need to express yourself on social media using the following types and percentages of content:

- Informing: 20 percent
- Entertaining: 20 percent
- Interacting: 40 percent
- Converting to business: 20 percent

If used seriously, consistently, and energetically, the Social Media Equation equals a positive ROI. We've worked with businesses and people all over the world—from restaurants to dentists to CEOs to nurseries, plus everything and everyone in between. The reason this equation works so well is because it applies to just about every business, every time. If you can inform, entertain, and interact in

> If used seriously, consistently, and energetically, the Social Media Business Equation equals a positive ROI.

the right amounts (which adds up to 80 percent of the time), then you can spend the last 20 percent of your time doing what we all came here for: to convert to business.

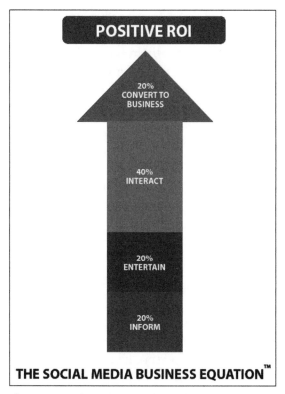

THE SOCIAL MEDIA BUSINESS EQUATION™

If you remember nothing else in this book, remember this equation!

Now that you know the Social Media Business Equation, let's break it down by category.

Informing: 20 Percent

When communicating through social media, the very first step is to inform. As enjoyable as the Internet is, very few of us sit down at our desks with a focused plan to waste a few hours surfing online. Typically, we get onto the Internet to learn something, fix something, scratch some itch, or fill some need. A friend is contemplating plastic surgery, so he gets on the Internet to research local doctors. A colleague is thinking about planting a garden, but doesn't have a clue how to begin, so she looks for tips online. My daughter just started soccer and needs new cleats, so I look for them online. That doesn't mean I'm not going to go to a shoe store with her and buy them in person, but I want to be prepared, so I go online first. In other words, people are coming to you for some kind of information. Don't let them down!

As with any relationship, you have to start by giving. With social media, you give your connections information they seek. It can come in any form, such as video, writing, etc. Whatever

> People are coming to you for some kind of information. Don't let them down!

form it takes, the information should come in specific, valuable nuggets that people can use right away, such as facts, statistics, steps, tips, answers, etc. It should be information your organization has that others want. For instance, if you're a garden center, you can offer tips about the best cuttings to plant for the upcoming growing season. If you're a plastic surgeon, you might post a short video of one of your patients asking you typical questions and you providing answers.

As you've learned, you should inform 20 percent of the time. The information portion of the equation serves as a "teaser" and a way to showcase special knowledge that your organization has. You can also serve as an aggregator of information that you know your audience wants or enjoys, putting it all in one little neat place for them. This information does not necessarily need to have been created by your organization. For example, if you are a doctor but you find a helpful blog on WebMD, you might choose to comment on the blog and highlight posts from it on your own blog because you know it will be of particular interest to your patients. (In these cases, you must always remember to give credit and link back to the original source of information.)

Another important point is to remain consistent. If you are an airline, include coverage of airplanes and other related subjects such as fuel, travel restrictions, packing tips, top destinations, hotel reviews, attraction information, or safety requirements. You should also cover subjects that you know your prospects and client base will enjoy. For example, if your airline caters to business travelers who fly to Asia, you could provide information about doing business in Asia or on cultural customs that should be honored.

As tempting as it is to be creative, don't throw in information about random, unrelated topics. For example, if you are an airline, don't give information about gardening tools. You'll only confuse your audience. They are there specifically for information about airplanes, topics related to travel, or topics specific to that group. By straying too far from the expected topics, you risk alienating your audience, which may cause its members to walk away from the relationship.

Entertaining: 20 Percent

Think back to the last really superb speaker you had the pleasure of seeing in person. Surely, this person was speaking on a topic that interested you. And she no doubt supplied you with the information you desired when you agreed to attend. But what made the speaker *truly* outstanding?

A good speaker can keep the attention of her audience because she not only informs, she entertains. An excellent speaker will hold an audience in the palm of her hand and keep it there. A good speaker can make you laugh or cry, but most importantly, she is entertaining enough that you actually want to hear what she has to say.

Social media affords your organization a very large audience. If informing is how you get your audience, entertaining is how you keep it. The best approach is to entertain your audience 20 percent of the time. How do you entertain them? With anecdotes, obscure facts, engaging statistics, little-known histories, funny videos, shocking photos—you get the idea. The goal here is to provide amusement, the same way you might at a cocktail party.

Once again, it's important to note that these gems of entertainment should always be related to your organization or to subjects that specifically interest your customers and prospects. For example, if you are creating content for your social media campaign and you are in the dairy industry, you might post a link to a story about an artist making a sculpture out of cheese, complete with a picture. Reusing great content in social media is allowed and encouraged, as long as the information is readily available online and you are giving credit where credit is due.

> If informing is how you get your audience, entertaining is how you keep it.

Here are some other ways you can be entertaining around your social media efforts:

- Use humor, the fastest way to create interest.
- Post quirky news that applies to your industry.
- Share strange or historic videos, audio, or photos.
- Use a play on words.
- Discuss little-known facts.
- Create imaginary characters.
- Create characters from employees, customers, or objects. For example, create a character or icon to represent an employee, such as "Judy" from customer service.

By all means, make them smile. Make them laugh. Wow them! However, do so in a manner that mirrors the tone and voice of the organization. For example, when it comes to entertaining, an artsy ad agency will likely have a much edgier social media voice than a prominent hospital. But even high-end, serious organizations and brands can and should be entertaining. Indeed, they *need* to be entertaining 20 percent of the time if they are to achieve positive ROI with social media. We have found this to be the correct percentage across the board, regardless of industry.

Interacting: 40 Percent

You get the audience with information. You keep it by entertaining its members. Then you get to what people go to social media for in the first place: to communicate and connect with others. We refer to that in our equation as *interacting*.

The most important thing to remember about social media is that it is simply communicating using new technology. The ability to interact and communicate is the only thing that differentiates social media from all other types of media that have come before it.

> The most important thing to remember about social media is that it is simply communicating using new technology.

Most books on social media are about the technology, such as video upload webcasts, or the vehicles, such as Twitter or Facebook, that you'll use in social media. But the challenge of social media is not that the technology is hard to master; it's that so few of us have mastered the art of communication. And it really is an art.

I keep going back to it, but this new development is so revolutionary, it's vital that you see it for what it is. Imagine being able to talk back to the ads in your magazine, or on your TV or car radio. Imagine being able to conduct an online focus group every day, all day. Imagine an open customer-service line 24/7 at every cubicle. By imagining these things, you'll get just a glimpse of what social media can be if you treat it like communication and not just another broadcast blast.

This is why I can tell you with certainty that social media is not a fad and will not go away: because humans will always be driven to communicate. Social media is the new backyard fence, where one can gossip, pray, cry, laugh, and share reviews about what's great, good, bad, or neutral. This need for communication is why, according to the Social Media Business Equation, you should be spending most of your time interacting. Interacting is the point where social media becomes a dialogue, where one-on-one engagement starts to turn relationships into business.

This is why I want you to spend the largest chunk of your time interacting. When it comes to using social media, your organization should spend 40 percent of its time interacting. This includes listening, questioning, and responding. This, in sum, is communicating.

If you are trying to get to know others at a party, how do you find out about them, what they like, and what they don't like? Do you do all the talking, or do you ask questions and let them respond? In an ideal two-way conversation, you are sharing and exchanging. It's called a dialogue, and it's exactly the same with social media! If you are spending your time doing all the talking, you don't provide any opportunities for interaction. Not only is this pretty boring for the other people, it may cause them to walk away.

Remember the young man at the Starbucks who, after blabbing on and on, said he enjoyed talking "with" us? Well,

I didn't get a chance to talk or ask questions, and certainly can't say I enjoyed it. It's the same with social media.

Here are some examples of ways to encourage interaction:

- Use a polling feature to survey your audience on their likes and dislikes of a certain product. Several social media vehicles offer polling features.

- Foster a discussion that is not about your product, but centers around a topic that is of great interest to your customers. For example, if you run a hotel, you might ask your fans to send in their best packing tips, in video, audio, or word form.

- Ask a multiple-choice question. For example, say you are in the recruiting business. You might ask, "What is the quality you most want in your next hire? Loyalty, hard work, brilliance, or something else?"

- Ask a controversial—notice I said controversial, not offensive—question. For example, there has long been a strong debate around whether the McRib Sandwich should be a permanent item on the McDonald's menu or a recurring one. McDonald's bringing up this topic via social media would stir up lots of conversation.

This list includes a few great ways to encourage your connections to interact with you, but here is the most important part of interacting: Listen to people online and respond. Listen earnestly and respond honestly. Yes, there may be times when someone is inappropriate or vulgar, and it is best not to respond. I am also not suggesting that you respond to absolutely every post. I *am* saying that you should truly listen to what your people are saying, and then respond as often as you can when a response or assistance is truly being asked for.

Often, these interactions are taking place in the public eye, which gives you a great opportunity to address concerns, questions, and even compliments in front of thousands of people/connections. For example, your company may be totally unaware of an issue that the public has with one of your products. When a customer brings up that issue in the public eye (via message boards, on feedback forums, or on a blog), not only are you made aware of it, but you have the opportunity to discuss, brainstorm, and solve the problem while your other connections watch and take

> The most important part of interacting is listening to people online and responding.

note. By proactively solving customer issues in the public eye, you establish credibility and build confidence—not just with that one customer, but with all other existing customers and potential ones. Even better, when possible, ask your online connections for suggestions in solving problems. Involving your online connections by asking them for help or ideas is a great way to build your relationship with them and make them feel that they are part of your brand.

Many people think that the power of social media is to spread the message of the organization. While that *is* true, one of the lesser-known powers of social media is a direct line of feedback that reveals exactly what people are saying, thinking, and feeling about your product. It is important for you to understand the message outside the four walls of your building— i.e., the customer perspective you wouldn't hear so easily otherwise. Wouldn't it be amazing to display in public the fact that you are willing to listen to the good, the bad, and the ugly—and respond?

How often has your customer-service department said it wished you could have heard a customer's phoned-in complaint? Or how many times have your salespeople tried to describe the passion in a customer's voice when he expressed his excitement about the latest release? Now a CEO or executive can be there virtually and can hear things firsthand, directly from the customer. That's why interaction is so vital to both you and your connections. It helps you gauge customer needs to know how to serve them better.

How long has it been since you listened to the music you play while customers are on hold? When was the last time you used a credit card to buy one of your products? When was the last time you shipped yourself a product and had to open it in a hurry? Chances are it's been a while. Well, your connections are on hold, using credit cards, and opening your packages every single day—and they're often quite vocal about these experiences on social media.

For better or worse, interaction means customers can tell you that the music you're playing while they're on hold is lame, scratchy, or too loud. They can tell you they had to click through six different screens to purchase a $9.95 CD on your company's web store—too many by far. They can also tell you how easy it was to open your packaging and how happy they were that it was composed of 60-percent recyclable materials.

I'm sure you'll agree that some, if not all, of this information is critical to your future success. Interaction via social media is valuable for discovering your customers' tastes and preferences so that you can keep your customers happy. If your customers are happy, they are more likely to stay in the relationship with you. If they are unhappy, they are likely to go somewhere else.

Interaction can also result in new product ideas, improvements on current ones, and other valuable revenue-generating opportunities for your organization. As but one example, consider this story about the Sheraton Fort Worth Hotel and Spa. After a guest used Twitter to complain about the hotel's pool hours—he felt it closed too early—the hotel responded within 48 hours to thank the man for his comment and to say they would consider it. A few days later, the hotel used Twitter to announce that the pool hours would be changed. They also publicly thanked the guest, by name, for his suggestion. Not only did the Sheraton Fort Worth Hotel and Spa respond to the needs of a valued guest in a timely fashion, they illustrated to the world that their guests truly are their priority.

When you engage customers directly to answer their questions and acknowledge their comments, your company becomes a living, breathing being to them. Through interaction, you build a stronger relationship with your customers and your prospects. Remember to question, answer, listen, and respond; in other words, spend 40 percent of your social media time interacting.

Converting to Business: 20 Percent

Imagine you've just walked into a networking event. You're thrilled to see a stellar group of 300 CEOs, business owners, and VPs. Naturally, you walk right up to the very first distinguished-looking gentleman you see. You can tell he's your type of client: nice suit, smile, handshake, the whole nine yards.

You shake his hand and say, "Hello! Would you buy my stuff?"

What? Talk about rude! I'm sure you can guess the outcome. He will likely make a kind excuse to visit with someone else at the event. Before you know it, he'll walk away, and that'll be that. No second chances.

Believe it or not, when it comes to social media, lots of organizations act this way. They get onto a blog or a video or a podcast and all they do all day long is say, "Buy my stuff! Buy my stuff! Buy my stuff!" They wouldn't dream of doing this in real life, so why do they think that just because they are using technology to communicate with people, it's okay to just sell, sell, sell?

Now, please don't misunderstand me. I am not saying you shouldn't ask for business. You and I are both here for the same reason: to create relationships that, ultimately, convert to business. However, the example I've given is not the way to do it—in person or online.

On the other hand, there are a lot of companies that do a great job using social media to inform, entertain, and interact with social media. Indeed, many social

> If you never ask to convert to business, you get nowhere.

media experts think you should stop there. They shout to the rooftops that the purpose of social media is simply to build giving relationships, and that one should never use social media to sell. I disagree. If you never ask to convert to business, you get nowhere.

Let's go back to Julie, your friend who needed your help moving her couch. Why did you so willingly move Julie's couch at 6 a.m. on a Sunday? Well, because she had earned it. She's a good friend, and you know she'd do the same for you. This wasn't just some stranger; you and Julie had built a relationship based on trust, and you knew that trust wasn't being squandered when she finally asked for help.

In any relationship, when you need help, you ask for it. That's what I'm asking you to do with social media in general, and with the Social Media Business Equation in particular. A full 80 percent of the time, I want you to *give*. You give by informing, entertaining, and interacting via your social media site/vehicle. But 20 percent of the time, I want you to *take* by asking for what you need.

What you need could be any number of things. It could be that your organization is looking for a new employee, business partner, or investor. Maybe you need to collect information on a certain subject or to get people to participate in one of your company's events. Maybe you want customers to read your blog. Maybe you have a need for a product or service, and you want to know who you should buy from. And yes, converting to business may even mean asking people to buy your stuff. The fact is, it is okay to ask people to buy your stuff some of the time. After all, you are giving them valuable information, you're entertaining them, and you're interacting with them 80 percent of the time. Asking for what you need 20 percent of the time means both parties get something of value out of the relationship. And isn't that what relationships are all about?

The right way to convert online relationships to business is to treat these social media communications and relationships exactly like the ones you have in real life. The right way to engage that distinguished CEO would be to walk up and introduce yourself. Say something like, "I'm Joe. I work with the ABC Firm." (This is informing.) As the conversation progresses naturally during the event, you might tell a joke to lighten the mood, or offer a funny anecdote from the seminar. (This is entertaining.) Next, you might add something like, "What's *your* name? Tell me about *yourself*." (This is interacting.) Then, at the end of the night, after you've built a relationship and learned that there is, in fact, a need, you might ask for a lunch meeting for the following week so you can pitch an idea. (This is converting to business.)

Now you know the secret to success with social media, and how to make sure all your effort in this big new world converts to business. Go and use it! When you do, I hope you'll share your stories with me.

6

THE ROI OF
SOCIAL MEDIA

So here it is, at long last, the million-dollar question—the question I hear from every CEO, CMO, VP, or [insert fancy title here]—"What is the ROI of social media? How does it pay off for me? What will I get out of it?" In short, "What's in it for me?"

I'll be honest, I've left this chapter for last because it's the most difficult to explain and one of the most important concepts we must tackle. The truth is, because social media is an evolving, rapidly morphing creature, no one can give a succinct answer on the return on investment it produces. There are just as many factors to measure as there are metrics to measure those factors. Why? Social media encompasses so many things that are typically measured in very different ways, it can seem really complex to assess.

It may not be so easy to apply a "cookie cutter" approach to measurement from some of your other marketing and PR divisions. For instance, there are excellent applications to monitor effectiveness in traditional print, TV, and even online and radio advertising, but you cannot simply apply these to social media because social media includes elements of both broadcasting and communication. Advertising measurements are not designed to measure the value of interaction.

Some organizations that are heavily focused on leveraging social media to measure customer service may turn to customer-service metrics (like net promoter scores) to apply a static form of measurement. However, because social media is a hybrid of marketing and communications, these measurements may not be accurate and will not always provide a clear picture of its effectiveness.

Even the most straightforward measurement of website traffic or online orders coming from social media vehicles will not tell the whole story, because it does not account for those customers who spend hours interacting on a company's social media vehicle and, because of that, later go to the company's site (or some other outlet) to purchase a product. In those cases, social media receives no direct credit for the sale.

That's the beauty, and the frustration, of using social media. You know it's working for you, it's just hard to snatch a hard, fast measurement like you may be able to do in a postcard mailing, a TV commercial blitz, or even a new billboard ad campaign.

Now that I've told you all the reasons why it is difficult to accurately measure the return on investment for social media, now that I've brought you to the depths of despair thinking you'll never be able to measure all this hard work you've committed to, well, now I'm going to contradict myself and tell you exactly how to do it!

The Two Keys for Measuring ROI in Social Media

It's a bold statement to be sure, but it *is* possible to measure the return on investment of social media—*if* you take two simple steps:

1. **Set a specific goal.** What, exactly, do you want to achieve with social media? Specificity is key. You can't just say, "Well, I want to make lots of money." That's fine; so do I. But *how* do you want to increase profits? Be specific. Say something like, "I want to increase sales of a certain product or service by 25 percent using a concentrated focus on a specific social media

vehicle (a blog, YouTube, LinkedIn, Twitter, Facebook, etc.) over the next six months." Now *that's* a specific goal!

2. **Establish a simple, safe, and effective way to track the achievement of that goal.** A tracking system will enable you to verify certain checkpoints along the path to achieving your goal at regular intervals—say, weekly, monthly, quarterly, or annually.

By creating a regular series of goalposts and a trackable method of measuring achievement at each of them, you can determine the ROI of social media. What I'm basically saying is that when you launch your latest, your next, or even your first social media campaign, you must start with a goal in mind

> By creating a regular series of goalposts and a trackable method of measuring achievement at each of them, you can determine the ROI of social media.

and a plan on how you will measure that goal at a regular frequency.

Measuring ROI: An Example

Imagine a hotel—we'll call it the South Beach Bed & Breakfast—that wants to use social media to increase room bookings by business travelers during the week. After reviewing their options, they've decided that Facebook is the appropriate social media vehicle for them. Facebook enables them to use graphics, post videos, and post information at their discretion. Plus, many of their guests have asked if they have a page on Facebook.

Having set a specific goal, the South Beach B&B must decide how, and how often, they will measure the results of their social media campaign. After all, they will want to know fairly quickly whether their efforts are paying off. To begin, the South Beach B&B can regularly monitor the traffic from their Facebook page to their home page or, better still, their reservation page using software such as Google Analytics (which, by the way, is free). In this way, they will be able to determine whether there has been an increase in traffic.

Having set a clear goal that involves using a specific social media vehicle and established a way to track the achievement of that goal, the South Beach B&B is ready to launch its campaign.

As you've learned, a social media campaign is only as good as the content around which it is centered. And like any other successful marketing campaign, it will require the correct frequency and the right audience. In this case, to lure more business travelers, the South Beach B&B would use their Facebook page to talk about things that might interest professionals, such as saving time on traveling for business, good business books to read on a two-hour flight, the best suitcases or laptop bags, stylish designs for business women, etc. Of course, the South Beach B&B will apply the Social Media Business Equation—meaning they will inform 20 percent of the time, entertain 20 percent of the time, interact 40 percent of the time, and convert to business 20 percent of the time.

In terms of tracking—which, as you know, is crucial to measuring the ROI of a successful social media campaign—the South Beach B&B can track increased reservations directly from their social media efforts by offering specials or promotions that send customers to a specific landing page or using a specific code that is tethered to only one social media vehicle. For instance, South Beach B&B could offer a special discount on their Facebook wall and require customers to enter a specific discount code, such as FB123, when making their reservation. That way, the South Beach B&B can track exactly where those customers were coming from (Facebook), enabling them to measure not only how effective their content and communications have been, but also the validity of their hypothesis that their prospects will visit the vehicle on which they are reaching out and will act on those visits. They will be able to determine whether their social media efforts are paying off.

Less Really Is More

Many companies get so overwhelmed at the prospect of juggling dozens of social media vehicles and managing thousands of connections—not to mention writing, editing, and posting (plus monitoring) tens of thousands of words of content—that they never get out of the starting gate. That's why, when starting out, I suggest that organizations use only one social media vehicle at a time. This may sound limiting, but by starting with one social media vehicle, by focusing all your efforts in one place, you can get comfortable with that vehicle and with social media in general.

> By starting with one social media vehicle, you can get comfortable with that vehicle and with social media in general.

After you find success with one social media vehicle, however, you'll no doubt be chomping at the bit to post more often on more vehicles. At that point, you'll be ready to expand to other social media vehicles, such as Twitter and YouTube. When you do, your message will spread at a rate you have never seen before! Note, though, that as you expand your social media realm, you'll want to ensure you use different tracking codes. For example, if you offer a special discount to

Facebook friends and Twitter followers, you should use a different tracking code for each one—say, FB123 for Facebook friends and TWEET123 for Twitter followers. That way, you can determine whether one channel is more effective than the other.

Parting Words About the ROI of Social Media

If your social media is difficult to measure, congratulations. That means you're doing something right. I'm not saying measuring social is easy; I'm saying it can be done with the correct amount of planning and monitoring.

The fact is, if you are *truly* interacting with your online network, it will be difficult to measure the ROI as a whole, just as it is difficult measure the ROI on the interaction your staff currently has with your clients and prospects. What is the ROI measurement of the last visit a customer had at your retail store? What is the ROI measurement of the last PR event you did to promote your technology company? Is it not exactly crystal clear? Exactly!

Understand that social media is big—I mean *really* big. Probably even bigger than all the buzz you may have noticed about it lately would suggest. Why is it so big? Social media is the culmination of marketing, customer service, and communication in real time in front of everyone. Any tool that affords you the ability to do so much and to reach so many people free of charge cannot be summed up with one simple measurement. The power, reach, and effectiveness of social media are why you cannot ignore it.

You must embrace it. *Now*.

Conclusion

So there you have it: *The Social Media Business Equation: Using Online Connections to Grow Your Bottom Line*. In this book, we've covered the why, the how, and the ROI of using social media. We've studied companies of all sizes sharing the truth about their business needs, challenges, and ultimate success with social media. Now it's your turn to start your next, or first, social media campaign.

Remember: First and foremost, social media is a conversation. The sooner you start talking—and listening—the sooner you'll build relationships that lead to business. You cannot control social media, but you can influence it. And since somebody, somewhere is already talking about your company right now, the sooner you start influencing it, the better.

I challenge you to take a deep breath and leverage this tool to achieve that goal you've been salivating over. At first, it will seem confusing—as if your company is bare for all to see. But then you'll begin to see relationships forming. What always has and always will build business are relationships. Now, with social media, you can build those relationships more quickly.

Go for it!

Acknowledgments

This book in its many forms was worked on a by a talented team of graphic artists, editors, proofreaders, writers, and staff: Rusty Fischer, Andi Reis, Jamie Nanquil, Amanda Montgomery, Amelia Clark, Angelo Fernandez-Spadaro, Mary B. Adams, Laura Hale, Katy Mendelsohn, Ruth Ferguson, Shilpa Nicodemus, Mitzi Koontz, Kate Shoup, Bill Hartman, Sandi Wilson, and Valerie Haynes Perry.

Thank you to my mentors, David Schmidt (LinkedIn.com/ in/ DaveASchmidt), CEO of Schmidt and Stacy Consulting Engineers, Inc., and Lois Melbourne (Twitter.com/ LoisMelbourne), CEO of Aquire.

Thank you to my amazing staff, who made serving our clients and creating this book simultaneously possible. Thank you to family, friends, associates, clients, and others who helped us countless times along the way. Thank you to the partners, clients, and companies who shared their real-life stories of social media success.

Thank you to Laura Hale, Ruth Ferguson, Mary B. Adams, Amelia Clark, Amanda Montgomery, Angelo Benito Fernandez-Spadaro, Katy Mendolsohn, Justin Hess, Shilpa Nicodemus, Tom Jackson, Tony van Kessel, Del Wratten, Robin Kruk, Gavin Head, Bob Willems, Melissa Kovacevic, Jamie Nanquil, Alan Evans, Desiree Buckingham, Vicki Jasper, Schuyler Thompson, Rosalyn Eishen, Umar Syed, and Petey the Gnome. Thank you Angela Schmidt, Dave Schmidt, Paige Schmidt, Grant Schmidt (future American president), Jemimah Wanjohi (Kermie), Degie Butler, Jillian Butler, Maria Martinez, Elizabeth Murdock, and Joe Murdock.

Thank you to Amanda and Monty Montgomery, for allowing me to finish my book at their beautiful lake house; my personal trainer in Dallas, Angela Smith (Twitter.com/angiefit404); my CPA, Wray Rives (Twitter.com/RivesCPA); Lane Bryant (Twitter.com/LaneBryant), for keeping me in style, James Wood Motors (Twitter.com/JamesWoodMotors), for allowing me to drive gorgeous cars; and Michael Schwartz (Twitter.com/MichaelVistage), who introduced me to the amazing CEOs at Vistage International.

Thank you to Patty Farmer, Fred Campos, Dr. Kent Smith, Dr. Jeff Roy, Anthony Eggleston, Amanda Williams, David Davis, Craig Scott, Lee Aase, TJ Schier, Wanda Brice, Lyn Scott, Haley Curry, Chad McDaniel, Paul Chaston, Rick Harrison, Craig Palmer, Chris Yates, Shauna McLean Tompkins, Mollie Milligan, Brian Fabian, Matt Parvis, Betsey Brailer, Heather McGarry, Nick Charles, Donna Mclallen, Mary Henige, Jay Dunn, Joel Denver, Fleetwood Hicks, Kimberly Hutchison, David Boyett, Julia Danklef, Mary Hoffman, Rafael Pastor, Tom Niesen, Mike Springer, David McGhee, Robert Wilson, Janna Wilson, David Gossman, Abbey Reider, Alyssa Waxenberg, Carrie Houston, Victoria Taylor, Mary Pomerantz, and Kathleen Lobb.

Thank you to 21st Century Dental, Anheuser-Busch, Bodycology, Cable & Wireless Worldwide, General Motors, In the Know Division of M.E.R., The Adolphus Hotel, The French Room, Mayo Clinic, The Women's Museum, Boxcar Creative, Huddle Productions, Live Hair Group, Stand Up To Cancer, Virgin America, Beauty Cakes, Acuity, Starwood Hotels and Resorts Worldwide, Pink Elephant, The Fresh Diet, the Sears Blue Blogger Group, and Cengage Learning.

Thank you to St. Joseph and E.D. White Catholic High School and the Nicholls State University TAG program in Thibodaux, Louisiana, for a great education. Thank you, Louisiana State University in Baton Rouge, Louisiana, for having an excellent communications and business school.

Special thanks go out to my mom, Ms. Kovar (my first-grade teacher), Geppetto (my childhood dog), and Brod Bagert (an author), who are collectively responsible, at least partially, for me becoming an author. When I was a child, Ms. Kovar, who was also my neighbor, lent me the book *If Only I Could Fly* by Brod Bagert. I was 10, and convinced that I was brave enough to camp out all night in a tent in the back yard. Of course, I chickened out during the night and my mom tucked me safely into my bed. The next morning, I discovered in horror that my Old English Sheepdog, Geppetto, had eaten the book, and I was in big trouble! My mom, always knowing how to turn things into an opportunity to teach me important life lessons, told me I would need to do some chores to earn enough money to replace the book. This was back in the olden days, before people had computers, so my mom couldn't figure out where to purchase the book. Somehow, she tracked down the author's mailing address. She had me write a letter to him explaining that my dog had eaten the book and asking how I could purchase a new book to replace it for my teacher. One night during dinner, there was a knock at the door. Brod Bagert had come to our house and brought me two auto-graphed copies of the book—one for me, and one as a replace-ment for Ms. Kovar. Bagert told me how much he liked my letter, and that instead of paying for the books, I should repay him by turning this story into a book and sending it to him. He said that maybe one day, I would be an author too. Later, he came and spoke to our entire elementary school. As a child, that event made a big impact on me, and I'll never for-get it. I have reserved the first copy of this book for Brod Bagert.

Finally, I want to thank my online connections and friends, who are the heart and soul of my online community and with-out whom this book would not have been possible or made sense. These 35,000 followers of my account, Twitter.com/LinkedInQueen, are only a few of the many people who con-tributed to my ideas and growth. Thank you.

Acknowledgments

@____I @____Crys @__haus @__mesothelioma_ @__sweetlady @__wahpapa @_7th_Chakra @_al_ @_alexyr_ @_AllyssaMarie_ @_AnilThakur @_Archie @_artemiy @_aryella @_AutomaticGeek @_ayudame @_BOWILD @_BTE @_caroloka @_chimes_ @_ClareOliver_ @_cloudgirl @_cmom_ @_cric_ @_darlene_davis @_DebbieRussell @_e_bomb @_EricLundberg_ @_Fast_ @_FNDS3000 @_GeorgeL @_iChRiS_ @_jul @_justthinking @_Kacee_ @_landscaping @_lauramckay_ @_LOVEMJ @_M_A_C @_MakeQuickMoney @_ManoelCandido_ @_McLaughlin @_NEAA_ @_Olga_ @_palomilla @_pathmaker @_Poschi_ @_praedo_ @_QFI_ @_Redux @_RickRage_ @_SEM @_seo_consulting @_Sheila_ @_ShoTyme_ @_Signalfire_ @_Sir_GaGa @_sivi_ @_SKSC @_so_so_ @_socialeyes @_spell @_TheBestOfMe_ @_thetwitguy @_toinfinity @_Umwelt @_webguru @_Why_Ask @_Woman_health @_WordGirl @_wwwafu @_Zweitverdienst @007Diva @007joectms @007LouiseOB @007phantom @01cypark @0bivan @0boy @0clickmylit @0Frank @0thevalentines0 @0utKast @1_Me @100lblogs @100lnoisycamera @100ltopwords @100acres @100days2victory @100KAMonth @100kMLM @100TopGeschenke @100x100net @103IExchangeNOW @104Tips @1055webdesign @1080Group @108antiaging @10yearsofbb @1154LillKC @116_Windhund @116thPanzer @11health9 @11kx @11taste24 @123_Refills @123movie @123peopleNL @123sexy_undies @123socialmedia @123teens @123top10 @1248webdesign @1337studios @1337windows @13rittny3 @1400words @140College @140LoveBird @140models @140twitstreet @1495bk @15pts @162030251 @16thDivision @173Sud @18002228477 @1800GETLENS @1800petinsure @1800pools @1800RUNAWAY @1854gop @18884PageRocket @1975jmr @19SIXTY5 @laurence @1BizLeader @1bluemarz @1BreakingNews @1brownmoUse @1Businessman @1BYBY @1CASTentertain @1CASTfinance @1CASTtech @1ChessKing @1chicgeek @1Chingishan @1christystoffel @1DanFeildman @1datarecovery @1esig @1FreedomFeed @1Green1Blue @1highlife @1HoustonNews @1jameshunter @1jasim @1lonelygal @1LosAngelesNews @1lovely_friend @1LX @1makemoney1 @1MCB1 @1miaan @1MiamiHurricane @1MILLIONBBMUSER @1mindone @1MonthFacelift @1mwilson @1NBUSINESS @1New_Life @1ok @1onlinestore @1opportunity @1PhillyNews @1picstory @1rene @1robward @1sassy_chick @1scottcarson @1securityguru @1Sky @1SocialMrkting @1st_Commentary @1stDUBLI @1stPositionMktg @1TD @1tolcoach @1txsage1957 @1webworld @1wisechick @2_Pears @2000thor @2010_APRIL @2010_FEBRUAR @2010_JANUAR @2010_JANUARY @2010_Vision @2010paradise @2010valentine @2012DeathWatch @2012files @2012revealed @2015wpfg @20Community @20somethingca @214Square @21CenturyDental @21cwr @21inc @21stlaur @220Generation @22Rockwell @23rmorandantejr @247hotinfo @247legaladvice @247tweet @24hourdad @2500group @256Mbps @2574Design @25dl @25sweightloss @26DotTwo @28DLA @29DayFacelift @2add @2addme @2ADu @2BidOnAWish @2big4mybuttons @2BitViews @2charity @2commonsense @2cre8 @2Debbie @2don @2DreamIt @2e2UK @2guyslawnmower @2helppeople @2hospitality @2jsmarketing @2kidswithcancer @2LittleShihTzus @2Marra @2mfox @2moroDocs @2morrowknight @2much2DOEF @2mysticmountain @2NeverWorkAgain @2osto @2PromoteU @2rise @2savelives @2SELLHOMES @2sleepbetter @2StayAtHomeMom @2tammytodd @2thespot @2tweetwitheric @2tweetyou @2urfuture @2weddings @2win1big @3_shera @3_wise_men @301STUDIOS @30dayturnaround @30wastedyears @312info @31DayFacelift @32Ideins @33_smile @333AutismNews @333AutismNews3 @360executive @360Mapping @360sxswi @360VideoMapping @360WebEx @360wellnessguy @36Terabytes @38_29_42 @380Dentist @39thStreetMedia @3amor @3dayme @3days_in_london @3dgamestudio @3dimensionalife @3DInternet @3dMildred @3dogmarketing @3DPorn1 @3elva57 @3fifty7music @3FOUR1 @3frogs @3GLebenskonzept @3iInfotech @3rdcorner @3rdpartyblog @3v3rytingiswack @3viewHD @3WDesign @3WDesignMedia @4_Squared @408Eric @411_HomeDecor @411bloggingude @440tv @451Heat @4BetWithAir @4BW @4byoung @4CloseYOURDeal @4Compression @4enterpreneur @4giv @4JustUsWW @4kaylin @4linkedlearning @4loveofcoffee @4PsMarketing @4ralph @4RealWeightLoss @4S @4SEMktg @4shish @4sqday @4theloveofmike @4tsubasa @4usaul @4wardfinancial @500Ksystem @506properties @509BeaderyNews @50boookchallenge @50champ @52Nine @52weekfootball @59minlearning @5bliss @5eo @5FiguresAMonth @5FtHighMktgGuy @5Great @5Ideas @5JKL @5pointedstar @5tevenw @5thStreetPizza @600conf @60plusfriends @617patrick @61surebet @62Labs @630info @666mkt1 @68bashirum68 @6FiguresForLife @71IRecruiter @714dragon @720Strategies @73K @74thnpark @7573Marketing @76sixer @777Stocks @7degreescom @7figures @7HUNNIT @7KeysToDeductIt @7LD @7NewsBRISBANE @7StarStrucks @7T8EET @7thscreen @7ucian @7wishes @847info @86food4thought @888jeffcline @888starmedia @88al88 @88PRINCEOFPOP @88BroadSt @8bdhd @8bjtny @8KeyStrokesTeam @8packabs @8thandWalton @8VisionsofHope @90sMillionaire @95millionaires @9INCHmarketing @9swords @9thwave @9xhot @A_Aviles @A_Big_Discount @A_Boogie24 @a_estrategico @a_greenwood @A_Lan @a_shoobs @a_smart_union @A1business4u @A1SURFus @a2zShoes @A3aanxl @a4567b @aaambler @AArena @AAAResumes @aabcdewi @Aadii_ @aajain @aakarpost @AaltoSpreadson @aamandabieber @Aan_Afdi @AandASocialMktg @aanetwork @AAOdds @aarfmike @aargenz1 @aaronabber @aaronadamson @AaronBiddar @aarond22 @aaronhackett @AaronHoos @AaronInTulsa @AaronMSanchez @AaronParsons @aaronpost @AaronRayo @aarrona @AAshmam @aatif_ahmed05 @AB_Thomas @abacil790 @Abadi_Access @abagailoorriaz @AbaloneHome @Abazy90I @ababell @Abbey22239 @Abbott2010 @abbybrown24 @abbylocke @abbyse @abbytaylor14 @abdulkarim @ABDWellness @abeahanfnp @abee2010 @abeles @abellastudios @Abendkleider @AberOnline @ABetterAnswer @ABetterResume @abfo @abfromz @abfsra @AbhayPatil @abhijitdas1982 @abhishek_gupta @AbidaNKhan @abie_maria @abigailming @abirb123 @abokroslife @abonadim @aboutbanks @aboutdietnews @AboutGameCheats @aboutinsurances @aboutpolitics @abouttimeshare @abovegame @abovethelevel @AboveTheStatic @abqbuilder @ABradbury @abrahamharrison @abrarach @abrownfarm @abrownplante @abrudtkuhl @abs4ever @absalam2 @absiemorrison @absolit @absolutamber @Absolutely_Abby @AbsolutelyJay @AbsolutelyPR @absolutpac @abssd @AbsurdistTaxi @AbsWorkoutsR @AbtGratitude @Abundance_ @Abundance @abundance4you @AbundanceBound @AbundanceExpo @abundantwater @AcademicDemon @AcademicHelp @AcadamicJobs @AcadianaEats @Acaiultimate @acastrillon @acatalanello @accaplus @access_basics @access_geeks @AccessAuto_Avon @accessbarbados @accessonora @ACCHBdotCOM @AccomandTravel @Accommotel @AccordionGuy @AccountancyGuru @accountingjobz @AccountPlanners @AccountPrepaid @AccountSitter @accrete @Acctg411 @AcctMgrJessica @AccuGuy @AccurateData @AccurateMailInc @AccuWxDallas @acedofcfan3 @AceFreeman52387 @Aceinternet @acelfl @Acenamers @Acentuate @acezadams @AchImO @AChelsian @AchFashion @achievereffect @AchimBurgardt @AchimMuellers @acholitek @Achordus @achristiansen @ACI_C5marketing @acid89 @acmcleaning @acmontgomery @acmsomyos @acnehelphq @aconvertshop @acoverthypnosis @ACPLAN @ACPundit @acquisio @AccrossTheDivide @ACTG @actioevent @ActionChick @actionczar @ActionGirlAPC @ActionManage @ActionREI @actionScript3 @actionwealth @Activ8business @ActiveHeal @ActivegameZ @Activelngreds @activeinterview @activenetwork @ActiveRain @activesearcher @actofficial @actonyourcallin @ActorAshley @ACTPLATINUM @ActuallyStinson @acuam @acutler @acydlord @ADA_KINGS @ADAH90068957 @adalys08 @Adam_Kraker @adam_mega @adam_smith233 @adam_thedad @AdamAdame @adamaltman @adamandstevesto @adamboyden @adamcandell @AdamChapnick @adamcohen @adamcowpersmith @adamfrench34 @AdamHoldenBache @adamjwhitaker @AdamLeeBowers @adamliskl @adamlucas25 @adamostrow @adamreiter @AdamRock @adamsangster @adamsconsulting @adamsherk @AdamSpiel @adamterw @adamwaid @adamwrichard @adaptick @AdastraPR @adbean_net @adbert @AddI000Follower @Adda_White @Addicted_Gamers @addictedtwit @AddinGeniue @additionsstyle @AddMeOnLinkedin @addoway @Adel965 @Adeah @AdeccoThailand @adelamathive @adeswellness @adevries @adformatie @ADHDcure @adhhyu973 @adi_Avi @adiaphoron @AdielLucas @adiletchaim @adillinger @adindustryvoice @adisnaan @adit82a @adityabhatt @adjollz @AdJou24 @adlt_lifestyle @Advance @AdManJosephG @admarketpros @ADMINotTix @admixsocial @adnzafar @Adogy @adolforosado @AdoptAPett @adoptedbabies @adoptingapet @AdrenalynnINK @adri72 @adriaanrainso @AdriAgus @AdrianaArvizo @adrianalove @adrianchira @adriandayton @AdrianeHigdon @adrianfleischer @AdrianLee @AdrianMelrose @AdrianneMachina @adriansoare @adriansutanto @adrianswinscoe @adrielhampton @adrienneaudrey

The Social Media Business Equation

@AdrienneCorn @AdrienneLJ @AdrienneRehm @adriereinders @AdriJ @Adrital @AdRockia @ads2txt @adsmove @adsoftheworld @adtrend @aDuchan @ADufriesVSS @adultorphan @AdvAmerica @AdvantageTaxRes @adventuregirl @AdventureLive @AdventurePass @adventurepeople @Advertising_UK @AdvertisingInfo @AdvertisingLaw @AdvertisingPR @AdvertisingSMS @advertlive @AdviceScene @advicesisters @advick @Advisor_Marcus @Advocate_LH @Adweek @adwrighty @AdzZoo_SEO2010 @adzzoocrew @AdzZooReps @AECarter @AegeanImports @AEKeleher6 @aellislegal @aemikel @aemmajg @aeohn @AeroAngels @AerobicsOnline @Aerocles @AeroFade @aerospacejobl @aetherstrike @afalk @AFasterPC @aff_cash @Affaircare @affiliantes @affiliate_buddy @affiliateaces @affiliatearmada @AffiliateDesk00 @Affiliatefaith @AffiliateFlower @AffiliateNews4u @AffiliatePro64 @affiliateprobiz @affiliates2 @AffiliateStar12 @affiliatetank @AffiliateTeam @affiliatetoday @AffiliateTrends @AffiloScott @AffiniaChicago @AffirmationBlog @AffirmYourLife @AffluenceNow @Affnet @affsum @afftraction @afieryphoenix @AfifaMasood @afiliatemarket @AFlirtYourself @afmasudivre @AFollowerForYou @afritainment @AfroditeLaceWig @AfroMarketing @AFrugalFriend @aftercurfew @afterdoorportal @afterschool4all @AfTranch @AftrHrsAutoGlas @AFutureWithout @afvanwingerden @Agabhumi @AGAconnection @agangulyy @Agape_Church @agapeglenda @agardina @agboise @age380 @ageasoft @agebackwards @AgelessSecret @agenceb2b @AgenciaCaffeine @AgencyBabylon @AgendaVoiceover @agentcesd @AgentDeepak @AgentJester @agentnews @Agentopolis @agentsmiller @AgentsOnline @agentspayforwrd @agentwealthproj @AgeoLopez @agguley @aghreni @AGICO @agideon @Agile_Cat @AgileDudes @AgilePoint @agiletechnosys @AgniCreative @agooddaughter @agoodeye @agoramedia @agquillinan @AGreenLady @AgribizNews @agriloka @agromaximum @agsocialmedia @aguitarguy95 @agunn @agus_setiyawan @agusbilly @agusnadhi @ahaddaway @ahall3649 @ahamany @aHappinessCoach @AHartFly @ahaval @ahblackledge @AHCSolutions @AHealthGuru @aheart4god @aheartforgod @aheneghana @ahhhgolf @AhhPhotography @AHLDickherber @ahmad94 @ahmansoor @AhomeZ @ahopton70 @AHPediatrics @Ahrnertyg @ahruman @ahsanmedia @Aianna95 @AidenWin @aidkits @aiesya69 @aigostyle @aihui @aikomita @AileenAvikova @AileenFlicki @AIM4Marketing @aimeecheek @aimeepilz @AimeeSilly @Aimegsinha @AIMIAqld @AIMTherapy @AineBelton @air_condition @air_cooling @air_cut @airIradio @AiraBongco @AishahC_Designs @AisleShops @aivalis @Aiye @aj_affiliate @aj_wood @AJ2D @aj313 @ajanijackson @AjayJacobsen @AJdigitalFocus @ajhalls2 @Ajidon @AjinkyaForYou @ajjoseph @AJLBank9 @ajuliano @ajwebmarketing @ajwilcox @ajwire @aka_mike @akalfa @akalous @akanaliga @AkankshaGoel @akearns @AkgeeSports @akhaleque @akikojes @akintibubo @akinyelestephen @AkiraMas @akleinschmidt @akmanda @AknieGirl @akoneill @AkosFintor @AKpicks @akquisefachfrau @AkramBiz @AKREMORFIN @akromanelli @akrongarber @AkronOhioHomes @AktieKrant @aktiff08 @AktivDigital @akuinginsukses @akula33 @AI3XIII @al999 @Alabye_com @alagirir @Alain_Lemay69 @AlaisterLow @AlAltan @alan_sharland @alan_sills @AlanaKarran @alanbobet @alanbr82 @AlaneAnderson @alange710 @alangent5000 @AlanGeorgeBrook @alanhaft @alanjenkin @alanjingram @alankerrigan @AlanLCaldwell @AlanLopuszynski @AlanMcGeeSay @AlanRae @AlanRainey @AlanSee @alanunderkofler @alanwhite101 @alanxing @alapplegate @alasandy @AlaskaArtist @alaskahwybb @AlaskaMoose @AlaskaSpeaks @ALauderdale @alawine @AlhamaePlant @albertagurll @AlbertoCuya @albertopayo @AlboNumismatico @AlchemyLab @alchimagica @AlcidesCF @AlcoheimersNO @AlcottHRGroup @ALD85 @AldaRRissel @ALDOI958 @aldsaur @alduque @aldyboy_03 @alead @aleandrade @alecberg @alecorreo @alejandrorcl @AleksAtanasov @aleksnrg @alemaksymon @alenhoff @aleqz @Aleska777 @AlessandraCo @AlethaMcManama @AleWriter @Alex_185 @Alex_Ionescu @Alex_Joungblood @alex_knorr @alex_marketer @alex_ping @Alex_Tomm @Alex_Veres @Alex14112412 @alexa86ab @AlexaAdrian @alexabi @alexaesthetics @alexanderbrom @Alexandermay @Alexandra_lo69 @Alexandra_Mary @AlexandraFish @AlexandraRyan @AlexandreBonin @AlexAndrei @alexandreruoso @alexandriaFry @alexandriarr96 @alexandrocastro @alexasamuels @alexasdad @alexbacks @AlexBlom @alexbobadilla @AlexDAllison @alexdc @AlexDogy @AlexDombroff @alexdrogeanu @alexgarcia @AlexGrech @Alexhamil @alexiaanastasio @Alexica73 @alexico_swim @alexingloire @AlexInHouston @AlexisCeule @alexisvandam @AlexKaris @AlexLelodLarrea @AlexLimInc @alexlockwood @Alexluvmusic @alexmatatula @alexnester @AlexPapaCom @alexpuig @AlexRansom @AlexResolutions @AlexSchleber @AlexShapiroWR @AlexSimpsonLOVE @alexsol @alexson @alextoul @AlFerretti @alfina87 @alfmarcussen @alfonsopineiro @alfonsoromans @AlfredoSMS @algoRhythmLabs @alhanzal @Ali_Dee @Ali_Kurt @aliayvaz @alibabaoglan @alicam @Alice200806 @aliceheiman @alicemurphie @AliceTChan @alicia_carlson @aliciacastillo @Aliciadawn2008 @aliciafalcone @alicialyttle @aliciamarie112 @aliciamejia @AliciaSanera @aliciaslander @aliciathephotog @aliciaXziel @aliabeth @AlienBeing @ALIENDIMENSIONS @alienguide @AlignProsperity @AlignYourEnergy @alihooper @aliinspired @AlikBarsegian @alikoh @alileenyc @AlilSunshine4U @AliMaynard @Alin_S @AlinaAlison @alinekefr @AlineLii @alingham @alinnearl @AlinsSonMullins @AlioGenetics @AlionaKJewelry @alisaa99 @alisfoster @AlishaGreen79 @AlishaTV @AlisonBLowndes @AlisonDoyle @alisondrake @AlisonHeld @alisonjns @alisonlaw @alisonrbcm @AlisPeraza @AlissaFereday @alissasadler @Alive_Dreamer @AliveNewZealand @AlkalineBuzz @AlkalineH2O @alkhemst @alkomy @All_A_Baut_HCMT @all_about_surf @all4freebies @AllaboutCroydon @AllAboutHer @allaboutpaws @AllAbtChristmas @AllAbtDogs @AllAbtFamily @AllAbtLove @AllaBurda @AllanBBeaton @AllanCrawford @allancurtis @allanp73 @allanpearlman @allanschoenberg @allantowns @allanwaldron @allcapetown @allcaughtup @AllDallas @Allen_Tx @allenbostrom @AllenCordrey @allenmireles @allenmowery @AllenRhoadarmer @AllenVoivod @AllenWebstar @allerent @alllfo @alliaalexander @allianceintl @Alliebrwneyez @alliemiami @alliey_marie @AllInOneOutlet @allison_w @allisoncrawfo21 @allisonmilton @AllThatIs @Allman_C_ @allneedo @ALLNEWSN @ALLLocalBargains @allonsdanser @allowinglife @AllSheriffSales @AllStagesMktg @AllTalent @AllTechTronics @AllTexanMusic @AllThingsGwen @alltopquotes @Allyaec @AllYap @AllYapp @allygill @AllYourDesigner @AllysePadden @allysimone @allysonmorgan @AllysonMorris @AllysonRKring @AlmaLasers @AlmaNova @AlmineSabia @AlmineWijsheid @almond_beauty @almondpeak @almostfearless @aloapur @AloeAloe2u @aloebiz4u @Aloe Tropical @AloftDallas @AlohaArleen @AlohaSales @alokc @alokrchy @alorluvin @alon_205 @alpha83 @AlpacaFarmgirl @AlPeggy @alpenwest @Alpha_Computer @AlphaBarter @alphaedefense @alphaengineer2 @alphahelicopter @Alphalist @AlphaMares @AlphaPie @alphatweet2 @Alprimocanto @alrai @ALRCoach @alsaprep @altacb @Altadie_JF @AltecLansing @AltEnergyWebPar @Alter_EgoxCMO @AlterianSM2 @AlternativeHeat @AlternativeNRG @althea_martin @AltMedicineBlog @altmktg @Altpap @altt1 @alucididea @alunrichards @alvaresotero @AlvesFilipe @alvinbrown @alvincbeyer @AlvinSchmitt @alvinycheung @alwayscatholic @alwaysfinance @AlWoods @AlxRodz @alyandrea @alysdrake @alyssawant @alyssagregory @alyssawalansky @AlzayCalhoun @amacowboys451 @amahouston @amalari @Amanda_vdGulik @Amanda_Warr @amandaavilesl @amandacdavie @amandachapel @AmandaDCMS @amandahawk @amandakathryn @amandakrill @AmandaMarieBlog @AmandaMCarter @amandasback @AmandaShares @AmandaVega @amandertising @AMAnet @amankumra @amapoda @amarc_afxisi @amarkule @amarrrg @amartintx @amasv @AmayaPapayasmom @amazedlive @AmazinglyAmara @amazinglyblog @AmazingPictures @amazingreality @amazingvidtours @amazonamit @AmazonSecret @Ambal @ambassador0112 @amber_design @amber01 @Amber69nf @amberbreannexo @AmberCadabra @AmberDeVille @amberpresley @AmberReiki @Ambitiouspeople @AmCapitalfundng @AMCForg @AmConsUnified @ameliachen @AmeliaEChampion @Ameliahomes @ameliawoods @Amenye @AmericaCalling @American_Bride @AmericanAir @AmericanEnt @AmericanExterio @AmericanIssues @AmericanLaser @AmericanMktg @AmericanWomannn @AmericasAgenda @americaspress @amesinora @amforever @amfunderburkl @amfurie @amgenove @amhartnett268 @AmHealthBeauty @ami_zhasayhu @Ami3251 @AmiAhuja @amiedigital @amihealthsvs @AminIuk @aminoff @amir2b @amirbq @amirk25 @AMIRSHAINKMAN @amitanigam @amitcpatel @amitgautam @amitibudhrani @amitm68 @amjadhkhan @amkl114 @AMLassociates @AMLIQuadrangle @AMm2studios @ammuappoze @amoils @AMORCII

Acknowledgments

@amorfar @Amorous_VI @amosays @amous @ampc @Amped4News @Ampiphy @ampli2de @AMPTAgency @amraxx @amrcon @amsandrewl @amsd2dth @amsonline @AmSpirit @amtower @AmUNESCO @amusingsexfacts @AMVdudes @amwatmovers @AmwayGlobal_IBO @amyanderson01 @AmyatMovingOn @amybeer @amygiambruno @Amygirl2006 @amyhammond @amyhasslen @AmyJantzer @AmyKinnaird @amykr @amylambright @AmyLinderman @AmyLynnAndrews @AmyMSimon @amyoutloud @AmyP00h @amys_bus_ticket @amysmlmfortune @AmyStark @AmyStarrAllen @AmyVernon @AmyVRO @AmyWSYX6 @AmyyMack @amzhealthcare @AnImalCrazy @Ana_Jam @anaas @AnaCarterOnline @AnacondaWOW @anadeau @AnaGirl22 @anahuac @anaknyte @AnaliFirst @AnaLoback @AnaLuciaNovak @Analytics_USA @analytixman @anamarquezl @Anan_Lashin @anandaleeke @AnaNogales @AnaRC @AnasaziStories @anbazhagan @anccricket @anchalsingh @anchorwomen @AndBreak @anddjournal @andgenth @andicurry @andiepetoskey @andikadewan @andilinks @andimarlon @AndMoreComm @Andrea_Wolo @andreabeadle @andreacarless @andreacook @AndreaDeaPachec @AndreaHoxie @AndreaJordanuk @andreamatthews @AndreaMeyer @andreamoffat @AndreaNowack @andreas_derksen @AndreaSatter @AndreaSJames @AndreasLeo @andreastenberg @andreaswpv @andreatarrant @AndreaVahl @AndreBiester @AndredeBeer @AndreGuay @AndreiCurelaru @AndreInfobase @andreitoup @Andreiuk @andremarujo @Andres_Luna @AndresD @andreseloynava @AndresFabris @andressilvaa @Andrew_Boyd @Andrew_Johnson @andrew_murray @Andrew_Skelly @andrew9963 @AndrewBates @andrewbrenner @andrewcbrooks @AndrewCiccone @andrewdaum @AndrewESikorski @andrewfoote @andrewhesselden @andrewjlingley @AndrewJohnHanna @andrewkeir @AndrewKuhn @AndrewLedford @Andrewlock @AndrewMarhevko @AndrewNation1 @AndrewOpala @andrewranwong @andrewrondeau @andrewspoeth @AndrewWSharp @AndriaStanley @AndroidPower @Andromeda95 @AndrosCreations @Andy_Burton @andy_dmxpert @andy_fuller @andy_proper @Andy_Stanczyk @andycarroll @andycooktellem @andyheadworth @andyhughes @AndyInNaples @andylloydgordon @andymac71 @Andymantweet @AndyMichaels121 @andymurd @andyraj @AndyShaw67 @andywallman @AndyWinchell @anechan @AnemosNaftilos @anepiphany @anerushprnews @anesiderman @anestatehunter @anetah @anewbook @Anewulivin @Angarastones @angarie @Angel_Oliverio @angel_voices @Angel4tweet @angela_nelson @Angela_Paige @angelabosscher @AngelaCrocker @angelakokorudz @AngelaLapre @angelambrown @angelarden @Angelatida @AngelaWills @angelic_fez @AngelicaLEvans @angelina54 @AngelinaMunaret @AngellaRaisian @angellr @angeloantoni @AngeloHall @angelovidiri @angelscassidy @angelscrews @AngelsDen @AngelsKnocking @Angelsoft @AngelvMaynard @AngelWardriver @Angesilva_ @Angie_Perez @Angieatcougar @angiechaplin @AngieElenis @angiefit4040 @AngiePaige_ @angiepeady @AngieStrader @AngieSwartz @AngieVistageFL @AnglumGroup @angrywhitedude @angshu_tnmg4u @Angus__McDonald @angusfraserDXB @anicho @AniChristy @AnideArt @anikabelle @anikogiampietro @AnikoLecoultre @AnilSalick @AnimalInside @animal @AnimalHolistic @anir27 @AnishKumarSingh @aniskhan1610 @anison_spirits @AnissaW08 @anissiddiqi @AnitaDFiouris @anitafiander @AnitaHampl @anitaideas @AnitaMatys @AnitaMHicks @AnitaNelson @anitasantiago @AnjaHoffmann @Anjawerkt @anjum121 @ankiep @ankitmendapara @ankurdinesh @ankush225 @AnkushKohli @Ann_imal @ann731735 @anna_dean @anna_rich @annabellalamp @AnnaJ31 @annalaurabrown @Annalilie @annalisabluhm @AnnaMarketAve @AnnaXYates @AnnaZ @AnnBotham @annbrine @AnnCollins @annconvery23 @anndouglas @anne_bain @AnneDGallaher @AnneEgros @AnneGogh @anneharpen @annejoyce @AnneliesVro @AnnemarieCross @annemariemilton @annemiejanssens @Annemieke_C @AnneMSwinehart @anneobarski @annesoul @annestockholm @anneterbraak @AnnetteatAlstin @Anngelica @annharrell @annholman @Anne_Fox @AnnieArmen @anniebananie76 @annielustig @AnniesBlogs @AnniesParadise @AnnieStrack @annievang @annika @annikaekTSD @Annita_Lee @annitot @AnnLuo1998 @annmariehanlon @annmarieWineset @annmartinphotog @AnnMcCaughan @AnnoyedByU @annpadgett @AnnRabson @annschilling @AnnTran_ @AnnualMusicWeek @Anny4000 @Anok_lmchen @anonymous1mill @anonymousjonez @Anorocagency @ANPaint @Ansaco @anscahomes @Ansolu_20 @answermen @AntHeald @anthemedge @AnthillMagazine @anthishiten @Antho_tompenk @anthodges @Anthony_Murphy @anthony_wilson @AnthonyB1 @AnthonyBasich @AnthonyCrecco @anthonycurtis @AnthonyGemma @anthonygunning1 @AnthonyKershaw @AnthonyKnierim @AnthonyMcMurray @anthonymcneil @AnthonyMoraPR @AnthonyNelson @anthonyonesto @anthonysanti @anthonyw_ent @AnthonyWenham @Anthrodigital @Anti_Pollution @antiagingnetwrk @antifoton @AntiGenre @antoine_c @antoinepatricia @antoniocuauro @antonioechols @antoniojana @antoniolana @AntonioRestaur @AntonioTalent @antonius0 @antonroy @AntonStetner @antonycw @antorio @Antoshka_Sk @antotea2 @antwanp @Anubhavspeaks @AnuffSaidInc @anumberIair @Anunciato @anupamrajey @anupchowdhury @anveso @AnvilPhilly @AnwarSafar @anxietyhelp4U @anyadowning @anybyscard @anylondon @anyotosetiadi @AnythingAnthony @anywaytosave @AOAweb @AOBA_TETSUO @AOD_Lois @aolado_com_br @aoljobs @AOLRadio @AomDAY @AP_THE_REBEL @apanafashion @apbyers @apegan @APejic @ApertureDaily @apfelmonster_de @api_mashup @apinkerton @APInt @aplacetobark @APLINK @Aplus_net @APMike @ApogeeCampaigns @apombalivre @Apostlemarvin @ApothecaryJeri @Apparelfan @AppAssure @AppetizersNOW @Appforthat_ @appitalism @AppJmp @Apple_Kills_PCs @appleifreak @AppleInvestor @applemacbookpro @AppQuotes @approachmarket @appshouter @appsourus @ApptmtJournal @appz6 @AprilBraswell @aprilbroussard @aprilgregory @AprilPust @APrince15 @aPrioriDiamonds @aprograms @AprStorm @AprylEhmann @APSSNY @AptsForRent @apurvarc @APYTJD @AQILITY @Aqua_Duke @aqua_spring @AquaBlueWeb @AquaDesignGroup @aquariumconcept @AquiferMedia @ArabObserver @aragoncalidad @aragornara @araujofabio @aravindbabuv @ARBetts @arbitainc @arbonneteam @Arborplex_DFW @Arcade140 @arcadedig @ArchHappyHour @architis @arctictrend @ArcyEm @ardakert @ardasakar @Arddrive @ardentisys @Area224 @arealestateplan @arelt @arena84 @arenosf @arethabest @Arethusa_Biz @arewers @areyouworthit @arfoodbank @argalabu @ArgentaArtwalk @argentbeauquest @argus27 @Argvineyardclub @ArianaStones @ariannekristel @Arias79 @ARich323 @aridoliveira @ArieBlokland @ariekbl @AriellaCalinPR @arifamca @Arigo_The_Movie @AriiadnaOJ @ArimaxPharma @aristotlebuzz @ArizonaFlooring @ArjanvanBijnen @arkarthick @arketi @ARKit_Plus @Arleen14 @ArleneTaveroff @ArlingtonAlerts @armadillostudio @ArmageddonBeats @Armando_Holguin @armandolive @armikoadm @armourcleaning @Arnab_Toronto @ArnaudJacobs @arnimadesign @Arno_muc @ArnoldBeekes @ArnoldMLM @arnoldseoung @ArnoldsTeam @arnonbu4 @arnonbu7 @ArnoudMeijering @AROMANDINA @arora_sunil @arounme @ARParty @Arrie24 @ARStateParks @art_of_chilling @Art_Tee @ArtArgenio @artbykimcook @artbythelake @artclubcaucasus @artechRoofing @ArtfromHeart @ArtGibbs @arthooker @ArthurAndSandye @ArthurB1955 @arthurbonora @arthurcooper @ArthurCVanWyk @arthurra @ArthurTubman @ArticleBackLink @Articlemark44 @articlemarket00 @ArticleReleases @ArticleSalad @ArticlesEngine @ArticlesFYI @ArticleSlash @articlr @Articoz @Articularnos @Artificialmktg @artikelprofi @artimpress @artistberrada @artistico @artixmartz @ArtJonak @ArtMktgMentor @artmonastery @artoflicensing @ArtOfOnline @ArtOfTweeting @artofwarMMA @artontile @Artook @artpainchaud @ArtPeterRoss @artretreats @ArtsCultureDFW @ArtseyC @artshirtdesign @ArtTileMosaics @artuntravel @arturocanez @arturoperalta1 @arturowow @ArtyClub @ArubaAwaits @arugbylife @ArumugamPitchai @arun4 @arunpattnaik @aruomiram @arvadayates @ArveeRobinson @Arvil_Lavigne @arysyahrial @arzzcom @AsAnuttara @asbestost @ASCCareerOffice @aschoolmutt @Ascottmuller @AScreenofSmell @asesita @asgoodandbetter @Ashl31618 @ashankumar @ashantifoods @AshB484 @asheville_nc @AshevilleFM @AshevilleHair @AshevilleVoIP @AshleeKeating @ashleekeep @AshleighBot @ashley_greer @ashley_wright @ashley0810 @AshleyAffeldt @ashleyapt @ashleydstanley @AshleyJJohnson @AshleyNetwork @AshleySI16 @AshleyTCaldwell @ashleyxlp @AshMaxGDI @AshMcdowel @ASHOK77 @asho2fun @ashrodriguez22 @AshtonKutcherFC @Ashvin176 @ashwinsanghi @Asiablues @AsiaCams @asiaimages @AsianArtStore @AsianRamblings @AsianStarGirl @asiawholesale @ask_larry @ask_mama @ask4ferguson @AskAaronLee @AskAboutTravel @AskAlicia @askarnett @AskAShopaholic @askbick @askbillmitchell @askbuyusu @AskChrisJensen @AskCRMA @AskDanThePRMan

The Social Media Business Equation

@Askdavidchalk @AskDrGeorge @AskDrRoss @askgeorgeyeocom @askjacki @askJayson @askjeffpaul @AskJerzijoe @askkencheung @AskKim @asklarry @asklarrynow @Askme2reshape @AskNannette @askrizzo @askrocco @asksail @AskShah @AskThatGuy @AskTheParents @askthewoman @AskTimWade @AskVic @askvincentfl @AskYourCoachSam @aslesinski @asmashah @aSmoothieQueen @aspelbernd @aspenbill @AspireShawn @aspoerri @Asriadi @AssaraLaser @Asselt @assetplanners @assistanttothe1 @AssistDiscovery @AssistTV @AssistWP @associatedesign @assuranceagency @AssurantCareers @Assureweb @ASSURX @ast3v3nson @AST750 @astbnboy @astdOC @astensby @AStepAheadMedia @asterdata @AsteriskCreativ @astonish_alicia @astrack @AstroBabes @Astrologer_raj @astronomymusic @astronomyrecord @ASTROVIGILANTE @asuntoasiat1 @ASusoeff @asvag @asweetp @atalieK @ATasteOfCandy @AtbattCares @AtbWebHost @ATC_SocialMedia @ATECTraining @ateenoie @AthaAliTweets @athealthstore @AthenaComm @AthenaEast @AtHomeMarketing @aThumper @ATI_SDVOSB @atimarketing @AtimKavi @atimothy79 @atkinsjennifer @ATL_ARTISTS @ATL_RealEstate @AtlantaMarketer @AtlantaRebath @atlantichigh @atltechgal @ATM_Machine @atmillermusic @atniz @atomic_jenna @AtomicDC @atomicegg @atomicjackie @atoneplace @atravelagent @atrealtylux @AtriaEspanol @atriskyouth2010 @atroya @ATsLady @AttagirlsAttic @ATTCottonBowl @AttendADHD @attJOBS @ATTMPress @attractionlaw42 @AttractMLMLeads @Attractorfactor @AttyDeniseBrown @AttysCounsel @atukbest @atxsme @AtYourLibrary @Auction_Action @Auction_Gal @auctioncar @AuctionDirect @Auctionscam @AuctionTweeter @audidriven @audiencemachine @audioconexus @audiolympics @audiomicro @AUDIOMUZIC @audiovideoblog @AudreyBJames @audreychernoff @audrog @aueueueboi @aufwandan @augieray @AugusteHS @augustfromhome @Auna_DenverMag @AundrayC @AuntMyra @AuPairCare @AuPairDanmark @Aura_Adorer @AuraDentalVegas @AuraGroup @AuraSustain @aurelieponton @AurelioSisto @Auriella @aurorabrown @auroraderi @aurorahealthpr @Aurume @Aussie_Geek @Aussie_Mossie @aussiechic @aussieissues @AussieLogos @AussieRocks @aussietechhead @AussieTomTV @austars @austin_mls @Austin_Williams @AustinBlvd_I75 @AustinGoodwill @AustinYC @AustralianDeals @AustrianEcon @austriannews @auswonderwoman @authenticsports @AuthorAlchemy @authorlaurasaba @AuthorNarea @AUTHORnRECOVERY @AutismTips @AutismWomen @auto4insur @autoaccessorywa @AutoBuilders @autofollowback @autografik @automatedray @automaticallyu @automedia @automotive_crm @Automotive_Jobs @AutomotiveLimo @automotiveman @AutomotivMotion @AutopilotMLM @AutoRevo @autos_insurance @Autumnsell @auwebmanager @available @avantgardeinter @Avasiare @Aventuramall @avenuegirl @Avenuehotel @AVerMediaUSA @aversitenteras @AveryCohen @AveryProducts @AveryTalk @aVg @avgconsumer @AvidBookshop @AvidCareerist @avigayildamm @avigenuine @AvilaNina @avilbeckford @avitalbez @avlcsfoundation @avmaster @AVMband @avocadogroove @AVONbyMindy @avondiva @avotaku_com @AVPpodcast @AVPvolleyball @Avramikas_Vas @avtopazar @AW_Systems @Awaiting2012 @AwakenDMarketR @awakeningaimee @AwakenToGod @awalshimaging @AwardEmployees @awarenessmaster @AwareNetConnect @AWClub @awcyber @AWEbusiness @aweome @AwesomeInchLoss @AwesomeROAR @awfulwaffle73 @awienick @AwigaMedia @awnawnow @AWOL @aworldforus @awscreative @axel2010a @Axepose @Axioneering @AxisCentral @AxisNewMedia @axpz01 @AxsysTechGroup @ayakoren @ayamanalo @AyannaMurray @AyBuey @AYCCarpet @ayegerl @AylinAhmet @Ayman250 @aymanIrshaid @aysegulru @ayseguru @Ayurveda_Today @AyurvedaSchool @ayurvediclove @az_awee @AZ_Wedding_Pros @Azbek @AZFamilyPhoto @AZHIAZIAM4life @azinuz @azjulia @azlocate @AZLotteryChicks @azquad6 @azueropanama @AzureMarcommTX @B_Hendrixx @B_R_Quillen_III @BI40Tweets @b2bdata @B2Bento @B2Bmallorca @B2BMARKETING_UK @B2CMKTGInsider @b2corporate @b46u5 @baababybaa @babajive @BabakDavani @babarkamranahmd @Babies411 @BabolatTexas @babsforsyth @babu2480 @BabyBlooze @BabyBonanza @BabyboomerGeek @babyboomerslife @babyboomincome @BabyButterflyB @BabyChampion @babyschickdesign @BabyComplete @BabyContests @BabyDinesOut @BabyLayth @BabyMadd0x @babyname4 @babyosphere @babysleepmusic @BabyWebmaster @BabyySavagePopp @bachelorhood @bachparker @back2 @backdoorman @BackdropsBeauti @BackFromRed @BackIlCenter @backpackcamping @backpacknews @backsidepick @Baconius @badal4u @Bad_Azz_Shoes @BadBoiiStarr @baddmom @BadgerCareerNet @BadParent @Badruddeen @BADST_8139 @baduku @baechtelcreek @BAFFREY @bagdah @baggzyue @bagnese @BagofLitter @BagsByColette @bilbo @bilai baripa @baijusolanki @baileyroy @bajarrells @BakeMeAWish @BalalNaeem @BalanceForce @balaramnayak @baliretreat @Ball_CUMango @Ballad_of_KVK @BallenaTuittera @Ballnacht @BalloonedBoy @BallysHotel @baloss @Balovnik @BaltoRadisson @balycooley @BamaSouthEnt @bambenek @BambiBlue @BAMMedia @bananagrabber3 @Banburyshire @Bandgard @BandMark @bandung @Bandung9 @Banff_Squirrel @bangggg @bangleandclutch @bangunbisnis @banknet @BankruptcyTx @banky @Bankys2 @banner_ad @BANowWhat @bapaintingdfw @BAPATT @BarackODugger @barakhullman @BarAmenities @BaranCLE @Barb_White @barbadel @BarbadosCarHire @BarbaraDougher @BarbaraDuke @BarbaraFriedman @barbarahof @BarbaraIreland @BarbaraLongo @barbaraluhring @BarbarasWorld1 @BarbaraUechi @BarbaraWayman @BarbDreger @BarberelliPhoto @BarbHADDAD @barbieangell @BarbieKilday @BarbInNebraska @barboraknobova @barbreindl @barbrogrindheim @BarbSaylors @Barc_alpha @BarCampParis @BarcelonaBandB @barcelonefc @barcenaformacio @bardsmith @barebottomsinc @barefoot_exec @BarelyBrown @BargainHome @barginsavers @BargainTweeter @BarginsForYou @BarkervilleBC @BarksdaleVa @barnews @barnetteric @barney2EH @barnsley_fans @barnsley_one @baronbuilder @Barrel27Wines @BarronSea @Barrueco @Barry_at_IMPACT @barry_brown @barrycarp @barrydewar @barrydot @BarryFlanagan @barrypeters @barrypotier @BarryRabkin @barrywilliams44 @barryzwahlen @BarterAustralia @BarterCoach @BartGatsby @bartosiewicz @bartvanmaanen @BaruchAttah @barunseo @barvica @basarabadd @basbrand @basebackpackers @basebot @basecadet @BaseHD @basementjaxx_ @BashirBilal @bashley @BasHoornBE @basicdesigners @basicq @basilandspice @basit0344 @basoftware @Bassalindos @BastetAsshur @Bastien_B @BastienCaillaut @basttiao @BasZundup @BATCOT @BatesNursery @batonrougeapprs @batterystuff @Battleborne @BaAukelien @BautisFinancial @BayAreaComRE @BayAreaDivorce @bayhawk @baylan @Baylor_Business @BayOfUndy @bayou_la_batre @BayouPerspectiv @BBA_Workers @bbasilico @bbcrisisaverted @BBCTheInterview @bbeautybar @BBECandles @bbfemme @BBGTV @BBLC @bblonchek @bblweb @BBMClub @bboekestein @bboggess @BBoyAirMax @BBQ_lover @bbrennanleads @bbvideographer @BBWClothing @BC4SM @bcadGroup @bcavoli @BCCarr @BCCF @bccthis @bcnadventure @bcromlish @bcrystal @bcswebdev @bcuban @BCVBenji @BDBOY55 @BdbrownRant @bdcsoftware @bduverneuil @Be_First_Media @be_present @Be1st @belup @Beach_Girls @beachgal @Beachlovers @BeachRealEstate @beachwright @beacon4training @BeaconZA @beadgirljewelry @beadiful4you @beadwoman @beagarcia @Beakerlife @BEANDIPCLOTHING @beaney @beaparmi @bearabledeals @BearBucketsClub @bearcampcabins @BearcatLair @BeardStacheNats @bearfanron @bearmycrossent @Bearnhal @BearReport @Bearscast @BeASurvivor @beatacne @beatbookstoreUT @BeateZastrow @beatingdiabetes @BeATopProducer @BeatrizMPP @beatsbeatsbeats @beatsmurfette @beatweek @BeauSoleilHome @beauthealthwell @Beautiful_BCN @Beauty_n_Health @Beauty_Salons @beautyinsiders @BeautyofWisdom @beautyorganic @beautyskintan @BeautyViewPoint @BeautyVintage @beautyxpertz @BebeBadddAzz @bebeotop @bebizzy @BecaOrg @becbucci @beccabernstein @BeccaM_Thompson @beccatalks @beckerg123 @Beckertime @becky_pittman @beckydjohnson @beckyericson @BeckyHolland7 @beckypearce @beckyromo_SHA @BeCloser @BeDelicate_cp4s @BeDogSavvy @BeDoTweet @bEdnaScandal @beebyhannah @beesfeeder @Beeftrain @BeegeJohnson @BeeLazyTweet @BeemOostervink @Beenaka @BeerConnoisseur @beercrafting @beermaven @beerphilosopher @beersatori @beerwars @BeesAwards @beeseen @beesham @beeyourfriend @beezmap @BeezPeanutz @BeforeShot @BeginnersBase @BehaviorMod @BEHRINGER @beiler @being_Social @beingmick @beiruta @Beirutiyat @BekaRomm @bekysu @BelAirFashions @BelAirMainSt @Belanda @BelarusDating @belfastangel @believer_007 @BelindaCarlisle @belindacheah @bellaeast @BellaPetite @Bellas_Pets @belle_juliette @belle4er @BelleKarper @BellevueNews @BellPerformInc @bellsex @bellytweet @belovedsnail

146

Acknowledgments

@beltal_com @BemDevassa @bementallyfit @BeMotivatedNow @bemycareercoach @Benaidan @benamails @BenAndEfrat @BenBarnesDaily @benbarren @benbeath @benbenmina @benckenstein @BeneaththeBrand @BenefactorsClub @benefit_hoola @benfox2212 @Benfranklin1 @BenHavoc @Benita_Charles @Benjamin_Finley @Benjamin_Reed @benjaminbradley @BenjaminMG @BENJAMINS4U @BenJJanssen @benlocker @BENNetwork @Bennorca @BENNY614 @Bennzy @benoit1502 @benpbway @benphoster @Benprise @benrobbins @benrobinsonband @BenSmit @BensonLaw @bensykes @benthemorrison @Bentise @BentleyK @BentoDutra @benton_quest @bentyers @Benvaughn @BenW20 @BenySchonfeld @benz_hot @BeOvation @BerberH @berddlou @bergerchris @bergs @BermanPost @bernadette1 @bernadettedoyle @Bernard_Artiste @bernardwong1 @bernatcomas @BerndRoettger @bernielandry @Bernstein_Rein @bernyalf62 @Berry_Smith @berrykingfarm @BerryLowman @BerryNetwork @berrysslave @BerryYummy1 @BertaArt @BertaCWimbis @bertilhjert @bertramnash @bertronda3 @bertsvensson @BertWright @Besag @besamegirl @BeSmileNow @besocialonline @BespokeSearch @BesratSolomon @Best_Bookmarks @best_webhosts @bestbizthoughts @bestbiztobuy @bestclicks @bestearner @BestEverYOU @Bestflightsales @bestfreesamples @BestFREEViagrA @BestGardens @bestgolfnews @BestGoodLuck @bestgrandfather @BestHomeBizness @besthomeremedy @BestInsurer @BestInvLeads @bestlinh @BestLoanDealnow @BestLovedHotels @BestofGuide @BestofMS @BestofTexas @BestProdReviews @bestraveldeals @bestresorts360 @BestSalesDude @BestsBets @BestSchmoozing @BestSearching @BestSearchingTV @BestSellerBob @BestSpaceDotCom @bestspinnerguy @bestvaluetoday @BestVGTs @bestwebstrategy @bestweddinggift @bestweetools @bestweightloss2 @beth_andrus @Beth_Barany @Beth_Lane @beth_potts @Beth08776 @BethanyDeines @bethbrodovsky @BethCPerry @bethdockins @BeTheBeat @BeTheMedia @BethersJR @bethflarida @BethFrysztak @BethHawkins @BethHewitt80 @BethLayne @BethSimonton @BethSMiller @BethVanVliet @bethweisberg @betito_ @BetsyBstreet @BetsyMunnell @better_health_ @BetterBizIdeas @betterblogging7 @BetterFit @betterjobsearch @BetterLivingNY @BetterMaya @BetterResumes @Bettor_GRacing @Betty_mom93 @betty_rolland23 @BettyBrand @BettyCrocker @BettyFellows @bettylovell @bettyoli @bettypenny @betwee @BetweenMyths @Betweeted @BevanWilde @bevbrossy @BeverlyBoston @beverlycornell @BeverlyHills1 @BeverlyMonical @BevFlaxington @bevisible @bevobeat @bevyhost @bexdeep @beyond40beauty @beyondbeauty022 @BeyondCaptain @beyonddispute @beyondweb20 @beyourownbossie @BeZensational @Bezmoney @bezumnyj_mir @bfaeth @BFMack @bfr3nch @bfreetomorrow @bgawk @bgleeson @bgriffen @bh3311 @BHA90210 @bhager5 @bhaktibabe @BHartMarketing @bhartzer @bhasenbauer @BhavaCom @bhaven @bhavna_j @BHBULLION @bhinn @BiabiaProductio @BianaBabinsky @BiancaMeijsen @BiasedGirl @bibdoopofddj @Bible_Guide @biblebeliever @BibleF451 @BibleTweetin @Bibliothomas @BibuBibuBags @bicefish @bicwarehouse @BidModo @BidOnProjects @BidReach @Bieberologizt @Biebs_Lover_ @biepm @bierkle @big_benford @big_daddy_paul @big_edlange @bigandyherd @BigAssBarCamp @bigassfans @BigBBrown @BigBillyGoat @BigBlendMag @BigBookofYou @BigBR_Net @bigbreakthrough @BigBrother323 @BigCityCloseout @BigCoastBrands @bigdad09260 @BigDaddy01965 @Bigdaddydallas @BigDaddyVegas1 @bigdan1122 @BigDBoatclub @BigDmrktgmaven @bigdogdaddy @BigDPlace @BigEFundraising @BIGfest @bigforegolf @biggapple18 @BIGGKEMP @BiggSherm @BiggSteele562 @bigguy4 @BigHitHogge @BIGideaguy @BigIdeasEvent @bigissuenorth @bigjondaniel @bigmama1276 @bigmarh @bigMLM @BIGovernment @bigpeoplesearch @BigProfit @bigpromotions @BigRayRocks @bigredspark @BigRIzzle @bigstepmedia @BigT2007 @BigThinkerJon @bigtimetweeter @bigtimsportsguy @Bigtravel76 @bigtruckman1962 @bigtwix @BigWealth @BIGWINNER1958 @bigzard @BigHealthcare @Bijgespijkerd @Bijoux_createur @bijouxleblanc @bijuc @bikerbar @BikersWelcomeUS @bikinifreak @BikramYogaDFW @bilalchebaro @BilingualXing @Bill_Griffin @Bill_Irwin @Bill_McRea @Bill_Warner @Bill_Welker @Bill4Jesus @Bill4Time @billabongcc @billandlisa @billbainbridge @BillBandit @BillBateman1 @billbateswins @BillBlase @billboardman @BillBoorman @billbrelsford @BillCarey @billcobb @billcush @BillDaley @billdavis_it @billdfowler @BillDoesLife @BillEatock @BilleBaty @billfishkin @BillFrieday @billgeist @billgluth @billhanifin @billhardin @BillHibbler @BillHurlbut @billjac @BillMaps @billmcintosh @Billmorrison35 @billpalmer @BillPath @BillPlaschke @BillPowell @billrice @Billrod2 @BillRomer @billrowe @BillRyanUK @BillSaveUK @billschaffler @BillSchu1 @BillSeitzler @BillShieldsTX @billsimpson19 @Billsopinion @billstheman1 @BillVick @BillWalsh360 @BillWixey @Billy_Com @Billy_Cox @billy_marcd @BillyCoxLive @BillyHallowell @billyheromans @billyj110 @billyjackson @BillyJulio @billymcline @billymitchell1 @BillZucker @Biltsurfboards @binaryclub @binaryrpc @binarystarmusic @bing20 @bingdevelop @bingfeng2 @binojxavier @binsnurich @Bio_Char @bionicalonline @Bioecig @biomagnetic @BioscienceNews @biosoccer @BioSolar @bipingaur @biraneyal @BirchBusinessIQ @bird505 @birdbathbuzz @birdiegirly2 @Birgit_Dondorff @BishopOwens @BishopsB2B @bisniopps @bistroprovence @biswasdiener @bitchgroup @BitchToHerJerk @bitslaw @bitstrategist @BittenbyBooks @BitterComic @Biz_Money_Blog @biz_oh @biz_tips @BizarroClinton @bizauthor @BizBazar @bizbuild2010 @BizBuilders_PA @BizBuildersUSA @bizbuyorsellfl @BizBuzzMedia @bizcard @bizchickblogs @bizchoice @BizCoachBill @BizDevTom @BizIdeaGuy @BizIncubation @BizInvestChina @BizInvesting @BizLaunch @BizLifestyle @bizMebizgal @bizmore @bizmum @BizNetNw @bizofdiving @BizOppAnthony @bizoppleadsfree @bizopps @BizOwnersOnline @bizplanner @bizprofit @Bizprov @BizSavings @BizSuccessInc @BizTeamz @biztechday @BizTek @biztelglobal @BizTipsDaily @bizvidya @BizWebCoach @BizWizTV @BizWomen2Day @bizzaroneck @bizzconfire @bjclan @bjenni @bjeya @BJJEngineer @bjoanmiller @bjohnsonremax @bjones17 @bjorn1981 @bjorns24 @BJsLasVegas @bjsmith @bjthebear @BjuanmaW @bkardon @bkhorwitz @BKInsurance @bkjrecruiter @bkkihega @bks4maggie @bkuhlsf @black_diamond86 @blackamarillous @blackballonline @blackberry140 @BlackBerryMike @blackbottoms @Blackdogworld @BlackFriday_09 @blackfridaybest @BlackHatBoy @blackhatceo @blackhillsgold @Blackjack11114 @BlackjackGuru @Blacklabrador @blacklacehh8 @BlackLotus40 @BlackPearlSEA @blackplunder @BlackPoorMark @blacksheepub @Blackskyradio @blacksonpalace @BlackSonia @BlackStoryBooks @blacktaz504 @blacktigersal @blackwatchmalta @blahblahblogger @blainovind @Blair_Serena_ @blairmacgregor @blake313 @blakeandwhite @BlakeCannon @BlakeGroup @blakenetizen @BlakeSunshine @BlakeWaddill @Blamewhat @blancameza @blancasie18 @Blanche55 @Blank_account @BlankMustDie @Blarlock @blassam @Blastcapboomer @BlastCapJuices @blastcreative @Blastoff_Ideas @Blastoff_Queen @blastoff_withme @blastoffep @blatantlybianca @blauehavik @BlaseWealth @bldwebsites @blehr11 @BlendedV @blendenergy @blenderlowprice @BlenzCoffee @bligh @blikkfangeren @BLINDACRE @blindguy55 @BlindscomCEO @blingandbuy @blingicedout @BlissBridalShoe @blissfulfun @Blitzpenny @Blizzard_News @BLKMGK01 @blm03 @blocheads @blochure @block7wineco @blockgreg @BlockSpirits @blockwood @Bloganize @BLOGBlokeTips @blogboy2 @blogbrevity @blogcerebrodb @BlogCoaching @Blogcritics @BlogDudes @blogfred @BlogFriendlyPR @bloggel @BloggerNan @bloggernott @bloggersbelt @bloggersblog @blogging4jobs @BloggingBetty @blogginginside @blogoingreport @BlogginNoggin @blogocial @bloggy_moms @bloggznet @BlogHer @bloghob @BlogKingGuy @BlogLuvr29 @blogmasterpoint @BlogMeApp @BlognBusiness @blogofsport @blogomomma @blogpaws @BlogPowerNL @BlogsByAnn @blogsofts @BlogSunnyside @blogtalkradio @blogtechnews @BlogWellDone @blogyourworld @BlokesLib @BlondeBlogger @BLONDEisLOVE @blonelynomore @BLOODFAREmovie @BloodQuantum @BloomCarrollton @blooomingthemes @blrmoneytalkz @Blue_Voda @blue234 @blueableblog @bluebamboo_ca @bluebayinn @bluebirdman @bluecollarlobby @BlueCollarTood @blueethos @blueferret @bluefog1025 @Bluegrass_IT @BluegrassPundit @BlueJessamine @bluelangroupinc @BlueM @bluemojodotnet @Bluemontoya @BlueMoonCandles @bluenove @bluepop13 @blueroofdesigns @Bluesake @BluesBrat @BluesBro @blueshoesmedia @bluesky03 @bluesnapper @bluestreamdsgn @BlueTroopl @BluewaterNPS @blufftoniancom @bluhofmann @blujam @BluJConcepts @bluenetwork @bluephoenix @BluRay_Inc @Blurst @BlushLingerie @Blydawg @bmacfinance @bmahfood @BMAMan @bmayorga @bmazza99 @bmeldrum @bmfalc @bmfuller03 @bmgioia @bmoyer83 @bmsoffices @bmtrnavsky @BMV_property @bmwatx @BMWMediaMaven @bmwMischelle @bnya_cc @BoardofAdvisors @BoatsShopping @bob_quartz @Bob_Raab @Bob_Schaffer @Bob_Willems @Bob409 @BobandKimber @BobBarclay

147

The Social Media Business Equation

@Bobbie1986 @bobbitt @BobbleDan @bobborson @BobBraswell @bobbrown06477 @bobbybackwoods @bobbygee @bobbygill @bobbyminor @BobbyNunn @BobCallahan @bobclark53 @bobdal @BobDBrown @BobF360 @bobfartall @bobfine @BobGarrett @BobHankins @bobhayward @BobHowardMktg @BobHutchins @bobinoregon @BoBJiGGy @BobKraft @bobloagirl @bobmaiman @bobmcdonnell @BobMilstein @BobNorton @bobodidil @BoBonner @boboto6 @bobphotographer @bobridgecrest @BobRoman @bobshirl5 @bobtv @BobWarren @bobweberemp @bocurran @BodieCzeladka @Body_Shaper @BodyBuildBlog @BodyMagic_Truth @BodyMagicOrlan @bodynutrition @BodyWisdomInc @Boehme @boekhoudingen @Boersenluder @Bofu2U @BoilerFootball @boisvert57 @Bojangles1977 @BojanKordalov @BojeEskildsen @BOKZILLA @BoldBizReport @BOLDfactor @boldspin @BOLGATANGA @BOLifestyle @bolora @BolzanGCC @BombBeauty5 @BondsLife @BonkBreakerNow @bonnaroonews @BonnetCreek @Bonni_C_Caril @bonniebagley @BonnieBishop @BonnieHoffman @BonnieMarting @BonniesSquires @Bontemedical @BonTempsLimo @boogieman50 @BoogieMom @boojigaengyi @BOOK4CHANGE @bookatonce_es @Bookcornercafe @BookDragon62 @bookieboo @bookland_net @bookLane @bookmark24 @BookmarkedByUs @bookmarkssocial @BookMyGroup @bookofwisdom @BooksXYZ @BookWarren @boom8088 @BoomDallas @Boomer1943 @boomerangdata @boomerblues @boomerbodycoach @boomerchicks @BoomerLivingNow @boomerwebwriter @booming @Boonido @boorambo @BoostDental @BoosterCash @boostfatloss @BoosturLanguage @BoostUrSitesSEO @Boostwave @bootcampmom5 @BoothMedia @BootsToSuits @Boozenik @Boozle @border_collies @borders66 @BorgeNielsen @Boriken @borislavd @BorlandGroover @bornagambler @borntru @Borrowedpencils @Bosman_J @Boss_Lady_Tiff @bossblogster @BossezUnlimited @BOSSmetroDallas @bossondaicus @BostonBOGO @bostoncareer @BostonLogic @bostonmike @bostonrecruiter @BostProvConnect @BoswachterFrans @BotanicalNews @BOTRecruiter @Boudro @Boulder_Lady @boulder_weather @bouldernews @BoulderSuZ @bouldertri @bouldertweep @boullekestrel @bounceceo @BounceEnergy @BouncingCoco @bounshee @bourbonblog @Bourne2share @BournemouthHot @Bournesocial @boutblack @BoutiqueBaubles @bouvankuyk @BouwMaterialen @bovespinha2 @bowenjohnj @Bowers_4159 @BowesLyonLtd @bowlgamer @bowlin @BowtieSouth_BTS @bowuuuu @BoxcarCreative @boxingcards @Boxtut @BoydGreeneArt @boydjane @BoydJones @boydscott @BoyntonBeachFL @BoyOrGirl @bozena @BPA_Consultant @bpblog2 @bpeasy @bpinaud @BPU_Sharay @Brad_bf @bradanddeb @bradattig @bradbechler @bradfallon @BradfordBaggs @bradgreenPR @bradhanks @bradhart @bradjhanna @BradKerstetter @BradKirbyPhoto @bradklaver @bradlanelove @BradLedson @BradleeBooty @BradleyDWatson @BradleyGauthier @BradleyLevinson @BradleyRoss @BradleyWill @BradLive @BradLowrey @BradLtv @BradOrlich @BradRHarrington @bradsdeals @bradshorr @bradtrussell @bradvenable @bradwjackson @bradwozny @Bradyofficial @BRAGdotcom @Braiden @Brain_Gym @braingain @brainline @BrainLover2 @brainrider @brampitoyo @BrandAmp @Brandastic @brandbull @brandcottage @BrandCottagePR @BrandDNAinc @BrandDynamics @BrandeeSweesy @Brandergy @brandguardian @brandguyblog @Brandilyn @BrandiNeloms @BrandingComm @brandingsalon @brandipal @brandirahill @BrandiTCU @brandlessons @brandmanagency @BrandNewWorld @brandon_glenn @Brandon_Kent @brandon_morton @brandonbontrage @brandonbowers @BrandonBreaks @brandonchicago @brandoncoon @Brandongio @brandonhawthorn @brandonle007 @BrandonMaseda @BrandonSheley @BrandonTuss @BrandonUTF3 @BrandonWArnold @BRANDONxy @brandpointe @BrandPoliceNYC @BrandRanter @BrandRepublic @BrandReputation @Brandrevolution @BrandsAnatomy @brandscaping @brandseo @BrandStrutt @brandteam @brandUNITY @Brandwise @Brandy_Long @brandyea @Brandylele @BrandYou @BrandyVinylLV @BranXTravel @BrascoWMR @brasshomedecor @Brat13 @bratawebmedia @brattonmark @BraulioPRI @BraveHeartWomen @BraxtonMedia @BraydensMom0724 @brazilproperty @brazilweb2 @brazoscowgirl @brdomain @BreakawaySport @BreakingBulls @BreakingMSNBC @BreakThruGuy @breakthrunow @BreannePH @breast__cancer @BREAST_PASTIES @BreastCancerAid @breastsize @breathingsince @brechtjedeleij @BREGI @bremantovani @bren3gold @brenblackburn @brenda_haines @BrendaAnderman @BrendaBoorman @BrendaFranzo @BrendaJeanWyche @BrendaJHook @brendameller @brendanhannan @BrennaElise @BrenSong @Brent_Jordan @brent_tucker @BrentBucho @brentcappello @brentcarlson @brentdore @BrentGray @BrentKlauck @brentnhunter @BretMcCormick @BretRowe @BrettBells @Brettconyers @BrettGreene @BRETTINGHAMS @Brettner @BrettRelander @BrettVanderH2O @BRETTWITHROW @brewercharities @Brian_A_Moore @Brian_Aldo @brian_clark @Brian_H_ @Brian_Hess @Brian_Howes @Brian_Kirsch @brian_mcguffey @Brian_Parker @Briana_von_Elbe @brianadrian @brianboyd @brianbreslin @briancarter @BrianClarkeNUJ @BrianCousins @brianeisley @briangiambalvo @brianhaberly @brianhorn @brianhouchins @brianjohnriggs @briankauffman @BrianKibby @BrianKurth @BrianLFoster @brianmcgui @brianmoline @BrianNewberry @BrianPrimeaux @brianrbrown @brianrobinson @brianrodriguez @BrianRogel @brianshumaker @BrianSmith_ @briansrice @briantercero @briantg01 @BrianTomkins @brianwilliams @brianwong @BrianWSelden @Bricklv @BrickMarkers @BRICKSBBQ @BrickworkIndia @BridalBazaar @BridalCoachUK @Briddick @BrideOfChrist @BridezillaTimes @BridgeOfAllen @BridgetAyers @BridgetDaly @BridgetteFife @BrieNadal @BrienCaldwell @briennamichelle @BrigBurton @brightasianstar @BrightEvents @brightfireview @BrightFuse @BrightMichelle @brightoakstudio @BrightonRag @brightttemehr @BriitishColoni @brilliantjeni @BrilliantTips @Brimbase @brin9000 @brington85 @BringMoneyweb @Briones2 @Bristol_PR @BristolEditor @BristolGva @britameric @BritCrit @BriteTab @BritishEyeFilms @BritneyBrush1 @BritneySpearsFC @Britta_SF @BrittAdamsPR @brittaniabigail @BrittanyFarina @brittanylothe @BrittanyPR @BrittneyGreene @britton96 @brivervideos @brlaredcross @broadspace @BroadwayBeat @broatch @brodieshostels @brogandt @Broke4Jobs @BrokenArrow11 @Broker_Resource @BrokerChange @Brokers4Charity @BrokersUnited @BrokeTycoon @broncodon @bronwynclee @BronwynSylvest @brookebrookins @BrookeKendall @brookelthompson @brookewalthall @brookfielddent @brooklynwino @BrooksBehrens @brooz109 @broozer7 @brownbowgifts @browndave07 @BrowneKevin @brqt @BRSocialmedia @BrstCancerNews @Bru5W @BruceBarber @BruceBarone @BruceBixler49 @brucecat @BruceTurkel @BruceTweets @brucewagner @BruceWood @brucker1029 @brugnolive @BruiseMD @brummyjobs @Bruna542 @BrunetteInBigD @brunnenwelt @brunoaziza @BrunoffWatches @brunohbrum @brunomaltais @BrunoSwell @BruteForceEvoll @brutonnb @BRXBondStreet @Bryan_Simkins @BryanAndaya @bryanbillings @BryanCWebb @BryanElliott @BryanEllis @BryanGT3RS @BryanHaleKGBT @bryanjacobs3 @bryankemp @BryanLongworth @bryanmarsh @BryanMHaines @BryanRicard @bryansays @bryanscolaro @BryBeats @BrycenMcCrary @BryceSutton @brynie9 @BrynJohnson @BrynnLarina @BSA439 @Bsagona @bsainsbury @bsak @bsctank1947 @bsdalton @Bsekhon @BSerjeantson @bsfero @Bshelly09 @bSherminsomniac @bsicomics @bsilva @bsm1970 @Bsmith_Home @bsouthern @BSquareWeb @bsrust @bstdiabetesinfo @bsteve76 @bstronge @btalonzo @BTarver @bthapa @btmVA @BtoBSocialMedia @BTopa_Smith @btroutman @BtrVacationRent @btwee @bubblecakesbaby @BubbleCow @Bubblelistic @Bubbleset @Bubbletoe @bubbmiller @bucaelectronica @BucannerThomas @BuckandTrish @buckeyeva @buckmuck @BucknellCareer @Bucky_Diggs @Budapestphotos @Buddhaworld @Buddiyenergy1 @BuddyBike @budeco @budgarmany @budget_camping @BudgetBlindsNC @BudgetDude @budiyantop @Budor @budsgirl11954 @BuffyGuyette @Buford_Mobley @Build_Followers @builddirect @buildingbrands @BuildItBigRadio @buildmybody @BuildProfits @buildrapport @buildwealthban @buildweb @bukisa @bukomir @Bukowsky @BukwithGege @Bulgarin @bulkcosmetics @BulkFoodsDirect @BulkSMS_Softwar @BulkWholesale @BulkyWebEU @Bull_Warrior @BulletProof_UK @bullfrogmedia @bullhunter @BullsandBeavers @BullseyeMktgB2B @bullseyevideo @BumbyBrook @Bumsbest @bungkiez @BunkerShotGolf @bunksmuzak @bunnytick @BurbMom @buretina32 @burgerhouse @Burgoon72 @burkeusa @Burney73 @burnmyfat @Burnsie_SEO @BurntToastDiner @burritoworks @Burst_Pistil @BurtonBrown @BurtWilkinson @BusDevU @business_finder @Business_Just @Business_Leader @Business_Wales @business4real @businessbuzz00 @BusinessCards00 @businesschamber @Businesscycles @BusinessDIY @businessed @businesshostess @businessisbusy @BusinessJack

Acknowledgments

@businessopps @BusinessPerfect @BusinessPlanBob @BusinessReach @BusinessSavvyOK @BusinessSysCo @BusinessTools4U @businesstweetin @businessworking @BusinessXpert @bustaro @bustedcelebs @BusterTheLlama @bustynurse @busy_moms @busygal @BusyMomsFitness @BusyMomTips @butch4senate @ButcherShopTX @Butler_For_You @ButlerBooks @ButterflyHerder @butterflylib @ButterflyMktg @butterflymoms @butterflyvan @buttonsftworth @buy_ebook @Buy_PepperSpray @buy_realestate @BuyBMVproperty @BuyersMarket @BuyFhaLeads @buymelanotanii @Buysilver_coins @BuySteroids1 @BuySuccessBooks @buythekindle @buytweats @BuyTwitAcc @BuyYourCarNow @buyzotrim @BuzlasCEO @buzonerre @buzyboyz @buzz_tweet_es @Buzz4Me @buzz4web @buzzboDFW @buzzbooster @BuzzEdition @buzzerize @buzzflash @BuzzFollowers @Buzzine @buzzinews @BuzzIt_TV @buzzitt @BuzzKillGamble @buzzmouth @BuzzPlant @BuzzProfile @BuzzRocket @buzzskill @buzzsonic @BuzzThreeSixty @BUZZTWITT @buzzvalve @BuzzwordPR @BuzzyPages @BVelvetDeluxe @BVIBOOTY @BVISailing @BwAbbeyInn @BWBTvShow @bwccreative @BwhoUR @bwozny @BWphoto @BWsocial @byAgah @byallwritesLori @ByeByeDWI @ByHold @BYNEWS @ByondBlckBeauty @bypassrider @byrnine @byrongray @ByronIngraham @byronlk @ByronNewMedia @ByronRLong @byscoach_remi @bywave @BZ_420 @BzionSalesCopy @bzsmith @C_arqdesign @C_DIG @c_hawkes @c_heffelfinger @C_I_Surfboards @C_OBrien22 @C_REISTROFFER @C00LSTUFF3 @c1girl @c2cmom @c2ros @c3forwomen @c4diet @C4Liberty @C4ssie @c4women @c54me2 @c5e @C8ConsultingPR @CA_Litigation @CA300 @CabinetGlobal @CableTV_deals @cabobrenda @CabotCoop @cabradio @cachingmaster @cacildanc @CactusCarl @Cadaverman @Cadazan @Caddyinfo @CaddyMarketing @cadelina @cadilacjax @Cadillac @caesarion @CafaLawBlog @cafay1 @cafbear @cafenurses @CafeThawra @cafeworldcrazy @caffeinezone @cag1223 @CAGOP @cailaburke @CaitDelphi @Cajun_Mama @CajunChefRyan @Cake55 @cakeorbed @CakesbyOrna @CAKEwebservices @calberty2k @calbosch @caleb20003 @calebdonegan @calebtromo @CalenFretts @calgrasley @calhardesty @calianatenley @CalianCareers @CaliberGroup @CalibrateRec @Calibrero @califgirl232 @caliwerner14 @callanrush @CallCCA @callcentersite @CallForKokesh @CallGeneration @callkathy @callmeacynic @CallMeAlva @callmeryanzoo @CALLOMES @CallUsNow_com @Calmingkids @calmlogic @calsheimer @CalumBrannan @Calverta @CalvinBenLester @calyen @cam_sex_chat @CAM7THDAN @CAMary @cambiotech @camcoconsulting @Camdal @cameliano89 @camelista @CameronForPM @CameronHawking @CameronHerold @CameronSoans @CameronToth @Camfed @camilavfranca @CamilleAThomas @CamilleRoberts @camilux @camilynn123 @Camlyn67 @CammdaCorp @cammicam @camojuve40 @Campaign_India @CampaignJobs @campbellheather @campbelljoshua @Campbellwil @CampingWorld @CampsterGuy @CamRanhOrphan @CamWithBarbie @CamWithHer @CamWLewis @canacopepuebla @CanadaHandymEn @Canadamortgage1 @canadianbacon09 @canadiangoddess @CanadianPl @CanadianPolice @canal_uem @canayjun @candacekaru @Candan76 @canDDylicious @candeepearson @candelwish @candh_sugar @candicejcurry @candicewalsh @CandidK @candidlyred @CandleRoyalty @candy @candycohn @CandyHouseGirls @Candyland87 @CandyLarou @canopybedding1 @Canterucci @CantHang @CantoImmersion @CantoniDesign @canyoncreeksoap @CanYouWin @caodata @caoimheenright @CapableManager @CapablePeople @CapeProducer @capflowwatch @CapitalBayConst @capitaleblogue @CapitolAnnex @caponelive @Caponocca @capsLol @captainjack63 @CaptainSEO @captic @CaptJacksCrabs @captkeating @CaptRobLee @CapturedMelody @CaptureItNow @Car_Parts @CarAdvice4Women @Caraizzle @caralynn @caravellawines @Carbon_Trade @carbonadvicegrp @carbonfeet @CarbonHeart @CarConnection @carcovered @Card_Counter @CardCycle @CarDecisions @CardiffOps @cardsfreak5 @cardsnow @carece @Career_News @career_tips @Career100 @CareerAdviser @CareerAssist @CareerAustin @CareerBranches @careerchatter @CareerConnected @CareerDesign @careerdiva @CareerDoctorUSA @CareerDRBlog @CAREEREALISM @CareerExplore @CareerGuy @careerhelp4you @careerjkm @CareerJockey @careermoxie @CareerOrigin @CareerPros @CareerRelevance @CareerRocketeer @careers20 @CareerSavvy @CareerSavvy101 @careerscoacheu @careersherpa @careerstyle @careertiger @Careertip @careertips @CareerTweet @CareerTweets4U @CareerVelocity @careervi @CareerVoyager @careetdesign @CareyZhen @cargecla @cargillcreative @carhughes @caribbeancostar @caribparadise @CaricatureFan @cariew @CariLMurphy @carimanis @CarinaSheng @CaringMom @carinsurance784 @CarisaMei @CariSchauer @carissaacker @carl_mogridge @Carl_Norman @carl2k2 @carl31wirth @carl5k @carlbadder @CarlChapmanSr @carluna @CarlEReid @CarlHoga @CarliHeartland @carlitosVenus @carllpaolo @CarlMotel @CarloMcknightWB @CarloPlatia @Carlos_ATL @Carlos_Shoes @carlos00murillo @carlosalston @CarlosAmaral @CarlosAponteJr @CarlosGil83 @CarlosInferi @CarlosJNavarro @CarlosMCedSan @carlosnevarez @CarlosPatcheco @CarlosStekelen @carlotta_valdes @carloXL @carlyoungnd @Carmen_Shearer @carmentaracila @CarmenVriesema @carmn10 @caroberry @carocc @carol_frans @carol_schneider @Carolcdt @Carolde @caroldeckert @Carole9073 @CaroleMyers @carolevans_skin @carolhagen @Carolina_Leon @CarolinaBeats @CarolinaMama @carolinebosher @CarolineMueller @carolinemytton @carolmartincpc @CarolMortaroti @CarolNoeLive8 @CarolWiley @carolyndonaghey @carolyndouglas @carolynishis @CarolynRusso @caroompasroom @Carousel30 @carpediano @CarQ_ @CarraRiley @carrepublique @carrieann @Carriecares @carrieimpactpr @CarrieLuver @carriere_info @carriewrFer @CarrollLavelle @Cartrotcomms @carry321 @Cars4Causes @carshownational @Carsroute @carstenkopinski @CarterMediaServ @CarusoApps @caryconrady @Carydc @caryganz @CarynBrown @caryngf @carynstat @casachevrolet @CasanovaDesigns @Caseldin @Casey_Container @CaseyandBella @CaseyChesh @caseylooney @caseymaeknox @caseypea @CaseyStanton @caseywright @cash_from_home @Cash4Affiliates @Cash4Laptops @Cash4uO @cash4youtoday @CashBizXpert @cashcloner @cashcure @cashel @CASHFLOWTUBES @CashForGoldCo @cashgarden @Cashinj @CashMagnetJan @CashMagnetQueen @cashmanpv @CashMasters @cashmentor_ @cashoncashdeal @CashOnline4You @CashOnlineMan @cashrebates @cashreynolds @cashsupply @CashSystems101 @CashTube458 @cashtyme @cashway1 @CasinoJack @casinomoondan @CasinosQuebec @Caso_Verdade @casper32 @Cass_Creative @cassandrawest @CassanosPizza @Cassi_Rod @CassieSTROM @cassiopea257 @casspa @castletuition @castyourart @CasualDating2 @CATALLOG_RU @catalystroi @catatar @CatBlogs @CateTV @catgirlva @cath0309 @CatharticDesign @CatchingLife8 @catherinecorona @CatherineDWhite @CatherineGrison @CatherineKaputa @catherineonline @CatherineWarren @catholicspirit @CatholicTV @cathpm @CathyDanahy @cathygoodwin @CathyScott @CathyWebSavvyPR @CatmanWebb @catmi @catsarebears @CauseWire @CautelaNetworks @cawemedia @caxdj @CayenneDiet @caymanhost @CaySedai @cb4us @cbarger @CBBigelow @cbcsouthwest @cbensen @cbgorden10 @cbhbusiness @CBourdelaise @cbpromo @cbreecopy @cbrown035 @cbruemmer @cbtdellc @CBujor @CBurgenstein @ccadenhead @ccadworks @ccarlson04 @CCCTechnologies @ccDallas @CCFCQuebec @ccICDallas @CCLeic @CCLinkedIn @CCMI_Telecom @ccnorton1 @ccoleman1974 @cconnell09 @CcoolwilliamyahF @ccopley @ccorskipc @ccrlibrarian @CCsCoffeehouse @CCSTHRIFTSHOP @cctvdomecamera @CCURTGO @ccw__cpl @ccwhittaker @CCWilmette @cdbond @CDivvy @cdmelor @cdproduction @cdshafer @cdsols @CDUniverse @CDW_RyanPil @CDWVisualSltns @cearainvest @CeaseTheDay @CeBT_pro @CeCiirawwwr @Cecila_Shea @Cecile_Costa @cecilemiranda @CeciliaCn @CeciliaMurrieta @CedarsLabJobs @cedeeturner @Cedric_Prince @ceejay_rvp @CEEjobs @CEEOA @CeesIngelse @cegeland @ceilpetrucelli @CEIRecruiter @Ceirysjewellery @celeb_babyscoop @CelebBDay @CelebrateAHero @CelebrateInPink @CelebrateWStyle @CelebrationsGB @CelebritizeYou @Celebrity_News @Celebrity_Pizza @celebritypizza @CelebrityURadio @celebshoppe @celebwine @CelectCEO @CelesteDee @celestine3942 @Celiaa_J @celinedionqueen @CellarsofSonoma @Cellcontrol @celldiscount @cellflare1 @cellflare29 @cellhphonerenta @cellight_muc @celloliza @cellsolNE @CellularGateway @CellularGuy @Cellularman @cellulitesux @Celrase @CelticTattooDes @Cenay @cenkbaban @centered @CenterdinDenver @CentHound @centripetalhq @CentriqSBT @centseller @Century21 @CenturyFinance @CenturyRockStar @ceoseo @CEOStrategies @cerebusboy @Certsonline @ces614 @Cesarcolme @cesarinou @cesbound @CescaK @cespringer @cestbeth @cezarmaroti @CFactoryDFW @cfagbata @cfalb @cfdtrade @fleury @CFOAdvisors @CFOwise @CFrancisVoice @cfsem

The Social Media Business Equation

@CG_OnlineM @CG_Servicos_TI @CGABookkeeping @cgajowski @cgawley @cgissler @cgmainwaring @CGme @CGMinfo @CGNCorporate @CGPublicidad @cgronlund @cgryp @CGTheGroup @cha_am_thailand @ChaaKraa @ChaChingage @ChadBooker09 @chadd_bryant @ChadDLindsey @chadebriggs @chadimoglou @chadlang @chadlhymas @chadmissildine @chadnilsson @chadromig @chadrothschild @ChadSemans @ChadTEverson @ChadVanNorman @chadwickgraham @chadycham @ChaimAlexander @ChainManFilm @ChairEET @ChairmanCorti @ChairoelMochtar @ChairsatWork @chaitisen @chalacuna @CHALCHIHUITES @chalkboarder @ChalkHillEstate @chamberlainwill @champagne_bar @ChampagneTap @ChampionLays @chanakyamedia @chanakyas @chancerussell @ChandeshParekh @chandlee @Chandlerism @chandrakumar @ChandraLee @chanesteiner @Change4aDollar @changemanagemen @ChangeNetwork @ChangetheWorldU @ChangingQuarter @changsookim1 @channelbermuda @channelhaiti @channelorleans @ChapmanForGov @chapperr @charalo @charanjit @charbrown @chard_fernandez @chardfernandez @Charge_Large @CharityCheeto @CharityDev @CharleneBrisson @CharleneMay @charlenepele @CharleneSummers @Charles_Georgi @Charles_Norris @Charles0532 @CharlesAmImage @CharlesCrosbie @CharlesEThibaut @CharlesGnilka @charlesharper @charleshdenney @charlesjo @CharlesNeer @charlesyeo @charleybravo @CHARLIE_BALLARD @Charlie_Large @charlie23412 @CharlieGilkey @CharlieGrounds @charlieisaacs @charliejarrett @charliejone @charlierein @CharlieSlang @Charliesview @Charlot_Weather @charlotedasilva @charlotte_niche @Charlotte4512 @Charlotte60s @CharlotteJBrown @CharlotteMenus @charlotteSPOT @CharlyMaiz @Charm_Charlie @CharmaineTucker @charmedbydawn @CharPennyAnn @charpentier @charris @ChartingACourse @chartzog100 @chas45 @ChaseCarrie @ChaseLettMusic @chasesagum @ChaseUrLion @ChaseYourLion @chasidyatchison @chasinghiromi @ChasingSolar @chasl @ChateauCabaret @ChatterBachs @ChatterboxMC @chattersondrive @ChattyFingers @chavesechapolim @chavis_t @cheapbuydeals @CheapHotPrice @CheapInsider @CheapInsurance2 @cheapmobilesuk @cheapquality @Cheapvalue_ @cheapwebtraffic @checktheboxer @checkthishouse @checoivan @cheekvanpersie @cheepstuff @CheeseBlocks @cheesetipped @CheezheadJohn @Chef_Matthew @chef_ragu @chef2nite @ChefBrookeCooks @ChefDean @chefferren @ChefJonAshton @chefmagana @ChefMarkGarcia @chefmartyrich @ChefMod @chefpaul9828 @chefsathome @Chefstales @cheftraveler @Cheilitis @chelmowski @chelseachoy @chelseagreen @ChelseaMoser @ChelseaPurifoy @ChelseaSmith057 @ChelseyVeturis @chelslevy @chelun @chemalara @chemistryoflove @Cheng2 @ChennaiSocial @ChequersSeafood @cherbchronicles @CheriAmour @CheriDouglas @cherishart @CherryBlossomJS @CherryKissies @chershberger @Cheryl_Antier @cheryl40inva @cherylberklich @CherylBrownlee @cherylcran @CherylCurrie @CherylCYoung @CherylHarless @CherylHRhody @CherylLeClair @cherylnoga @CherylSmith999 @cherylta @chessblogcom @chesskillertips @chesspics @chesspolls @chessqueen @Chesterfield_MF @Chesterontheweb @chestyle @cheth @Chettl2 @chetthaker @chevrolet @ChevyIndonesia @ChevyTexan @ChevyVolt @chewmeiling @Chey_Pet_Food @chezeelet @chiana_ireland @chiaopi @chibisoft @chicago_events @chicagoama @ChicagoDesign @ChicagolandHR @ChicagoLumineer @ChicagoMoms @ChicagoPetPhoto @chicagopizzacaf @chicagosinfo @chicagosnews @chicagosweather @ChicagoTVChick @ChicagoW_eather @chicblvd @chicFABu @ChickensOnCam @Chicklix @ChicksLuv_Me @ChickVacations @chictopia @Chiczofrenic @ChiefHotMomma @ChiefSparkler @ChielSogeti @ChiemeeConsult @ChiFdn4Women @Chikkichik3 @chikquintans @ChildAnxiety @ChildCancerInfo @ChildCareA @ChildhoodwayBtq @chilihead @Chilis @Chillami @ChilliDipr @chimsenet @ChinaBizWatch @chinadreams @ChinaTraveling @chip_de @chiplambert73 @ChipMahaney @ChiqitaMJ @chiraggawde @ChiRestaurant @chiro_marketing @ChirpFactory @chirpspot @ChirpTweet @chirpysam @CHISocialMedia @chitowngreg @ChiWeddingVideo @CHIwtp @chixxxstore @ChloeCreams @Chloee_yang @chloesupercat @chngitall @chnvn @ChocAddiction @chocamaca @ChoccieJohn @chockman @chocola_puur @Chocolate_Chick @ChocolateWellne @Chocomize @chocophile @Chodidees @choiceeldercare @cholled @choosechanges @ChooseWork @ChoosingBeauty @ChopraYoga @choreotogo @Chow322 @chowhoundgta @chowkyadgar @Chrapka @chrclmnky @Chris_And_Julie @chris_fell @Chris_Ledbetter @chris_naylor @Chris_Stapleton @Chris101W @chrisabradley @ChrisALavery @chrisaperry @ChrisArts @ChrisBonanne @ChrisBowserEbay @chrisbrogan @chriscabrera849 @chriscducker @ChrisCelek @ChrisChase @ChrisClickZ @chriscolston @ChrisCommando @chriscostner @ChrisCree @chrisdenker @chrisdigital @ChrisDockery @ChrisDovetta @chrisgarrett @ChrisGaudette @ChrisGenoPR @chrisgeorge4 @chrisgomedia @chrisgomez @chrisgutafson @chrishalbohm @ChrisHillsc @CHRISHOTMAIL1 @ChrisHudgins @ChrisHusong @chrishutson14 @chrisinla1 @chrisjacobs7 @chrisjans @ChrisJDenman @chrisjhallett @chrisjsewell @Chriskilber @chriskilian @ChrisKnight @ChrisKominiak @ChrisKrysinski @chriskuech @ChrisLahay @chrislara @ChrisLevinson @chrislmarsh @chrisloft @ChrisMavis1 @chrismckinley @ChrisMReid @ChrisNewstead @ChrisOzcan @chrispenner @ChrisPJr @chrisramsey @ChrisReimerSTL @ChrisRHires @ChrisRudd @ChrissieDM @chrissiejoy @ChrisSilveira @ChrisSpagnuolo @chrissstone @chrissundberg @ChrissyMorin @christakeizer @ChristianaNYC @christianblab @ChristianCochet @ChristianDebt @ChristianeCooke @ChristianFrend @Christianity333 @christianjoly0 @ChristianMcM @ChristianRep @christianslave @ChristianWheel @christiborden @ChristieJarvis @christienev @Christina_Gomes @christina01_d @christinaarcher @christinajacksn @christinakb @ChristinaOn3PR @ChristinaSchaub @Christine_4_ @christinealcott @ChristinedWyer @ChristineEBell @ChristineG @ChristineGreen_ @Christinekorda @christineLg @ChristineMiller @christinerob @christiswhite @ChristmasWish75 @christmodo @ChristopherBuc @christopherxyz @christuttle @christy66 @christybeckett @ChristyDutilly @ChrisVanBuren @chrisvary @CHRISVOSS @CHRISVOSSSHOW @ChrisWilde @chriswilz @chrisyates11 @ChrisYoungUK @chriszweber @ChrMll @chryssy67 @CHSHeather @ChubbyFlyers @Chuchubells @Chuck_G @chuck_mac @chuck999 @chuckaikens @ChuckAinsworth @chuckbalsamo @ChuckBlakeman @chuckcullen @chuckdalby @Chuckdizzle78 @chuckgosh @chuckhester @ChuckieLe123 @chuckjaxonjr @chucklasker @chuckm33 @chuckmartin1 @chuckmarunde @ChuckNeuschafer @ChuckOliverNews @chucksnt @chucksrant @chuckvegas @chucky_sambouw @chumbonus @cHuMeeee @ChungTang @chunxia @ChurchHumanLife @churchloop @Churchoh @churchtweet @churreol121999 @CHustleMusic @chuyrod @chyams @CI_SocialMedia @ciaobella50 @ciaobella7 @ciaranTduffy @cibelestuff @CicerosComedy @ciciliya @CicisPizzaVegas @cidadaomaluco @CiganaECIG @cigarchick @CigarPlayer @CigarTwits @CigReviews @cigsmoorecom @CIHumanity @CileaLash @cimatruck @CIMBaby @CIME4 @CINA_Global @CinchCast @CincinnatiBOGO @CincyRecruiter @cindifletcher @CindyB @CindyBie @CindyBillington @CindyCarriger @Cindycindy12 @CindyColoma @cindygreenway @CindyHartman @CindyKing @CindyLeavitt @cindymariej @cindymiller20 @cindy2 @CindyMorus @cindympickens @CindyPapale @cindyspivack @CindyWMorrison @cineandreea @Cinemeo @cinequix @CinnamonEdge @cinnamonhotel @cinnic9 @cinocinvirgin @cinportilla @Cinzia_ @CIOCoach @cipher_online @Cipollone @circlemedia @CircleReader @circuitparty @circuscircus_lv @Cisco_X1Concept @CiscoTP_Video @cisnationwide @CitizenPower @citizenshipcd @CitizensIntel @citrixreadiness @citrixsupport @CitroenTechTips @City_Guide_Mike @city7life @CityChicStyle @CITYPUBLICITY @cityspur @CitySquareMiami @CityTavernDFW @Cityxxi @civis @CIZZLE @CjandMerly @cjaysauriya @ChuckBlaster @cjbowker @cjferrer @cjkatte @cjrock @cjromb @cjsantiago @CJsKidsClub @CJToyo @cjuon @cjweb @ck_2 @CKaldenbach @ckburgess @ckfoot01 @ckieff @CKochster @ckollm @CKR_Interactive @ckroks @cksyme @ckw09 @Cla_Gagliardini @claceltete @Claim_4_Injury @ClaimAttorney @ClaireDobinson @clairelight @clairifycanada @ClareWebDesign @clarissel_03 @clarissa600 @clarissathymes @ClaritreeAndy @claritysurveys @Clariziita @Clark_King @clarkeinvest @clarkkentclub @classic_chevy @classic_movies @ClassicCarsBits @classiccarshows @ClassicFence @ClassicRockGuru @ClassicUrbanHms @classyCEO @ClassyLingerie @ClassyModlTrain @clatko @Claudia_cbus @ClaudiaBroome @ClaudiaEpaz @claudiafalt @claudiagmodel @claudiagoen @ClaudiaSamson @ClaudiaX5 @claudioalegre @Claunel @ClavelChris @ClayOxen @claytonmcdaniel @clcrow @cldegoede @cleandailyjokes @CleanJourney @Cleansing_Coach @CleansingGuru @clearclutter @cleardebtfinanc @ClearedJobsNet @ClearpointPR @clearverve2 @ClearViewTrips @clemenselia @clementbryant @ClementonPark @clementyeung @Cleopatra789 @Clerisy_Hillary @Clevastin @clevemarine @cleverbusiness @cleveronline @CLEVGOSPEL

150

Acknowledgments

@clgdistribution @clgoodman @click2ink @Clickaholic @clickbankbiz @clickbankdiva @clickbanker @clickbankguru @ClickBankPros @ClickbanksBest @ClickBizNow @ClickDeal @ClickDeal003 @clickfire @clickforclients @clickforseo @ClickingForLove @clickmycoupon @clickperpay @CLICKsharron @ClickTips @clicktosell @clientonomy @ClifCoSolutions @Cliff__Clavin @Cliff_Meyer @cliffhayes @cliffordsound @cliffrnewby @Climate_Bill @ClimateDebate @ClimateScam @ClimaWorld @Climax_C @Clingerman @ClinRecruiter @clint_galliano @clint_hughes @cliptheory @cliqology @clivehyman @CliveMaclean @CLLC400 @cllctor @clmejia @cln172 @CLNunn @CloakAdotcom @cloaker @ClockFox @ClockWorkCEO @clode_m @clopezi @closebys @ClosedStacks @closestcloset @closesttodisney @ClosetCon @ClothCoutureLLC @clothes_hangers @clothesfree @ClothesObsessed @CloudBreakSurf @cloudliving101 @CloudNewsCenter @cloudninepet @CloudNineRec @cloudsuite @CloudTap @cloudthinkn @CloutMachine @CLposters @cltaylor8 @Club500k @clubdeliphone @clubdesoleil @ClubFemina @ClubGamer @clublezlife @clubofsurf @ClubRec @ClubSportiva @clubzazza @clubZoneVan @Clued_Up @cluelessaff @ClueMe_In @cluttercoach @clutterdiet @ClydeBoom @ClydePRM2 @CMarraccini @CMatignon @cmatthews58 @CMBeaudet @CMCAtlanta @cmchadwick1 @cmcheatham @CMColeman_OBM @cmelder @cmenzani @cmetweet2 @cmgarcia @cmh512 @cmic @CMIJobs @cmkrescue @cmmllp @cmnathanson @cmoexec @cmoments @CMR_Church @cmrajeshkumar @cmsgstockton @cmurphy7780 @cmused @cmutrie @cmvbconsultor @cmwalker25 @cnadeau @cnarcisse @CNotejr @cnpsupport @CO_Creatives @CO_WheatRidge @Coach_Colette @coach_lloyd_ @coach_marketing @Coach_Works @CoachBehnam @CoachBernardo @CoachBeverly @CoachCavanagh @coachclaire @CoachDawn @coachdbrown @CoachDQ @coachestraining @CoachForADHD @Coachforyou @CoachGenie @CoachHeather @CoachIanScott @coachingmums @coachingtrain @CoachIyabo @CoachJaneLee @CoachJennie @CoachLaura @CoachLynDee @coachmrob @CoachNetwork @CoachNewberry @coachpak @coachstefan @CoachStuart @CoachTanya @coachtomking @coachTsvetanka @coastalclicks @cobaltonline @Cobbman1212 @cobeyparnell @COBfan @cocareerconsult @Cocktails4Cure @COCOandREMY @CocoanutLady @CoCoaSunshine @COCOCARMELCREAM @cocomele @CocomoRetreat @cocteaulab @codearachnid @codebluerun2 @codec123 @codella @codenamemax @CodesUK @codexhelp @codias @codisedlacek @CodSpot @codyproperty @codysbrown @cofacio @coffee_tweets @CoffeeCupNews @CoffeeForLess @CoffeeGroundz @coffeekiwi @coffeemakerpro @Coffeemate49 @coffeemaverick @CoffeeNate @coffeetablepoet @coffeetonight @coffeezen @CoffmanMedia @coggno @Cogniance @Cognitiongroup @cohwill @COINMERCHANT @coinsclub777 @coisinha_ @cojentmarketing @cokeaddslife @coks @colalife @colbyculbertson @colbywright @ColdCallScripts @ColderICE @COLDFX @coldhardtruth @ColdStoneNOLA @coldwellm @coleenjackson @ColeLive @ColemanMichael @colettefeinberg @ColetteLesage @collabcreators @collagen @CollChris @collectivesavvy @ColleenGainey @ColleenKRich @ColleenLilly @colleenlockwood @colleenpence @colleensspark @ColleenSoehnlei @ColleeSoehnlein @college_studnts @CollegeADboard @collegeessaynow @CollegeGrad201 @CollegeLady1 @CollegeStockPro @CollegeTownTalk @CollenMcGee @Collette_Jones @collier1960 @CollinDouma @CollinsConsult @colloquy @COLmilwaukee @ColocationUSA @Colopril @coloradoartist1 @coloradocartoon @ColoradoEyes @colorcutwax @coloritpurple @ColorWorksPaint @coloursinternet @Colpurin @colttrickle @columbiasc @Columdevine @colungadens @com_marketing @Comaea_NL @comaford @combi31 @comediapolitqro @ComedyinLosAng @ComedyNutter @Comedyscreen @ComedyZoneJax @ComeRecommended @cometoroanoke @comfortserenity @comfycrafter @Comfyrene @ComfyShoes @comic_artist @comicer @comicscavern @comittees @CommaPR @commerce_e @commercial @CommercialMash @commercialMash @CommerclBreak @commrgirlSA @Commnwlthparent @commodityguy @CommonPointMin @CommsChat @CommsCrusader @communications9 @communitychange @CommunitySoul @commutiny @Company_Law @company_logos @companyofhealth @Compare_hotels @comparecredit @CompareTights @compassdesign @completeb2b @completely_geek @CompNetworking @comprend @comptonstore @computaal @computer_geek10 @computeramade @ComputerGeekz @computerprice @Computertweeds @computii @CompUtrader @ConceptHub @ConceptMama @concepto05 @ConcertSquare @conchdev @ConchoVia @ConciergeQ @concisetraining @ConcreteImmort @concuchara @concurso24h @Conduit @ConExec @ConfessionsMom @confluentforms @confuciustally @connecsean @connect2wealth @connectedcampus @connectedclaire @connectedwomen @connectfriends @connectingqueen @Connections4U @ConnectivityPro @connectuscan @ConNews @ConniDKaree @Connie_Podesta @ConnieGreen @Conor_Knight @ConradCrash @ConradSwailes @consciousriver @consensiowine @consensustechno @ConservationNH @ConservativeRed @conservativeroo @Conservatives @Constancebenzua @Constantinec21 @constructionlaw @ConstructionNow @ConsultAndrew @ConsultantCPA @ConsultCary @consulting @ConsultingChick @Consumer_Wire @ConsumerBuzz @consumerdad @consumermate @ConsumerVoices @ContactContact @contactgov @contactjeff @containerplants @contatow2pod @Contemplari @ContemporarySTL @ContinentalLoan @Continentalrlty @contmortgages @Contractor_Dad @contractoraccts @contresita @Control4 @controlanger @convergewireles @conversiondoc @conversition @ConvertBuster @Convrtnow @Conxport @cookiechefs2010 @CookieLTreasure @cookingblogger @CookingItaly @CooksAndCaters @cookwell @cookwithpraj @Cool1Guy18 @CoolIMike88 @Cool2Earn @coolbot @CoolCashTools4U @cooldads @cooleremail @coolfanpages @coolfoster @cooliphoneapps1 @coollider @CoolMovieQuote @coolmusicTV @coolnjax @CoolOscar @coolsi @coolsportstuff @cooltrade @CooperAerobics @cooperativismo @coopercox @CopelandsATL @copetersen @copong @copsicon123 @copycash @copycraft @CopyDimitri @copysnips @copywritemaster @CopywriterTO @CoralKittyCat @CoralooStudio @CordeliaMendoza @CorderoCanchola @CorePurpose @CoreSolution @CorettaJackson @COREYANDREW @coreygt3 @CoreyJSanders @coreylittle @Cori_Rizzo @corinne08 @CoriolanoAC @coripadgett @corjanmusic @CorkyKyle @Cormacaroni @cornbinder @Cornel @CorneliaHR @cornell140 @cornellchen @corner6labs @Corp_Prophet @corpalia @CorpNet @CorporateClass @CorporateImpres @CorporateWell @corposolar @corposolarsm @CorpSecrets @Corptravel @CorraFilms @corrientes @cortcase @Cortney_plus2 @corvetteBeth @coryaidenman @coryalan103 @CosmeticConsult @CosmicCowPie @CosmicGrunge @CosmicRami @costalifestyle @CostaRicaA1 @costaricacondo @costasmandylor @CostSavingsGuy @Cosylove @CoThrive @CoToYpieprzysz @Cougar_Candy @CougarsandCo @couldwork @countcologne @CountMeInSays @CountryDiscount @countryrealtor @countUP @CountXero @coupon_tweets @CouponBot @couponcodelady @CouponCrazyKC @coupondivas @couponlovin @couponsbycmc @CouponSherpa @courtenaybird @Courtney_182 @CourtneyAThomas @CourtneyBanks @courtneyengle @CourtneyParham @CourtneyWilding @CourtneyZito @courtordered @COURTYARDDFW @CovalentMedia @CovenantTab @CoverGround @coverlover111 @cowartandmore @cowboy_stadium @cowboyGary @CowboyJWS @Cowboys_News @BowdyWiseman @cowgirlbb3 @coworkAustin @coworkers @CoyDavidsonCRE @CPACoachNow @cpamadeeasy @cpapro @CPBADAZZ @cpcnet @CPGSupergroup @cphelpdesk @CplHRJobs @cppj @cprofit @cpudan @cpullumkiki @CQScafidi @CR_Financial @CR4_News @crabbywabby @craftylildevil @Craig_O @craigastley @CraigBBurns @craigdfreeman @craigdrew @craigedmonds @CraigGFrancis @craighcollins @CraigKausen @craigklein @CRAIGLSANDERS @craigmo2 @craigoldham @CraigProSpeaker @craigpsmith @craigsdickson @craigvickery @crandle @cranendonk @Cranleys09 @CrashCustom @crashsitenews @crauert @CRAVEamsterdam @cravingsavings @crawfishmedia @CrawlerPromo @CrayonsInc @crazedmom @Crazy_Felix @crazy4health2 @crazybat @CrazyBuyNow @crazyeyestudio @crazyvotes @crcbarney @CRBlackmon @Cre8tivegang @CreaComu @CreateandInvent @CreateMyWebPage @createpei @createyourmind @Creationtips @creativeacclaim @CreativeCaringC @CreativeConsult @CreativeDireX @CreativeEdgeInc @CreativeFeed @creativefood @creativeinaz @creativejohnny @CreativeKidstuf @CreativeSEO @CreativesInDFW @creativestride @CreativeWisdom @creativIive @creatorsinfo @Credit_Coach @creditanswers @creditfinder @CreditHitman @creditsvs @CreeksideFarms @creeping_snayle @creill @CREEindex @creolediet @CREOutsourcing @CrescentSEO @cresolvis @crestcafesd @CrestCapital @Crewlink @CRFConsulting @crickyman @CrimeAlerts @CrisalidaURB @crisbradshaw @CrisBuckley @CrisJobCoach @crismitchell @crispytalk @cristadelacruz @CristalFlo

151

The Social Media Business Equation

@Cristian_Lungu @CristinaCaverly @cristinariesen @cristobalfarias @cristy_fl @criticaldmg @CritSolutions @CrittyDougherty @crizatudzd @CRMbrussels @crmetrics @CRMtutor @crnc @Croaghie @crochetstitch @CroixSather @CRoss5252 @CrossComm @crosscutpr @CrossKit @crossplus @CrossRefSearch @CrossView_Inc @crowdSPRING @Crowneplazanc @CrownePlazaNOLA @CrownLoyaltyEnt @cru_ms @Crubini @CruiseLineFans @CruiseLog @CruiseOceania @CruisePlan @cruiserail @CRUISES_INTL @Cruiter @crunchbid @crunchdot @CrunchNow @CRUSADER4CHRIST @Crushtweet @crxstal_OsiRis @crydecker @crys_richards @Crystal_Mason @crystalbroyles @crystalbutterfl @CrystalClearBuz @CrystalCree @CrystalDLeonard @crystalline_ree @crystallyn @CrystalOutlet @crystalweb @csalisbury @CScottCrider @cscstudio @CSEnterprises @csharo @CSI_Talent @csilberman1 @CSMcMahon @cspenn @csramma1 @csswebsiteaward @cstechcast @cstegmaier @CSUFcareer @CSuiteAdvisors @cssunk @csutton624PR @CT8888 @CTGOP @ctiedje @ctlesbians @ctothelee @ctpvu @CTSAmerica @cubanalaf @CubanDiva33 @Cubbon17 @Cube2485 @CubeClips @cubeGATE @CuccioniR @cucky @cueblocks @CulinaryChef @CultCROC_Cancun @CulturalCompass @culturaltweets @Culturatist @culturevore @cunhamary @CupcakeCaps @cupcakes_a_gogo @cupcakes5 @CupidMan73 @CupidMarket @cupidzclozet @cupojoe_blog @cuppycakeboutiq @Curahee_KT @curbsideprofits @curestress @CuriosityDiva @curle09 @CurlyandClever @CurlyBrown @curranmedia @currency8 @currencynews @current_biz @currodelapyme @cursosjavier @Curt8888 @curtbuthman @curtisfinancial @CurtisPhelps @curtjonestweets @curtmercadante @CurtVisek @Curvatude @Curvezilla @CurvyGirlChic @cusherr31 @cussy @customerexplabs @customerone @customeyesz @customsign @CynthiaA @cuteangela2010 @Cutebutwild69 @cuteupdate @cuvee_corner @cvancecast @cvedulla @cvitello @CVMINC @cvray @cvcul @CWaarum @cwaterhouse @cwatv @cways @cwcafc @cwghyt @cwmcleveland @CWOOsr @CWPatriot @cwynnes @cxpz03 @cyamanak @Cyanide68 @cyber_web @cybercivilian @cybercourt @cyberdad @CyberElectronik @Cyberhub @cyberkid_CJ @CyberKind @CyberlandGal @CyberMark @cybermum101 @cybernautic @cyberpastor @cyberpoint @Cybertegic @cyberwar @cyBURsleuth @Cyclehouse @Cycleit4ward @CycleitForward @cydtetro @CyndiWilliams @CyndyTrivella @cynelson @CynthiaCavoto @CynthiaDeVelvis @CynthiaGoranson @cynthia1947 @CynthiaLasVega @CynthiaMedinaM @cynthiarichards @cynthiarowland @Cypear @cypnignite @CyprianoHawaii @cyprus_property @cyprus_villas @CyrusPastera @D__M @d_breshears @D_Desperation @D_Doyle @D_Elms @D_Mac_Biz_Plan @D_N_Ls @dd13vk @d3niies @d4rKn1ght @DA_MOSS @da1cbiz @DaaanielD @daanbrinkman @daavisn @dabbadie @dabdes @DABieberLovers @dacapo @DacianaRenee @dacrie @dadae @dadarocks @daddyclaxton @daddydew @DaddysToolbox @DADfurniture @DadLabs @dadre @DadsTrains @daegan_smith @DaemonTWO @DaffronMkt @DafjeTurbo @dafnan @DaGentleman @dagh @DagmaraPostelle @DagmarBleasdale @DaGreatest_ @dahara @daichulinas @DAILY_FREEBIES @Daily_Hotties @DailyAngelCard @DailyChat @dailydanet @DAILYDEALINDEX @DailyDollar @dailyebooks @DailyEngHelp @DailyFlowerInfo @DailyInfoOxford @dailymediazone @DailyPokerFix @dailyrover @DailySkew @DailySource @DailySourceNews @DailyTopStories @DailyUprising @dailywave @daimanuel @DairyQueen @daiyaan @dakitchen @DakotaRae @DalDubya @Dale_Lawrence @daleagainey @DaleAtES @DaleAThomson @dalebrown06 @DaleJrFanClub @DaleKamp @daliaamor23 @DaliaPHRJobs @Dallas_Brehaut @dallas_hotels @Dallas_iphone @dallas_mls @dallas_news @Dallas_Observer @Dallas_Realtor @Dallas_Roofing_ @DallasBarReview @DallasBizOpp @dallasblack @DallasBlackcom @DallasCyr @DALLASDANCERS @dallasdemocrats @DallasDesign @dallasdivorce @DallasDoctor @DallasFoodGuy @DallasFun @dallasgeekly @dallashappyhour @dallaslawyers @dallaslinks @DallasLive @DallasLoanGuy @dallaslovesdirk @DallasMeetings @DallasMetro360 @DallasPlanoTXRE @DallasQuad @dallasreal @dallasroadster @dallasseoguru @DallasSocials @DallasStockGuy @Dallastexasatty @DallasTexasUSA @dallastips @DallasTXLawyer @DallasTXrss @DallasTxWeather @DallasWiMax @dalm8ton @dalton_bodywork @DaLuvHat @DamasoD @Damayanthi @DameMintPattie @Damenwaesche @damian_watson @damianstweet @Damien_Diaz @damiensaunders @damienstjohn @DamMagazine @damndarling @damon7young @DamonHuynh @dan_baker83 @dan_cote @dan_coyle @Dan_Holden @dan_kuschell @dan_nelson_blog @Dan_Rapp @DanaBarfield @DanaCullum @danafreeman @danager1 @danalarsy @DanaLDunn @danaminter @DanaMNelson @daNanner @DanArgento @DanaSFisher @danasowrite @danatstout @DanBodybyVi @DanceClasses @dancemusicnews @dancer4u @dancergirl66h @dancermarketing @DANCESHAPE @dancingbudha @dancingelephant @dancingfrenzy @DancinginLife @DanClark17 @DanConniaMedia @dandenone @Dane_Gay @danejrobertson @DaneStevson @danettemcmahon @danfoleyusa @dangelorebecca @danger53 @dangerdiabolick @dangerous21 @dangerousmeme @DanHamilton1 @DaniaEdibleHl @DaniBabb @danicacolic @DanicaLea @Daniel_Lafrance @danielabarcelo @DanielAlfon @danielbdc @danielbegun @DanielBenevides @danielbenton @DanielBKimball @DanielBoix @DanielBoom @DanielBrackins @DanielBrunoSanz @danielbyrnes @DanieleAttias @DanielEgan @DanieleMathras @danielgansle @DanielJankovic @danielkatz @DanielKFoisy @DanielKlatt @daniellamegan @DaniellaObregon @danielle_nguyen @DanielleDALi @danielledrummer @DanielleHelms @daniellemmiller @daniellesteph @danielliu @danielpowers @danielpuljic @danielrayong @danielrmccarthy @danielromanonet @Danielsroth @DanielStoicaTax @DanielSWnst @danielvnw @danigranatta @DaniiiCp @danilomiedi @DAnimalRecords @DaniMediaS @danisinthenews @DanitaBlackwood @DanJB @DanJDecker @DanJoseph @DanLHays @Danlinked @danmoreno @DannetteLewis @DanNieves @danno1962 @Dannuroo @Danny_Fr @dannydevriendt @dannydkellman @DannyJJohnson @DannyMcFarlin @dannymckinney @dannymonk @danynokazaki @Dannysheikh @dannytopping @dannywhitehouse @Dano196301 @danoreilly @DanPlasticMan @DanRiehl @danromejuliana @DanSandercock @DanSchawbel @danschmoll @DanScott @dansdugout @danseyer @dantc @DanteHarker @DAntion @dantoren @danvoices @danweik @danweik1 @DanWorksfrmHome @DanyiViktoria @DAOLLC @DaphnesCovers @DaphneSt @darbydarnit @DarbysEnt @darcangeloCPAs @Darcybev @Darcymason @DaRealTomHanks @daream @dareber @DareSomething @DAREvolutionary @darianoreilly @DariaSukman @DarinCarter @DarioBenitez @darissaVistage @DariusDaquan @dark_skyzz @DARKEYE2 @darkfaerydovy @darkwzrd7 @darlasycamore @darlene_g @DarleneZiebell @darlingseo @DaronBabin @darrahl @Darrell_A_Smith @darrellfinney @darrellhudson @Darrelllssa @DarrellRhoades @Darren_Moloney @darren_robson @darrencrawford @darrencurrin @DarrenFarris @DarrenGibson @darrenlinkedin @darrenplester @DarrenWMoody @darrromusic @DarryleP @DarrylRMSG @Dartanian22 @DarthVaider @DartingDogs @darrenwingfield @DarrenWMoody @darrromusic @DarryleP @DarrylRMSG @Dartanian22 @DarthVaider @DartingDogs @darupprecht @darwineco @DarylMather @DarylTurner @dasaples @DasGeheimnis @DashaBushmakin @dashkk @dashtonwagner @dashwood @dAshx4 @Dasit @DaSoccerEssntls @DasPoetica @data2save @dataatwork @Dat @DataInfoCom @DataToProfits @DateCover @DatenTecnologia @DatesRUS @dateup @datewithyou @DatingTipsBlog @datingtipsite @daubale @Daud_A @dave_carpenter @dave_darby @Dave_Nicholson @davealtstrat @DaveAndHeidi @DaveAwl @davebasulto @DaveBates2 @davecleinman @davediotalevi @DaveDube @daveg65 @davegray11_7 @DaveGriffith @davehashley @davehassellband @DaveHearld @davehucker @DaveIreland10 @DaveJRaven @davekim @daveknowsall @davekusek @davelakhani @davelawrence @davelewis @DaveMalby @davemhuffman @davemorse @DaveMurr @davenervi @davenjan @davenorona @DaveNotes @daveoffen @davep21 @davepenny47 @davereinhardt @davesag @davesnape @DavesTakeOnLife @daveswellness @davetown101 @davew66 @davewest1 @DaveWestfall @davewoodson @daveyaguinaldo @Davezeller @davezichos555 @Davezilla @david_aim_histo @david_alecock @David_Alli @David_Allinson @david_bdml @David_Lanning @David_Lyfe @David_Mariano @David_North @David_P_Mullins @david_puippe @David_RGray @David_Tesla @david_waugh @David_White_ @davidl965 @David1McDonald @DavidAHaines @davidahood @davidaknapp @davidalston @davidamoore @DavidAseMosley @DavidBaeza @DavidBailey_LSU @davidbates @davidblevitsky @DavidBloom @davidbohan @DavidBortman @DavidCarleton @davidCarlson1 @DavidCarreno @DavidDogTrainer @DavidDuree @davidedwards64 @DavideScialpi @DavidFarq @DavidFinch @DavidFlom @davidfung @davidg406 @davidgerzof @DavidGraziano @davidgregtaylor @DavidGutting @davidhallstrom @davidhblair @DavidHolzmer @DavidIanGray @DavidJCorr @davidjguyton @DavidJohn_son @DavidKamatoy @davidkluge @davidkubicek @davideemax @davidlombard @DavidLRowe

Acknowledgments

@davidlsharp @davidlsharpe @DavidMadow @davidmarkslade @davidmccadden @DavidMitchell11 @davidnour @davidomni @davidp98 @DavidPaulDoyle @davidrankin @davidrepka @davidreske @davidrosuero @DavidRScott @davids127 @davidsancar @DavidSandusky @davidsbain @davidschirmer @davidsiecker @DavidSinghiser @DavidSitto @DavidsMind @davidsteel @davidsthompson @davidthomas38 @DavidVallejo @DavidVerrill @DavidWedemire @DavidWeedmark @davidwenger @davidzielski @DaviesWriter @DaVinciDeb @davines @davisco @davitydave @davor_fasaic @dawizonline @Dawn_Abraham @DawnBertuca @dawnbricker @DawnCullo @DawnDarner @DawnDeGarmo @DawnGartin @dawngilcrest @dawnmarrs @DawnNLang @dawnpappas @DawnSandomeno @DawnTO @DawnTongish @dawntrenee @dawsonbarber @dayatto @dayenmama @DayJobGone @daylight2416 @dayn @DayNurseriesUK @dayonhaynes @daysoutinfo @DaytonSEOservic @DaytonWebDesign @daytradingfella @DazedNTattooed @DazyDayWriter @db2dba @dbarnhart @dbashyal @dbenders @dbensur @dberney @dbgl @DBinBigD @DBJAssociates @dbk @DBoscoW @dboss @dbost10 @dbroos @dbrowell @dbruce1 @dcagle @dcartwr2 @dcchallenge @dcdecker @dcemkt @dchoneybear @DCL_Real_Estate @dclobbyist @dcnoc @dcp511 @DCPatient @dcpickett @dcSportsGuy @dcstarr @dcstpaul @DCWebDude @DCWeddingDJs @dcwillard @DD_2010 @dd0dg @ddbarker @ddbell03 @ddeclemente @DDGriffith @DDixon5821 @ddkurcfeld @ddma_nz @ddmecce @ddotcdotvdotme @ddpizza @DDPokerPlayer @DDPWeddings @ddrrnt @De_Risky @dead_media @DeadGameTM @deadheadland @deadmartin @deadonoptics @DeafMom @DeafTV @deal_queen @DealCanada_TO @DealerDx @dealitlivecom @DealmapDenver @deals4caribbean @Deals4Orlando @deals4u @dealscout @DealsInDallas @DealsInFrisco @DealsInPlano @dealsman @DealsThatHeal @DealSwift @DealUniversity @dealwithpeople @dean1192 @deanboedeker @deancousin @deandelisle @DeanGrove @DeanHolmes @deanhopkins @deanklotz @deankosage @DeanLaGrow @deanlindsay @DeAnnaCochran @DeannaRaymond @deannasworld @deanopriasa @DeanPerrone @deanpickering @DeanProchnow @DeanSorenson @DearAl @DearNiamh @deauxmain @debasispradhan @debbernat @Debberzz @Debbie_Martin @Debbie38133 @DebbieBarth @debbiebess @debbiebush @debbiedefreece @DebbieDonner @debbieelicksen @debbiegrayson @DebbieJJohnson @DebbieLBennett @debbielonergan @DebbieMarchok @debbierenee @DebbieSummers @DebbieTraum @debbieturner @DebbieYoerg @DebbieZachry @debbmestre @Debbora @DebbyBeachy @DebCE @debdebss @debdobson @DebGarraway @DebiRen @debiwalker1 @deblaqua @DebLawrence @DebloisLu @DebOGrim @DeboraBoeckel @deborahbravandt @DeborahBurris @DeborahTekkbuzz @debracurl @debraldaily @DebraMorrison @DebraParisi @debrareble @debrargrossbach @DebraTemplar @debratwitt @DebsDragons @DebSivard @debteasyhelp @debtfreeguy @debthelper09 @debthelpirstax @debtloansecured @Debtma @debtseliminated @debtsettle4me @debTUSA @DebWeinstein @debwink @deCali @decalogXXI @DECinDublin @decker_chris @Decorator_Style @dederants @DediKatedVA @DEDLINES @dedrashahan @DeeBishop @deehec @deejaatee @deekay21st @deenamorton @DeepDishCreates @deepkelvin @Deepu_DJ @deerheart7 @definitionmoder @DefMex @deforgenicolas @DefyTheMind @DegrayAustralia @DeGrooteBiz @deheldere @dehydratorbook @DEITRIX @Dejan_Kosutic @dejanromih @DeKoning @DeksDaka @Delacruz_279 @delamarketplace @delareviews @delcacornelius @delenafanmatt @delfreez @deliberateang @Delichelle @DeLiteTweets @DellU_AZ @DellU_CA @DellU_CT @DellU_KY @DellU_MA @DellU_MO @DellU_NJ @DellU_RI @DellU_VT @DellUniversity @DelMarPilates @DelMarVaSurf @delmonifieth @DeloitteGradsNZ @DeloresandCo @DeLoresPressley @delove100 @Delpack @DelphiLeaders @Delphinus_swim @DelPrado @delta40 @deltagirl2 @Deluxelimo1 @delwratten @DemagogzSty @demaijr @DemandCaster @DemetriosDallis @demetritzortzis @DemingHill @demis @demiwood @democrats2009 @DemondJackson @demonlism @DemoWell @dena33 @DenaMillerter @DenaWetpaint @denawhitebirch @dencena @DenianW @denicetex @deNieSaNL @denis_0bet @DeniSch @DeniseDeVries @DeniseEleuterio @denisefernandez @DeniseFolkerts @DeniseFraser @DeniseGabbard @denisegriffitts @deniseras @denishirst @denissowitsch @denmeister @DennisCode @DennisDaugherty @DennisLLynn @DennisMHayes @dennismstevens @DennisPeters @dennistubbergen @DennyCoates @dennyheinonen @dennykropka @DennyLyon7 @DennyMcCorkle @denoto @Denrealtor @denstank @Dental_Puebla @dentalplanusa @DentalSpaGC @dentalturk @Dentoris @denverartsygal @denverbardudes @denverbroker @denverbusiness @denverchefdude @denvercorealtor @denvercrime @denverdogworks @denverflips @denverfoodguy @denverfoodnews @denvernews @denverpete @denverpokerdude @denverpolitics @denverpost @DenverPostPicks @DenverPR @denverrei @denversnowdude @denversolarguy @DenverTwitr @denyseduhaime @deonderneemster @Deoxydoesit @Departer @depressividade @Derek_Haines @derekantoncich @DerekBrad @derekjoesoto @dereklacroix @dereksemmler @DerekStolpa @DerekTampa @DerfMagazine @Deri_light @Dermacut @Dermaxin @DeRosaImports @derrickcarlisle @derrickruebusch @Derricktodd @DerrolConnor @desdeCantera @DesertRealtors @DesertSunNudist @deshocks @desigg @designink @design_crawley @design_more01 @Design_Pro @Design4people @designandvoip @DesignDolceVita @designdune @designer_sarah @designerchoc @DesignerDepot @DesignerG @DesignerSecrets @designfollow @DesignsbyKoko @designstormgirl @Designstudiouk @designtwit @desireebanugo @DesireePaquette @DesireeScales @DeslockDarkstar @DesmondChild @desole @DesperateHighwa @DesperatHighway @DessertsRecipes @DestDaily @destinynefx @destockmode @DeStressCDs @detaildevils @DetailXPerts @determineddirk @Determinism @detobey @detourshirts @DetoxTips @detrick @Detroit_Alerts @detroitautoblog @DetroitPR @detstylereview @DetVendetta @Deuce2ProCEO @deuhlig @deusexcomputer @deutche @DeutscheOnline @DeVeauDunn @deveshd @Devils_Workday @DevilsRadioNY @Devindelane @devinemarketing @DevinHunter @devinjoncarlson @devKhalid @devon_jordan @devonbrown @devongall @DevoraRhoads @Devoted2HR @Dew95 @dewhurst4texas @Dewydeeee @DexterAddict @dexteralbrecht @DexterJr5 @DezignersDen @dfarnsworth1 @DFBrouillette @dfw_dance @DFW_HOMES @DFW_Joblist @DFW_Mama @dfwama @DFWAreaCadillac @DFWAssistant @DFWBabyplanner @dfwbargames @dfwbars @dfwbizlink @DFWcon @DFWDANCE @DFWDanceTalk @DFWGuide @DFWHIPHOPEVENTS @DFWHomeRentals @DFWHotBizTalk @DFWLeaders @DFWMoneyMatters @dfwreupdate @DFWSOCIALMEDIA @DFWStuff @DFWTRN @dfwvideo @dfwwebdiva @dfwwp @dg @dghgbooth @DGAT @DGilabert @DGL45 @dglobalnews @DGoddardLive @Dgreatone @dgupta5150 @DHA_2010 @dhanimu @dhanishth @dharmacharya @DharmaTalks @DHarmer4USHouse @dharrison47 @dhatfield @dhayes3396 @dhf70 @dhglen @DHills_Realty @Dhirley @dhlindemann06 @dhnaves @dhollings @dHolowack @dhsmith24 @dhudiburg @dhyarga @di_mobile @diabetes_help @DiabetesPosts @DiabetesStream @DiabetesSupport @DiabetesTreat @DiabetesUSA @DiabeticinSF @DiabeticSingles @DIADetroit @DialemupRVA @DialemupVA @dialogprofi @diamondalign @DiamondButterfl @Diamonddebyoerg @DiamondDiveFilm @diamonddjl @diamonddj4 @DiamondSharp @Diamondsongrass @DianaColley @DianaEnnen @dianafreedman @DianaIngram @DianaOrgain @dianarowe @DianaSebzda @dianaseovirtual @DianaSepielli @DianaSmiles @diane_nagel @diane_potter @DianeBourque @dianecallaway @DianeChamplin @DianeConklin @DianeGahagen @dianegiesy @DianeRayfield @DianeRines @dianesmall @dianewolfepr @diaska @diasloo @diaz_comms @DIBayliss @dibonafide @dichen @dichroicglassuk @dick_olmenius @DickAmateur @DickDeals @dickentweets @dickfrankenberg @DickieArmour @DickPrice @DICX @DIDARKHALSA @diddyc_ @DiDi_Dometilie @didisurf @Didjugetit @DIE_keitaro227 @DiedreBraverman @diedreggkto @DiegoDeNotaris @diegocasazza @diegoortizpr @Diehl @Diesel_Parts @DietDownNow @DietGourmet @DietingZone @DietInsiders @dietmaster1 @dietmaster101 @DietPlan101 @DietSlimPills @DietTipsFit @DietTools @Dig_Literacy @Digi_Designer_ @Digilava @DigiCameras @digigaia @DigiGirl @DIGIKIDSChildID @DigINAnchors @Digivalerins @Digisecrets @digital20s @digitaladtools @DigitalArtFem @digitalCamerasW @digitalchalk @digitalcreati0n @digitaldean @digitaldigs @DigitalDoug @DigitalDripped @DigitalDynamo @DigitalEngage @digitalfprint @DigitalGFs @digitalgolfer @digitalhause @digitalista @digitalkvan @DigitalLeader @DigitalLinks @digitalmediabiz @digitalmediabuz @DigitalMediaPR @digitalphotobuz @DigitalPhotoTip @DigitalPivot @DigitalSummer @digitalteacup @digitalwomen @digitmedia @digitmediastorm @Digitoad @Digitronx @digiVOX_SA

153

The Social Media Business Equation

@DigLiberry @DigMo @DigMyPersona @digthemoment @DihydrogenOxide @Diiiamond @diije @dikedrummond @DilaraEsengil @dileeshus @dillanos_Meli @Dillanos_VP @DillardTools @dillonburroughs @Dim3_O @dimag_money @dimitrieross @dimitrify @DinaEisenberg @dinag @dindasheeva @DineDelicious @DineDownUnder @dineshdoshi @dinform @DinhoCasanova @DinnTrophy @DinoHerbert @dinorealty @DinoVedo @dinowhite @dintravel @dinyah @DioFavatas @DionGeBorde @dionne02 @DiontraeHayes @diosacomm @diptoe @Direct_Tweet @DirectCapital @directory_links @directorysolar @DirectSalesCJ @directtraffic @DirkinDallas @DirkStrauss @dirman28 @dirtbikedude_NZ @DirtyEnid @dirtysalsa @disability @disableddating @DisastersAlerts @discgolfingl @Disciplanner @DiscipleMyChild @DisciplikeJesus @discoradiodance @discountblgrs @DiscountCoffee1 @discountdiva_ca @DiscountE @discountperks @discountsighter @DiscountTire @discountwhere @DiscoverClocks @discoverRB @DISCProfiler @diseaseaday @dishkarma @dishPit @dismay22 @Disney4Babies @DisneyDean @disneytips @disneyupdates4u @DisneyWorlds @Displaced_Texan @Displayxpress @DissertationRX @distressedreia @District13art @ditesco @diva_squad @divasexy3993 @DiVASolutions @divatoolbox @divatymejflo @DivaUSA @divercities @divercitybiz @diveresolution @DiversityMBAMag @diversitymn @diversitymnjobs @diverze21 @DividendStocks @DivineMissWhite @divorcedivorce @DIVSA @divvuhosting @dixie451 @DixieDynamite @dixonsj @DIY_Geek @diyhomester @DIYPR101 @dizzydentfilms @DjAjm_ @DJAndyPost @djaspeth @djavolo @dJazzit @DJCOMEOFAGE @DjCurtisRock @DJDaJam @DJDiG @djelski @DJfan1 @DJFerdinandi @djgreetings @djhornsby @djjeffyjef @djkiger @DjKingAssassin @DJKura2 @DJLecheNYC @DJLenny14 @DJM_Training @DjMarcoAndre @djmaxis @DJMorrisFitness @DJNeilHunter @DJofAtlanta @djroyaltykingme @djs2661 @djsamhouse @djsavel @djschultz @DJSibbald @djsoulless @djtechnasty @DJThistle @djtystix @djules @djwaldow @DJWISPAS @DKerken @dkholland1 @DKKipp @dklpacific @DKMahant @dkny12386 @DKTConnected @dkupras @dkwebconsulting @DL101 @dlbncalifornia @DLClark @dlloydcrazy @dlloydthemlmpro @Dltoolman @dlueking @DMAC451 @dmaher @dmaxcreative @dmburrows @dmgerbino @dmgsouth @dmiamSIC @dminson @DMMayland @dmncuts @dmschab @dmscott @DMurrow @dmuse @dmwdirect @dmwevents @dmwnews @DNA_Dave @dna4dollars @dnbeatcreative @dness @dnewman @dnjcouture @DO_Designs @do_ecoliving @Do_Well_Today @Dobbo52 @DobelsteinLaw @doc_bill @DocJerry @docmarkting @DocSibylle @DocSpallone @DoctorGlyco @doctorgorrell @DoctorGrass @DoctorLarry @doctormapache @DoctorProfits @DoctorsChoice @DocuMentors @documentpros_GA @DocumentZone @dodgecity2004 @DodiesPlace @dodmartil99 @dodosedky @doesgodexist @DoFruitPDX @dog_lovers @dog_tips @DogCorner @dogday1975 @dogdazed @DogDollarStore @dogfood_coupons @doggyblog @DoggyPals @dogloverme @DogMotel @Dogopolis @Dogos @DolHaveACase @doingpoker @doitnowromero @dokov @DolceFugo @DolceMeetings @dollars5 @DollarSignSir @DollarsInside @DollaThug @dolphin_swim @dolphin001252 @dolphingroup @domain360 @DomainBELL @DomainNameValue @DomainPros @DomainsDomains @DomCrincoli @domination2008 @DominicBelfiori @DominicFarrell @DominicScott @dominichales @DominiqueJ @DominiqueMainon @DominiqueNYC @DominosPizzaLa @domozychmedia @domsitowski @Don_Biron @Don_Crowther @Don_Fausto @Don_Jalbert @don_simmons @don21stc @Don411_com @donabby @DonaldBellGam @donalddotfarmer @donaldhooper93 @DonaldTrumpFans @DonalTravers @donatetimeshare @DonChounard @DonCrow @DondiScumaci @donetag @DongFang87 @DonHalbert @DonHutsonLive @DoniaPepita @DonMacAskill @DonMai88 @Donna_Price @donna84062 @DonnaAntoniadis @DonnaDahl @donnadilley @donnafeldman @DonnaFrindt @DonnaHBurns @DonnaKozik @DonnaLynnS @donnambruschi @donnamct @DonnaMLehman @DonnaNewDay @donnapenland @DonnaRagland @Donnaseries @DonnaToothaker @Donnette8676 @donniehoover @donniepie @donniesully @donnkidd @donnunn @donnygamblejr @DonovanCreed @DonRJeffries @DonRoberts @donrock1 @dons_deals @DontDuitOrg @DontDumpOnTexas @dontechnology @donttaxmebrosep @DontWorryMommy @DonValenteTexas @Doom82 @doomna @DoorToDoorCash @doppelraish @DoraNikols @doreendilger @Dori_Etheridge @DorianDickinson @DorianHarnage @dorishelge @dorksterdave @dornobdesign @DorothyDalton @DorothyNed @DoryanOliver @DosClicks @doshel @dotco @DotComExpertise @dotcomtalk @dotdotdotcomic @doterraoil @DOTeSTATE @dotjas @dotjenna @dotmusic @DOTProduct @DotSauce @Dotster @Doubleclutchca @DoubleDBill @doublerainbow7 @doublereds @doubletreestl @doug_hoff @Doug_Kelly @DougBarger @DougBrooks @dougbuchananjr @dougcoleman @DougFirebaugh @douggrady @DoughPizzeria @DougKBrownl @Douglas_Burson @douglasbass @douglasi @douglasmkting @DouglasNeer @DouglasWhite @douglehman @douglescchan @dougmcsorley @DougMummert @Dougoukolo @dougpmd @dougpowell @DougRitt @DougS_online @dougschorr @dougwinnie @dougwittmann @dougzipevski @doulail @Dove_Chocolate @Dovescorner @dowelltaggart @DownForLife @downhillskater @downloadbuyer @downloadsgame @downshiftingPOS @DowntownAnaheim @DowntownFord @DowntownMtz @DowntownWoman @dowwhiz @DP_Gates @dpbkmb @DPBradley @dpeacockstudios @DPerrys_iTools @DPete4 @DPHealthyLiving @dpillie @DPracz @dpsiphone @dPuncher @Dputamadre @dq4 @dquitsmokinguru @Dr_Guy_Cox @Dr_kinky @Dr_Lorentz @dr_nitha @DR4WARD @drabruzese @Drackomarin @DrAfzal @draganmestrovic @Dragon_Chairoel @dragonblogger @dragonflycoach @dragoterziev @DrAlan718 @DramaFreeWork @DrAnthony @drarunsatheesh @Draxford @DraytonBoylston @DrBarbier @drbenlo @DrBermant @drbloem @DrBrianWilliams @drchadfaulkner @drcheckitout @DrChenette @DrChessov @drcoreymaas @DrCoursaris @drcraig @DrCyberspace @drd2 @drdrahahn @dreadfroggod @dreal_seun @Dream_it_Today @DreamAlchemist @dreambizcoach @dreamcodder @Dreamfans @DreamflyProd @dreaminghope @dreamonkeylove @DreamREIProp @Dreamsagain @DreamsEnt_Inc @Dreamspacecom @DreamStreaming @dreamsystems @DreamTeamMoney @DreamTexan @DreamWorthy @drango @DrEilmanhasya @dressbarn @dressesu @drew_castic @DrewMcLellan @drewmgriffin @drewmiller @DrewskiBabii @drewstatsabout @dreyfus_marion @DrFernKazlow @DrGaines @DrGelb @drhenslin @DrHitmanPR @drhousingbubble @drimington @DrinkChile @drinkFLAVIA @DrinkItEatIt @Drinksology @DriveAwayBob @drivebid @DriveDownPrices @drivefishcom @DrivenAffiliate @DrivePower @driversdrive @driversedguide @DrivingSafety @DrivinMedia @drizler @DrJaniceE @DrJeffersnBoggs @DrJennifer @DrJerath @drjoesDIYhealth @DrJohnB @DrJohnMcGinn @drjohnscobeymd @drjosephnemeth @drjoyce_knudsen @DrKatay @DrKatka @drkisane @DrKraszynskaMD @drlam @DrLenSchwartz @DrLuz1 @DrMiaRose @DrMichelleRobin @DrMikeFleischer @drminkoff @DrMonaLove @DrMosesCPC @drmrakesh @drnatalie @DrNickMorgan @drnicomartini @drobnick @DroppingPoundz @Dropsofreign @drossignol @drp_pr @DrPam @DrPepperArena @Drplove @drproactive @DrRamsey @DrRaulRodriguez @DrRichardVisser @DrRickGoodman @DrRobAnderson @DrRobM @DrRonaldBeach @DrSamRizk @DrSchempp @DrSchurger @drscott33 @drscoundrels @DrSharonMelnick @DrSinghBooks @DrSmallBiz @DrsPeter @drswebmaster @DrThomasBarnes @drtiffanybrown @DrTimlrwin @drtirado @drugfreehealth @DrugSavings @drugspills @DrugStoreCowboy @drumming4you @drummondgolf @DrunkyClaus @drupal_builder @drupalhash @drusilabemol @DrVanessaDallas @DrVarenikova @drvincewong @drwarwick @DRyan327 @dryanhair @dryeyecare @drypen @DSaruwatari @dsbeautysupply @dsbthemovie @dsburgess @dscweb @dsennerud @dsenyard @DSignage_EU @dslava @dsm012 @dsmfood @DSRoe @dsteel @DSW_Vodafone @dtchssofkickbal @DTcomputers @dtdpilates @dtfpress @dthorpeJMS @DTJobe @dtp8 @dtpxpress @Dtracyr1322 @dtsportsfan @Du2012 @duane_rich @DuaneForrester @DuaneHallock @Duanns @DubaiLife @Dublia @DubliAlive @DubLiBestDeals @DubLiiOz @DublinTrail @dublinwebsummit @DuboisLucas @DuboissetB @ducatinewstoday @duckwhacker @ducttape @dudedotdad @DudleyTabakin @DuelingPianos @DueNorthComm @duffer47 @dugriss @duhism @duispydotcom @DUIVoid @duly_noted @dumbassity @DumbingAmerica @duncanday @DuncanWierman @Duncdiddly @duncraft @DunkinDonuts @DunningDesign @DuongTangua @duranaca @DurhamDad @DurhamMortgageS @Durrani @DurrellT @DustDBugger @Dustin_Bates @DustinAskins @DustinCase @dustinrd @dustinT1ong @DUSTtoDIAMOND @DustyReins @DustyTrice @dutchcowboys @DutchDivaOnline @dutchfeltart @DutchRecruiter @duxiaoshan @dvautier @dvd_movies @dvdamade @dvdburg @development @dwade828 @dwainawood @dwassociates @dwatson27 @DwayneDStevens @dwayneWa @dwbrint @Dwcwiak @dwellbeauty @DwellingStyle @dwhl40

154

Acknowledgments

@dwhite770 @Dwight_Thelisis @dwightbain @dwightcook @DwightFrindt @DWILLZMUSIC @DWMarketing @dwoodward @Dwordpresstheme @dwsuccess @dwukropek_ @DYCharters @dyhatchett @DylanCombsTV @Dylandoe @Dynamicarthouse @DynamicDialogue @DynamicFutures @DynamicwomenFth @DynamiXWD @DZHEDZHULA @dzifah @dzinetipsbyanne @DZittel @E_Wall @E_XCelerate @e2conf @e2mentoring @e3dlr @e4myJob @e71nokia @E85_recruiter @EAE_ @eagibbs @EagleChris @Eagleshams @eagleyejohn @eamcc @eammon @eandmphoto @eandtsmom @earldsmith @earlegurl @EarlPdxPearl @EarlRobichaux @EarlWallace44 @EarMitts @EarnByHelping @earnnow @earnxmoney @EarthPeaceHome @EarthtoAmber @earthXplorer @earthzen @EarwaxDigital @eashlforum @EastAtlVillage @eastbrunswick @EastCoastAuto @EastCoastBob1 @EASTeam @easternmedical @EastieGal @EastSidelnk @eaststyria @easy_family_law @Easy_Places @EasyBlogging @EasyChatNow @EasydisplayCN @easyecar @EasyFollowBack @EasyFunStuff @EasyHomeForex @Easyleads @easyloansuk @easymoneygal @easymoneymaker @EasyMusicPromo @EasyOnlineJob @easyplaces @easysalesonline @easytogrowbulbs @Easyunderwear @easywealth1 @Eat_Organic @Eat24Hours @eatastic @eatensomerice @eatinginweb @EatMeMagazine @EatNearAtlairpt @EatSleepRide @eazysmoke @EB5investorvisa @EbayBlog @Ebaycheapdeal @ebaymotorsdaily @ebaynetcash @ebayonlineshop @ebaytips4u @ebaytips4U_07 @ebbyhalliday @EbbyHomesApt @EbelingHefferna @EbenezerDaniels @Ebentwittes @eBiz_Consultant @ebizenterprise @eBizUniverse @eBjorn @ebkcoach @eBlasterPro @eblenerator @ebono @ebook_software @ebookbays @ebookgigant @ebooksand @eBooksFree @ebooksnsoftware @ebooksolutions @ebooktruth @eBootCamp @eBossWatch @ebrucigdem @eBusinessArts @ebwriters @Ebyrnebiz @eCashBusiness @EccoPrints @Ecendant @echo_stream @EchoBusiness @echogarrett @echoliving @echomms @ecito @eckohills @Eclectic_Times @Eclectopedic @ECLiveYounger @Eco_Costa_Rica @Eco_Earth @Eco_Energy_ @Eco_nomy @ecoach1 @ecoactions @ecochange @EcoCigarette @ECODOGNYC @EcoExploration @EcoFamilyTravel @EcoFriendlyMRTG @ecoglominerals @EcoGOP @EcoInteractive @EcoInvest @EcoJoe @Ecole20 @ecoml31 @ECOMAN2K10 @EcommerceJunkie @ecommercetalk @EcoMom @EcoNakano @economicsnz @EconomyHeroes @eConsumersearch @EcoOrganizer @ecoresume @EcoSafeCanada @ecoseek @EcoShredding @ECOSONNY @ecoteer @ecotpdotcom @ecowarriorusa @ecowind @ecraftpatterns @ECRetail @ecsuperhero @ed_han @ED2419 @edani_ela @edapina @edbisquera @edcabrera @EDCEurope @EdCleary1 @edcortina @EdDeCosta @Eddie_Christina @Eddie_Godshalk @eddie_saenz @Eddie_SaenzJR @Eddie_TopGun @eddieacsee @EddieForster @EddieLsc @eddiemart @EddieReeves @eddiesaenzjr @eddieturnerjr @EddieVsDallas @EddieVsFtWorth @Eddy_Williams @EddyGos @eddypiasentin @EdelOMahony @EdenFantasys @EdGandia @Edgar_Rodriguez @edgar_sanchez @EdgarCorley @edgarMart @EdgarMontanez @EdGedvila @EdgeSmart @edheiland @ediaz33 @EdieGalley @ediesel @EdiKurnik @edinburgh_ @edisonave @edith_blacksoul @Editing4U @Editoresweb_es @EditorTXBiz @editspot @EdLovesSumo @EdLucia @EdMartin4MO @EdMcarth @edmeeroche @edmpro @eDoorways @edorcutt @edotter @edscreenworks @EdTaylor08 @EduardasGricius @educationdebate @EducationNut @EducationNYC @Educator @EduFuraste @EduGuide @EDUITorg @edunham823 @EdutopiaBetty @EdwardEh @edwardesco @EdwardFelson @EdwardGoldsmith @EdwardMoore @edwardperry @edwardsWilson88 @EdWills2 @EEA_Org @eeadpi @eeakdss @eearning @EeeGeee @eeeyan @EelcoSmit @eeordogh @eepalmer @eeUS @eExecutives @eexist @eezeer @EFCANOW @efcusnews @EFDixon @EFFaXo @EffectiveMktg @effectsbay @efficientva @EffortlessChick @effortlesshr @EFinkelstein @eflorida @eFootPrintInc @efr0702 @EFratAghassy @EFTCoachJane @EFtours @EfusionElite @eGadgetGeek @egadirect @egagunawan @EgbertOostburg @Egehead @eglobalbuzz @eglobaleyes @egstrup @ehagglebids @EHayen @eHealthTips @ehesla @ehrenseim @eiaculazione @eikeollech @EiKids @EileenBonfiglio @eileengriffin @EILEYEUEM @EinarRice @einminutentexte @EINSTEIN14 @Eiro_Fit @Eiro_WeightLoss @EiroFitness @EIROresearch @eisenhofer @EitherOrFilms @EivindHeiberg @ejbwbiz @ejecant @EJM421 @EJMorris @ejnatuta @ejoiner @ekaffee @ekarff @Ekaterina @EkklesiaDetroit @eklaus @ekta_shah12 @Ektron @el_bergo @El_Campos @el_mono @elaadZ @elagrew @ElaineDodson @elaineshannon @elalisrael @elamar @ELAMca @Elan_Sassoon @elanbes @ElanorWaverlyHY @elatedca @elbasiliogmas @Elbst23 @elCHELSEAo @ELCircle @ElderCareStLMO @ElderOptionsTX @eldoen @ElDoradoSEO @eldridge2m @EldridgeJenkins @Elec_Generator @electar2010 @ElectraJoClair @electric949 @ElectricityGrid @Electromedicine @ElectroRC @eleesha @EleganteDallas @elegantfemme @eLegolas @ElekT @elektricblue01 @elementofspeed @elemprendedor @elenaemma @ElenaH13 @ElenaKazanova @ElenaKovist @ElenaLoC @elenamusician @ElenaShapiro88 @ElenaStudio @EleniLiapakis @elephantik @elevate_ca @ElevatorMusings @eleventhedition @ElGradoTequila @elguiri @elguszah @elhathaway @eli_lieberman @ElianeCarbajal @eliassengroup @EliCsAll @elienassour @eLightBulbs @EliminateMyDebt @elintao @eliotfrick @ElisabethKuhn @ElisabettaTweet @ELISE215 @elisimone @EliskaF @elissapr @Elistprovider @EliteAccounting @Elitedance @elitedesigner01 @EliteFinancial @elitegudz @elitemate @EliteMedSpa @elitepro @elitead @EliteSolutions_ @elitetrader @EliteTravels @eliz_edwards @ElizabethBastos @ElizabethDClark @elizabethglau @elizabethhannan @ElizabethPoppen @elizabethricca @elizabethsosnow @elizabethstiles @ElizBeskin @elizcohencnn @elizharrington @elizhurd @Elizioso @elizlaprade @ElizObihFrank @eljane @ElkeScheffler @Ellagrandi @ellahodeh @Ellany @ellawissa @Ellen_Brown @Ellen27 @EllenAFeldman @ellenfweber @ellennyc @EllenSwanson @ellenvanree @ellerbestyle @elleroi @ellies58 @ellindokid @Ellionaire @elliottdotorg @Elliottmarkc @elliottp123 @Ellipsse @ellismourant @ellissanjose @Ellunes @EllyElzBaby @Ellys411 @elmbathnbody @elmundodemando @ELnSMediaExpert @elocalise @elocio @eloko @Eloqua @elpoderde @elrosetweet @elroy2k @ELSimonds @elsom @elton_sbo @elucidmarketing @ElvinTiong @Elvis_Souza @elwin99 @elwoodbybryley @Elyse_D @ElyseTager @elyshemer @ElysiaBrooker @elzamguyen @em_designandi @Email_Strategy @emailace @EmailCopywriter @emailm @emailpunch @EmailTrayNews @emailyogi @emaliz1021 @emallpaysyou @Emanuelle_M @emarketgirl @eMarketingCubed @emarketingtwips @eMarketSchool @Emateinc @EmbarkCreative @EmbassyLoveFld @EmbeddedDIRT @EMCConsultingUK @emcpadden @emcsearch @EmcsMedia @EmergingFeeds @EmerMcCourt @emeyerson @emgcoach @EmGillette @emielli @EmilioKaram @Emily_Kirby @Emily_Morgan @Emily_Sings @EmilyANichols @EmilyCarterS @emilycsimmons @emilyfoshee @EmilyFun @EmilyHaHa @Emilyjhall @EmilyMcKay @EmilyMedvec @emilyrlong @emilysandford @EmilyThaler627 @Emiratisation @emleach @eMLMSecret @emma5374 @emmagoldberg @emmamediaCC @emmapureflavour @EmmaSpykid @EmmaWarren1 @EmmEffJr @EmmyWinnerMoses @EmoFreeAlan @emotionalaffair @eMotivMarketing @EmperorDarroux @Emperoroffun @emperoroflove @empireofthekop @Empleosti @EmployIT @EmployMeBCVic @EmpowerLTCI @empowermentdiva @empowermephoto @emprendedor_mx @empress_lee @EmpressN @EmpressOfDrac @empstudio @EmpyreMedia @EmpyreMedia_com @emreerbirer @Emsxiety @emtainplaylists @emuboots @eMusing @EnchantedMedia @EncounterGen @Endeavour2m @endreality @endrebarath @enduracom @EnergizedCopy @energizenj @energy_secrets @energy4virginia @EnergyAuditATX @energybec @energybodies @energyme @energyongdemand @Enerjize @EngageConsult @EngageLearnings @EngagementExpo @EngageStrat @engagingwork @engineering_uk @engordar @engr_emerson @EnjoyCelebrity @enjoyhuman @enker1i @enkhtorb @enklings @enleger @enlux @EnMotivate @EnnChayy @ennect @ennisander @enomaly_ecp @Enoxh @enricosnews @enriquenavarro @EnRo04 @ens7piper @ensamblador @EnsanityBiz @EnsleyValentine @enspired @ensuredsuccess @ENT_and_Allergy @EntAdvisors @enterprise20 @EnterSuccess @ENTITLEDIRECT @entrecon @entreesontrays @Entrepreneur @EntreprenAuthor @entrepreneur567 @entrepreneurDFW @EntrepreneurHI @entrepreneurlaw @entrepreneurpro @entrepreneursnw @EntryHR @EntryLevelJob @Entwinelnc @enunezcrm @envisionGood @ENVISIONProcess @EnvisionTweets @envymetips @EODDC @eoinos @EONpr @eotuteye @epallai @EPBEATS365 @epc28 @ePharmacies @Ephinity @EphinityCEO @epicevents @EpicHelicopters @epiman @EPKproducer @eplastino @eplreprblog @EPSclimate @epyk @equalman @equicktipsblog @EquineBandB @EquineChronNow @equintanilla @Equte

155

The Social Media Business Equation

@ERA_Florida @eranb @eranederland @ERATE @ERbelts @ercairo @ereadworld @erealestate_ @eRealEstateNet @ereleases
@Erfolg_Zitat @erfolgs_wissen @ErfolgsWeg @ErgoChairDepot @ergonomicstore @Ergotron @Eric_anthos @Eric_Burnettl
@eric_pusey @eric_su @eric_sullivan @Eric_Urbane @erica_holloway @Erica_Michelle @ericabiz @ericacampbell @ericapijs @ericarki
@EricaToelle @Ericatwitts @ericavandenberg @ericaverner @EricaYoh @EricBlumthal @EricColburn @EricDye @EricEgozi @ericEsilva
@ericeustaquio @ericfdouglas @ericfleming @ericfletcher @EricFontaine @ericgoldstein @EricGourmet @ericgrandeo @EricGreenspan
@ericherman @erichmiller @ErichMoor @EricHouwen @erichrapp @EricJAst @ErickAckles @erickdelafuente @erickosia @EricLofholm
@ericmooij @ericrasmussen @ericright @ericrosen75 @ericsbaldbytes @ericsingerl3 @ericstandlee @ericstips @ericstm @EricWorre
@eridgel @Erika_Henson @erikabarbosa @erikacheah @erikahansonbrow @ErikaLafata @ErikaLehmann @ErikaOBlanchard
@ErikaOlson2 @ErikaPryor @erikcecil @erikdorr @ErikFoss8 @erikgl @ErikLoebl @erikluhrs @erikwiklund @erinassist @ErinBlaskie
@ErinDonnelley @eringlass @ErinInBA @ErinKCasey @ErinKennedyCPRW @erinloz @erinmccune @erinrbreedlove @erinrea
@ErinSander @erinstockwell @ernady @ernestososa @ernestschweit @ErnieFowlke @eRocketFuel @erotao @ERrisk @ErwinFelicilda
@ErwinLitsenburg @erycked @erymobile @Esamu @esandow @esawdust @Escamotage @EscapePollution @escapethematrix
@eschlosser @eschreyer @Escondido_Wx @esdresults @ESgraphics @eshanfaaz @esjournalist @esm4 @EsmaaSelf @ESMtraducciones
@esotericsociety @esp_universal @Esp4Dads @Esp4LDS @esp4Moms @Espanoll @espeago @Espider2 @espnscrum @ESpotlight
@ESQCoach @ess_aar @EssenteeWeb @EstateSalesUS @EstBieberLee @estebanibarral @estebanramirezj @EsteDiaVA @estelleflaud
@esthergoos @EstiLensoN @estoesunajena @estrayhorn @Estreetloans @esukop @esunatrampa @eSurvive @eteamz @etenbroeck
@Ethan_Rayne @EthanTemianka @Ethekwinigirl @etherk @ethicalernie @ethicalhomebiz @ethicmarketing @etiennechabot
@etiquetteexpert @etlapl @eTOMGeek @EtoroFXTrading @etot_mir_moj @etouches @etradecash @etravelpros @eTravelUnltd
@ettaL @eTweetTanker @eugenelee @euniceseow @EurekaJanet @eurobaumarkt @eurodance4all @EuroDollarMan @EuroHandCraft
@europe24me @europortal @eutology @Eva_Abreu @Eva_Fit @Eva_Smith @Eval_Source @EvaMcWriting @evandenbranden
@evangelinewhite @EvansMediaGroup @evansmichaelj @evanswebdesign @evasandy @Eve_69_7 @EvelienSnel @evemayerorsburn
@evemorris @EvenCamerasLie @Event_Updates @EventCloudPro @EventElephant @EVENTjournal @eventmktr @eventmood
@eventphotogirl @eventplng @events_chicago @EventsJoe @EventsMarketer @EventsTicketsDE @EventusIT @Evergreeni
@EverlastingREOs @evernote @EvertonBlair @everybloke @EverybodySafe @everydaylotto @everyhomeremedy @EverythingBiz
@EverythingNYC @everywun @EvieBPat @eviejewelry @EvikaSystems @evildeath @EviMoreland @evo_terra @Evogard @evoklarry
@Evolution_Guy @evolutionfiles @evolutionshift @Evolv247 @EvolvHealthcon @evpac @evxmedia @EwaGusta @ewaldauto
@ewayhelp @EWDest @eweknitwits @ewhitmore @ewhitney25 @ewisdomcom @EwoutLK @examinerstone @eXapath
@ExcelRecruiting @Exclusivelygo90 @exdell @EXE_MoreCash @ExecAdvisory @ExecSpeak @executiveoasis @Exetimbo @eXExec
@exhalechicago @exhaledallas @ExhibitCraft @ExitAshburn @exmttravel @exogroup @ExoticLingerie @expandabuck
@expansionexpert @Expedia @ExpensiveGuy @experienceads @experiencemme @ExpertResumeMan @expfollower @Explainnation
@explicitmemory @ExploreDallas @ExploreHTown @ExplorePassport @ExploreReality @explosivechildr @ExpoDisplays
@exponentialpr @exposeliberals @exposingthelie3 @Express74 @ExpressHome @ExpresWorldwide @ExpresYourself @ExPrTMary
@Extra_Nieuws @extraincomenews @ExtremelyAvg @extremewealth4u @extwarranties @ey_me @eyarikkaya @Eyebetwitty
@EyeblastTV @eyedesignstudio @EyeFiCard @eyeflow @eyemagic @eyeondesigns @eyeshopwatford @eyesofobserver @eyespeak
@eyesplash @eyetoeyeteacher @EyeTraffic @eyoste @eYuliya @Ez_Money_Magnet @EZ_PC_Fix @Ez37 @ezadsncash @Ezbbiz
@EzBuyPerfumes @EZClickbankcash @ezcreditrepairl @EzihAlive @EzineProfits @EZLifestyleCtr @ezonlineincome @EZPayroll
@ezPoachedEggs @EZSportsPicks @ezwealthman @ezwealthmlm @ezwealthmoney @ezwealthtaxi @ezyhelper @F4binhosk8 @fabfas
@fabianalaura @FabianKern @FabianTan @FabKimberly @FabLifeHacker @FabNSexyDoll @FabulousAndFit @Facebook_Tricks
@facebook4u @FacebookBiz_4u @FacebookPetitio @FacebookPro @Facethesunmovie @FaceTwittLink @factpile @fadeyifemi
@FadiSemaan @FaelHenri @faethefirst @affiliate @fafnews @fahadzaheer @Faheemrazaa @fahriferdian @fahrradel @failingenglish
@FailWhaleBook @faineg @FairfieldDesign @FairmontDallas @Fairmoon @FairyBlogMother @fairygirlII1 @faisalmasoodCOM @faisk
@faistech @faithfulpoet @faithgoddessl7 @FaithLegendre @faithpeterson @fattachepills @fatwallet @FatWireSoftware
@FaulknerStrat @Faultlinellc @faultlineusa @Faux_Joe_Moore @fauxpanels @FavoriteBlonde @FavoriteTickets @FavorSA
@FavorsbyDorinda @FawnKey @faybe @faydra_deon @fbrglssmnfsto @FC_Barca_Fan @fc3arch @fc3architecture @fc3art @FCathala
@FCBsportscards @FCEtier @FCFH_DALLAS @fchurcerd @FCJohnsen @FConceptsLLC @fdaggerz @fdaly @FDASM @fdipays
@fdomon @FDRRESORTS @FearBustinSales @fearlesscomp @FearlessFactor @FeaturedBug @FeaturedUsers @featurethis1
@FedericoArreola @federina @fedner36 @FedorDeBock @feedbackagency @feedsme @feicipet @Feiring @FeliceDunas @FeliceTilin
@FeliciaStacker @FelipeZeni @felixferdi @fellipem @FeltstarsPoker @FemAJH @FemaleCyclist @FemaleEquality @FemaleFactor
@FemaleMenopause @FemininePower @FengShuiKarma @fenixenflames @FennelDesign @FenwayWest @Fergal_Crawley @fermikos
@Fernan984 @fernandoex @FernandoPerezB @fernandosahagun @FernGable @FernandaCareer @fernyit @FerreeMoney @Fesdantas
@FestivlAcadiens @fetconnect @feteish @fettymulya2005 @FezelryJewelry @fezztv @ffin09 @FFLmemphis @ffoschiani
@FFWDBrands @fgaeg @Fgermes @fgfinat @fgfu70 @FGrau @fha232lean @Fibrotoday @fiction4dessert @FidelityFirm @fidelsotelo
@fidimeru @fidjo @fidracula @Fierte @FightingGadfly @Fijiradio @figuretstudio @Fijitrader @filebarter @FillMyProperty @film_ebook
@FilmbugTweets @filmecasamento @filmedvdbluray @filmenoi @FilmGuyLA @filmm @FilmNoirCafe @fimihan @finance_tip
@financeandfun @financedival @financegurus @Financeman1980 @financialFraud @FinancialMogle @financialrescue @FinancialUAE
@FinancialWell @financing_guru @FinbarrMcCarthy @findajobresumes @FindAnyFloor @findcouponcodes @FindDomains
@FindingCharm @findingzealots @findmexicaneats @FindWorkSoon @FindYourCoach @FindYourSearch @findyourstoday
@FindZerona @FinePrintNYC @FineProperties @finethingsnyc @finesse140_info @finesse140IL @finkcards @finnishgreen
@finntastico @FinTel @FionaArt @FionaBondH @fionasdesigns @FireAlley @FireBellyLawn @firecatsue @FireDrumIntMktg @Firefares
@FireflyVodka @FireHost @FiREiCEBoston @FiremansCo @FirePathInc @firetown @FireWalkLeader @FirojBD @First_English
@First_Patriots @firstaidtopics @FirstAlertStock @firstAmTech @firstclassmlm @FirstForCopy @firstthomeguy @FirstJobsInst
@FirstPlaceOM @firststep2your @FirstTracksNH @FischerFinance @fishdogs @fishermarketing @fisherofmen @FishFry @fishingtalk
@fishingtweet @fishmark @fishtalesmkt @FishTopsites @FitaDewanty @FitBusyPeople @FitCoachCarole @fitforamom @fitipper
@fitlifecash @FitMenu @FitnDietCoach @Fitness_00 @Fitness_4Her @Fitness_PT @Fitness2050 @Fitness4Her @fitnessbest
@fitnessschick @fitnesscoffeeus @FitnessFitness @FitnessForHer @FitnessForHim @FitnessInfoMan @fitnesslion @FitnessRules

Acknowledgments

@FitnessSpot @FitnessTown @fitnesstrick @fitnesswtloss @FitnessXExpert @FitnesTrainer4U @FitPass @fitsnews @fittnessforever @fittolive @Fitz @fitzroychedda @Five2NineVA @fivebadges @fivedirections @FiveStarSite @fivewithflores @FixComputerNOW @fixcv @FixedOpsGenius @FixUrCreditNow @FixxerCompany @fjalonsom @FrJayHall @fjsman @FkltPurple @Fl_Broker @Flair4Marketing @Flamster @flannelbrighton @Flash_Site @Flash_website @Flatvision @FlaviaZule @flavioni @Fleming5b @FleshnChrome @FletchMcGull @fleurdeleigh @FleurtyGirl @FlexAwareFit @FlexibleMomJobs @flexjex @Flexlewis1 @flexpencil @FlexPlexico @FLFLori @FLGPartners @flicka47 @flid2 @fliderman @FlightSearch @flint_jj @flintbankowned @Flip_Video_Tips @flipandgrow @flipandtumbleoz @Flipbooks @FlipVideoBrand @Flitardo @flixelpix @FLNewHomes @flockpad @flocktweets @flodner @FloJohnson @floodlight2010 @FloorMall @floorplans @FlorenceShapiro @FloridaCRE @FloridaPutts @FloridaRVParks @florisuka @florizelmedia @Florvarga @Flow_StellaFame @Flowerpodsg @Flowers_Jewelry @flowersophy @Flowersplus @FlowTimeLtd @Flowtown @floydkim @floydkolb @Floz12 @FLPhotographer @FluentInGreen @FluffyWigglyBum @flugrausch4u @FLYCADE @flyfromdallas @flyfromDFW @FlyGirl0050 @flygirl737700 @flyingdog @FlyingPatriot @Flyingsaddle @flyingspeed @flyingspringbok @flynate @FlynPenoyer @FLYthingTon @FLYyouthDC @fmgifts @fmillionaire @FMOmusic @fmtb @fmunozj @fnazareth @FNicoleHebert @FNLawFirm @focus_nutrition @focusadgroup @FocusGears @FocusOnChrist @focusoncruising @focusonthelord @foleypod @FolketJublar @follow_alexis @Follow_Ring @Follow_U_Back_ @followandmoney @followback420 @followbackpleas @FollowBFollowU @followbsmith @FollowDeborah @Followe_r @followergold @followergrowth @followers24 @Followers9 @followeveryday_ @FollowFeeder @FollowFilm @followgary @followgenerator @FollowHound @followmania @FollowMe_RnBE @FollowMe4Cash @followmeback @followmonsters @FollowNYGiants @followshouts @followstevegord @FollowTHESTEPS @followupcards @followupsmart @followwithme @FollowYoo @FOLLOWyouFRIDAY @FolsomTweetUp @foluke @fondalo @fondsbank @FoneHomeEnt @fooch_media @food4thought @foodaction @foodandrecipes @foodchat @Foodelz @foodiemomma @foodienet @Foodimentary @foodprovider @FoodsForThought @foodmo @football_news1 @football_scout @footballcardz @Footballcareer @Footballguy843 @Footprints4you @footprintsat50 @For_Cats @For_Dogs @ForAHealthyU @forbiddengem @forcemarketing @forces2 @forchocolate @Ford @Ford_fanz @fordad @fordrm @forecloseshield @foreclosureknow @forestonia @foreverulove @forex_article @forex_ology @ForexBrokerGuy @forexed @ForexFreedomNow @ForexGossip @forexhourly @forexmoneygirl @forexpro2009 @forexstrategi @forexsuper @forextradercat @forextradi4 @forhirejobs @ForlIllinois @forkflydallas @formationsol @FormationSPR @Formstack @FormulaBlog @forneymichael @forrestkoba @forsakengen @forsaleontwit @forsgrens @Fort_Worth_Car @FortHardKnox @ForTheFisherman @FortheLifestyle @fortunedenim @FortuneMktgCo @FortunesInForex @fortyplusandfab @forumdoamor @forwinelovers @FosseesShoes @fotistikatv @FotoAltaCalidad @fotopost24 @foued @foundonmars @foundub4 @FourDoubleOne @Fourpointsstl @foursquaregames @fox5newsedge @Foxandra @Foxification @FoxNewsVideos @FoxstoneFinance @FoxworthCRE @foxyiom @FoxyMarketing @fpaynter @fr_profession @FRAccountants @Fragrancevelly @Fragum @fraisl @fraizerbaz @FramesDirect @Framsyn @france4homes @FranceDubai @FranceHouseHunt @Frances__Farmer @Frances427 @Francesca_LA @FrancescaOliva @francescsoler @FrancesFlynnTho @FrancesHui @francesk0 @FrancesKosak @FranchiseKing @franciscoaraujo @francoasousa @francisfetherby @francishopkins @francismarantal @francisotolo @franck_thery @frandrescher @franjeann1 @frank_barto @frank_souders @frank_tentler @FrankBauer @FrankBernardo @frankedwardz @FrankEves @frankfurness @FrankFusion @FrankieSportBar @frankieteo @FrankieVuitton @frankinferno @FrankKamadin @FrankKnipschild @Franklin_Adam @FranklinBell @FranklinDelk @FranklinLasalle @franklintello @franklogic @frankodell @FrankPMichael @franks_glasses @Franmccully @FranNetHQ @franokeefe @franpenwillcook @franteractive @FranYorio @franzidee @frasercole @FrasPartVictim @FrauFranke @Freak4Marketing @freakzappeal @frecklescrafts @fred24Live @fred7004 @FredBarretoc @FredCamposJr @fredcannon @FredCuellar @FREDDYFABULON @Frederick52 @frederickwebpro @FredErnsting @fredevincent @FredGarvin_ @FredGriffin @FREDHASSEN @fredherbert @fredinchina @FredKidd @fredkrautwurst @FredMcMurray @frednavarro @FredParrish @fredranger @fredricles @FredricSchwartz @freds4hb @Fredyblast @free_andpwrful @FREE_NKOREA @Free_R_E_Info @free_wordpress @Free_XboxPoints @free4ten @freebabycoupons @freebhouseplans @freebies4life @Freebies4Mom @FreeBirdsFlyHi @Freebiza @FREEBOOKS4U @FreeCalifornia @freecash23 @FreeCashGifts @freecashman @FreeCellularGuy @FreeCokePoints @Freecomnet @FreeCopyWriter @freecreed @Freedawn2010 @Freedom4unow @Freedom4USnow @FreedomAlliance @FreedomCoach @FreedomFounders @FreedomHeals @FreedomNowCom @FreedomOffshore @FreedomRotator @freedomsoft @freedomtogo @FreedomtoreIax @freeebies4You @FreeEnterprise4 @FreeEventsVegas @freeforallyaa @freefreebies17 @freeheart252000 @freeholdreos @FreeIMResources @FreeItunes600 @freejapav @freelancecampH @freelancemomcom @freelancerpro @freelancesquad @freelancesupmrk @Freelead @freelifepower @FreeListAds @freemarketgrip @freemoneypoker @freemoneytweets @FreeMusic999 @freemystics108 @FreenZone @FREENTERPRISE @Freeonze @freeonlineradio @freepokernz @FreePsychicHelp @freerollss @freesampletimes @freeseminars @freeSEOadviceUK @freeseoguides @freeshirish @freesnatcher @FreeStuff4Free @FreeStuffSurfer @FreestylePR @freethinkeruk @freetimes4u @FreeToSki @freetrafficgen @FreeUpdate @FreeVideoRoom @freeway2wealth @FreeXpedia @FreightDiscount @FremontSunMarkt @Frenchism @frenchman88 @freocorp @freoreviews @freshreleases @freshvibemedia @FresnoDad @freudianic @freymans @Freystaetter @frezcoming @frezkid @fridaamma @Friebs @FriedrichSchirm @friendandfollow @friendsaround50 @FriendsFoodFam @friendsforyou @friesenk @FrikiTV @frilokis @FriNigtCybPunk @FriscoJeff @frith64 @FrittsFord @FrkHjortland @FrogHater @FroilanOng @fromprices @fromthepoint @fromvlee @frontdesk500 @FrontRowCenter @FrontStrat @frostmiller @FrostyOs @Froyogirl @frubob @FrugalBookPromo @FrugalExercise @FruGalFriday @frugalife @FRUiTZOOM @frumpymudgeon @frumsatire @FrusMarketer @FSCnola @fsdigital @fshift @FSSimon @ftrigueroster @ftrouill @FTUK @FTWNightlife @FTWorthLapBand @fuckingAtweety @fuegoconnect @FuelLines @fulingu2 @Full_Movies @FullCustodyDad @fully_catholic @fun_cash @fun_jokes_video @funaudio @FunCityChief @fundanceruiter @funfraiserhelp @FundraisingGuy @FundRaisingNP @FuneralExpert @funfelt @FunFlying @funjoypower @Funkalarmanlage @funkytrend @funloverz @funmarketingtip @Funny_Bits @funny_forwards @Funny_News @FunnyBloke @FunPearls @FunTrack @funtravelforyou @funwithgames @Furious_Island @furnace_guy @FurniturePlaza @FUSEalbumNEWS @Fusework @fusiblenetwork @FUSIONb2b @FusionHqReview @Futrellautowerk @FutrFrmrFatGuy @FuturAD @Future_Growth @FutuRecruit @futurecruituk @Futureglu @FuturePowerGen @futures_mentor @futurespacemag @futurevisionari @futurization @fuuuckiiit @fvroengl@F @FWISHINE @FWBaseball @FWritingDesk @FWSheraton @Fx_Signal_ @fxeareview @FXHenri @fxp123 @FXStefan @FXtradingcourse @fysaen @fzipperer @Fzz869 @G_D_4Biz @G0utham @GICreative @gln0bIII @G2AExecSearch @G2GRealEstate @g33kdom @G4PL3 @g8marketing @gaaTyrone @gab_div @GabbyBernstein @gabdenny @gabeansel @GabeElliott @GabeLee @GabrielaKortsch @gabrielavcunha @GabrielBryanSEO @GabrielGrimes @GabrielVaraljay @GabsAX @gabyarocha @gabycastellanos @GabyDurgomz @GacFranchise @gacsolutions @Gadgetcom @gadgets @GadgetsWorld @GadianSociety @GaGuerreiro @Gahanco @GaiaFlowYoga @Gail1983 @GailBongalis @gaildoby @GailGrannum @GailGupton @GailKasperPark @GailsTwits @GAINLifeCoach @galagon @GALAGON @GalaxyMaker @galenaridge @galew2 @galileorecords @galinahelpme @GallagherMeow @Gallagherstar @GalleonB @galleriagifts @GalleyCreative @gals4free @Gamble2win @gambler100 @gamblingsports @gambrill @game4lifetweets @game4quotes @gamebittk @GameGlide @Gameloft_Italy @Gameonsportgirl @GamePlayerz @Gamer7882 @GameReporter @GamersIreland @GamersPlaceTv @GamesRUS @gamework @Gamienator @GamingComputer @gamingwrld @GanchoRusev @gandroid_co_il @GANEaudiences @gangaroots @gannotti @ganxiaoyan @GAPeach1210 @Gapfillers @garagejulio @garagewineco @garancommercial @gardelinoagency @GardenAdvice @GardenFocus_net @gardeningfun @GardenLOVIN @GardenMemos @gardenofliferaw @gardensnhomes

157

The Social Media Business Equation

@GardenWow @GarenThoms @garetare @GarethIngham @garethreynolds @GarettGoldsmith @gargirl @GARIFUNATRAVEL @garimadutt @Garmoe @garry_hill @GarryArasmith @garryleigh @Gary_at_PROSOCO @Gary_Foreman @Gary_McGeown @Gary_Webb @GaryCGriffith @GaryColemanGhst @garycozin @garydale @GaryGil @GaryKnows @garylhall @GaryLoper @garyPlanetEarth @garyschmitt @GaryTheMentor @GaryWGliddon @gaskinbiz @gasoffgloves @gasparem @gaspari_nz @gastricbands @Gate6Agency @gateoperator @Gatopard @gatot09 @GATropheywife @GauthierMgmt @gavinharkness @gavinherd @gavinmccaleb @GavinPoynton @gawthrok @gaybars @gaybenz @gaychat @GayFlirt @gayforums @gayfreechat @GayFriendsyyc @GaylandAnderson @GayleBuske @gaylejack @gaylemerka @Gayvan @GazaliAhmad @GBayliss @GBDaly @gbgexperiment @GBGnutrition @GBizzo @GBLiquidations @GBLShoes @GBLshoes_STYLE @gboban @gbocast @GbrilliantQ @gbrrealtytours @gburgio @gbussmann @GCAJapan @gcgreg @gchadwick @GCompass @GCSocialMedia @gDASHmo @GDCinspires @gddlive @GDI_Success @GdiMembers @GDInternational @GDMagas @Gdowling @GDuham @GE0STAR @GeaKoleva @GECamerasAus @GeDesPi @GedichteGarten @GeelmJoe @geek4data @geekbytez @geekeriesfr @GeekPolice @Geeks2tr @geekscouk @GeekSoapBox @GeekSpeakIMC @GeekToday @geekysarah @geemetal @geeni_in @GeeRen @gekkeikansakeus @gelbevideos @GeldGratis @gemanian @geminieast11 @gemlyte7 @GEmpireKing @gemsie @GemsSolutions @Gemstars @genaresr @Gene_Boyd @GeneAndJulie @GeneLura @General_Counsel @general1987 @genevaexplorer @Genevieve_Marie @GenghisGrill @GenieBenson @genieteam @genio_marketing @genius2genius @GeniusRocket @Gennarulz @Genny_Barrios @genomega @genomepop @Genosworld @gentleffort @genuinechris @geocentury @geochirping @Geoff_Snyder @geoffairfield @geoffc11 @geoffdutton @GeoffHardy1 @geofflaughton @geofflord @GeoffPeterson @geoffroigaron @GeoffRyan @geogeller @geokath @Georg_Grey @george_marion @George_Tr @George_Williams @GeorgeAtha @georgeb48 @GeorgeBarckley @GeorgeBobrovski @georgeclegg @GeorgeErbele @GeorgeFarrell @GeorgeKao @GeorgeKiss107 @georgelgonzalez @GeorgeMadiou @GeorgeMcJackson @georgemetzger @georgemoen @georgescifo @georgesdlvb @GeorgeWalters @Georgewhite_22 @georgia_dogs140 @GeorgieBedworth @Georgina_Lester @GeoScarborough @geosotal @geosteph @Geothinkers @gephaest @Geppettosounds @Gerald_B @geraldebner @GeraldMaio @geraldpilcher @geraldromine @geraldshaw @GERALDSWEALTH @GerardoFlores1 @gerardsese @gerenciavzla @gerenciaycambio @Gerhard_Kaiser @gerhard20 @GeriKleeman @GermannaCC @germanpv @Germzp @GerrieFerris @GerritBausG @gerritsenlars @gerrycramer @GerryGrewal @gerryhoch @GerryTweeter @GerryWieder @GertChappellUK @gertjan_g @GertjanBaarda @gertkoot @Geschenke_ideen @gesund_bleiben @Gesund_Expert @get_round @get2click @Get2KnowGVO @getads2txt @Getamazingabs @getambITion @getatraveldeal @getawayrentals @getawebsite @getbuttonedup @getcreativeinc @GetDeals @GetFit101 @GetFitGetFree @getfnews @GetFollowed @getfollows7012 @getfoundintown @GetFoundOnline @getfreepspgames @GetGlamorousNow @GetGoogleSniper @getin_it @GetItDoneGuy @GetItHowUPlay @Getleanwithme @GetLuckySurveys @getmarriedLA @GetMeOffTheDole @getmep @GetMoneyOnline @getmoneyzone @GetOndotCom @GetOnFast @GetPC_TV @GetResults @GetRippedATL @getseenhere @getsellingnow @getsocialconf @GetThePart @gettinricher34 @getwebusa @getxplan @getzookspro @geull @gewna @gezhacha @gezprila @GFBewerbung @GFEchecker @gFiras @gfwelch @ggasp @GGateFengShui @GGGBook @GGHomes @ggizelle @ggrigg @GhadaLancer @ghhts @GHMconnect @GHOST2UCE @ghostpressbed @ghostwhowrites @ghwen @GI_RESEARCH @giaiphapso @GianLightRock @gianna_b25 @giannatos @Giant65 @giasausse @giascott @gibsar @gibsonguitar @gibsonpatt @GiddyUpGDI @Gienna @gifaen @Gift_tours @GIFT4Tw8 @GiftCard01 @giftforyouandme @giftideasdirect @GiftIdeasHelper @Gigagroove @gigan_yamazaki @gigapig @gigaruga @giggsoid1 @GigiBelmonico @GigJuggler @gihomeloans @gilbanesf @Gilbanzo @GilbertTownSq @gilbsy123 @GildaAwesome @gilfordgreen @GILL_Media @gill_partner @gillardg @gillashl @gillat @gilldelia @GillesCollette @gillesgrisanti @Gilleslacones @gillianbritt @gillianchung91 @GilliansFoods @GillianWhale @gillispritchett @GilPizano @gilscorner @gilvan_cardoso @GilZanella @Gina_Drennon @gina_rice @Gina5280 @GinaAbudi @GinaAlzate @GinaAtPPG @GinaBell @ginabella @GinaManzzila @GinaParris @GinaRubel @ginarudan @Ginaschreck @ginasmith888 @GinaUncensored @ginaunfiltered @gingerbiscuit84 @GingerBurr @GingerGOP @Gingerlatte @GInGeRLicKS @GingerRJ @ginidietrich @ginstual856 @GioLovesYou @giovanni_carlo @gipsyblood @Girblee @girishmungra @girlbonus @GirlBug @GirlFridayHQ @GirlFriendly @girlfriendology @girlgetstrong2 @Girlie_tazmania @GirlinYourShirt @girlmovies @girlopinion @GirlOrangeCoat @GirlScoutsGSSGC @girlsgetaways @GirlswithGoals @girlwithnoname @girlzoo @Gis4Girl @GiselleBell @GiterdoneDave @GittleBos @giulianomlf @giuroocha @GiveMeCapital @GiveMeGrits @givemeservice @GizmoAlex @gjindrich @Gjrvial @giwatkinsir @GKBusiness @CKDallas @GKGnet @GKMen @gkrue @GKStill @GLainiotis @Glam_Mother @glamorousshots @GlamPhotos @glamurius @GlanceNetworks @GlanzAn @GLaraLopez @glarronde @glassbeadgamer @GlassBHalfFull @Glassesnest @GlassRiverJewel @glbonafont @GLBTblog @GleeClubOnline @glenbeer @GlenBradley @Glendadu @glene @GlenGilmore @GlenGilmoreEsq @glenizett @glenjacobs @glenlloyd @glenn__crocker @glennarcaro @Glennarm @glenndanker @GlennDesign @GlennEades @GlennHafler @glennhudson @GlennMadden @glennmward @GlennPegden @GlenoreMc @glenrice @glenscooking @GlenSmith @GlenTownsend @GlenWoodfin @glenysethompson @glenzgolfmmbr @GLHoffman @glintadv @glitirla @GlitterfulFelt @glitzeria @glmyers @Global_Trend @Global247Income @globalbeerco @globalcopywrite @GlobalCrossing @GlobalFin @GlobalFranGroup @GlobalFXAcademy @globalgeeknews @GlobalGiving @GlobalHealthMgm @GlobalMentoring @GlobalNetworker @GlobalNewHomes @GlobalPeaceFtry @globalresults @GlobalStreams @globaltalkradio @globalthoughtz @GlobalTownhall @GlobalTwitizen @GlobalVA @GlobalVision360 @GlobeCast @GlobeRunnerSEO @Globesters @GlobeTaskVA @GlobeViews @globfreelance @glorelys @gloriagemma @glorialynnglass @glorjane @GlobWPaint @GLucciano @glugster @glutenfreefox @glwallace @glynhenderson @glynott @GMaffeo @Gmarchess5 @GMblogs @gmcabee @GMCustomerSvc @gmelling @gmgmeva @gmhomebiz @GmiG @gmiller5227 @Gmoney52 @GMTexas @gmtgiftbaskets @GMTLife @gmurrel @gnldnews @gnomesatwork @go_around1 @Go_Chicago @Go_Green_Shower @go_usa @go2bostonsays @Go2DavidLeFevre @go4games @goaasim @GoABRA @GoAbroad @goaccelerate @Goal_Coach @Goals_Coach @goaskmarti @GoBeyondIT @GoBizClass @gobucki85 @goclichetysplit @godalley19 @goddessvixen7 @godessaf5 @GoEdChina @goldcevita @GoDominique @GoDpuncheDmeh @godsent247 @Godwish @gofastseo @gofigureskate @GoforNo @goforwardplan @goforyourdream @GoGabble @gogogreengadget @GoGoHubbit @gogreenbeth @GoGreenEnergy @GoGuerrillaGirl @gohewitt @GoHomeMARKet @GoInfluence @GoingGreenToday @GoInterview @GoIBG @GOLDANNE @goldasich @GoldCoinPro @golddateblog @golddinosaur @goldenebay @goldengirl717 @goldenic @GoldenTech @goldentweeter @goldenTwine @GoldenWayMedia @goldinpr @goldmedalmel @GoldNDesigns @Goldstanderd @GoldStrategie @goldtrail49 @golf247couk @GolfChannel @GolfChimps_Dave @golfclubs4sale @GolfersQuotes @golfin @Golfing_Nut @golfingupdates @GolfLessonVids @golfmrc @golfnovels @golfsecrets01 @golftitbits @golfworth @golocalphx @GoLondon2012 @gomaja @Gomblue @goneupandwent @GonzaloAlric @gonzelius @GoochyFBaby @goOCTA @good_question @Good_Quotes @Good_Sky_Today @goodcoin316 @goodmarketing1 @GoodMillwork @goodnewsrev @GoodOpportunity @GoodPilotNews @GoodSense @GoodThymes @goodtimesroller @goodtugo @goodwill4u @goodworknetwork @GoodWorthy @googirls @google__top_10 @Google_Money @Google_PPC_SEO @Google_Wave_Inv @GoogleGoop @googlegurul @GoogleJuice @GoogleLocal @googlenetcash @GooglePPCDom @GoogleRanking1 @googleslave @googlewavely @Goose_TV @GooseValley @GOPaholic @goparchitect @GOPlatforms @GOPNetwork @Gopons @GOPWhip @GoranAPP @GoranRistic @GordiansKnot @gordon_bowen @GordonBengston @GordonPlutsky @gordonwhite @GordWeisflock @GoreckiMike @GorgeousStyle @Gorileo @goriol1206 @gorjuzliz10 @Gormaya @goseedo @GoSociable @GospelGladiator @gossipgirl90 @goswamir @gotfax @GothamLimousine @gotmelik @GotoBus @gotolouisville @gotta_see_this @GottaBuyPC @GottaWantBieber @Goulding_Photo @GoUmbria @GoUp @gourmetliving @GourmetNews @goutamsathia @gov20radio @GovCloud @GovCon20 @GovernorPerry @GoVoskos @GovRecords @GOWITFLOW

Acknowledgments

@gpahia @gpetap @GPFdospuntzero @GPGoyne @gpidesign @Gpocialik @GPShockley @GPSstuff @gqwilson @gr1innovations @gr8futures @Gr8REALTORinAZ @grabbingtoast @grabresults @graceandcharm2 @GracieAndCo @GraciousPantry @Gradle @GraemeMenzies @GraffitiBMXCop @Graham_Winder @grahamallcott @grahamjones @GrahamY @granadatheater @GranCanaria123 @Grandblusystems @GrandmaMaryShow @grandmapeg @GrandPerfumes @Grant_D @GrantCriddle @GrantGriffiths @grantshapps @GrantWuellner @grapechick @GrapevineDental @graphdesign @GraphicAlliance @graphicly @GraphicMail_fr @Graphicster @Graphixlink @GrappleSmart @grapplica @graskinchylas @GraspEnglish @GrassRootRevolt @gratis_ebooks @gratiscosmetica @grattongirl @gravityjack @GravityPush @gravitysummit @gravyontherice @graydensn37 @GraylinSanders @graymccarty @graystonetrader @grazianig @grazingportal @grcohen @Greatbearwoman @GreatBigStuff @GreatCreater @GreatCredit @GreatDadNews @GreatDegree @GreatestHomeBiz @GreatestQuotes @GreatFlowers4u @greatgolfing @GreatHiking @greathunting @GreatLakesGreen @GreatMindsLtd @greatmovienews @greatorpoor @greatospatravel @greatpate @GreatScottGetaw @Greatspiritual @GreatTips4You @GreatTShirts @Greatvine32 @GreatWebDesigns @GreenWolfLodge @greecetraveling @Green_Realtors @greenandhealthy @GreenAwards @GreenBidet @GreenBnB @greenbusrpt @GreenCarReports @greencoax @greeneating @GreenEmbalming @GreenEnergy2050 @GreenerCleaning @greenerLA @GreenerMachine @greenerNYC @greenertrends @GreenEyedDottie @GreenFlshGarden @GreenFootJobs @greenhatseo @GreenhousEfect @GreenIslandMktg @GreenIsTweet @greenjenschultz @GreenJobIdeas @greenkelly @greenlightad @greenlightjobs @greenlinux @greenlivingblog @GreenLogistics_ @GreenMach5 @GreenMoneyTree @GreenMust @GREENOLAstyle @greenprofs @Greenraising @greenroomshow @greensbury @greensisters @greensquirel @GreenTrainPrjct @greeNuvo @greenvenues @greenwayprint @greenwerks @greenwtiffany @GreenyarnLLC @Greg_Christian_ @greg_savage @Greg007Collins @GregAtGist @GregBaleson @gregburch @gregcangialosi @gregcole81 @gregdpowell @greggackle @GreggDavison @greggfraley @GregHerder @greghsnow @gregjarboe @gregjon @gregjonesonline @GregKnottLeMond @GregKThompson @greglemke @GregLuchak @GregMartin_ @GregMattison @gregmyer @gregneo @GregO09 @gregoryanne @GregoryBryant @GregoryDCollins @gregorydwhite @GregoryMJackson @gregoryparson @gregostendorf @gregrobber @GregRyan1211 @GregSBarrett @GregSoffe @GregThomas44 @GregWHoward @gregzencoach @GreigWells @gretablackburn @GretaHP @gretawells @gretchenbenes @gretchenbostrom @GretchenGary @gretchenrubin @greyeyegoddess @greyhawk13 @GreyVisual @grhines @gribemont @griffin666 @GriffinPest @griffinsgarage @griffithworks @GrillAdvantage @Grimlaw @Grimmmachine @Grindhousemobil @grishi77 @grits4me @grivno @GrizzlyFeed @GrizzlyJacks @grjenkin @grkerr0311 @grnenergypwr @GroceryShopFREE @Gros_sq_tm @grosocial @Grossbauer @GroubalFounder @GroubyDallas @GroundsGuysCa @Groupon_Milano @Groupon_Roma @GrouponBristol @GrouponDallas @groupY @Grouve @GrowAndMake @growaplant @growingcoaches @growinggold @growline @GrowMuscleMass @GROWNFAMILY @groworganiks @GrowSocially @GrowthNation @GrowYourList @GRPasswater @GrueneHallTX @GRUPO_HL @GruveOn @grymill @gsaboe @GSEVENMD @gsmcellshack @GSocialMedia @gsohomes @gspadoni @gssahni @gsunil @gt1987 @gtbizdesign @GTBundy @GTDtweets @gtea @gthead @GTMazlen @GTPie @GTPRlocal @GuacimaraGlass @GuardAngel3 @guayjubb @guekeb @GuerillaNest @guernseyweb @Guerrillawar @guerthiel @GuessWhoJQ @guestjames979 @GuestPulse @gugubird @GuiasLocal @guidedmouse @GuideGecko @GuideNetworking @Guidogo2 @guilhemmaury @Guine_Beto @GuitarChordsGuy @guitardetails @GuitarNews @Guitars321 @gulfclearup @Gulmohar @GunDogBroker @GUNGACartoons @gungski @gunz4sale @gupromos @Gurdonark @gurdy_net @gurpnage @guru4online @GuruBrian @Gurutropolis @guruwife @gusauga @gusandjadee @GusLeo @GustaafVocking @Gustafer @gustavodudek123 @guy_finley @guy_smith_light @guy_vroemen @GuyanaX @GuyBoulanger @guyglover @GuyHagen @guymallinson @GuySie @guystarbuck @GuySTRIJBOSCH @guyversplace @GVExperts @GVOConferencing @GVOToday @GVOworld @gvyshnya @gwac @GwenDille @GwenLombardi @gwhitely @GWIZ_LM @gwmatthews @Gwopsolot @GWPStudio @gwsmedia @gypsybreezes @gypsymediagroup @gyutae @H_Clinton @h_farb @h_marketing_seo @H0STGAT0R @h20_Healthnut @h2cm @ha55ett @Haaboom @haareigenzaak @habboweenhotel @Habibies @hackettconsult @hackhealth @hackhype @Hadeed1 @hadiyahofford @haforhope @Haibarachan @Haidaman @haidarpesebe @HaideeSocialBiz @hainguyenV @hair101 @HairBoutique @HairbyDina @HairCareAdvice @hairdivas @HAIRUWEAR @hakansidali @Hakicoma @Hal_Good @HalcyonDays360 @Halcyonelle @halemary @HalcyoneLife @haleyrenee @HaleyVeturis @halfbrown @halfcenturyman @halfspoon_com @Hallie_Janssen @HallmarkBiz @halloshawn @Halloween_Etc @Halloweeniverse @HALOtc @HaloweenCostume @haltopgun @halupki9 @halze @Hameed_Hemmat @hamillauctions @Hamilton2 @HAMISHSCOTT @hamlesh @hammyhavoc @hamptonhasit @HamptonInn_PV @Hamptonlrving @han_m @Handango @handbooklive @handlinglife @handmark @handymanboise @handyprolink @HaniMasgidi @hanimourra @hanhblank @hankoo9 @HanksThinkTank @hanktweets @hankwasiak @hankwrites @HannesKuehn @HannibalBray @hannush @HansAHCdeWit @HansTerhune @hanul30 @HapiAct @happinesschick @happyblogger @happyches @HappyHealthyHip @HappyHedonist @HappyHourWeekly @HappyJoyJoyBlog @happymakernowco @HappyMamaGifts @happymomscoach @Happypleasures @HappyScience1 @HappySwim @haprees @Harald_Nick @HaraldKlein @hardertobreathe @hardierlime @HardlyBearFilms @hardwoodbrokers @hariandja @haribnair @harikherold @HarLanLawOffice @harlau1 @HarlemVoice @Harlette @harleyapparel @HarmonicLife @harmonizingTFA @harmonyhols @HarnessTheNet @HaroldAventSr @HaroldThiele @haroonharry @HarperVA @HarperWells @HarpInstitute @HarpInteractive @HarpoonBeer @Harriet_T @HarrietteJ @harrisnsonnet @HarrisburgSMC @HarrisImage @harrydabroker @HarryDelgado @HarryTucker @harsh6641 @Harsumi @HartHooton @harttwohart @Harufer @harukadanyaaan @harynovianto @HASHTAG_ORG @hashvideo @HaskinsInsure @hatmani @haukepetersen @HausmanLLC @HauteCoutureDiv @HauteFlash @HaveFaithInGod @havefunatwork @havefundoingit @havemoremoney @havenner @haveNOdoubt @HaveSomeSense @HawaiilslandRec @HawgNSons @HawkBiz @Hawyia @HaydenStone @hayinvestments @HayleyDoyle @HaynesvilleFilm @Hayrobley @HaythemSALHI @HaywoodStubble @HcfGnews @hclondon @HCMSanMarcos @HCPLive @HCRGroup @hculbertson @HCWReview @HDemiral @hdolan01 @headacherelief1 @headhunter212 @headhunterbrian @HeadOfTheBoard @HeAintGottaKno @HealingWithin @Health_Coach @Health_Life_Hap @health_promos @health_today @health29 @health2wealthy @HealthBeautyDr @HealthBeautyFit @healthcarenuts @HealthCareOz @HealthConvo @healthewoman @healthfest @HealthFit2Day @healthforuminfo @healthglobe @HealthGuy8 @HealthitMatters @Healthpreneur @HealthStation @HealthTopNews @healthweek @healthwikinews @HealthyAnimals @HealthyChefDani @HealthyFastrip @HealthyFeeds @HealthyGurlz @HealthyIncome @healthyinformer @HealthyInOside @HealthyIsIn @HealthyLifeMan @healthymcm @HealthyNetwork @HealthyNewsFeed @HealthyPassion @Healthysparx @healyconsult @hearingspeecstl @hearkorea @HearMickey @heartbeat1 @hearthofthehome @HeartLinkLaura @heartlites @heartmoolah1 @heatertom @Heather_Cooan @Heather_Bianchi @heatherbowlresci @heathercolby @HeatherEColeman @heatherlloyd @HeatherLynn11 @heathermadder @heathermcgowan @HeatherO @heatherpolivka @heatherrast @heathersmemo @HeathersMusic @heatherstclair @HeatherVale @heathesh @heavenlynaids @HeavenWeddings @HEAVY666 @hebertjet @HEBHealthIns @heckersdev @hector_alfonso @hector_eldoctor @Hector_M_Torres @hectorjarquin @heddyt @hedy7 @heeren @Heidi1163 @HeidiEKMassey @HeidiFeemster @heidimoon @heidipr @HeidiRichards @HeidiSiefkas @heidithorne @HeightsCat @HeikkiHallantie @heinhofman @HeinSidVR @HeinWine @hejfires @heisberger @HeishmanFM @HelaineBorquez @helbertm @helenanzalone @HelenaRitchie @helenashu @helencrozier @HeleneThituson @helengaitanakis @helenhames @HelenLindop @helenpengelly @helenschmelen @helewix @Heligonix @HelixWeb @hellaPR @HelloHelloGuru @HelloLT @hellomynameise @HelloNorthGA @hellosmalldog @hellosplendor @helloval @HELLRIEGEL @helmitch @help_triumph

The Social Media Business Equation

@Help4Engineers @HelpAnimals @helparussian @helpburner @helpbusinesses @helpfatloss @helpingmom @HelpingYouHelpY @helpitcrashed @HelpMeCableGuy @helpmeRhonda11 @helpmyresume @HelprinLaw @HelpYouHypnosis @HemalRadia @hemmons @hemmorx @hempbagmonk @HempNews @hendersonof5 @HenerySchaffer4 @Hennalondon @henrikMSL @Henry_Griner @HenryAssociates @henryjcjc @henrynatalie @HenryPQ @henryramirez @HERALDDay @heraldhsehotel @herbert68 @herbertharris @HerbFirestone @herbhealthgeek @herbiekk @herbmason @HerbNarcissist @herbndvelopment @HerbPastor @HerbSuperb @HerChevrolet @HerCouponCodes @herdlinger @here4cause @HereIsTheLink @herfuture @heritagebruges @HeritageInc @HermanCoessens @Hermanita_ @Hermanns @HermanoGeoff @HerMedia @Hernan_Ovalle @hernannadal @herrenhof @herrintech @hershbhardwaj @hervaljunior @HesDaD @hessiej @hexbomb @HeyComputerGuy @HEYGOTOcom @HeyJoshGrownUps @heykim @Hfuhs @hgetson @hglondal @hgroom @hgshrionhg @HHAcademy @HHDesign @HHKingOfContent @hhtong @hi5bkk @HiceRE @HickoryNCHomes @hickoryspeedway @HiddenGemStocks @hiddenground @HideMyIP @hidihidi @HiDollarDesign @hieuiee @highballsport @HigherNews @HighGrowthForum @HighImpactMom @highjac1 @highlanda @highlandasound @HighOctaneCEO @highpercentage @highpointseo @highpop @HighPosition @highpr @highriser @HighSchoolShow @Hihotweet @HilaryJ @HilaryKennedy @HilaryMcA @HileyMazdaDFW @hiligpinoy @HillCountryNY @Hillhaus @Hillustrated @hillwood @Hilmar_Nierop @hiloaloha @hilory @hilquiasdarcley @HiltonAnatole @hiltonat90 @HiltonSandestin @hiltonsd @HiltonSedona @HilzFuld @himikichan @himikosama @himvik @HinduPuja @Hip_M0M @HIPAA_explained @HipHopBuilders @HipMamaSales @HippoArmy @Hire_Profile @Hire120 @HireEzySoftware @HireFinders @hiremax @hiremyparents @hiretheworld @hirewheels @hiroaki81 @HisBoysCanSwim @HISCEC @hisdates @hispanianetmlm @Historianizer @Historyday @HistoryGamer @hitdigger @Hitman206 @Hits_Club @HIValicious @HiyaJoyTracy @hjfalk @hjthompson @hklong @HKotadia @HLBuzz @hlooman @hlsdk @HlthCoach_Julie @hluette21 @hmandp @hmantri @hmaust @hmbascom @hmikail @hnn_hotnewsnow @HOBDallas @hockeycrew @hogcatch @hoimoon @HOJEseja @holdingofwrist @holeinthewalltx @holibyte @Holiday_City @holidaygeek @HolidayLightz @HolidaySage @holidaysgermany @HolidayToursInd @HolisticHealth0 @holistichealth1 @HolisticHolly @Hollablackent @holleechadwick @hollib @hollischapman @hollismatise @hollisthomases @Holly083 @hollydolly11 @hollyhauge @HollyPavlika @hollypowell @HOLLYWIRE @Hollywood_Tweet @HollywoodBV1 @hollywoodpride @HollywoodSBlog @HollywoodTheo @holtecyou @HolyCowSauces @HolyGod @homaid @Homanbv @Home_Aid @Home_Loans_ @home_solar_sys @homealone3r @HomeAndHolidays @HomeBiz_Profits @homebizadvice @HomebizTrainer @homebiztriumph @HomeBusiness411 @Homebusinessadv @homebusinessb @HomeBuyerRebate @HomeBy3 @homecomokme @homefreeorg @homegetaways @HomeInternetBas @HomeInvestorAZ @HomeJoy @HomelandSecNews @HomeLocators @homemadebeer @homemadevino @HomeMotivation @HomeOrganized @Homeprodigy @HomeProductsInc @homeremedieszl @HomerSapiens @HomerTwits @HomeRunners @HomesAustralia @hometownesuites @HomewdSuitesCol @HomeWoodworking @HondaMcKinney @homedamer @homestkr @honestriches @honeydippable @HoneyFox4u @HoneyMacLipz @honeymom378 @hongkiat @Honoree @Hoodez @HOODSURVIVORTV @hoodtech @HOOPLAHcom @HoopsUpdates @HoosierMommas @HootersTexas @hootratings @HootSuite @HootyMcB00B @HooversTrainers @Hope_Shines @HopeChat @hopeforjoyals @Hopp2Shopping @HopperNYC @horacesorob @horaciolm @horizondirector @hornbet @horneto @horseheadtheatr @horsemoon @horsetalkgirl @Horsevitamin @hoscom @HOSFELDinsuranc @hospitalityhub @hostalert @hostalerts @HostDiscussion @HostedCRMApps @HostedMnSApps @hosteltrail @hostgatordeal @hosthunters @HostileTwitness @Hosting8 @hostingaccount @hostreviewer @hostscout @hosttips @hostx @hot_gossips @Hotel__ @hotel_lucia @hotelblog @Hoteles_Safi @Hotelinfosystem @hotelmarketers @HotelMktgROI @hotelmonteleone @HotelRescue @hotelsbooking @hotelsreviewed @Hotelstostay @HotelStream @HotelWebsitesIT @hotemplate @hotglitz @HotGloo @HotInternetMe @hotjvgiveaway @Hotmoviestube @hotpennystockss @HotPickUpLines @hotpursuit @HotSociety363 @HotSociety555 @hotspotjo @Hotspur_Argyle @hotspurs2009 @hotstockchat @hotswflorida @hottiecarmen @hottweeterspy @Hotvegaslegs @hotvogue @HotZombieAction @HourglassAngel @HouseholdMom @househunter7 @houseofbalsamic @HouseOfJerky @Housephire @houserherel @HousingReporter @HoustonCenter @HoustonGold @houstonmacbro @HoustonREexpert @Houzz_inc @Hovmodet @How2GetRich @How2MakeMoney_ @howard_aslain @howard_delain @howardl1792 @HowardKaplan @howardLDN @HowardScott @HowellMarketing @HowieBruce @howieward @howsolarpanels @howtobeabro @HowtobeInvestor @HowtoCCCC @Howtofreebie @howtoguidebook @howtohideip @HowToKnowledge @HowToSteve @HowToUseSN @HowToWP @howzit4u @HPAR @hpdArchitecture @HPNOTIQDFW @HPSelf @HR_Beth @HR_kerensa @hrbartender @HRCaz @hrelax @HRFishbowl @HRH_Ololade @HRMagUKProjects @HRMargo @HRMexplorer @HRPeopleNews @HRPUK @hrreporting @HRSolutionsUK @HRThoughts @hrycyszyn @HsiuPharmer2423 @hsmailax @HtdWebMarketing @HTELECOM @htmlslicing @htran841 @hubcitylowin @hubeiren @hubpages007 @HubSpot @HubZeCard @HuckFinnister @Hudsonkm72 @HugePreLaunchDE @hugh009 @HughesPR @hughett @HughJOrdeal @HughMcMarlin @hughnorstrom @hugodwarf @hugstacie @huitter_com @HulaCafe @HullyandMo @hulmevision @Human_Cap_Grp @humancapleague @HumaneSociety @HumanistExec @Humannova @Humberto2210 @humbertomx @humbertotassoni @HummingBirdCars @Humorvideos @humphreybo @hungfict @hungkyo @hunJONASfan @huntedoptics @huntelar1976 @Hunter_Wellies @huntergreene @HuntFishTX @hunting_heads @HuntingAGhost @huntingNfishing @HurdontheWeb @hursty_231 @hushiqi @hussy26 @Hustle247 @HustleMom @huffhafa @hvwinegoddess @HW33 @HWCaregiversDFW @hwilcox2010 @hwmaust @HWoodHomemaker @hwyl01 @hwyhotel @hyacinthgroup @hyattcareers @HyattDallas @HyattNDallas @hydechen @hydrosonic @HyeYunLee @Hyken @Hylkee @Hypeman_Q @HypeManSam @hypeonline @hypeoutlet @hyperadvertiser @HYPHYROCKSTAR @Hypno_Tweets @hypnomarketing @hypnosisaudios @HypnoticMuses @HypnoticYogi @HYSTA @Hyundai @Hyundai_ @I_Am_The_Mob @I_am_ungeeked @I_do_know @I_KnowHow @I_learn_spanish @I_learn_tagalog @i_meet_food @i_Squint @I_Tconsultant @I_Will_Follow @ia2clip @i5city @i5cityb2b @i80equipment09 @iabshane @iacovides @iadapt @iaJimenez @iam_milner @iamamogul @iamarkus @iambicinc @iamboricua @iambuster2 @iamChuckHarris @iAmCloud @iamclydetubac @iamconsulting @iamdayman @iAmDroBoy @iamGlenLove @iamJeffCohen @iAmJhoni @iamKeyLay @iamKimAnderson @iamLAUNCH @iAmLovable @iAmNotLucid @iamoffended @IAMPowerInc @IAMPowerWiz @iamPramit @iamSantilli @iamscottpatters @iamsin @IamSNIPEbro @iamsource @iamwilliams @iamwinnu @Ian1966 @IanAspin @ianbissell @IanBNorris @ianbrodie @IanCook @ianfarmer @iangbrown @IanGGoulding @IanHarm @IanHightonIFA @IanJGallagher @ianlopuch @ianmoomie @IanMRountree @iannarino @IanNorris54 @ianwpeters @IASocialMedia @iate_ @IBEAMGREEN @IBelieveInStyle @ibherdz @iBidcondo @IblduaFollowing @IBM6654 @IBMCliff @ibnportal @iboatscom @iboy @iBoyWonder_ @iBuildBlogs @iBusinessGuru @ibuylogos @icanewfriend @iCANhazJOB @icantinternet @icantstop @IceCreamGuy @iCedric @iceIcebaby_85 @iceJacket @iceman65 @IceMystDesigns @iceotope @iCHATBY @ichikawa51 @iChillDave @iChristina2010 @icingandAprons @iCitadelLive @iclimber_smo @icoachingcircle @icobuzz @IconPresentsAV @iContactPlus @IconTourism @iceryan @ICOTBO @icprofits4u @icruisebecause @ICTAlliance @ictip @ICUSA @idaMRivera @idarober @idea2delivery @ideabiz @ideaFS @ideagin @IdeaDrove @iDealExtreme @idealo @Idealonlinepro @IdealPitch @idealway @ideas4rent @ideascale @IdeasConLegs @IdeasCulture @Ideasforav @IdeasForSuccess @ideaswoman @ideesdesiteweb @iDen_21 @IdentityCred @IdentityG @IdentityG_Steve @idevron @idewan @idfoss @IDGAFclothing @IDGary @iDiary1 @IdiotsGuides @idLOOP @idnplace @idntlds @IDoBeauty4U @idobiradio @idobliss @idowebmarketing @IDProtectBlog @IDTAL @IdTheftBarrier @idtheftbusters @IDUniversity @iearnbigmoney @ieditandwrite4u @IEGNation @IEGroup @iEllie @iempoweru @IEnjoyMyFamily @ier_network_com @IESsuperstar @ievutte @ifbbprogym @ifeelgod @ifeoluwadebo @ifileonline @IfindDeals @firedmyboss604 @ifollowallback @ifollowbackboy @ifonlyblog @ifotbol @iFratellipc @ifucould

160

Acknowledgments

@Ifyouujustsmile @IG_Auto_News @IG_Media_News @igenero @iget2work @iggypintado @igivenoquarter @IgniteDallas @Igniteva @IGNN @iGodMind @Igoriy @Ihadnochoice831 @ihatecraigslsit @IHatePeople_ @ihatestickers @ihbsonline_com @iheartcircle1 @iHeartFaces @iheartwordpress @ihelpyouwithtax @iHiredMe @ihospitality @IHustleHarder @IIBSolutions @iimaonline @IITweetDesigns @iizLiz @iJacky001 @ijeff_ @iJPWeb @ijumpers @ijustinj @ijustlikecigars @ikallmeyer @ikeoo @ikerbill @IKLIPTIC @iknowa @ikooos @ikovannoy @ikra2news @ikstrimist @Il_Principe12 @IlacoinMusic @ilamaneez @IlaTexas @ilchenko @ilearntoearn @iliad09 @ilianora999 @ilinc @iLincBuzz @ilitygroup @iliveisl @ilktomi @ILLASTR8RADIO @illumiNETMedia @Illumnative_Vis @ilostmyjob @iLOVE_Scooter @ILove2Live @ilove2PACNSODMG @ILoveBlogs @Ilovefurrypets @ilovemarketing2 @ilovemobos @ilovesolar @iLoveYouJody @ILuvM3_24 @iluvMarthasVY @iluvmy3grlz1boy @iLUVvegies @ily_GAGA @im_rishi @IM_TOOLS_TODAY @IM_World @im75social2 @imaaik @imadnaffa @iMAeStore @iMagDB @imagefusionDFW @imagg @imaginalplain @imaginestudios @imago_mundi @imannounce @iMantouch1 @imarketiing @imarketman @iMasterTechniq @imatakutin @imBenJanke @ImBigChampion @imbriton @imbuzzcreators @IMCashSaver @imchrisjaeger @IMCNZ @imdevil @IMDiner @imdrmak @imdude @iMeetzu @ImFacebookQueen @IMFreeHelpGroup @IMG2009 @ImiKozma @IMJ_Ireland @ImJessieJones @ImJimGrant @Imjustdesia @imkcyrus @imlisadu @IMLuv @immasterminds @ImmigrationPost @immigreat @immo44 @Immobilien_neu @immoverkauf @ImmuneQueen @imnizzura @imonline2 @ImOnlyBlessed @MorningZoo @iMoseyPhone @Impact_Rob @impactROI @ImpactThinking @ImpactVisual @ImpassionedCat @impdwife @impe83 @impeppy @implementeasy @impo_condiang @improfits @ImproveYourRoom @impulsemagazine @iMRacHeLXo @imrankhanseo @IMRelations @IMresults @IMRobertdm @imryanmickley @IMSoNewb @IMspintheweb @IMTOMKENNEDY @imup4it2day @imurangel23 @IMviraldomain @In_Emmas_Memory @in_your_shoes @in4profit @in90sec @inatoS @inblurbs @InBoundMktgPR @IncentIntel @InceptSaves @Inchomphu @InCliss @Income_For_Life @income4school @IncomeCreation @IncorvaiaTeam @incslinger @independentball @India_Hindustan @indiabucket @indiagames @IndiaHobson @Indiana247 @IndiaNewzPortal @IndianFriends @indiDenim @Indie_Elf @indiescott @indietravel @indigo1745 @indobatik @INDOMEDICON @indonesiatogo @INDT @industrialarts @IndyApartment @IndyChamber @indymike @indytrac @indywoodFILMS @ineedhits @Ineedjob_09 @iNeedMyVisa @inekeve @iNetExecutives @inetin @inetmanual @iNETSEO @iNetVideo @iNetworkYouNow @inevergrewup @infidelsarecool @Infinitaire @InfiniteGrind @InfinityDollar @infinityimages @Infinitynews @infinitypg @InfinityWebHost @InFioreWorks @InFitnessMusic1 @inflataparty @influenceLA @InfluencySW @Info_4U @infoadvantage @InfobaseBR @Infocept @infocheapit @InfoComm @Infoexxpert @InfoGeek01 @infoholiker @infohoreco @infoimp @infojakarta @infologic @infolosophy @informationbook @Infosoftx @Infotech1s @infotechusa @InfozBlog @infusecreative @InfusedWeb @IngaBroerman @ingeekim1984 @IngridElfver @ingridfuller @inguiryate @IniquityClub @injurylawyertod @inkcarts @iNkDrEbeL @InkedBeth @inkfoundry @inklesstales @inlifeawareness @inlinegirl @inliving @InmanNews @inmyinsurance @InnaLA_RE @Innenrevision @innerman @InnerMastery @InnocenceNkt @Innocoach @Innofresh @innomgmt @innovadia @innovativcp @InnovativeMan @InnovativeSMM @InnovativIT @innuo @InocenteTequila @inoutgarden @InOutPlumbing @inovedia @Inphotek @INQMobile @InquisArchiver @Inquisix @insideoutbound @insider_page @insidethegames @InsideVox @InsightPSI @insightsempire @insomniacbruce @InsomniacGamerZ @inspectorsarit @inspiralic @InspirationDay @InspiredEnglish @inspiredesigner @inspiredguru @InspiredHousing @Inspiredscents @inspiredwriters @Inspiresalon @inspiresuccess @inspiring4all @InstinctiveLife @instyroch @InsuranceAnswer @insuranceforum1 @infidelsarecool @InsuranceInter @Insurancemavs1 @InsuranceMHQ @InsuranceSite @insurancexpertz @Insure_TravelUK @Intacct_Peter @IntegreonEDD @IntegrityKelly @Intendance @Intenders @intenselovers @IntenseWeb @Intentdotcom @interactEgypt @InteractiveDay @interactiveo @InterExec @InterLearnForum @interlinkedin @interlinkONE @interlopergolf @interloperinc @intermac @InterMarkdude @internet_dating @internetcapital @InternetCoachFR @internetcontent @internethelfer @internetinfomed @internetinq @internetmaster7 @InternetMktgTst @InternetNews1 @Internetoffer4u @internetools @InternetProTech @InternetTrainer @interNETworkWiz @InternQueen @internweb @InterOperator @interpellation @InterviewAngel @InterviewIQ @InterviewQs @InterVisaPC @interxion @intimatetimetab @IntLogic @IntlSocialMedia @InTouchCreditU @intrapromote @IntraTeam @intridea @intriguedinrva @IntrstngTweeple @INTRUSTkate @inventhelp @inventorsdigest @invest2008 @InvestigatorGuy @investigatorUK @investingnow @Investor2050 @InvestSteps @InvestWithIman @invincibelle @Invincible_Blog @invinciblePOP @InVinoCharitus @InVirgo @invisiblepeople @InvisiMarketing @InVision_brand @invitefree @InvokeResults @InWordsFanClub @iokijo @IOLmotoring @IOLsport @IOMScreens @ionices @ioninteractive @lonosphere @ionproductions @IONRyan @iorr03 @louis_vuitton @IowaHawkeyeMeg @IowaHeadlines @IPAC_IAPC @ipadappsoutlet @iPadDaily @iPadNewsBlog @iPadPlaza @iPaulGipson @ipayyou @iphone_develop @iPhone_NL @iPhoneApps_ @iPhoneAppsStore @iPhoneDentist @iPhoneJerkOff @iPhoneKidsApps @iphonemart @iphonesocmedia @iphonity @ipodiphonenews @ipodplaza @ipointwebdesign @iPolitics @ipolitis @ippokosmos2 @iPresent @iprichu @IProcureDirect @iprogram @iprosperity @ipunlock @IQ_test_UK @IQRsearch @ira9201 @iradeje @iraexpert @IRAtrainer @irayana @IreneHouston @IreneKoehler @IreneOfford @iRestaurant @IRGnews @irielinkz @IrinaWardas @IrisDesign @Irish_Pikey @IrishBreak @irishealthyguy @irishfitman @IrishSmiley @IrisRounds @Irissillygirl @Irlandia @IrmaBarrios @irobhere @ironbellgym @ironsworker @IronTender @IrrigationInfo @irsandroid @irte21 @IrunMonmouth @irvandisana @irwando @isa247 @IsaaFox @IsabellaSkye @IsabelleBano @isabellemathieu @isabelmontoya @isabelsabadi @isadag @IsadoraVail @IsagenixAngel @isaiahmustafa @ISaidIDoToday @iSalesMax @IsAllAboutYou @isasbread @ISBOnline @Iscariot79 @ISESDallas @ishaka @iShareGospel @ishirdigital @Ishmael2009 @ishootinraw @iShotMachine @isidorusweb @Isla_paradise @islandprincess2 @IslandVogue @IsmaelCraner @iSMTV @ISNoA @isoconsultancy @ISPMedia @ispytim @Israel_Anderson @Israel_Garcia @israelimom @IsraelProducts @IsraelRVarela @IssaMitchell @istanbuladvisor @IstanbulTWSTVL @iStation_staff @istepweb @iStratBuzz @Iswirls @iSwS_Music @IT4GenY @italianfinishes @ItalianMktDFW @italianpassion @italogeo @ITBankzitter @itchairpro @itchfer @itechnosoft @itekwrks @itemstoday @itevent @ITexpress @ithreedots @ITJil @ITMinefield @ItokkClick2Call @iTradZ @itraveliearn @itravelnet @Itrios @its_Oneshot @Its_Our_Choice @its_veck @ITSAGRINDCoffee @itsallgood3sm @itsallsuccess @itsallyour @ItsAndru @itsbubblecake @itscindy @itscouts @ItsCrucial @Itseasy2begreen @itsFunJoinToday @itshumphrey @itsjessicadi @itskellykim @itslikelyn @itsmeEdward @itsmeteddyb @itsMrsL @itsonlywords @itspatrickg @itspaulomahony @itspgalv @ItsPrimp @ItsRici @itsRobynwithay @ItsSeanRoach @itssuzziemay @ITSTHEMEDIA @itsupportdallas @itsybid @ITtainer @ittozago @ituneiphone @ITValueCreator @itvibes @iTweetArt @iTweetOp @iTwiddle @ityim @itzabitza @ITZsammentzer @itzuvi @iUEBO @Iulian_J @iulianj @iulienel @iukxl @iuliusg @iUmesh @Iva57 @Ivan_Jones @Ivan_Leon @ivan_life @ivan_nunez @iVanbsac @IvanCampuzano @IvanLeon @IvanMedvedev @IvanSantiagoSam @ivanwalsh @ivettemuller01 @IvieInc @ivmweb @IvoneteAlmeida @ivoryjohn @ivyapotomus @IvyBakery @IvyDoolittle @Iwanjka @IWcrew @iwearyourshirt @iWebHound @iWebU @iWoodpecker @iWorkwell @iwym @ixigo_fan @iyadb @izahoor @Izerah2010 @IzuKawa @IzzyEdible @J_BieberLoveYou @j_britta @J_Dahla @j_dubs @j_henriques @J_igor @J_La @j_lavalley @j_luis_moura @J_Spady @J_T_Ray @J_Wlodarczyk @j00st @j2bmarketing @JAAKYU @jaanaijas @JAAndrews @jacadams @jackagnew @JackAlanLevine @jackalert @jackalopekid @JackBeddall @jackbergstrom @jackbosch @jackcupp @JackDanielsFans @jackmaitlonjr @jackhar @JackieBiz @jackiebustios @jackiecuyvers @jackiejthompson @JackieLennartz @jackiequinn @JackiesBuzz @JackieTEwing @JackievStubbs @JackieWeber @JackieYunTweets @jackjbrandt @JackJiao @jackkuhry @jackmaj16 @jackofoley @JackpotGraphs @JackRobertson1 @JackSonCJI @jackpass @Jack5The5itten @JackWagner54 @jackweb316 @jackofoley @jackzaar @jacob_p @jacobathompson @jacobfreitas @JacobJSmith @jacobkotze @jacobLpeck @JacobMarinko @JacobMJordan @jacobshare @JacobyHemphill @JacquelineAnnPR @JacquelineGreen @JacquelynAldana @Jacqui_K @jacquichew @Jacquitac @JaDavid @JadeBarclay @jadehandy @JadeLT @JadeRNRecruiter @JadeYG @JaeEsButtah @JaeHoLee2010 @jaffejuice @jafonso @jafvisa

161

The Social Media Business Equation

@jaguardata @JAHeinlein @jaholin @jailguide @jaimealmond @jaimedrinksin @jaimekaufman @JaimeOikle @jaimesanchez @jaimeskelton @jaimesteele @JaimieField @jairmorsellis @jaiyan @jakegreene @jakelangwith @jakemwright @JakeRosen @jakoneval @JakusREALTOR @jalanbelakang @Jalexanderphd @jalexromero @jalishree @Jam_Sugar @jamaal_jayz @jamaicajuice @JamaicanTravel @james_clarkin @James_E_Jones @James_Halbard @james_jessup @James_M_Fann @james_patrick09 @James007157 @jamesacannon @jamesaharner @jamesalancaster @jamesashley @JamesatBabySpot @JamesB003 @JamesBasbas @jamesbaydiva @JamesBeingFrank @JamesBlond00 @JamesBlute @JamesBruni @jamesburchill @JamesBurgin @jamescapetown @JamesChenFX @jamescoe @JamesDelnort @JamesDeNitto @JamesFahey @JamesGowers @JamesGunnSEO @jameshannan @jamesherd @JamesJHooper @jameslamarr @jamesleesupport @JamesMed @JamesMelat @JamesNorman @JamesonMgmt @JamesonRocks @jamesoweng @JamesP_ @jamesparton @jamespmedd @jamesprussell @JamesResort @jamesroughton @JamesRyanJ @jamessarian @jamesscaggs @jamesvasanth @JamesWeddle @jameswoodmotors @JAMI_HIRSCH @Jami_Rae @jamieadams76 @JamieAHBGal @jamieceloti @JamieCrager @JamieGator @jamieharrington @jamiemurphy23 @jamiePRszwiec @Jamieroy @jamiew1136 @jamiewalden @jamisonb @jamjarwilkie @jamorel @JamshedWadia @jamylle1234 @jan_anderson @Jan_B @jan_borg_larsen @jan_moore @janagan @janainamesquita @JanakMehta @JanalynVoigt @JanamInfosystem @janappenzeller @janbelcher @JanBench @JANDA13 @jandrewstein @jane_firstclass @janebixler @JaneDoesCards @janefinnis @Janelle_Wooten @JaneMeetsTarzan @janepenson @janepulido @janesblogs @janesmithhere @janet_johnson @janetdcarlson @janetfoust @JanethD @janethebert @JaneTips @JanetSlack @janettefuller @JanetTilford @janewii @janger @jangutz @janhudson @janica @Janice_Clark @janiceacosta @JaniceEVolpe @JanieWible @JanisMarshall @JanJanzen @Jankovitch @Janlady6 @JanLAshby @janlgordon @janmalloch @janmariedore @jannahtesl @janya226 @JanRagnvald @JanSimpson @jansosa @jantallent @JanVermeiren @Japan_Clouds @japanesehorror @jaquesfotografo @Jared_Guynes @JaredOToole @jarettr @jarilove @jarom @jarosezell @JarrettHolmes @Jas0n_Myers @JAS13 @Jase_1234 @JASEgroup @jasku @jasluder1 @JASMINE_pietila @Jasmine_Sage @Jason__Ramsey @jasonalba @jasonanderson @jasonandjodie @jasonarcemont @jasonaverbook @jasonbenefield @JasonBKendall @jasonbradshaw @JasonBraud @jasonbreed @jasonbruno @jasonbucholz @jasonelewis @jasonellisons @JasonFalls @JasonFrovich @JasonGan @jasongsanders @JasonHadley420 @JasonHoeppner @jasoninchi @jasonkerchner @jasonkiddoz @JasonLappe @jasonmcwaters @JasonPerry @jasonpinto @JasonRecord @JasonReliv @JasonSilvestri @jasonsmithatl @JasonThibault @JasonTrenton @JasonTriboda @jasonyormark @JasperOng @jaspersilvis @jassim01 @jattyofficial @java_3dsmax @JavaJoeMyspace @JavaUsers @javi_mendoza @Javier_Ramos @javierge @JavierLZavala @jawaada2 @jawamo727 @jawconsulting @jawsgirly @jay_visaya @jay226 @JayatiTech @jaybaer @jaybenoit @JayBower @jaybranch @JayCataldo @jaycbee @jayceodpromoter @Jayctee @JaydeeSchiller @JayDunnOnline @JayElkes @Jayeshvasava @JayGaddis @JayGilmore @JayHazel301 @JayLink_ @JayMcLean15 @jaymorrisshow @JayneMcc @JayOfTheShow @jayosborn09 @JayPeete @jayperezz @jayphilips @JayRodChicago @jayscott10 @JaySwag_SODMG @jaytheanalyst @JayTheFordGuy @jaywilk @jayyjust @jazlai @jazzbird2100 @jazzgirl4 @JazziShow @JazzRF @JazzSalinger @JazzTalk @Jb2096 @jballardw @jbcat @JBCStyle @jbella07 @jberkowitz @JBF_CPA @JBGuru @jbhl6 @jbherrera @JBHigherEd @jbiancamrktg @JBieberFansTX @JBiebsBoy @jbiesenberger @JBinSanFrancisc @jbj_investor @jblackthorne @jblm @jbmagal @jbode @Jboreyko @JBPERFECT @JBPlayers @JBrentl911 @jbripley @JBryantWrites @jc_dawkins @jcastell3 @jcbl23 @jcchancellor @jccj4uu @JCDaydream @jchomesforAl @JCIAustralia @JCinQC @jclawgroup @jclutch @JCMcKnight3 @JCMedinaV @jcmeister @Jcoenen7 @jcooper225 @jcosola @JCSaintJohn @jctec @jctexas736 @jctownend @JCVdude @jcvr777 @jcx27 @JD_Glover @jdarrenlister @jdaykin @JDAZE @jdbasketball @JDBiHeartYouux3 @jdblue40 @jdcasa @JDeragon @JDEsajian @JDewiel @jdfireman @jdgem @JDGreer @JDieker @jdinsmore @jdlusan @JDMarvin @JDMstrategies @jdn318 @jdomangue @jdrmichigan @JDubyew @jduuham @jdw919 @jdworldly @jeanaharrington @jeanannvk @JeanBansemer @jeanbedel @jeanclaudeb @jeanddiaz @JeanElizabethl @jeanestreet @Jeanette_McVoy @JeanetteCates @JeanetteJoy @jeangandelin @jeaniehornung @JeanineHeller @jeanjeanhe @JeanKlett @JeanLevi @jeanlucr @JeanMarcBegin @JeannaGabellini @jeanne16254 @JeanneMale @jeannepinchard @JeanneQuereau @JeannieMcP @jeannieodza @JeannieWhyte @JeanPierreLevac @jeansopinion @JeanYves @jeb0921 @jebcoolkids @Jedera @jedi_roach @JediJunkie @JediMaster_OPS @JediMasterWhite @JediMindInc @JeeSouza @jeetrainers @jeetseo13 @jeferans @jeff_a_brown @jeff_cox @Jeff_Durante @Jeff_LaFave @jeff_larson @Jeff_Machado @Jeff_Oster @Jeff_Ringnall @jeff_russo @JeffAbram @jeffallenUT @JeffAshcroft @jeffbetts @jeffbilbrey @JeffBruneau @jeffbullas @JeffCole53 @jeffdance @JeffDrudge @jefferymartin @jefffaldalen @JeffFowle @JeffGoesGreen @JeffHargens @JeffHerring @JeffHurt @jeffjaner @jeffkolodny @JeffLee @JeffLevine1959 @jeffmarmins @jeffmetcalfe @JeffMindell @JeffMontana @JeffNetworks @jeffprice @jeffrasansky @jeffrey_clarke @jeffrey73 @JeffreyFeldman @JeffreyFriend @jeffreygoodwin @jeffreyhansler @JeffreyHartmann @JeffreyHayzlett @jeffreymlovell @JeffreyMMartin @jeffreypjacobs @JeffreyRomano @jeffreysgrubb @JeffreySummers @jeffreyvaneck @jeffroach @jeffSanGeorge @JeffSaville @jeffschwiekertl @JeffSheehan @jeffstrater @jeffthesensei @JeffUnderwoodTV @JeffWend @jeffwhitfield @jeffwiedner @Jeffy_LL @jeffzaret @jeiol @jejer @jellegxk @jellieTiemersma @JellyfishStudio @jembahaijoub @JEMcCrae @JEMDevelopment @JEMHealth @JEMTraining @Jen_Gilbert @Jenafa @jenajean @jencrochet @jendara @JendisJournal @Jenevalynne @jenhale @JenHolistics @Jenicagrondahl @Jenicaivy @JenieceGibbs @jenifferkwan @JeniseFryatt @JenKaneCo @JenKristinCox @JenLankow @JenLDoyle @jenlynch @jenmfes @Jenna_Goudreau @Jenna_Toms @JennaAtBlackSky @JennaGold @JennAllen @JennaLloyd @JennaLS @JennaRiedi @JennB1979 @jennfrancine @jenniedwards @jenniesjursen @Jennifer_Fish @jenniferbarbee @jenniferbesser @jenniferbourn @JenniferBoyes @JenniferBull @JenniferBunker @jennifercannon @jennifered @JenniferFlaig @jennifergosse @jenniferkateab @JenniferLKeller @JenniferNTaylor @JenniferPointer @JenniferPriest @JenniferReviews @Jennifertuener @jennihilton @jennimacdonald @JenNipps @JenniProctor @JenniRyan @JennIsLovex3 @jennsanz @jennsmith2010 @JennWilsonPR @Jenny_Berlin88 @jennybethm @jennybloghog @JennyCraig @JennyDeVaughn @jennyferns @JennyFlintoft @jennykutz @jennynavan @JennyQ @jennyweigle @Jennywrites @JenSeaSolutions @jenshilger @JenSinger @jensKsorensen @jentsl23144 @jenypoke1 @Jepara @jepok @jepsteinreeves @jer327 @jered_jones77 @jerell @Jeremy_Andrews @Jeremy_Jenkins @Jeremy_Sandy @jeremy3102 @jeremybelter @JeremyCampbell @JeremyDBrown @jeremydumont @jeremyfrandsen @jeremyjanes @jeremyjbloom @jeremyorbell @JeremyDeYoung @JeremyRobertsHR @jeremyrobo @jeremysaid @JeremySaville @JeremySpiller @JeremyUlmer @jerichohr @jerilynmcdonald @JeriVespoli @jeroennagtegaal @jeromemccall @JeronKerridge @Jerreko @jerry_ihejirika @Jerry_Remy @JerryBroughton @jerrycoen @JerryDRussell @Jerrylwanski @JerryKetel @jerryvokrie @JerryPelletier @JerryRenwick @JerryRrans Grill @jerryscannyon @JerryThomas @jerryyZambrano @jerseyhideout @jersoninsurens @JerzYY @jescbird @Jeselite @JesHag10 @jeshooge @Jesilea @jessbrigs @JessCWill @Jesse_Guthrie @jesse_willis30 @Jesselll @jessel957 @jessechou @jesseguitar @jessewight @jesshunterl @Jessica_toms @Jessica731 @JessicaDonlon @JessicaDotCa @JessicaFajans @jessicafatima22 @Jessicajnly712 @jessicalearning @jessicamalnik @JessicaMcAnally @jessicanight4 @JessicaNorthey @JessicaPierceAZ @JessicaRMurray @jessicarrrx @jessicasimko @JessicaSmooth @JessicaSturges @jessie_thegreat @JessieDates @jessiegetts @jessiemorris @JessiHeartsJDB @JessiJohnson @jessjohannes @JessKalbarczyk @jesslynteo @JesSofiaValle @jessperate @jest_staffel @jesre @Jestrun @JesusBibleStudy @JesusBranch @JesusChrist52 @JESUSENERGY @JesusSuarz @JesWal4 @JET739 @jetemple @jetittogether @jetpackit @JettAdvertising @jeurope8 @JewelleryGal @Jewelry_J @JewelryCrazy @JewelryForever @JewelryforYou @Jewelrymania @JewelryPlace @jewelrypop @JewelryShoppers @jeykigee @jezis @jezzerlloyd @jezzyhills @jfanfan @Jfannmann @jfarside612 @jfinley @jfkpix @jflyons @jfmori @jfouts @jfrederick96 @jfruiz @jfryer2000 @jfsays @jftoutant @jfwag @jg_howard @JGadFly @jgaler @JGchloooe @jgillardi @jglowacz @jgm77 @jgmambuscay0 @jgptec @jgraziani @JGTwitting @JHAguiran @jhamon @jharlaar @jhaubein @jhcustomhomes @jhelogfurn

162

Acknowledgments

@jhenn02155 @jhephit @jhertzberg @jhibbets @JHillRecruiter @jhmeek @jiansh @Jibinclt @jibinfo @jidawil @JIDF @jilevin @jillanjay @JillChristopher @jillelswick @JillFBrown @JillianPattee @JillKoenig @jillkrasny @jillmcfarland @JillRStevens @JillTheTrainer @Jillwriter @Jillybob @Jim_BoB52 @Jim_Collens @Jim_Grant @Jim_Hammons @Jim_Kernan @Jim_Marketing @Jim_Montgomery @Jim_Razz @jim_turner @jim_wilcox @jima54 @jimbarbagallo @JimBeamFans @jimbompensa @jimbonim @Jimboroks @jimbrowning @jimbulian @Jimcer @JimChelmowski @JimChianese @jimdose @JimEverett @JimFeistSports @jimfinwick @JimFortin @JimGillette @JimGrygar @JimHHoutz @jimhong @jimibratt @JimiJones @JimKitzmiller @jimknaggs @JimKorioth @jimlvy @JimMacMillan @jimmcnees @jimmeffert @jimmhughey @jimmycraig @jimmyelliott @jimmygilmore @JimmyKyriacou @JimmyLaSalvia @JimmyLel @JimmyPatronis @jimmyreeddotnet @jimmyrwilliams @JimmyTalbet @jimmytam @JimmyYoung @JimNardone @JimOdom @jimodonnellnh @jimogle @jimoreillyPR @JimPelley @JimQuillen @jimrcummings @JimRea @jimsignorelli @jimspcrepair @jimstrit @jimsutton5 @JimTNY @jimwarnold @jimwebster @jimwrench @JimZAda @jinasi @JinniDotCom @jiodarseo @JiriMajkus @jitkasame @jituppal @JivewiredMike @jjamitabh @JJantzen @jjarmoc @jjasminj @jjaylad @JJBramill @jjfortin @JJHomeBiz @jjividen @jjjinvesting @jjkk72 @JJMADSEN @jjprojects @jjspelman @jJK13 @jk590 @jk858 @JKANIDIA @JKapps @jkblack08 @jkellie @JKern_MOD @JKHarwood @jkheaton @JKirts @jkjohns @jkloren @jkoeber @JKoumpouras @jkraar @JKRSOTHY @jksilver @JKWgrowth @JKWinnovation @jL @jlandells @JLaWH555 @jlboissonneault @JLesThomas @jlevans @jlgaudy @JLipschultz @jlisak @jllarson3 @jlmarketing @jlock @jloonthego @jlriesco @JLTuttle @jlwgreg @JMacMarketing @jmajka @jmalmberg @jmanzitti @JMarie615 @jmathree @jmbloom @JMBthatsme @jmbventures @JMC_Ministries @jmckeever @jmctigue @jmd1220 @jmdmlm @jmediamaven @JMerinoH @JMFI957 @jmfmarketing @jmgmarketer @jmhgraphics @jmholewa @JMJb2bleads @jmk64 @jmmyers @jmoberg @JMorrison2103 @JmpseatTherpist @JMusica @jn0rth @jnanagroup @jneisse @JNExotics @JnfrFowler @jnickles @jnmedien @jnosal @jnunez142009 @JoabNg @joana_varon @joanikin @joannaakins @JoannaBTV @JoannaErnest @JoannaFuegobut @joannarobbins @joannawarner @joannayarrow @JoanneLuke @JoanneMcCall @JoanneMcInnes @joannguida @JoAnnLefebvre @joannlipton @JoannMoretti @joanschramm @joanthedogcoach @job_list @Job_Tipps @Jobaba @JobAngels @jobbala @JobBoardDoctor @JobCareerAdvice @JobConcierge @JobFairUSA @JobHits @JobHuntOrg @JobingFortWorth @JobingTampaBay @JOBINTHAI @JobMarketAccess @JobMarketSucks @JobNewsFlash @jobs_inIreland @jobs_texas @jobs_web_design @jobs4friends @jobsasia @JobsAtAdamNYNJ @JobSavants @jobsearch @JobSearch4Women @jobsearchassist @jobsearchforums @JobSearchUS @JobsEastMids @jobsETCC @JOBSetcom @jobsfrom_blue @JobsInClerical @jobsinfashionbe @jobsnonprofits @jobsofamerica @Jobsonica @jobspeaker @JobsPlano @JobsProgramming @JobsTwitting @JobsWithNatalie @jobuch27 @joby_semmler @jocelleuntalan @jocelynbenet @JochemKlijn @Jocian1 @jocotoo @jodey_smith @JodiBogle @jodiebeckphotog @jodierecommends @JodieWilson @JodiMaas @jodiontheweb @jododds @JodyLand @jodymal @JodyUnderhill @JoDyZvv0rLd @joe_charles @joe_kirkpatrick @Joe_Marketer @JoeAbbascia @JoeAbreu @joeantonucci @joeatsea @joebobhester @joecalloway @joecosa @JoeCostello @joedanwilson @joedark @joegabreu @joegallant @joegotomow @joegottii @JoeGruters @JoeGuitar33 @joeguty @joehul8 @joej2uk @joekiddone @joeknaack @joekozak3 @joelabarnes @joelannesley @JoelBlock @joelchristopher @joelcomiskey @JoelECarlson @joeleyba @JoelHadley @joelkight @JoellePEYRET @JoelPlanner @joelraitt @JoelWarady @JoeManzone @JoeMattes @joemsie @JoeMullally @joenormal @Joenunes @JoeNYLaw @JoePhilippon @JoeRassenfoss @JoeReneeVizi @joergsieber @joergV650 @joerobertson @joeshartzer @JoeSixpackSays @JoeSkiBum @joeslaughter @joethegolfer @joevick @JoeWelsh @joesfreedom @joomblocks @JonnyRumble @jonnysilcock @JonOnFireDotCom @jonoringer @JonTiegs @jonvick @JonWelsh @joolsfreedom @joomblocks @Joomlaink @joomlavideos @JoomlaWatch @joomli @joonggoworld @JoooryPub @Joost2everyone @Jord_Greenberg @Jordan_Crowder @Jordan_JAH @Jordan56vk @JordanDWinter @JordanKasteler @JordanMeehan @JordanMitll @jordicollell @jordinsilver @joreenlye @jorgeavilam @JorgeLuisCampos @JorgeMGalvan @Jorgesalesgenie @JorisEyck @JoRobisMusic @Jorrian @JOSE_FRESH @jose922 @josefmartiello @Josefpau @josefschinwald @JoseGAbreu @joseguerra24 @josekaufman @JoseLopezPonce @josemambo @josemariagil @josenewmdm @JoseOleCentral @joseph_hedary @JosephaEdman @JosephAlbarez @josephbrady @JosephBushnell @JosephDickerson @JosephDPuckett @josephjett @josephjhett @JosephLlorca @JosephMcDevitt @JosephStorch @JosephTX @josephweaver @josephwhyte @JoseRusso @JoseSotillo @joshauroma @joshbecerra @JoshBoxer @joshcarroll @JoshDruck @joshhersh @joshhinds @joshhodgson @joshkulba @joshlam @joshmaness @JoshNikle @joshpaiva @joshpeak @joshspencer28 @JoshSuth @Joshua_Lynch @Joshuabizley @joshuacamp @JoshuaColbert @joshuanulan @JoshuaOConnor @JoshuaWaldman @joshwulf @josieinthecity @josippetrusa @josschuurmans @Josstayner @jota_doria @jotaprojects @journalism_mob @JournalistaLtd @journeytv @journik @Jovenez @jovonni @Joy81BB @JoyASloan @JoyCash @Joyce_Embree @JoyceAuteri @joycebooth @joycecherrier @JoyceLayman @joycelindner @JoyceOwen @joyceramgatie @JoyceSchneiderl @joycesohn @joycesschool @JoyDoctor @JoyfulBiz @JoyfulNan @JoyGayler @joyhays @joyniemack @JoyofLivingBlog @JOYOFTODAY @joypackard @JoyTHood @JoyWebber @jozegr8 @jp__ @jpaduchak @jpage @jpj @PALMERPHOTO @JPAscarrunz @jpbpublications @jpearlstein @jpirrello @Jplsabelle @jpostman @JPratas @jprazen @jprpublicity @JPSchwartzINC @jptander

The Social Media Business Equation

@JPWilsonOnline @jratkins @JRBuckley68 @jreandino @jreejmt @JReyns @JRFrim @jrgcomm @JRGriggs @jri111 @jriveros @Jrjetset @jrlabs @jrmehle @jrnoir @jrobinsonRN @jrogersgray @jrollerson @jrsocial @JRStratford @jrtweetmooi @jryan9307 @Js3721 @JSACREATIVE @jschmeling @jschwirian @jselss @jsenft @jsentel @jshanley @jshuey @JSL301 @jslconsulting @JSLMarketing @JsMasquerade @jsmuseum @jsncafe @jsoriano21 @jSteVe_MD @JstnCase618 @jsvautier @jsxtech @jtdachtler @JTeeter1 @jtevanshaulage @Jtheprintguy @jtmartin @jtoddb @jtodonnell @jtperman @jtrophy @JTsPartyBoat @JTStwit @juancarloslujan @juanenjoyslife @juanfranlopez @Juanhellou @JuanitaBerguson @juanitakiesler @juanlechuga @JuanLo12 @juanmaroca @juanmolina @juanstubbs @JubileeCampaign @jubileokr @jude_d1 @JudeCaserta @judecper @judena_wrap @JudeNewcomb @judgep15 @JudgeRoyMoore @judgethejob @JudgmentCash @JudiCogen @judie01_ @judisheehan @judithcantor @Judy_LC @Judy_McKee @JudyAnnFoster @JudyCoaster @judycocherell @JudyConway @JudyHWright @judyiannaccone @JudyLubin @JudyMick @judyrey @JueL @juhotunkelo @JuleMai @JulesBaxter @Juli_K @julia_rl983 @juliaerickson @JuliaFeel @JuliaHallin @JuliaHsia @julialilly @JuliaMcDonnell @JulianCharles @JulianPerez123 @juliaS2k10 @juliasmola @julie_archibold @Julie_Fontaine @Julie_Gallagher @julie_horn @Julie_No @Julie_Tweeter @JulieAbel @julieannevanzyl @JulieBauke @JulieBooz @juliecrislip @JulieDiazAsper @JulieFarin @JulieGallaher @JulieGammack @JulieGaroni @JulieHennrikus @juliejulie @JulieLakehomer @JulieLucas @julieminevich @julien_simon @julienduprat @JulieO65 @JulieSabbatis @juliesalgado @juliesmith_os @juliesmithdavid @julietacuadrado @julietaustin @julievaiz @juliewyndham @Julio_SPFC @Julio_Valentim @juliolins @JulioMario_com @JulioSilvaJr @JuliusDavies @JuliusTrujillo @jullieanne @jumpman211 @JumpStartJim @JUNEOFF35TH @jungborn @JungleDisk @JuniorLeagueKC @JuniperProperty @JUNJI @junkmydatessay @Junkuu @junokughler @Jupattanakul @jups_ilhabela @jurgenweller @juscott @juske @just_d4ns @just_facts @just_jenny24 @Just_T @just08in @just1nus @Just1Word @JUSTaDADokay @justaddbourbon @justafive @JustAskGreta @JustAskJean @JustBetSports @JustCallMeGoose @justcareers @justcoachit @JustEden @justfara @justformom @JustGettNItDone @JustGoJoe @justgoodfriend @JusticeJonesie @JusticeMitchell @justiceworldlaw @JustifiedRight @JustifyLeo @justin_king @justin_popovic @Justin_Stolpe @justincresswell @justindclark @justindnewton @Justineter @Justinevdberg @JustinFlitter @justinglover @justingroy @justinhuntsman @JustinJONeill @justinlevy @justinmacgonal @JustinMcNeil @JustInOttawa @JustinPhillips @justinvincent @JustinWaldrop @justy3w3ls @JustLawJobs @justmenga @justMouse @justnotlast @JustPayShipping @JustSweetAngelz @JustTellKeith @JustTweets @Justyna71078 @Jusuru @jutawanakhirat @juttarund @JuusoPalander @juvylyn @JVA_Janine @JVariscoEvents @jvcorner @jventrella @jvijz @jvoyage @jvremec @jvRina @JV_MLM_SUCCESS @jw39 @jwcraw @JWean @jwestwood @JWilfong @jwilliambrogan @jwsokol @JWTatl @jwtheblueprint @jww61 @jydesign @jyi @JZAkundi @jzkundi @JZmcBridePR @jzzctv @K_BENZEMA11 @K12SpiritWear @k2whino @k3vinsmith @k4thybrown @k7ahd @k7dugan @K8EBartlett @k9centrum @K9Ring @kaaliss @KaanSEO @kabakoip @kablysb @KabuteMonster @kachuchu19 @KacieFaye @Kaelynfppuppf @kagaspring @Kai_89 @Kai_Zee @kairaca @kairos_Zedtlitz @KaiserCz @KaivanDave @Kaiwright @Kajslare4 @kakupan07 @KalaAmbrose @kalabrock @kalangenberg @KaleidoscopeSol @KaLeMiehet @kalicz @Kaliczynski @KalkanOguzhan @kallayanna @KalleKlein @kalooz @kalvinchong @KamaaianINC @Kambodscha @kamigray @Kamikazelnc @KamiTheWriter @kammarketer @kamper @kamyousaf @kandikreatives @KaninaJohnson @kanipk @kannataylor @kansansforlife @kansaschief @KansasLatina @KansasLimuLady @kanta_sharma @kantaramagna @Kanttila @KanzIei_Rudolph @kaoru_ari @kaosar_1986 @KapaKFoods @kapeezle @kapheroph @kapil_dev @KaplangDesign @kaposlogisztika @Kara_O @KaraChow @Karahm21 @karakenio @KaraNessian @karaoke2ph @KaraokeNinjas @karasmamedia @karatershel @KarateUpdates @karawelch @karecristobal @KareemHarper @KareFreeman @Karen_Jenkins @karen_newman @karen_voshol @karenabbate @KarenAndeso @karenarandolph @karenbuell @KarenDeadrick @karendemmery @KarenDenovich @karendivenanzo @karendunlapdc @KarenEman @KarenGowen @KarenJune @karenklam @karenkwilliam @KarenLangston @karenlatham @KarenLKay @karenmarrow @KarenMarzo @KarenMaunu @karenmaywrites @KarenMcKennaVel @karenmcnaughton @KarenMSiettmann @KarenONeil @KarenPowers @karenpwheeler @KarenRJenkins @KarenRosenzweig @karenrothmsnc @KarenVizer @KarenWadeOnline @Karenzwriter @KariAndCompany @karidbn @KariewithaK @karikorkiakoski @Karikuy @karimacatherine @karimbassiri @karinajim @karinbosveld @KarinDFW @karinericard @KarinGrasley @KarinHousley @karinnz @KarlaMorasca @karla_porter @KarlaScott @KarlDetkenProDJ @KarletonThomas @karlfoster1 @karlfulton @karlgoldfield @karlkellerltm @karlrohde @KarlSydow @KarlWolfe @KarmaloopSales @karmart @KarmicMarketing @karnadiutomo @KarriannGraf @KarrieRoss @karriesue @kartonoiqbal @karvetski @KarvFashion @karyrogney @KaseemSuleiman @kasevay94 @Kasey2oo8 @KaseyaITToolkit @kashishkaushik @KasiaRachfall @KasperDeWijs @kasthomas @Kastingkrowns @kasutimpian @kasyyoung @kat_rosales @katahdinme @katalink @KatapultEnt @katarzynagola @KatawuthEarth @Kate_Hudson @Kate_Saunders @Kate_Voth @katebilling @KatedeCamont @katedish @KateGardiner @Katelanta @katelizdee @KateNasser @Katerocksbabe @KateRuze @KateWilson00 @katfarmer @Katgear @katharnavas @KatheKline @KatheStanton @kathhaug @KathiJGriffin @kathiminsky @kathleengage @kathleenlowes @KathleenRubin @KathrynCloward @kathrynlindsey @kathybabb @kathybaka @KathyCaseyChef @KathyClark @KathyCondon @KathyDV @KathyHadley @Kathyhavingfun @KathyHerrmann @KathyJWest @KathyKamauu @KathyNelson @kathyoreilly @kathyperry @kathypop @kathystover @katiaspeck01 @Katie_Howard_TX @Katie2u @katie84 @KatieAMcD @katieatvintage @katiebcosmetics @katiebustin @KatieEghinis @KatieFelten @katiehaag @katieinspires @katiekauai @KatieLooneyCA @KatieMcCaskey @katiepessnecker @katiesheadesign @katiewinchell @katiey424 @katiraymond @katjaib @katjarvel @katmandelstein @katonahgreen @KATrGEEK @Katrina_adams @katrinabikini @katrinadegruchy @KatrinaGregory @katskloset @KatTansey @katybarrilleaux @katydaniells @KatyFeggins @KatyinIndy @KatyMendos @Katyx0x @katyzachbow @kauaikiel @kauf @kavekadm @kayadd @kaydas @KayDee022 @kayeflack @KAYENW @kayla2000 @Kaylynreve @KayMLeMon @kayodster @KayoTheGod @kayrina @kayross @KayTokner @KayValentiino @kayvanwey @kaz747 @kazionetworks @kazispence @kbadandy @kbarw @kbaxter @KBBusiness @kbward29 @KBHomeSUCKS @KBJB1010 @kbkmarketing @kboon @Kcancer @KCBolt @KCGPR @KCinMontreal @kcinnamon @KClothier @kclowlife @kcltd @kcmarshall @kcolaco @kcpickett @KCPub @KCSourceLink @KcWebGeeks @KD_Churchill @kdelucia @kdevito @KDL77 @kdragon87 @kdrewien @keachmore @kearnspalmbay @kee313 @keefy01 @KeeganLarson @keenumus @keenancobb @KeenanWellar @keeneonlife @KeepAustinWierd @keepexpanding @keepitglos @KeepPetSafe @keeskamsteeg @KeesMulder @Keethlnk @keg711 @kegeluniverse @Keidi_Keating @keiichiroseto @keikofalcon @Keith_Brown @Keith_Shay @keithar105 @KeithBansemer @keithbobrien @KeithBorgnet @KeithKamauu @keith_e_m @kelleyob @KellieHosaka @KellieMyHS @KellisArt @kellischwall @keithyoung @Kejii @KeleaDenmark @kellcurtis @kelle_m @kelleyob @KellieHosaka @KellieMyHS @KellisArt @kellischwall @keithyoung @Kejii @KeleaDenmark @kellcurtis @kelle_m @kelleyob @KellieHosaka @KellieMyHS @KellisArt @kellischwall @Kelly_Growley @Kelly_Langston @Kelly_Long @Kelly_Price @kelly_smith01 @Kelly_StrayCat @Kelly_Whyte @kelly2277 @Kelly4Congress @KellyAnneSmith @KellyBean76 @KellyDavis1 @KellyDiels @KellyGalvin @KellyITJobs @kellyjcameron @kellyjkit @Kellykoz @KellyLux @KellyMarsch @KellyOlexa @KellyONeil @KellyTirman @kellyverwie @kelseycarver @KelseyCottrell @kelseydickson @KelseyHelgeson @kelton2009 @kelvin8048 @kemblepdx @KemEng @kempmagi @KempEquine @ken_dr @KenaRoth @kenashley @kenblackwell @KenBurge @kenbcyber @KencoRealty @KenCoscia @kencurtin @Kenda @KendaMorrison @kendenace @KendraPearson @KendraRamirez @kendroy @KenE3C @KenEngland @KenFach @kenh78 @KenHanscom @kenjiro @kenkaiseo @kenkrauss @KenLegler @kenmaier @KenNadreau @KennedyIAm @kenneth_tweets @KennethFoster @KennethTanch @KenNewman @kennygregg @KennyKaramo @kennysburgers @kenon3 @KenPickard @KenrickC @KenRobbins @kensaku63 @KentAllen @KentBeatty @KenTheTrainer @KentHuffman @KentSchaefer @kentsm @Kentspeakman @KenWallin @KenWellsIED @Kenyaescortgirl @KenyonBlunt @Keppie_Careers @kieralita13 @Keri_Mellott @kericrawford @KeriJoRaz

164

Acknowledgments

@kerina @kermit_wallace @kerrigoldsmith @KerriJ @Kerry_P_Tavons @kerrybeck @KERRYDOWLING1 @KerrySOMalley @KerrySullivan22 @KershWellness @kerstinIFS @kerstinmueller @KerwinIfill @kesambi92 @KeseGreen @kesoh @kesomackan @ketaketi @KetelboeterPR @Ketsugo_John @kettlewell @KetyE @kev2719 @keva42 @Keverw @Kevin_Connell @kevin_homer @kevin_irwin @Kevin_Lee_QED @Kevin_Martyn @Kevin_S_Doherty @kevinalexBIZ @KevinAndrewL @KevinBevan @KevinBooren @kevincottrell @kevincox1 @KevinCruise @kevindasilva @kevindc @KevinEikenberry @kevinfunnell @keving31 @kevingodfrey @kevinhasley @kevinhokoana @kevinjryanLIVE @kevinknebl @kevinLangan @kevinleversee @KevinLindgren @KevinMcHaleFans @kevinmcnabbintl @kevinmesiab @KevinMihm @KevinMoss5 @kevinpackler @kevinpalmer @kevinpaulk @kevinplantan @KevinPuls @KevinRSmith @kevinrthompson @kevinschwab36 @kevinsenne @KevinTacher @kevintylersmith @KevinWGrossman @kevinzinniel @KevLLindgren @kevnbarnes @KevRightWinger @KevStatham @Key_Parliament @key4387 @KeyAudio @keyawashere @keybaksa @keycity @keycollege @keyleadermarket @keyplacements @keyrelevance @Keys2Twingdom @KeystoChina @KeyToRevelation @keyworddoctor @KeyWordEliteNow @keywordspeak @KeyworkerDirect @KezzaDY @kfcatoe @kfom @kgarland @kgmarketing @kgoyette @khaberni @KhadijahHolmess @KhakiBrands @khalilaleker @khaw_far @kheamena @kherihines @kherrajesh1 @khmer10 @khmerbird @KhrizWar @khuntley @khyi953fm @KiahDube @KianaGerman @Kibitzette @Kibler @kickapoofolkart @KickAssRE @KickCancerOvrBd @KickMix @kickofftopic @KidDictionary @kiddinaroundusa @KidneyRegistry @KidsActivewear @KidsAreHeroes @kidsdesk @kidsdirect @kidshealthtweet @kidsheartdoc @KidsMealDeals @kidsroomdecor @KidsTodayInfo @kidsvancouver @KidtoGrownUp @KIDZMEALCLUB @kielculture @kierantong @kieshaspeech @KiestwoodGarden @kihuns @kikolani @Kill21 @KillaaBADD @KillerBeeez @killerwebs_info @KillMyDayNow @kim @kim_cre8pc @kim_fields @Kim_Wesley @kim_willis @kim_yoon_hee @KimAClark @KimandCharles @kimanddutch @kimandphilstone @KimB @KimbaGreen @kimbergjohnson @kimberly_jones @Kimberly_Roden @kimberlybates @kimberlycandle @kimberlygold @kimberlyhughes @KimberlyVonD @Kimbirly @KimBrater @Kimbriel @kimbrotoo @kimchandler @kimclarkbiz @KimClink @kimdarcy @KimDeYoung @kimdoyal @kimduess @KimDushinski @kimferrell @KimGregory @kimgriz @Kimh2h @KimiKent @KiMiStRyCOS @kimkl01 @KimKiefer @Kimknopper @kimmar @KimmLoutey @Kimmoy @kimmybess @kimnow @kimonhorseback @kimonthefly @KimPadgett @KimPossibleX @kimprohaska @Kimpton @KimScavonni @KimSchuenman @Kimthomashomes @KimTTDavis @kimwang1 @kindcutesteve @KinderEric @Kindle_by_Tony @kindlejournal @KindOffensive @kindredspirit76 @kinerenterprise @KinesisInc @KineticalDummy @kingbillionaire @KingCourage2 @kingdom_Info @KingdomAssets @KingdomMagic @KingdomPlanner @Kinglet62 @kingomar21 @kingpin_seo @kingscashflow @KingSharukhKhan @Kingstadub @KingXXI @kingzly @kinoge @Kinomobile @KINSEYs @KioskSignup @Kiowah @KIPL @KipLyn @kiprep @kira_kenzie @kira_morehouse @KIRATIVE @Kirbyboy1der @kirchieJHB @kirifue @Kirkkim @kirklindner @KirkMichie @KirkPaterson @KirksNews @Kirsten_Dunst @KirstenVonk @KirstGoo @kirstiscott @KirstTreth @kirtsy @kiruba @kisatterwhite @kishau @KISSFMPhoenix @kisslaci @KISSmetrics @kissmygumbo @kit2kat @KitchenAssist @KitchenKop @kitchensluxury @KitchenUtenzils @KITEPLAYER @KiTtyCrysTL1991 @Kiva @KiwiGordie @kiwindahl @kixgroup @KiyosakiQuotes @Kiyoshileo @kizzlethizzle @kjardim @KjartanAlvestad @Kjellyn @KJenNu @Kjmastaw @KJohnWise @kjoneskc @kk23wong @kkonotchick @kkoolook @KKRSeattle @kkthornton @kktm @KKtres @KKyno @KlaireBlack @klams1 @klasikfatale @KLATAFIRST @klaus2go @klausbandisch @kleimkuehler @klempit @klhcrew @klich @KlikotUniversal @KLImageGroup @klingaman @KliLatAP @klkestner @klopmp @KloudSocial @Klovecruise @KlusOpdracht @KMacMortgage @kmallan @kmartdesign @kmburnham @kmburu @kmcusick @kmeghana @KMelen @KMJPro @Kmo_Chirp @kmorisp @kmorrison @KMPriest @kmsdesigns @kmwoodke @kmyrvold @knan @KNBR @kneereplacement @knelita @KnHall @Knieriemen @KnieriemEric @KNIFECOACH @Knight2701 @KnightCop @KnightGlobal @KnightMovesBlog @KnightsDisney @knitterpreneur @knitzees @knkenterprises @knockbuckle @knockoutmusicLA @knotjustjigs @knovial @knowem @KnowFree @KnowItAll1 @Knowledge_City @knowledgebroker @KnowsEbay @knoxkeith @KnoxPub @knreichert @KNSSsecret @knuotio @knussbaum @Kobe24Official @kobepray50 @KobyLuedtke @kochschwinger @kocosports @KODAKIKI @KodakSave110 @kodebreaker @KoenvdZanden @koganpage @kohlben @KoinoniaMI @Kokaneofficial @kokoforkayak @kokswereld @KolbySlocum @kolcoo @KoldCastTV @Kolibrix @Kolton_Kuhns @KongHendra @KontraCreative @koocci @KookyBirdcage @koolbenny @KoolRigAPU @Kooolessst @kootenayborn @kop48 @Korban__Odessa @KoreaDiscovery @KoreanHorror @KoreSocialMedia @kosamabody @kosiv @kothi_com @kotobato @kotusenko @Kowshik_Islam @kozakdream @KPAction @KPerrotteRHI @KPKC @kpkfusion @KPNewman @kprfund @kpsourcecareers @KPVancity @KQQL1 @kraigrbrown @kramermark @KranKgear @KRAPPS @kreativekaur @kreativoli @KrechExteriors @Kredit_Beratung @Kredittkort123 @KreeBeau @kreg_atterberry @kregobiz @krgwrites @krhodey @Kricketeer @kriley19 @kris1911 @krischislett @krisdiamond @KrishnaDe @Krisiku @krisitha @kriskarafotas @kriskiler @kriskishan @krismap @KrisSchCom1 @Krissy_71 @Krista_Abbott @KristaFlock @KristaJarvinen @KrisTalk @kristalmorris @KristalSergent @KristaNeher @kristencruz @KristenDaukas @KristenJacoway @KristenMcNally @KristenNicole2 @KristenObaid @KristenRidley @Kristi_Beckman @KristianDaniels @kristibernard @KristiinaMeme @KristiLeBlanc @KristiLynMiller @Kristina_Mia @Kristina_R_Youn @KristinaCraig @KristinaCrowley @KristinaJSchulz @KristinaLibby @KristinaMills @kristinahoades @KristinaVittas @KristinJArnold @KristinKopp @kristinsteed @kristiwl @KristK @kristy_campbell @kristybluebaby @kristyejy @KristyRNinAZ @kriswarner @KrisztinaCseri @krksupplements @KRLD @KRodd @krumlr @Kruti @krystle_green @ksablan @ksavelyeva @kschoeck @KseniaCoffman @kshaidle @kshaoran @ksmall1 @KSmarq @ksparkles @KStarry @KSTaxlady @ksuzan @ksyl0 @ktacsocal @KTCaroline @ktindfw @ktkiwi @Ktownclassified @KtownLandscaper @KTPatt @ktwit2009 @Kuanyin @KuanYu888 @kubotatools @Kucumber @KueC @kufarms @kuilee @kuiperactive @kuchawheels @KuliBiz @kuligina @kullztips @kulraj12 @KulturWest @kum72 @kumaresan_88 @KumpulJakarta @kunaalus @kunalsharma @Kundenpfad @KungFuRobert @kuni920 @kunthi3 @Kurtissl @kurtroswell @KurtScholle @kurtweissphoto @kurtwvs @kushal84 @kustom_sa @Kutano @kvangs @KWALSH30 @KWamser @Kwand1 @kwbridge @kwbsteo @kwells2416 @KWmarketing @kwoodpartnerjo @kwoodpartners @kwri @KXAN_News @Ky4TaxReform @kydos @kyio @KylaMaeCutie @Kylaquino @KyleBlakeAllred @KyleCarpenter @KyleeLane @kylegary @kyleglanville @KyleH186 @kylemacrae @Kylenelson24 @kylerodeck @kylespencer @KylieDoak @kyliefd V88 @kymhuynh @kymme @kyrstenrue @KZaxundi @L_AWeather @L_Cappelli @L_Hawkins @L_Teezy @L2_ThinkTank @L2008D @L2LGroup @L3LEADERSHIP @L8est @LA_DATING @LA_PartyHelpers @La_Puntilla @la_vacation @la15SecondPitch @Laanetweets @LaBahnsLscape @Labedzki_Art @LaBelleCosmetic @labmag @labrute @LacedWithJava @lachaudee @lacitigal @lactorbeau @LaCountryGirl @lacouvee @lacretia @ladansusan @LadaRasochova @ladevjob @LadieoloGistPKF @LadiesWhoBrand @ladolcetati @lady4zen @ladyal09 @ladybead @LadyBizBiz @Ladybug4Freedom @LadyEz @ladygagaconcert @LadyGagaPlanet @LadyJhia @ladylibertas93 @LadyLumineux @LadyMissMBA @LadyNNN @LadyOTrout @LadyPuppe @LadySalesDog @ladysilvina @LadyT_32 @LadyDevorah @LAEAMERICA @LAfactor @Lafayette_Alert @LafayetteTravel @laffytaffy57 @LagoonBand @Lagwolf @LahainaDotCom @LAimport @laineybirdy @Lainie_Bradshaw @Lainin @LaiStirland @lajilla609 @LaJolla_design @LaJollaHomesPro @lakerfan24kobe @LakeSideMarket @lakevilletruth @laksh @laksshaybehl @LaLaBoyd @lalawag @Lalolow @lalunamaul @lamademe1 @lamalterie @lamanlibrary @LAMARCOMMLLC @LamarSmithTX21 @LameDuck2010 @lamekiffin @lamiebretonne @LamNuwin @LAMP_AFTRS @lana_berry @LanaHodges @Lance_Blackburn @LanceBAnderson @LanceScoular @Land4Less @LandaBooks @landinedward @LandmarkHQ @landon_long @landrushnow @LandscapeLights @LandUseXperts @lanebryant @lanee2 @LangdonStPress @Langevin @LangoDallas @LaniVoivod @LankaBusiness @Lanray @LansbridgeU @LANSystems @LANTS @lanzigiuseppe @laonline @laoyang945 @LaPeregrina @lapocketrocket @Lapp @LAPRESS @Laptoptaschen @LaRainbow @laralaine @laramarsf @LaraOhara @lardito @LArecruiter @LargestLibrary @LariKB @LarisaBelliveau @LarisaWl @larissaelou @larissainnyc @Larry_Weight @larry2x2 @Larryathome @larryathomebiz @LarryBenet @larrybrauner @larrycolangelo @LarryCorbi @larrycrossley

165

@larryczerwonka @LarryDevine @larrydrice @larryjackson09 @larrykim @larryloik @LarryLugnut @larrymwalkerjr @Larryphoto @larryprevost @LarryRuvo @LarryTolpin @LarryWentz @larsdigerud @LaserFocusCoach @lasermaze @laserspine @LasoSteReO @Last_Valhalla @lastinglipstic @lastminutestay @LasVegasBuffets @LasVegasHilton @lasvegaslimopro @LasVegasPro @LasVegasTimesRE @latechcouncil @LAtechnology @latenightmovies @latestACDC @latestBeck @latestmuse @latestOasisnews @latestPearlJam @latimestot @LatinaBeautyBlo @latinaprpro @LatinoCleveland @LatinoLifestyle @LatinosAtWork @LatishaSimmons @latitudetools @LaTorretta @LaToyaReports @LAtraders @latronepic @latte4u @Laugh_lots @LaughingCrow @LaughNYC @launchagency @launchclinic @LaunchManagers @LaunchOrbit @LaunchSales @laura_bey @laura_ml986 @laurabwilliams @LauraCatherineO @laurachillman @lauraduhaime @LauraGainor @LauraGoodrich @LauraGuthrie @laurajordan @LauraKennedy @LauraLabovich @lauralaydss @LauraleeGuthrie @LauraLFournier @lauralhale @LauraMcPeck @LauraMears @lauramoore @LauraN546 @Lauraperillo @LauraPorterHaub @lauraposey @LauraSherman @laurashort @laurasimas @lauraswatson04 @laurathornton @LaurelinMadison @laurelpine @laurelreynolds @LaureLuxe @lauren_howe @laurenamcmullen @laurenbenson @LaurenCandito @laurencoppage @LaurenCotner310 @LaurenCoulman @LaurenGav @LaurenHickson @laurenhuston @laurenkgray @LaurenSleeper @laurenswaling @LaurentBerry @LaurentBour @laurenthain @laurentvg @laurenwuscher @LaurianaZ @Laurie_Monahan @Laurie_Tossy @LaurieArnston @LaurieBerenson @LaurieDaly @lauriefoley @LaurieHenry @LaurieHosken @LaurieLTaylor @LaurieMacomber @LaurieMeisel @LaurieNowland @LaurieSheppard @LaurieShook @lauriewajda @lauriewang @LauriSYoung @LaurMandu @lavasite @LaVenusBallard @lavon_temple @LavRunWalk @LawForum @Lawminatrix @lawnguy384 @LawNinja @lawrence_fbt @LawrenceBland @lawrencechan @Lawrencelp @lawscomm @lawton_chiles @Lax102fm @LAXgirl @LaydeJ @layeronline @LaylaBeth @layn50l @LayneFisher @lazarinkroni @Lazcano @lazysupper @LBbreakingnews @LBiLondon @Lboogie2000 @LBsoftware @LC_DesignMedia @lchrisray @lcilmi @lcurrie @lcwontheweb @ldesautels @LDguyMN @LDIinAZ @ldiomede @ldistefano @LDRCoach @LdrshpCommunity @ldscott @LdsNana @ldwalton @Le_Brenda @Le_Vagabond @Leachka @leacycorley @Lead_By_Example @LeadClick @leaddiva @LeaderBook @LeaderChat @LeaderCoachTM @leadernewspaper @leadersbeacon @LeadersCircle @Leadership1 @Leadership2050 @Leadership4 @leadershipcoach @Leadershipfreak @LeadershipMuse @LeadershipWired @leaderswanted @LeaderTalk @LeadGenLab @leadingdigital @LeadingReporter @LeadingResource @Leads_Success @leadtheteam @LeadToday @LeahsGotIt @leakedtoday @LeanBodyCom @leandro_ojuara @leanerbodynow @LeanFitLife @LeanneF @LeanneForshaw @LeanneLipworth @leapCR @LEAPdirect @learn_and_earn @learn2earnnow10 @learn2earnwithd @LearnBright @LearnFromLance @LearnGuitar321 @learning_ceo @learning2live @LearningGerman1 @learningtocook @learnmktingsim @learnthat @LearntoBlogroll @LearnWithLauren @lease_equipment @leaVictoria @LeavingSBI @leavitt9 @lebray @lebrun @lecairn @lecastle @Lederfreund @ledboss @ledsaint @LEDWatchStop @LedZeps @Lee_newmedia @LeeA39 @LeeAase @LeeAnne_Orange @leecoopers @leedbolt @leedman @LEEDme @LeeFarb @leeforcongress @Leeftnugezond @Leeharmon @leehyung @leejoned @LeeKahler @LeelaSavage @LeePryke @LeeRosen @leesabarnes @LeesChicken @leesmallwood @leezabiz @lefreddie @left_handesign @LeftoverPenguin @LegacyConnect @legalbear @legaleagleMHM @LegalFormsBank @LegalizedGreen @legalninjaKris @legalnotransito @LegalRiver @LegalZoom @legizz @LeglessLush @Lego_Girl @LEGOROCKBAND @legrah @legrandsecret @leif_n @LeighAnneRamsey @leighcgilly @leighgrace @leighkm @leighmayo @leighpod @LeighStouffer @LeilaSamoodi @leldfw @lelhouston @lelphoenix @LemmingHerder @lemondrizzle @lemonknickers @lenablackswf @Lenaistewart @lenapple @LenCarson @Lender_Reviews @lenderapartment @lene477 @LENetwork @leniden @LenK7l @Lennar @LennarAustin @LennarDallas @LennysAtlanta @LennysSubsShops @lenorajoseph @Lenscapper1 @LentzBoykins @Leo_Pusateri @LeoCredo @leogoyk @LeoMatch @Leon_Kestel @leonardoodns @LeonardSquare @leonele @leonware @LeoThooner85 @leotomita @leplan @lePrecoceFeroce @LeRey @Lermont @lertman @les_the_mess @les_tontons @lesb3 @LesFonk @leshannepretty @lesintellos @Lesley_Johnston @LesleyDewarl @lesleyjudge @LesleyMorgan @Leslie796y @LeslieCoty @LeslieGilmore @leslielinevsky @LeslieMarshall @LeslieMcLellan @lesliescales @lesliewhittaker @lesliezengler @LessaT @LessonzGuitar @lessweight @Lesterbuddy @lesterg @LeszekTumkiewic @LetDallasThrive @LetDogsOut @leter_buck @letgohealthy @Leticiacarlar @leticiafre95605 @Letizialuggo @LetJeffHelp @LetMeGoCFG_esp @letorrivacation @LeToyaNEWS @LetraNova @Lets_Reflect @letsdojava @LetsGetupNgo @LetsGoOutside @letsgoshop4more @letsmarketbiz @LetsTalkIM @LetsVote @letswatchmoviez @letsxcel2gether @lettalondon @letterpress_se @LettuceRejoice @LevBurda @Level3Media @LEVEL5DALLAS @LevellandEDC @LevelTen @LevelTen_Colin @LEVELTWO @LevequeThots @LeverageSuccess @Levi_Pinnacle @Levi9company @LevineDany @levitanl @levs_a @LevyMcCallum @levyrecruits @Lew_Jetton @LeWirrya @lewisclayton @LewisHowes @LewisSLewis @Lexi_Carter @lexilooo @leximo @lexipatha @lexusofrenoblog @LEXXtech99 @LeyLucas @LezzBeLib @LezzBuzz @lfamous @lfer @lfom @lfootprint @lgerrits @lharrison @LHAworld @lhvillasana @LiamAWalsh @LianneHassen @liasophiabeauty @liatmyers @LiatTsarfati @LibbyGi @LibbyGill @LibbyJulia @LibbyRobinson @libertyforex @libraryfuture @libraryhag @libraryladyjane @licekniga @LiddleMonsta @lidelu @LiemNguyen @liesbethjansen @LiesbethR @liezeltassina @LifeatBlake @LifeCanBeDffrnt @LifeCoachBuzz @LifeCoachMary @LifeFromAbove @LifeGoalsCoach @lifeisawesome @lifeissupreme @lifelessanxious @LifeMasterSS @LifeOfDNA @LifeOnBlast @LifeScoop @lifeseek @lifesgoldenrule @LifeSpoke @Lifestyle2050 @lifesuccess96 @lifesystem1 @LifetimeDancer @LifeTrax @LIFETUBERS @LifeVerse @LifeWinnas @LifStyleUDeserv @liftmoveandstor @LightingBalloon @Lightning_Man @LightOverLife @Lightroomers @Liight_ning @LikeMe @likeomg @likestoplay @LikeTwolink @LikeWear @likiran @Likwid_team @Lil_Giz @Lil_Name @lilachbullock @Lilaylin @Lilchick1001 @lilchrissofresh @LilFairyWings @LilFatTony @lilliajanelle @LilianTavares @liligo_ES @lilkaraokediva @Lill_Any @LillieReibold @LilMissMusket @LilPatt @LILRHEEDOTCOM @LilRockerSteve @lilwildbuck @LilyB444 @lilybella @lilydustbin @liman_zx @limbar @limberg9l @limbtec @LimerickLover @limsteve @LinaEgutkina @Linda_ADAO @linda_miner @LindaAllen @LindaAllen @Lindacbarksdale @LindaCFlores @lindaclairepuig @LindaCork @LindaDuffy @LindaEskin @LindaEskridge @LindaForSenate @lindahancock @LindaHuaAnswers @lindajhutchinso @lindajvetter @LindaKayLens @LindaLocke @lindamiller @Lindan9 @LindaPTaylor @lindastanley @LindaThieman @lindawhite @lindenhurst @lindsaybaish @LindsayGTweets @lindsayjhopkins @LindsayJNichols @LindsayMac1 @lindsaymain @LindsayMAllen @lindsaytweets @lindseycholmes @LindseyGraceOU @LindseyHayzlett @lindseypaolucci @lindseyrmeadows @lindseytorbett @LindusCon @LindzeeLindholm @lineaumts @lingojob @linibiz @linikerpires @LinkageOD @Linkatech @LinkBid @LinkedIn_Ads @LinkedinConnect @LinkedInDiva @LinkedInExpert @linkedinguy @LinkedInKing @LinkedinLimits @LinkedInMaster @LinkedInNews @LinkedInPhoenix @LinkedInProfile @linkedinromance @LinkedinTips @LinkedInTrainer @Linkedportugal @LinkedTips @linkibol @LinkInfinity @linkmoneydotorg @links2trust @linksdedesign @LinkToPro @Linkz @linnea459l @LinuxForYou @linuxwebnews @LION500 @LionelatDell @lionelfumado @LioneServices @LionessMe @liorabear83 @LiposculptureSD @lipsticking @Liquid4All @liqwda @Lirtraining @lisa_dmblover @lisa_in_nz @Lisa_J_Lehr @lisa_ritter @lisal248 @lisa3boyz @Lisa4l798 @LisaAAdams @LisaABastian @lisaallenbrown @lisaberquist @lisabuck01 @LisaCherney @lisacrymes @LisaDouglas1 @Lisafolger @LisaGemini @LisaGillamMusic @LisaGoin @LisaHaruki @lisahickey @LisaLarter @lisaluxus @LisalynSchaffer @LisaMarieDias @lisamariesings @LisaMcCartney @LisaMcKenzie @LisaofArabia @LisaOffutt @LisaOnTheLoose @LisaPOswald @LisaPreston @LisaSaline @LisaStone @LisaTMartin @LisaVanAllen @lisaverde @lisdlA @LisenbyK @LisiSilveira @lisnagol @lissa_anne @LissaDuty @Lissarankin @listbuildingief @LitChat @Litegreen @LithiumProducer @LitleMisWheeler @Little_Soya @little12a @little12toes @littlebit80222 @LittleDebbie @littleerikking @littleg2010 @Littleshivaa @littlestinker @LittleTechGirl @Liturgy @liuboursiny @LivAmazingGrace @liveadventurous @LiveCareer @livehealthy_50 @LiveIfYouWantTo @Livejobscafe09 @LiveLean @livelive99 @LiveNationDAL @livenetwork28 @LiveNewOrleans @LIVEOUTLOUDWD

Acknowledgments

@LivePartyScene @livestrongofdal @livetechnology @livethelushlife @livetothemaxl @LiveTranslate @livewithtelisma @LiveWorkLove @livexpertweet @LiveYourBrand @livia_v @liviacowell @LivingCareers @LivingChiangmai @livinglocurto @livingmaxwell @LivingSocialBOS @LivingstonSmith @livingtruenatur @livinlime @livinteractive @LivioRadio @livlewis @Livvie_Matthews @lixaATX @liz_greene @Liz_Money @Liz_Silver @lizacosta @lizarddawg @lizcable @LizCappon @lizcorreia @lizdutoit @LizFrerich @LizH07 @liziarahza @lizkelley @lizkline @lizkupcha @lizpugh @Lizrenteria @LizSonnanstine @lizstrauss @LizSwiftHR @LizThompson_TEN @lizwagner @lizwalk @LizzHarmon @lizzy_breen @lizzybm @lizzys54 @LJacobwith @LJCSC @LJJSpeaks @LJSchafer @LKnerl @LKNSavings @lkwebbiz @LL4G @LLAmos @LLDA @llflorez @lllivingston @LLLivelovelife @LLOnline @lloyd1990 @LlsieuX @llUprisingll @lmaddoxla @lmalloy77 @lmedcroft @lmet @LMHill @lmitch324 @LMM_Merch @LMovements @LMRestplaetze @lmtforexsystem @lmurtagh @LMVCompanies @lnando2006 @lo2345 @LOA_Lover @load58 @LOAmanifest @loanapartment @LoanLeads @loanshooter @loantribe @loatutor @LobbyLand @LobsterandChick @LocalConsultant @Localeze @localizations @LocalPoint360 @LocalSearchPro @localseocanada @Localtweeps @localvorekid @LocalWebDesign @LocalWineCo @Locasun_uk @LocateMeACrib @Lochranns @lockard7 @Lockology @LockwoodChris @LoCoForHooping @Loebette @loesencialprcom @Loft_Dallas @loft1024thehome @LoftyDream @Log__Homes @LoganBestAgents @logannathan @LogicalD @logik_direct @logoscoaching @LogoTalkz @LogotypeTV @lohansarah @LOHASForum @LOHershberger @lohumideepak @loisgeller @lorenmorris @lorenpmatthews @Lorenzosendar @Lori_Randall @LoriCainRE @LoriDicker @loriforney @LoriGama @LoriJ_VA @LoRiKooP @LoriMoreno @lorimurphykoala @loritraylor @loriruff @loritokunaga @loriwill @lorizidell @lornali @LorneDaniel @LorRainesInfo @LoRunShield @lorygold @lose_weight_10 @LOSEWEIGHT_1 @LoseWeight_182 @loseweight318 @LoseWeightIndia @losmusicgroup @Lost_Initiative @lost_liszt @LostRoll @lostsolz @LostZombies @Lotay @lotion4you @lotterycracker @lottomagic100 @lotusjobs @lou_dubois @LouDornbach @LoudStarBazaar @LoudyOutLoud @loue @louiebaur @louiejr23 @LouieLighting @Louis_Batides @Louis_Michel @louis3105 @louisagoldstone @LouisColumbus @LouiseCollier @louiseheasmanuk @LouiseJames10 @LouisianaMoms @LouisPagan @louistm @Louiza12 @loumanna @LoungeKittens @LouPage @LouVettel @LouvettWatches @lova_stva @LovableWords @Love_Amelia @Love_Weddings @love2golf @love2homeschool @Love2Inspire @love2read4kids @lovealiblue @lovebenidorm @LoveCanal2020 @loveeeeeheather @loveinus @LoveKungFu @loveleestudio @lovelifemusic @LoveLifestyle @lovellpr @LovellsLager @Lovellyinc @lovelyk @Lovelylili808 @LoveMeLingerie @lovemorenow @lovemydogs2 @LoveMyPhilly @lovendancing @Lovenestparties @lovepethealth @LovePlanetaBy @LovePlanetaNet @lovepublishers @LoveRockstar @Loves2Twit @lovesays @LOVESDIGITAL @loveSHEE @lovethearth @LoveTheGulfRE @loveuranimals @loveshate_band @LoveYachts_com @Lovin_Life @lovina @LovingMommaBess @lovjoyhop @lowcarbthis @lowcostINS @LowellDaisley @LowerOakLawn @lowrateca @lowrobb @lowryagency @loyal2_me @LoyalKNG @LoyaltiePAYS @Loyalty360 @loyaltytoday @LTNa @lovealiblue @LPNational @LPNtweets @lpruden @lprufino @lpstkjunkie @LPT365 @lquerel @lrbray @LRHand @LRLF4Texas @LRothschildPhD @LSA_Home @LSA_WorkStyler @Lsaraj @LScribner @LSCullyPromoZ @LSDGROOFING @LSheka @lspearmani @LStephenCleary @lstexasnews @lstreams @LSWO @LT_Interns @LtGenPanda @Lu_Leite @LubbockPM @lucaonofrio @Lucas_Wyrsch @LucasCookMusic @lucasdrew33 @lucasfelipecost @lucaspedroza @lucassevilla @LucasWeber @LucBernouin @lucdupuy @lucenticok @Luciaa_JB @LuciaMitro @lucianacns @LucidFans @lucienbechard @LucilleBurn @Lucindap22 @Luckboxx @Lucleabauer @lucky_Card @luckydave3 @luckypenny @luckysplayhouse @luckytamm @luckytom72 @lucnathebest @luculent @lucyintheskyih @LucyWaters @lucyx_ @LudaDrummond @luduran @luemob @LuhMe_ @Luiggio @luigifilograna @luigisilveira @LuigiTorres14 @Luis_Garg @luis2010 @luisa2098 @luisacramirez @LuisdoAmaral @luisluque @LUISODLH @LuisSandovalJr @lujeansmith @Luke_Oatham @Luke_Sutton @luke_w_ellis @Luke69 @lukealley @lukeferrar @LukeRomyn @Lukes_Locker @LukeStratford @luketullos @lukstruk @Lumino_GmbH @LuminologyNet @LunabeanMedia @LunaBoston @lunadenoche5 @LunaLeigh @lunarfly @Lunch_com @lunchboxbunch @Lunisol22 @lunnucear @lubreinternet @LuRiLu @lurkey @Lusianacarolina @LuTroo @LuvHouses @luvleey @luvmylatte @LuvSocial_Media @luvsortho @luvthatcoffee @luvyaa @LuxeAustralia @luxeworldwide @Luxuo @LuxuryBeachRent @LuxuryShop @luxusweib @LVGrkGrl @LVIllinois @LVLG @LvrOfDisney @lVVVVVI @LXLEE @ly0nsd3n @lyal @lydiarambuyon @lydiavandemade @LynandPeteKelly @lyncadence @lynchy321 @Lynda_Susan @LyndaAJohnson @LyndaRamirez @LyndsayCabildo @LyneTum @LynleyP @Lynn_Murphy @Lynn911 @lynncatwalters @LynnCleverley @LynnDessert @lynnecor @lynnegordon @lynnfishman @LynnHarrisberg @LynnHillen @LynnPerron @lynnpholman @lynnreidl @LynnSerafinn @lynnterry @lynnyap @LynxsterGroup @lyrablackcats @lyricacopy @lyricsent @lyssachttr @lyssajaney @M_Albee @m_demena @m_gilles @M_Helm @M_Hickinbotham @mm_highfive @M_Isenberg @M_K_Reynolds @m_powermktg @M_Slater @m_tst @mlhalg @M2Walker @M3AMORE1983 @M3Brands @M3Publishing @M3Summit @m5NewHampshire @malgosia @MaarcyR_ @Maarten_v_vliet @maartendeclercq @mabielam @mabvertex @Mac_Station @Mac20Q @Mac27111960 @macaddict75 @MacallanDallas @macaroniandglue @Macaveli85 @MachenMacDonald @macherman31 @machomatcha @macjay @MACKatDAYMAR @MacKCollier @MacKenzieWBrown @macleoness @macnchuk @macronichie @macstarr @MacThorsten @mactricks @Mad_Hatter_Tea @MadAboutHealth @madaerodog @madaiqu @MadalynSklar @MadamePrimula @MadameTwit @Madatsara @madbushfarm @MADconsulting @MaddAdder @maddisonfoster @madebyhippies @madefelice @madeinmelmac @madejadomuelta @madel_21 @madelineearp @MadelineLaFave @MADforpeace @madhollywood @MADhusar @madicella @madisonbrooks87 @madisonloesche @madisonman @MadisonSMC @MadLeadsDiva @madmain @madmariner @madmentvshow @madmickmad @MadowGroup @madrugadorc @maejessica @Maelle_Ricker @Mamennerschuhe @MaHenal @mafiahairdresser @MAGDRL @magentaresearch @Maggiacomo @MaggieAnn09 @MaggieDennison @MaggieDeptuck @Maggiehaskell @MaggieHibma @MaggieHolben @maggiekbennett @MaggieMoos @maggytyger @magic_soil @MagicalKingdoms @MagicalNdeavors @magicalnoob @MagicBlogs @MagicClub2012 @MagicKreations2 @magiclogix @MagicSauceMedia @MagicShovels @magicskincare @magicsupertips @magicswebpage @magiesplace @magnethk @magnoliapr @magnotti @MagnusHaga @magnusmattsson @magnusmedia @magnusone23 @magsbyrne @Magsedoyle @mahalo @MaharishiU @MaharishiVideos @mahatab20 @mahbobbd @mahoganyt263 @maiimmaii @Maikeme @mailbagmedia_tx @MailOnline @Mainca @MainGig @mainstreammos @mairishahid @MaitlandWalker @MajedNachawati @MajesticBartend @maji01 @major_sohaib @MajorBreakthru @MajorExtreme @MajorsCareersOH @makaan @MakaMoreno @makbouli @make_money @make_moneytweet @makealifechange @makebuks1 @makefastcashnow @LizzHarmon @makeit @makeitwork @makemesomemoney @makemoney22 @makemoney4fun @makemoneymil @MakeMoneySimple @MakeMoneyStore @MakeMoneyTeach @Makeover_Diva @makepaydaytoday @MAKErain @makesomeonesday @MakeTopRetailer @makeurmoneynow @MakeWavesBonnie @MakeYoursNow @Makey_Money24x7 @MakeWeightIndia @makula_macula @malarchuck @MalaysianTwit @MalBryc @Malc0 @malcolmo77 @malhacao @malibucoltribun @maligariani @maliksoft @MalinMasterMind @MalloryAngers @mallshopping @mallybiz11 @MallyJames @malpaso @MAltaee @maltaserus @MamaCapps @mamakatslosinit @MamaLoveU @mamaweirdo2 @MammothAdams @man_health @Manage_Better @ManagerGuru @managerservices @manamica @ManassasMotels @ManateeApparel @manbargains @mancevic @MandaBlogsAbout

The Social Media Business Equation

@MandAMarketing @mandcinsurance @mandeewidrick @MandeWhite @MandieCarrusERZ @mandurahealthy @ManduraLeader @ManduraTopRep @Mandy_Kerr @Mandy_Vavrinak @maneishsaagar @Manfred2112 @Manganolcon @mangelesdiaz @ManhattanDallas @manil515 @ManiacMoe @maniagrawal @manifestfuture @ManifestingWall @ManifestWest @ManitobaCottage @ManitouBnB @MANNMITBRILLE @mannose @mannsworld @MannyHunni @Manon_69 @ManonLeroux @MansiiShah @Mantis_Media @ManTripping @mantychchristin @manualforliving @ManuelaSawitzki @manueljim @ManuelMontaner @manukanaturals @manyanasj @ManyHManyC @MaOneGosia @mapa70 @mapattorney @mapfood @maplemusketeer @maps4pets @maquiron @marablecq @MaraCod @maradanielle21 @marae02 @MaralaScott @maramamous @MaraPearson @Marble001 @Marc_Beharry @marc_reppin @marcandangel @marcapplewhite @marcbodenstab @marcbrowne @MarcDeCaria @marcelasuonski @marcelloorizi @marcelmend @marcelocbacchi @MarceloPCEns @marceloug @MarcelTeunissen @MarcEnsign @marchalpert @MarcHindley @MarchMadness2 @marchofdimes @marchon @Marci_A_Aurila @Marcia_ms @marciahansen @marciahoeck @marciamalucelli @marcie_davis @MarcieCasas @marciemacari @MarciJames @marcioalmeida @marcioluque @marcireynolds12 @marcjward @Marckow @marclevin @MarcLucas @marcmawhinney @MarcMGraham @marcnarine @marcoboersma @MarcoCarbajo @marcofaraci @MarcoHendrikse @marcokozlowski @marcold @Marcome @marcomessina @Marconi_SUCKS @MarcoNunezJr @MarcoSantarelli @MarcosCaldeiraa @MarcosPizzacorp @marcosthecuban @MarcosViladomiu @marcpoirier @MarcSalinas @marcsampson @marcshome @marcus_fielding @Marcus_Grooms @Marcus44137 @marcusapassey @marcusclarkus @marcusmessner @MarcusSchmidt @marcvidal @marcylauren @Mardanpalacecom @MarDeck @MardiLoFaso @MarDixon @mardonnavalta @mardotcom @Marek_W @marenhogan @marenkate @marfreaky820 @margaret_baylon @Margaret_F @margaretlewis56 @MargaretMarston @MargaretMolloy @margaretstock @MargaretWallace @MargaritaMatt @MargaritasCam @MargHamp @MarginUp @margorose @margryan @mari_lagares @maria_hilton1 @maria_muir @Maria7e0f @MariadPDC @mariagudelis @MariahKeith @mariaKappen @mariakitano @MariamCook @MarianaCardier @MarianBWood @MarianneKalland @Mariannsch @marianodealba @MarianSchembari @MariaPulice @mariarmcdavis @MariaSanz @mariashapiro30 @mariashriver @MariaSimone @MariaSmiling @mariatchijov @MariaVistage @maricarmenmar @Marie_Ang @marie_claire_au @marie_elg @marie_remedies @MarieAndreeW @MarieBenard @MarieDenee @marieespiritu @marieeved @marieforleo @MarieLasVegas @marielle722 @MarielleL @marigoy @Marii_xxx_ @marijevh @MariJoHarding @Marikablog @MarikoHulme @mariliaborges @marilyn_messik @marilynbohn @MarilynTDowning @marinashemesh @Marinds @MarineTechMike @marinic @Mario_Marketer @mario_photo @MarioAlcaraz @mariobox @mariocabrera @MarioKaestner @MarionDeDemos @Mariop72 @mariorodriguez @mariosolanoSEO @maris_life @MarisaCorser @marisacp51 @MariSmith @marisoldiaz @marisolmaribell @Marissa_J @Marissa_stone @maritune @MariusOna @Mark_Campanale @mark_charlotte @mark_crase @mark_earle @mark_ellam @mark_fallows @mark_koenig @Mark_Sheldon @mark_tetzner @Mark_Vaudreuil @mark_warner @mark33 @MarkAllenOnline @markanastasil @MarkAPatten @MarkARodriguez @MarkBakerEvents @markbaxterdc @markbel3 @MarkBilton @markbnorwich @MarkBowser @MarkBrimm @markcahill @MarkClayson @markclement @markcolless @markcreaser @MarkCWinters @markdanshaw @MarkDavidGerson @markdeldegan @markdgibson @MarkDimension @Markedia @Markedon28 @MarkEricJohnson @Markerter @Market_Articles @market_expert @market_mastery @market_talk @MarketBistro @MarketeersCLUB @marketer_jobs @Marketer_UK @MarketersShop @MarketFX @markethinks @MarkEThurston @Marketinehoude @marketing @marketing_4_u @Marketing_Apes @marketing_biz77 @marketing_gal @Marketing360 @MarketingAlly @MarketingApes @MarketingArmada @MarketingBrian @MarketingBtrfly @marketingbus @marketingbykat @Marketingdonkey @MarketingDonut @MarketingEpsert @marketingfem @MarketingFool @marketinggrl @MarketingInFL @marketingisus @MarketingJedi @marketingldr @MarketingMav @marketingmiguel @MarketingMikeR @MarketingMobi @MarketingMoma @MarketingMud @MarketingMuscle @MarketingProfs @MarketingPulse @marketingseo2 @marketingstatic @MarketingStrtgy @marketingsurfer @MarketingTipsGR @marketingtwitts @marketingwa @marketingyudai @MarketingZen @marketjrb @MarketLikeAChik @MarketMavenNYC @MarketMeSuite @MarketResults @Marketri @MarketsNYC @marketstrategy @MarketThis @MarketWithHeart @MarketWrapDaily @MarketYrSuccess @MarkFairbanks @markfarmer @markflax @markgammon @markgarfield @markgiggsy11 @MarkGoren @markgungor @markgyles @markhankinson @markharbert @Marki_Lemons @markidguru @MarklsMusing @markjstonham @markjuelich @MarkKaplan @markkerr @markket @markkjaer @MarkMatiszik @markmcculloch27 @markmeyer @MarkMHarrison @marknagy @marknhopgood @MarkNkids @markoharephoto @MarkoMinka @markotu @markpinney1 @MarkRCameron @markrice03 @MarkRMatthews @MarkRobbins76 @MarkRRoberts @MarkRRobertson @MarkScamardella @markscuderi @MarkSimmering @MarkSmithart @marksstuff @markstencel @MarkTHook @markusmh @markwalters @markwalton_uk @markwesig @MarkWesthead @markwilliams @MarkWLein @markwschaefer @markyto @marknet @MarlaMorales @MarlitaH @marlys1230 @Maroundit @Marq_Von @marqueeent @marquesdepaiva @marquis1955 @marquis1955live @marriageissues @MarriageMan @MarriageNFamily @marriamb @marriedaffairs @marsadvice @marsan1973 @MarshaCollier @marshafriedman @marshallblake @MarshalSylver @marshmedia @MarsVA @marsya @Martenlemstra @MarthaAYoung @MarthaGiffen @marthalisa @MarthaTucker @martigirl @Martin_beaulieu @MartinaCurtis @martinbastin @martinblonk @martinehunter @MartinFaulks @martini777 @martinlee33 @MartinRnchWine @martinschecter @MarTrelong @marty_desmond @MartyDavis26 @MartyGriffith @martyk @MartyKoenig @martymjm @martynik @MartySuijk @martythornley @MartyVettel @MaruxaMurphy @MarvelaHGrizzar @MarvenReyes @marvid101 @MarvinsWineClub @MarWarrender @Mary_Ballard @mary_thayer @marya1986 @MaryamLovesJazz @maryanncando @MaryAnneNagy @MaryBudge @MaryCallie @Maryellenc @MaryEllenGibson @maryettat @MaryFKrueger @MaryFlaherty @maryharlan @maryhenige @maryheston @Maryjean_Howe @MaryJoWagner @marykayhoal @marykellyspeaks @marylove99 @marylynn3 @marymac @marynix1 @marynyoung @maryscandy @maryscsandy @marysfreebies @MaryVincent @MaryWbn @Marzbymarz @masahiroglobal @Mashable @mashedvegas @MASHMALLOWMEN @MashupChristine @MASisMore @mask6543 @MaskedMarketer @masnganten @MasonSpeak @mass_ebooks @massaboutique @massageenvydfw @massagemanly @massimokamal @massin @massmoneymaker @massoutsource @MassTweetsPro @mastabootwrecka @mastadon @Master_Builder @Master_Grill @mastercreating @Masteris71 @masterlocksmith @MasterMarketers @MasteryCoaching @MasterYourMoney @MastiAsk @mastoyshop @matau22 @MatCendana @matchmoneytree @MatejVarga @Matersys @materteral @matheusti @Mathieu_Roberts @MathieuBisson @mathildalando @mathteachers @MatildasPlace @MattRempitPJ @Matrixah4u @MatrixGroup @MatrixTycoon @MatShepSEO @Matsony @MatsStromberg @matt_heindl @matt_houston @Matt_Lenzie @Matt_Matey @matt_tritico @matt_which @matt_wimberly @Mattaffiliates @MattArndt @mattasamuels @MattBasically @MattBinder @mattcase @MattDickman @MattEder @matteandrew @mattesM @matteswho @MattFindsDeals @matthewbrabson @matthew_d @matthew_ferry @Matthew_Kramer @matthewbjohnson @MatthewCoast @MatthewCooney @matthewjhoward @matthewleitz @MatthewLiberty @matthewmaiden @MatthewMichuda @matthewneer @MatthewRusso @MatthewSato @matthewtdoyle @matthewwiese @MattHope_ @mattial @mattiasis @mattmixten @MattJavit @mattjgoodman @mattkassulke @mattkrantz @MattLaClear @MattLawton @MattLevenhagen @mattlisk @mattlloydonline @MattnCatWillis @MattOnAir @MattPenna @mattpowersmusic @MattRauch @mattress_giant @MattSapaula @MattsAttic @mattscherb @mattscutt @mattsingley @MattSlavenov @mattuniwestmin @mattwadsworth @mattwarman @MattWeitzman @matty1999 @MattyMo34 @Matvee @Matwilson1 @Maudeonline @MauiBentley @Maureen_Tseng @maureenbridget @maureennaisbitt @maurelita @MauriceCFlynn @mauricefreedman @MauriceHam @maurilio @mauroferri @maverickdigital @MaverickMastery @maverickwoman @MavH @mavrikmoney @mavrodievv @Max_Marketing @Max_Miecchi @Max_Success @max_titanium @maxamizelifebra @MaxBateman @maxcamsnet @MaxCashFlow @maxfightmaster @maxfrag @MaxGilbert6

168

Acknowledgments

@maxifier @MaximeDeGreve @maximediastudio @maximestp @MaximumMarketer @maxinemaxxy @MaxKhazanovich @MaxKohler @MaxMotorsDirect @maxOz @maxrosenthal @Maxs_Books @maxsearchengine @MaXsiM @maxsportsplus @maxusmedia @maxwellfinn @maxwellnewage @Maxyourvoice @may_ha @Maya_Charmed @MayaCoupons @Mayah_Riaz @Mayakovskij @mayarend @mayaweb7 @MayBelFire @maychch @mayhemstudios @maykyyue @MayoClinic @MayorSamAdams @mayrangely @mayukh_11 @mayuraw @mazaldiamond @Mazukins @Mba_anjali @MBA_Channel @MBAGeekDotCom @MBAHighway @mbahsurep @mbarnn @MBartloff @mbdunnusa @mBeyond @MBGroupSusanB @mbiance_ @mbirch_cma @MbitoGee @MBKSarah @mbl @mboaman @MbonoNet @mbrettcurtis @mbrinkerhoff @mbtalent2 @mbtoon08 @mbwconsulting @mcassem @mcassettari @mcastel @mcbidz @McBookPro @mcbrundage @mccJustin @McClarinPlastic @mccordweb @mccrackenc @mccurtin @McD_NorthTexas @mcdermott_billy @MCDolphens @McDonaldBryan @MCDouwes @Mcdowell_87 @mcemilywrites @MCENTURY @MCergo @Mcfixit @mcgawco @mcginnco @mcguiganm @McGuireLock @McKearin @McKeenMatt @mckennasmark @McKinleyMovie @McKinneyConnect @McKinneyFamLaw @McKinneySuzuki @McKinneyTXAlert @McLaren_eShop @mclaughlinchris @mcmilker @MCNAffiliates @Mcnet_Dipp @mconstruction20 @Mcontemporanea @mcort @mcp111 @mcphillipsP @MCR_FANS @mrcolorado @mcsinn @mctstreetteam @mcullison @mcviolin @McWhipkey @MDAI_UK @mdalton999 @mdavisl @MDCentral @mddelphis @MDE_STAR @MDelaCalzada @mdelcid @mdh47 @mdhtoday @mdjack @mdkhairu @mdkhairun @mdmolzen @MDREPros @MDREPROS1 @mdresort @mdrfl @MDSTraining @mdtoorder @mdtownsley @mdwaterfront @me_angelonearth @me2everyoneIT @me2everyonenews @me2everyoneNG @me2everyonePLC @me2everyoneRO @me2everyoneZA @meadowleap @Meaghery @meandthewww @MechanicalPtnrs @mechawebmaster @mechlin @MEdAdvisory @MedalShop @MedCareerVillag @media077 @media55 @mediacafeAU @MediaCluster @mediacoach @MediaEdAssc @Mediagirl007 @mediahunter @mediaman64 @mediamanx @medianmarketing @MediaOutletHere @MediaPowerTools @MediaScott @MediaShouter @MediaSidekick @mediatemple @mediatwo_social @MediaweekDotCom @Mediaworkslre @medical91 @MedicalMile @medicalmlisting @medicalneeds @medicalnewsal @MedicalSoft @MedicVuecom @medienkongress @Medindia @medinsurance @meditationzx @MediterraneanDi @MEDixon215 @MedNewsReports @mednewswise @medoo23 @meeboii @MeeGoExperts @meepbobeep @meera_kc @Meerim_O @meesposito @meadowleap @Meaghery @meandthewww @MechanicalPtnrs @MCarron @meetanshul @meetDonnaMcRae @meetings_LA @meetingwizard @MeetJohnFuller @meetmikemorgan @MeetMyBusiness @meetthebosstv @MeetTheTweets @meetthewalkers @Meetup @MeetYoLe @MeFile @Meg_Store @meg2day @MegaHealthCoach @megaira @megamarketer @megamcc @megamentor @MegaMike09 @Megan_FoxGirls @MeganBacon @meganfoxjr @MeganKGreen @MeganLawler @MeganLeap @meganmonique @MegannePrice @megansforbes @meganshoee @MeganWoods @Megapixcameras @megapremium12 @megarespsone @megashare @MegasysHMS @megcalnan @megdavis00 @megenheslip @MegfromCT @meggiluvian @MeguGuiseppi @MeghanLeeArnold @MeghanMBiro @megheuer @megmark @megnjackyip @MEGoldberg @MegOyanagi @MegRange @megsterr @megvoice @MehboobKhan @mehndipatterns @MeHottyNaughty @MehrEuro @meili_chen @meinzuhause24 @meiolitro @MekDaSneak @mel_mayhem @Mel_White_ @Melanie_Parish @melanieann79 @melaniebardot @melaniedaigle @MelaniedeJonge @melaniedye @melaniejohn @melaniejor @MelanieJRadford @MelanieKissell @MelanieMinnaar @melaniepeters35 @melanievotaw @melaniewoods @MelanyTexas @MELavine @MelCarlton @melchlepp @melcoach @Melekdesigns1 @melenie @MelGadelha @MeLikeGoodMusic @MeliMoore @MelindaCopp @MelindaFlood @MelindaJane @MelindaStone @melisproject @Melissa_Albers @melissa_c_cowan @melissa_snow @MelissaBrandt @melissaearlyoun @MelissaHourigan @melissainfo @Melissaloul @melissamade @MelissaMcCreery @MelissaNicholso @melissaonline @MelissaPazPR @MelissaUWD @MelissaWaldon @MelissaWilmot @mell8509 @melleefresh @mellieReed @MelMcClendon @melmilletics @melodeedailey @melonus @Meloyul @Mels1 @melstamper @MelvinEverson @MelvinJacksonII @Melvinjames18 @memathews @memci @memelspeak @MeNameLast @menardsguy @MendoFilmFest @meneldur @Menamayzar @mensdomain @MensGrooming @mensweddingband @MentalHealthUSA @mentalista @mentorconach @mentoringlab @MentorKen @MentorMichelle2 @Mentoropolis @MentorPlanet @MentorPortal @Menus4Mums @meonitcom @mercatopartners @Merchant_Metrix @merchant91 @MereCorte @MereElainePR @meretajma @MeridianMex @merleped @merlijne @MerlinDigital @MermaidHel @meroveiasco @MerrieMarketing @merrybubbles @merrygourmet @MervynDinnen @merylkevans @MesaAzHomes @Meschede @MESHagency @messagemasseuse @MessageSpreader @meste48 @matabolicsystem @Metacowboy @Metalnik621 @MetalRoofingVA @metalsnews @metatube @meteorit @MetricsBoard @MetropolisTweet @MetroPolitics @MetroVW @MettlerToledoPA @Meverick @meVikash @MeWriteForFun @mexiaPR @mexicool713 @MexicoTimes @MexInsurance @mfascette @mfb83 @MFBissett @MFCollier @MFDragon4 @mfeil @mferna @mfernandes83 @MFF999 @MFinMedia @MFinney @MFKtoday @MMKMuenchen @mfreise @MFRhymes @mfriedman01 @mgallops @mgarcia_KOV @mgavoor @mgharavi @MGHurston @mgiarrat @mgk_ae @mgm3c @mgmli @MgmtGrp1 @mgpogue @mgrydahoak @MGroenevelt @MGStults @MH_Youth @mhappyb @mhcharter @mhemig @mhequalities @MHewitson @mhorne @MhzQuiros @mi4m @MI5HRA @miafia @MiaFredrickson @MiahMarker @mialeenasofia @miamiadschool @MiamiAdSchoolSF @MiamiEstates @miamifavs @miamikeyshomes @miamiolivia @miamireal @miaph74 @miapride @MiataJenn @mibizin @MiBuzz @Mic_lasamahu @micahboswell @MicFarris @micfo @micgus @MICH_GREG @michacha101 @Michael1Green @michaelk @michael_arndt @michael_duvall @Michael_Ghezzo @Michael_Hoffman @michael_n @michael_nelson @michael_oakes @Michael_RE @michael_rushnak @michael_vaclav @michaelb061 @MichaelBelba @michaelbristol @MichaelButlerSR @MichaelCantone @MichaelCasida @MichaelCasnji @MichaelConquest @michaelcroweTFK @michaeldavis777 @MichaelDinoff @MichaelEck @MichaelEdwards0 @michaelemlong @michaelfieldcom @michaelgass @michaelgold @MichaelHartzell @michaelheiniger @MichaelHyatt @MichaelJKillian @michaeljohns @MichaelJordanYo @MichaelJSubhan @michaeljzimmer @michaelking4023 @michaelkoldham @michaellunsford @michaelmccann @MichaelMcCurry @michaelmcminn @MichaelNeubarth @michaelnewhouse @michaelnobbs @michaeloon @michaelpahl @michaelrburcham @michaelrlitt @MichaelRoland @michaelsdugan @MichaelSpiro @MichaelValez @MichaelVanV @MichaelVorsatz @michaelvorel @MichaelVrijhoef @MichaelWillett @michaelwolfe @michagabriel @michalminarovic @MichChat @MichDdot @MichelaKaren @micheleborba @Michelee1433 @MicheleJory @MicheleKersey @MicheleNewcomb @micheleoreggio @michelhovenkamp @michelkronthal @michelleagredo @michellegoldb @MichelleBargain @michellebeckham @michelleclode @MichelleeWagner @MichelleFF @MichelleGamradt @michellegaribal @MichelleGtv @michellejenn_HR @MichelleKelly33 @michellerabell @michellericsson @michellerigg @MichelleShaeffr @MichelleSpivery @michelleStephPR @MichelleStewart @michellestonge @michelletripp @MICHELLETWOME @MichelleYamine @michelreverte @michfredericks @michi_mikou @MichianaRealtor @michic @MichielGaas @michiganfe @Michiyu @MichWorksAssn @MicJohnson @mickdarling @mickelous @mickeymantas @mickiejames01 @MickMonroe @MickMoore @micknsk @micksay @MicroBilt @microbizfanatic @microcleaner @MicroFoundation @microkarma @micropr @MicrosoftSales @Mid_Ngt_Trucker @Mid247 @MiddleNameIsFuN @MidlifeRoadTrip @midnightads @midnightexec @MidoxJebrane @Midphase @midtownweb @midwaylabs @MidyAponte @miekevh @miekojapan @mierdadepajaro @MightySmalls @miguellasso @MiguelMassey @miguelsytem @Miharu @mihalylaszlo @Miharu5 @mihhirnayak @mihmarketing @miiaakkinen @MiiGomeeez @moines @MiakFoss @mihkaku @Mike__Sheehan @mike_Clough @Mike_Cotton @MIKE_DA_SINGER @mike_gingerich @Mike_hts @Mike_Igartua @mike_kohn @Mike_Kunkle @Mike_Paturel @Mike_Rodriguez_@mike_seneschal @Mike_Stelzner @Mike_Trk @mike.me @mike2977 @MikeArgi @mikeasaunders @MikeBallantyne @mikebarker007 @mikebausman @MikeBehler @MikeBoehler @MikeBoehmer57 @mikeboylen @MikeBredthauer @mikecamarillo @MikeColbourn @MikeCorak @mikeczerwinski @mikedammann @mikedmerrill @mikedspringer @MikeDubrall @MikeDuering @MikeElgan @mikefay @mikefinn_tweets @mikefixs @mikeflanny @MikeFrankel @MikeFreyParadux @mikefroccaro @MikeGeffner @MikeHale @MikeHanbery @mikeshankey @MikeHaydon @mikehenrysr @mikehobbs @MikeHood215 @MikeJMonroe

The Social Media Business Equation

@MikeJody @mikejweber @MikeKalil @mikekemp @mikekmcclure @mikekumpf @mikekwan @MikelCortes @mikelking @MikellaB @mikellespot @MikeLloydOBrien @MikeMacLeod @mikemayhew @mikemcguff @MikeMehring @MIKEMILLIONZ @MikeMueller @MikeMulla @mikemyatt @miken_bu @MikeONeilDenver @mikeperras @mikepfs @mikepouraryan @MikeRamer @mikerass @mikerbrt @MikeRuffles @mikeryanman @mikesemple @MikeShawTV @mikesireci @MikeSKing @mikesmarket @mikespindle @MikeStaar @MikeStaff @MikeStover_ @MikeStuder @miketon944 @MikeToombs @MikeVanDervort @mikevermillion @mikewarren129 @MikeWaterton @MikeWhitaker @mikewhitmore @mikewillam @MikeWilliamsPro @mikewittenstein @MikeWize @mikeycunningham @MikeyLotts @mikeymushi @mikeyoung @mikimarkovich @mikki_cabot @MikkoMann @MikoTech @milanaxx @milbiz @MilCivX @mileese @milenaregos @milesaustin @milesb @mileslovegrove @mileymursal @MilitaryBenefit @miljenkob @MilkmanBog @MillCreekResort @Millenefaria @millerheavy @MillerPierce @mikesireci @Million_Mentor @MillionaireGC @MillionaireMimi @millionaires20 @milliondavid @milliondollar22 @MillionDollarJV @millionlikes @millionsofmyles @milloggerz @milnearts @Milo_Moon @Milogh @MilwMoments @mimi529 @MinahRempitKL @MinataurGroup @minavocal @Mind_Brain @MIND360 @mindandbodyscri @MinDavidWilson @mindblob @MINDBULLY @Mindclay @mindcomet @mindeliver @MindFortune @MindFrolic @MindfullyChange @mindoverweight @mindpom @MindPowerCoach @mindproject @mindsatori @Mindsetdefect @mindsetmillions @mindstirmedia @mindtalk @Mindtrekker @mindtube @MindyJay2009 @MindyLanders @minervatees @Minervity @mingleeasy @MinhQuang_07 @MiniAnne @minigarden @MiningForumAust @miniroom549 @minkbh @minnesotajobs @minnixs @Mint_LA @MintCool @mintyjam @mintzwebdesign @minxdragon @miprd @MiquelC @MiracleFruitPlu @Miracles4Kids @MiraclesGoddess @miragreenland @MirandaRyan @MIrealestate @MirelaMonte @miriambuhr @MiriBe @mirithomas @MirjamSpronk @MirkoGosch @mirkohumbert @Mirman1978 @mironasee @MisaHopkins @MiseryXchord @Mishon8 @misizjackson @miskinlaw @MISNIUIL @MisplacedBoy @Miss_Behavin @Miss_Friday @Miss_Poker @MissAddict @missbad22 @MissBeckala @MISSBELLINI @MissBooker24 @misschattychica @MissChiaraGee @missCRMpixie @missdetails @missflynius @missgillygrace @MissGinger26 @MissieLaura @Missilonka @missionmauve @MissionOakGrill @MissJamieSwartz @missjennybar @MissKatieAngel @MissKiaa_ @misskpatel @misslailah @misslori @misslori2 @MissMalaprop @missmaryelliott @MissMediosa @MissMichelleAZ @Missmissyport @MissNeilaB @MissPoudrette @MissSallysPC @misssmaris @MisssThickyy @missstbrownatl @misstoddX @MissTwittter @missusMSP @MissVontheScene @MissWall @missy5ft2 @Mista_Montana @Misteism @mister_tarobe @MisterNatural2 @mistertelecom @misty_browning @mistyblue2255 @MistyKhan @MistySutton @Misupilami @Misz_Gii @mitalikhanna8 @mitch000001 @MitchBaldwin @mitchellashley @MitchellFrom @MitchellMcKenna @MitchMeyerson @MitchSchneider @MitechTrading @Mithbecca @MithiBhatia @Mitragrad @mitsuyamazaki @Mittagskarte @mittenshatesyou @Mittkontakt @mitusen @MityDad @mitzilewis @MIURAmusic @miwalabo @Mixtur @MIYOMIYO34 @MizJaxon @MizQui @mizzbabygurll @MizzSocial @MizzyB @mjbwolf @MJCherdyle @mjeannet @mjesales @MJExec @MJGSocialMedia @mjherbert @mjkramer @MJMudd @mjoyce71 @mjoypekas @mjuliat @MJvDoorn @mkal9 @MKCallConsult @mkebiz @MKELive @mkellner @mkemegs @mkganda @mkgunnoe @mkilmurry @mkimarnold @mkjmc @mklankenau @mklein818 @mklubok @mKounelakis @mkregel @mksmither @mktgbill @mktgDIGITAL @mktginsolutions @mktgmediamaven @mktgqueen1 @MktgTourGuide @MktplcCoach @mktvitortavares @mlauritzen @mlayna @mlcfactor @mLehua @MLFNOW @mlhujber @mlinson @mlittles23 @mlkeone @mllemire @MlleNB @MLM_Absolute @mlm_failproof @mlm_leads @MLM_Leads_4_u @mlm_luegen @MLM450DOLLERS @mlm4ever @mlmathome1 @MLMAttractXpert @MLMBigProfits @MLMbyTheNumbers @mlmcampus @mlmcashsecrets @MLMCat @MLMchamp @mlmerotic @MLMfromHome @MLMgeek @MLMguideFreedom @MLMLeadsMastery @MLMMoneySecret @MLMNoobie @MLMOnlineHelp @mlmpirat @mlmrichesnow @MLMRocker @MLMSuccessGold @mlmsuccessstory @mlmsuccessytem @mlmsummit @MLMSuperCharger @MLMTopCoach @mlmtrainingbase @MLMTravelNetwrk @MLMTriumph @MLMtwitWealth @mlodba @mlomb @mlperryny @mlrockwell @mlsdonkey @mmadamba @MMakersClub @mmangen @mmartoccia @mmateju @mmBrains @mmealing @mMediaFX @Mmelisse @MmeSocialMedia @MMGALLERIES @mmid1 @MMidas @mmilstead @mmituk @MMMInc @mmoleculedotcom @mmontplaisir @mmonz @mmordecai @mncahill @mnjobs @Mnmissy @MNOGOSISEK @mnorthcott @mnsrainbow @mnurws @moanaboutmencom @Mobeca @mobienthusiast @MobileBarcode @MobileCouponNow @mobilecoupons @MobileEyeGuy @MobileMarketNow @MobileTraffic @mobiltelefone @Mobiltwit @Mobious_2012 @mobiqpons @mobs_chahat @mobyminnow @mocha_guru @mochan42 @Moda_Italia @ModaMags @modaonline @MODDFW @modeling22 @modelmodels @modelwealth @modenews @modernetc @modernhood @modernmediaman @modernmethods @modowd @modyandmody @MoeneekH @moesslang @moey63 @moezone3svq @Moffly @MogheesTahir @mogobogo @mohajan @MohamedHashim @mohitdhiman @mohsinabbas007 @MoiraGeary @moiraop @Moiseslopez @MoishesMoving @mojara @Mojo2Go @MojoMaxted @mojopath @mojuu @mok_oh @mokasti @mokpovia @mokyuhiko @MolaahDotCom @molechilango @molfamily @MollieJohnso @MollieWat @mollycgaines @mollydcampbell @MollyDugganLLC @mollyhound @MollyThornberg @MolsonFerg @Mom_Daughter @mom2summit @momac88 @momager1 @mombizcoach @mombloggersclub @momchats @momdadcanwetalk @momentify @mominthecity @momlogic @MommaDJane @mommaude @MommyBagsDFW @MommysForJesus @mommyswishlist @momo_ok @Momofangelgirl @MomOfTeen @MomOnTheVerge @MomsRising @momstownGuelph @MoNaboulsi @monatwt @MONDOprint_com @mondster @MonEbrown @monedays @Monetize_Twt @Money_Hunt @Money_Report @Money1000 @money2kcom @moneyadda @MoneyAndYou @moneyartist @moneybizonline @moneyedup @moneyfellas @moneyforloan @moneyfreeonline @MoneyFromNet @MoneyIsKing14 @moneyjo @moneylender4u @MoneyLifeNetwrk @MoneyMaker777 @moneymakerbrat @MoneyMakerGroup @MoneyMaking123 @MoneyMakingDude @MoneyMakingTim @moneynerds @moneyonline19 @moneypowertips @moneyries @moneysavingdeal @moneytalkdotcom @MoneyTreeMom @moneytwitting @monfdz @mongabay @Monica_Rafiq @MonicaDayPhotog @MonicaLushale @MonicaMcPherrin @MonicasAcaYAlla @MonicaWB @moniebagsnt @moniquelester @MoniqueRamsey @moniquesavin @moniquew @MoniqueWoodard @Monir9 @Monitium_by_Deb @monitoringblog @monitoringsoft @Monitronics @monk2be1 @monkeyhillbar @monkmusic @monmouthp @monnienielsen @monolithicdomes @Monster_Quest @MonsterMusic @monstrocity @montagecomms @MontereyCoins @montpellier_fan @MontPR @moo0k @Mook_LWH @mookentooken @MoolaGang @MoolalaFroYo @moomike @MoonApe @moondogfarm @moonlighthk @moonlitesocial @mooredon @Moorius @MooseHaven @moosedooley @Moovzon @moowebsites @moowhackbeef @MOOYAHBurger @Mopec35 @mora57music @MoreFamousThan @Morehotconcept @MOREMarketing4U @MoreMoneyLady @MoreSpaTraffic @moretips4u @morferro @Morgane_R @MorganFletcher @morganleeonline @morganmeador21 @MorganPR @MorgansSupport @MorgansWndrlnd @morganwesterman @MoringaMax @morinjean @mormon_news @MorningstarCDN @Moroch_Movies @MorochPartners @morphT @morrison1982 @MorrisTed @Mortgage_World @Mortgage123com @mortgageadvise @mortgagecorner @mortgager2 @mortgagerelated @MortgagesBook @mortiz @mortjac @MortysComedy @mortyscomedytx @MosaicTile @moseslee @MoshiAndKibo @Moshtarak @Mosley23 @mossappeal @mossinterest @MostLucky @MOSTraining @Motek_Diamonds @motercalo @motherducts @motherfluffer @motherpucker @MotionAudio7 @motiquoter @motivatingmo @motivationlive @motivcoach @MotoCMS @MotorcycleShows @MotorcycleStuff @motormaven @MotownDan @mottibez1 @Motts @moue @mountain14 @mountainlaneman @mouselink @mousleyki @MoussliDotCom @MouyyadA @movaio @MOverseas @movestudio @MOVETHECROWD @movie_trailerco @MovieBum @moviecarmania @MovieMERCENARY @moviepoorch @moviesepisodes @moviesstore @MovieWallpapers @MovingMavins @MovingStorageHQ @Mox_eMediaGirl @moxionmarketing @MOyanagiJP @moyegirl @mozy @Mozzie99 @mp_green @mp3_fiesta @mpaines @mparent77772 @mpaynknoper @mpenwarden @mphillibert @mphthuy @MPIDFW @mpondfield @Mprintmedia @mprosceno @MQAlumni @mqtodd @Mr_1Liner @Mr_Cosmic @mr_linkedin @Mr_Oneliner @mr_onions @Mr_Pinkerton

170

Acknowledgments

@Mr_Psychotic @Mr_RPBrown @Mr_Syria @Mr_TMontgomery @Mr_Write @Mr_X10 @mr903muzic @MRahlenbeck @MrAkashSharma @MrAlanToaca @MrAllround @mrALReza @mramaneo @mrazfans @mrbensays @MrBentoCasillas @MrBlogl @mrbodidly @MrBrandonMarcus @MrBrooksGCNews @mrbunltd @MRBuslT @Mrcarl007 @MrCGWhatitdew @MrChrisKennedy @MrCompGuru @MrCouchp32Money @mrcwalsh @mrDaveyGuy @MrDeeDuncan @mrdeleted @mrdeveraux @mrdigydigy @mrdjamesrice @mrdOLIVE @mrdonmac @mrebay @mrenlightenment @MrEricCole @MREX @MrExquisite @MrFatFighter @MrFreitag @MrGeorgeBrown @MrGoodGoesHard @MrGreedyDJ @mrgreennz @MrHammertonSEO @mrhaneysr @MRHolidaysl @MrHybridCar @MrIanBass @mritsch @mrjeffvo @MrJimPatterson @mrjke @MrJMassey @mrjoeromero @mrjohndonnelly @mrjwhite @mrkdw35 @MrKnowsBest @mrksagor @Mrlae @MrLeeLawson @MrLinna @mrlogek @MrMarketingMan @mrmarketology @mrmartye @MrMichaelFowler @MrMichaelTucker @MrMomWorld @MrMovieReviews @MrNuttyChris @mromea @mrpaulmiller @MRPaulSimon @MrPhat @MrPigglesworth @mrPilat @mrpingation @MrRayNichols @mrrelic @mrrichclark @MrRoachie @MrS_mR_mOo @mrsaferide @MrSangVal @MrScottEddy @MrsD_Winchester @mrseniordan @MrSevan @mrsF5 @mrshawntkiley @mrsKBautis @MrsMoonsDiary @MrSocialMedia12 @MrsSteveoftheOC @mrst_cruises @MrStealYaChsCke @MrVance @mrverloc @mrvestek @mrwhittington @mrwillw @ms_alessandra @ms_effective @Ms_Glambert @MS_MURDA @Ms_PerleNoire @ms2weathergirl @MSAdvertising @MsAlexander @MsApelthun @msasearch @MsBail @MsBentleyBee @MsBiffys @mscator @MSCFoster @mscfranchise @mschleini @mschoder @MsDehAlves @MsDMosley74 @msebeling @MSEFenley @msegedie @MSFTBizBuilder @msftnyheter @msgatoradr @MSGiftCompany @MSGiro @MShahab @mshaynehall @msheehym @mshraybman @MSiek @Msieur_Eddy @MSJA_888 @msjag @msjourney @MsLeisure @msmaso9 @MsMaxOut2010 @MSMF2 @msmorrisonspks @MsMyria @MsNicola @MSOfficeResKit @MSpight @mspinpoint @MsPlaymaker09 @msponhour @MSreview @MsShrinkxHIPS @mst_seedonplaza @mstajduhar @MsThinutopia @mstrategiesinc @MStreetBar @msummers75 @mszot @MT4offshore @MtAdamsADesign @mtaram @mtbenson @mtcrookshank @mtdreamaker @mtgfinancebuzz @mthinker @mtillman_l3 @Mtnmd @mtritt @mtrufant @Mtsprofits @MTVTwit @MTw1tter @MTWblog @MuahBlogger @muazzuhdey @mubasheir @muellertime @Mugil @mugilanc @MugsyRusso @Muhadeeb99 @Muhamad_IS @Mukaika @MukhrizMahadir @mukkuTheMan @mulberrybush @mullenunbound @multihb @Multimarathon @multimedia_talk @multiplaza @multiplytraffic @multisvchr @multitoool @mulyoo @MumJennifer @mumpvt @Munatyze @MundoAcosta @mundodrogado @muneerl @munsoy @muracevic @MuralMan @MuratUnkar @MurphyKlinger @murphymaizedays @MurrayMelb @Musclegal @MUSCLERABBIT @Muselnks @MuseumNext @mushmushmush @musicdenver @musicdomain @musicextension @musicfestival @MusicHolster @MusiciansPage @musiclovingguru @musicmavenrsa @MusicMicetro @MusicMyMedicine @musicnacho @MusicPortal @MusicSkins @MusicSkinsVic @MusicTubenl @musikamade @MustangTeam @musthavemenus @MustLoveWine @mustrack @mutaharisst @mutlu20tr @MutualityClub @MuVar2009 @muyifei @Muzachan @Muzition @mvassistant @MvdVeen @mverdemhumano @mverver @mvkumarvijay @mvpombogdi @mwarnersmith @MWCAshley @mwerner022 @MWGEnt @mwpatrick @MWR_Esq @MWreckazRadio @mwrenelt @mwsmedia @Mx7Goldrush @MxNCinema @my_advice @My_Blog_Review @my_dog_ate_it @my_gold @my5pillars @myaaachoo @myadventureguy @myairwaves @MyAirZero @myalli @MyAlt @MyAppleStuff @MyAtlantaFord @MyBabyBeds @MYBELARUS @MyBestCasino @mybestnews @MyBidShack @mybigcrazyworld @MYBLASTCAPBIZ @myblogusa @myBoboBags @MyBrainEnhancer @MYBRAINSELLS @mybrandz @MyBridgesNet @MyCaricature @mycents_today @MyChatToText @mychicagomommy @MyckeyFinns @MyCollegeOnline @MyColorCopies @MyComputerTek @mycontent @mycorporatmedia @mycraigslister @MydaddySaid @mydailydues @mydailywine @mydala @Mydancepro @mydesignpod @MyDFWMommy @mydietchef @myDigitalGadget @MyDigitalSafety @MyDiningSpot @mydogjerry @MyEbisu @myen @MyEntredex @MyEventGuru @myfashionqueen @myfirsthome @myfirstrobot @MyFitCoach @MyFreelancePaul @myfreshberry @myfriendniro @MyFxTrading @MyGamingworldUK @mygetaClue @mygiftsecrets @mygirlcass @MyGizmoRocks @mygreencard @MyGuru @myharleynews @MyHarvestUSA @MyHawaiianHome @Myhealthybreast @MyHipHopRadio @myhipoksearch @MyHubTV @myihotels @MYIL1 @MyIPhonics @MyJobScope @mykieoyler @MyKuteKid @mylender @MyleneDuffy @Myler_ZZP @mylesbristowe @MylesConnor_Fan @MyLifeAsMonster @mylifebydesign @MyLiquorCabinet @MyLogoSource @MyLondonGuide @mylovepoetry @mylv8 @mymaktabaty @mymarketingnews @mymentortools @mymiaomiao @MyMichaelB @MyMillionaire @myMonstera @mymoxxor2009 @mymt @myMuse @mymxm @mynameisbrooke @mynameiskimy @MyndersGlover @myneurotica @MyNewMediaIdeas @MyNextRehab @myniftynappy @myob247 @MYOBTrainer @MyOLCEA @MyOngobee @mypaintedthings @myPause_app @mypeopledb @MyPerfectGift @mypersonalvalet @MyPMExpert @mypoliticalzon @mypoliticscdn @mypowerfulmind @MyPRGuide @MyPrivateBank @myprofiler @mypure @mypusaka @myrealtorkarmen @MyReincarnation @MyRFC @myrollingstocks @MyRonNoeLive @MyrtleBeachSEO @MySacredEnergy @mysalesrep @mysemicondaily @MySexHealthTips @MySexification @mysheernaturals @MYSIMONESTARR @mysitenews @mysleep4sure @mySMBcommunity @mysmilenews @mysocialgroup @MySocialManager @mysocialpolicy @MySOdotCom @MySoulCafe @Mystachoo @MYSTERLINGHOME @mysteryinvest @MysteryMeetBOS @Mysterymessage @Mystic_Jewels @MysticalArt @mysticdave @mysticventures @MyStoryBookLady @MySupercuts @mysystem24 @MytaraE @mytexasgarden @mytexaslege @MyTieNecklace @mytiff @mytimematters @mytinyphone @mytinytots @MyToolbox @mytradingcoach @MyTravelPlan @MyTunez @MYTVBIDS88 @mytweetmark @MyTwitShirt @myvaspace @MyVBO @myvideotalkoz @Myvidsonline @myvinespace @mywe8watchers @MyWackyFamily @MyWayOnNow @mywealthcreated @MYWEBBIEcom @mywebgal @mywebguytaylor @myweblog2u @MyWebYellow @MyWebYellow_com @MyWifesHusband @myworksearch @Mz_DivaStar @mzayfert @MzdhrJourney @Mzlrk @MzJay2u_ @mzjaygee @MzKecia @MzMarketing @mzs @MZSHONDABABII @mzusan @NABAQC @nabihamalik111 @nacampbell @nachbarslieblin @Nachhi @Nachtgedacht @NacolLawFirm @nadaaay @nadeemd @Nadegda @NadiaParker @nadinegerber @nadinekahlon @nadinekf @NadineTouzet @NadiraHaniff @nadjica @nahars @NAHBhome @NAIGlobal @NAILAHISM @nailatty @NaiveAbroad @NakedElephant @Nakedincome @nakedjoker @nakedMAYOR @NAKEDOWNGuitar @NakedPizza @nakeva @nalle09 @namaste_vayo @namasteshopper @NamePlays @nameswing @nametagscott @namethatmovie @NamgoongYon @namowmai @NamsDomestic @namtrok @NAMUAPhysicians @nanaclay21 @nanawilltweet @nancerellababy @nanceyh @nancyadkins @NancyBrown09 @nancyburkebarr @NancyFraser @nancyhunt @NancyJBorgia @NancyLovesPets @NancyLuvsDogs @NancyMancini @NancyMarmolejo @Nancyemcatqq @nancymccord @NancyMyrland @NancyPerez @nancypricer @nancyquinn @nancyrubin @nancyrush @NancysCorner @nancysiniard @nancysperalta @nancytrustin @NancyWard6 @nandaroep @nandinizg @nandolindinho @nanland @nanlive @Nanniil3 @nanoKnowledge @nanopanel @nanotraveler @nansen @Nansouille @naokits @NaomaDoriguzzi @Naomi631 @naomidole @NaomiDowney @naomiestment @naomilever @naomimeran @NaomiTrower @NAOMultimedia @NapervilleLink @Naptownkid @narannual @naratiwas @narmidyear @naro @naromirra @nash8686 @nashis @nashpropst @Nashy @Nasir_Hayat @NasrulEam @Nasty_sweet @Nat_Mich @Nat_TV @nataliajackson9 @natalie_crane @natalie_f @Natalie_Revell @NatalieCrue @nataliegbw @NatalieJayW @nataliemacneil @NataliePeluso @NatalieRuth1 @natalietweets @NatashaAstrid @natashagholo @NatashaHall2005 @NatBourre @nateal33t @NateatFFWD @NateBallard @nateforrestmlm @NateHolland @NatesParty @NateStockard @natfinn @NatGreenOnline @NathalieBonnard @Nathalief @NathanBryce @NathanelMohr @nathanfast @nathangriffiths @NathanielDame @nathanielstott @nathankievman @NathanLatka @nathanreep @nathanstower @NathanWatsonl @nathershlag @Nathon_Willy @NationalBarter @nationalconvey @nationalcorp @NatJsworld @NatliaGarcia @natlsurboard @natrelle @natsukawado @naturago2 @Natural_Tam2l4 @naturalovens @naturalskinHQ @naturcounselor @naturecaretaker @natures_corner @naughtydred @NauraNaoru @NauticalBid @navahk @Naveen6 @Naveenlivein

The Social Media Business Equation

@NavesinkGroup @navetspot @Navigatorin @nawabawaab @NAWBAW @nawlinswoman @NAXART @nayeems @NayeriNan @nazaraliev @nazmisheriff @NB2point0 @nbarron @NBAtwitbunny @nbr1sportsfan @NBridgeVillage @NCDM_DMA @ncmpublishing @ncmusclecar @NCTaxPro @NCVacations @nCynthiS @NDB_DX @ndesp @NDGEditor @NDStoreFixtures @nducoff @Neal_Schaffer @nealcross @Neale_Evolution @nealffischer @NealSchaffer @NealsYardLady @NeatShitILike @NeazMH @NebProd @nectarios @NEDayCrafts @NedFetch @neecie4ou @Need2makemoney @Need4skills @needacfo @needACTIONnow @needgraphics @Needimages @NeedItKeepIt @needletwo @NeedMyCall @needweightloss @NeehalBrito @NeelamPatil @Neelsdl @neelyadkins @neerajtramp @neeshahothi @NeffKnowsPhilly @nehal321 @nehemiaaahhhh @Neifre1 @NeighborGoods @NeighborNorm @neighborsgo @neighborsgobiz @neighbour4all @Neil_Grippa @Neil_Lemons @Neil_Rubenstein @neildevries @neildrewitt @NeilHarkin @neilipearce @NeilKayJones @NeillGibson @neilmarsh @neilminetto @NeilRussellNCK @neilsisson @neiltwitz @NEJobShow @NelidaCapela @nellyulima @NeloSolutions @nelson_brazil @Nelsonmiller @NelsonSola @nelsonwee @NEMoney @nemopsy @nencetti @nene790 @neobion09 @NeoCon @NeoJeric @NeoNebu @Neonester @neongorilla @neoshon @NeoSpire @neptunecityreos @nerDallas @nerdcoaching @nerde @nerdenterprises @nerie_1115 @nerry1984 @Neseret @NESocialMedia @NespressoMakers @net_profit @Net_Strategist @net360sa @net4wiseowls @netaid @NetBizForNewbie @NetBizopps @netbuy @netdoc66 @NetDrifter @netdruide @netflixforporn @NetHosting @NetInfluencers @netjelly @NetKungFu @netmanianz @NetMarketer @netmarketinglv @NETmcgroup @netmillionaire @Netpartner @NetProfitQuest @Netrafic @netsalesman @netsfinest @NetTips4 @NetWaiterOnline @Netwayitalia @NetWealthOnline @netwerkTV @Network24 @Network4dollars @Networkbyrich @networkerplus @Networking_Lini @NetworkingCEO @NetworkingFool @networkingnsd @NetworkingJane @networkingmlm @NetworkingPhx @NetworkingPro @NetworkingSite @NetworkMarketer @NetworkMaverick @NetworkPartners @NetworkPlus @networksurf @networktrump @networkz @networlding @netzender @NetzReport @neudesic @Neunus @neusportas @NeverTheTwains @New_federalists @new_houston_job @new_hustle @new_panda @NewActors @newageaquatics @NewAgeLeadGen @newbie_friend @NewBloggerTemp @NewCenturyCo @newcityofladies @NewCommGlobal @NewDawnCoaching @NewDomainName @NewEdinburgh @newfiction @NewFreeSamples @newgameoflife @newhaitiproject @NewIslandPix @NewJerseyNissan @NewLeadTool @newmarketing30 @NewMediaFreaks @NewMediaGenius @NewMediaMaiden @NewMediaPR @newmediawave @NewMindMirror @newmother @newoctavian @NewOrbOrder @neworldcoaching @NewOrleansAlert @neworleansbars @NewOrleansPrint @NewOrleansRum @NewPcGames @NewPontiac @newproxysites @newraycom @newreachonline @NewRenaissance @NewRichWealth @news_april11 @news_google @News_Of_Hope @NEWS_ONLY_ @news_THoM @NewsAndCoffee @newsaustin @newsbanks @NewsCafeVibez @newschoolresume @NewsCollective @NewsConnoisseur @newsfishuk @NewsFlash707 @newsfly411 @newsgeeks_info @newshourly @newsinfotweets @newsleader @newsletterguru @NewsletterGuy @newsmediaimages @NewsOccult @NewsOfChelsea @NewspaperGrl @NewsQld @newstodayohboy @NewSugar @NewSunNetworks @NEWSUNSEO @NewsUSAUpdates @newswineflu @newswise @NewsWithViews @newt4potus @NewTechBooks @NewTerraLiving @newwaytogrow @Newwebby @newyorkcityvine @newyorkforex @newyounow @Newzworth @nexalogy @nexleveladvisor @Nextel_com @NextHolidaysInd @NextHotThing @NextMashable @nextnewsroom @nfloresy @nflpreseason @nfredericks_AR @nghype @NgKait @ngoanhminh @ngosindia @ngurnik @NHansen @nhaqueoi @NhatPham @nhc1987 @NHDFW @NHHealthyLiving @NHLA_Dave @nhodgescpa @nhprman @NhuQuynh70 @NiagaraCityNews @nialldevitt @niallomalley @NiamhNiCh @NiaPhommavong @NIBAnet @nicadler @nicasalvacionPH @nicehealthy @niceman4u @niceteethnet @niche_building @nicheblogsetup @nichegenerator @NicheIntMktg @nichemktgguru @nichepackage @nicheproduct @nicheworld @NicheWriter @nichobrown @Nicholas_Klein @nicholasfane @NicholasFBray @NicholasJLord @NicholasLoise @nicholaspatten @NicholasVitale @NicholeB128 @Nicholls_Rich @Nick_Hofer @nickcarnes @NickCharles507 @NickDevious @nickemannen @nickgoodrealtor @NickGVIT @nickhealy @nickimayes @nickjungman @NickKellet @NickLaBran @nicklight @nicklogantv @NickPang @nickrick32 @nicksideris @nicktadd @nickwillcox @NickyB28 @NickyFeller @NickyNorah @NickyRamos @nicnatdan @nico_tache @NicoCoetzee @nicolagrayling @nicolaquinn @NicolaRBLClubs @NicolaSciortino @NicolasMas @nicolasmithPR @nicolassuarez @Nicole1515 @NicoleBraden @NicoleDean @nicolefincham @NicoleGwiazdows @NicoleLynnHdz @nicolemarie4 @NicoleMickle @NicoleNeagoe @NicoleRaphael @NicoleRiel @nicolesafley @NicoleScherer @nicolesimon @Nicolettaa @NicoletTlatHP @nicolexxooxx @NicolineDeen @NicollPR @NicoMarquardt @nicorette @Nicotine_Free @NicoWiekenberg @NicPalin @nidaulia02 @ninabrazan @NinaGoya @ninalabs @ninaspringle @Nindira @ninebookshop @Ninefoot @ninepointten @NinjaCavars @ninjateletubbie @NinoMagzoon @NischalShetty @nishanjoomun @nishio @nishit_kotak @NishMoney @NISSANandVW @nitedreamer1 @NiteNation @nitinbarman @NitishP @nitrowz @nittaryo @nittwitsea @nittyGriddyBlog @NIUPRSSA @nivgariani @Nixie @NixiSpeak @nixnew @niyomter @NizamPierre @nj_hbusiness @njchesney @njdevmgr @NJeatsNOW @njection @njfamilymag @njmotocross @njmovingguru @njobryant @njones1920 @NJonesH @NJSocial @njunemployed @nkarnas @nkinnefick @NKYJennifer @nlbctim @NLCotter @NLCSocialMedia @nlinton @nlpconnections @nlplearn @NMACCommunity @NMandelaBay @NMNbiz @nmcandle @NMFFFFD9 @nmfourwheeler @NMSNetwork @NMTAutism @nmyniche @NNChick @nndever @NnennaReviews @NNIFTwits @no_arbitrage @No_More_Day_Job @No1ForexGuru @Noa_Adamsky @NoahMallin @noahrinkle @NoahsArkClub @NoamKrig @noberg @Noblein @NoBullBroker @nocky100 @nocojobseeker @nocoparalegal @NoCoRentals @nocovoip @NocturnalAnimal @NoDebtU @noelbellen @noellebydesign @Noetical @NoFadFitness @nofilnaqvi @NogaYinon @nogueiradiana @NogueraNeill @NOH8Campaign @nohairsports @NoJonas_NoLife @nokl219 @nola_freebird @NOLAComedy @NOLAforFREE @nolan2u @NolanBailey @nolannaidoo @NolaOut @nolf @noluies4me @NoLimitsAsia @nolimitsforme @nologymedia @NoloLaw @nomadicnotes @NomadsLand @nomee @nomorebrains @nomorecellbills @nomoredayjob @NoMoreDedicated @Noname_Face @NONchan15 @NONchan51 @Nongling @noninvasive1 @NonPC_Cartoons @NookyLiverpool @NoosaCrest @NopalJuice @NoPanicAttack @NoPickles @NoPlateaus @norandi @Norbert_Kloiber @norbertorlewicz @nordy389 @NoResultNoFee @norm_noordin @normah1 @NormanAsher @NormanFrenk @NormRiceRealtor @normsrestaurant @norrisebooks @norskealbum @northernstocks @NorthstarAV @nortonsoft @NorwoodDavis @nosalesneeded @nosmoking6days @NoSmokingDay @NotAProBlog @Nostradamus36 @Nostringslovin @not_beige @NotAProBlog @NotEasyToForget @NoteQueen @NotesOnDesign @notforeveryone @NoTieIn @notjustagranny @notmarcocollins @NotNowNigel @notoriousGIG @NouVeauGeek @novaisweb @novamir @NovaScotiacondo @NovaWtloss @NoVegans @NovotelMoscow @novowriting @novrealty @novronturkey @NowdinyGrind @NowDiningVeggy @NowDiningWine @nownen56 @NowHiringJobs @Nowiphones @NowIsTimeForYou @Nowplaying_4u @NowYouBeYou @NPI_purchasing @NPSocialMedia @NRGtheory @NSDFrisco @nsharp506 @NSHconsulting @nshn @nsikub @nistarga @nsnyteinc @NTblog @NTctorworld @NTJ @ntrofounders @ntrotter1 @NTSuperBowl @ntxcopperheads @nubeerja10 @nubeerja3 @nubeerja5 @NucodeMedia @NuCreativTalent @NuDigitalMedia @nudist_resorts @nudistclubhouse @NuErives @NukeMusic @nukonuko_P_ @Numa100 @Numanalnc @numanity @numbuz @numismiami @NunezPR @nuntapol @NuPDataFlow @nur45euro @nuriman08 @nursemom90 @Nurul54 @nurvnumedial @NuSkinNow @Nusoxmedia @nutrexcuritiba @Nutrisystem @Nutrition_00 @Nutritionalfun @nutritiondave @nutritionworld

Acknowledgments

@nutshellcards @nutshellmail @NutTheSquirrel @Nuvota @nuwav @nuwegeskiedenis @nuweigh @nuwestpro @nview @NWJmedia @nwleary @nwolf38 @nwtwebsitescom @NWXBend @nxting @NXTMedia @NYI0112 @NYC_LElgirl @nycareerfinder @NYCBD @nyclq @NYCRedhead @NYCREMilton @NYInjuryLawyer @nykorean @NYLibrarians @nyoyjohn @NYPDretCOP @nyrealtorteam @nywellnessguide @NZAfro @nzjoybelle1 @nzmortgages @nzpis @nztourismblog @NZVel @o_jaimes @o_Ouija @O2AcademyLeeds @o420o @OA_Inc @OAHall @Oak_Arrow @oakweb @oakwoodcleaners @OarFan5 @obamacarelemon @ObamaEpicFail @obamaflipflops @ObamaLifeWatch @obamunism_us @OBankalDeWit @Oberhauser @obesechihuahua @obiokere @object59 @obrubsfelix @ObserverDallas @ObstructedViews @OBTPJewelry @ObviousExpert @OC_DanceNews @OC_Monica @occasi @occultfollower @OccultSecrets @oceanbutterfly7 @oceancitynjnews @OceanDoctor @OceanEchoes @OceanEdu @oceanic_art @Oceanisleinn @OceanMarketingg @OceanParkInnSD @oceanriver @OCGente @Ockumsrazor1 @OCMomActivities @ocp_advisor @OCReport @octalmage @OctalSoftware @Octaviano @Octisage @octofinder @odailydiscounts @OdedNoy @odeolivia @OdessaAhmadC @odgreen19 @odh_00 @odigma @Odin1 @Odinaka @odonnell @OdorZap @odtfc @oenologist_com @oexmaster @offback @offcost @Offdeadline @offering @OfferStrategy @Office_Live @OfficeArrow @OfficeDivvy @OfficeExchange @officemate @OfficeVA @OfficiaLLoStar @OfficiallyPerry @OfficialManish @OfficialManLaws @offlinegoldguru @OfflineWebCoach @offroadwarrior @offshorePT @OffshoreTrans @OffThe_Record @offtheroad @ofhandandsoul @Ofiget @oghme @oghydamara @OGIConference @ogochukwubenson @ogunquitelectrc @OguzSerdar @ohh_la_la @OHHHkevin @OhioBroadcast @OhioDanielle @ohjerika @ohlundonline @ohmannomma @ohmarestrada @ohMariana @OHMichael @OhSo_Jazzie @ohwhatfun @Oil_Leaks @oilsuwit @OInterestMortg @oissubke @oj1 @OjaiVisitors @okazii_gadgets @okaziiro @OKD2Houchen @okkyangga @okmillion @okphotobooth @oksecurityguy @OKtobeWEIRD @ol_paris @OldBieber @OldFunnyJoker @OldMagazines @OldMrBill @oldschoolseo @OldSpice @OldWorldLimited @Oldymoldy @OlegSomin @OleHippie @OlfaSoudani @olgachk @OlindaServices @olitreadwell @olivas34 @olivejpage @oliveoilshop @olivers @olivetiger @oliviamyles @OlivierCarron @ollieandforbes @OllieRelfe @Ollyoco1 @olmertyair @olotwittwoo @olsenspeech @olsonnd @oluhenry @olustewart @OLX_English @olyfilmgirl @olympicchamp2 @OM4Biz @OmarCaf @omarelmohri @OmarHaRedeye @OmariOneal @OmariTaylor @omarjonathan @OmarraByrd @OmegaLocksmith @OmGaGaBitch @omgfaks @omgjes @omgsell @OMGStacks @omgxnehemiah @Ominos @omniadagencyIL @Omnific_Design @OMNIWOW999 @omobono_digital @omettechnologies @OMTMagazine @OMtweets2 @ON_COMM @On_The_Vines @OnAfricanSafari @onbloggingwell @onboardingcoach @OnceUponADollar @ONCEVision @ondineb @One24WeShare @onebayo @onebrightlight @OneCoach @oneDivineSPIRIT @onedroMyaJ @OneEpiphany @oneforty @OneGreenGnome @OneHourHVAC @onehundredjobs @ONeill_Africa @OneLifeGoals @OneLifeNoFear @OneLineWorld @OneMFriends @OneMoreFollower @onepercent @oneplace @onestopefusjon @onestopplus @OneStopWebSolut @onetosix @onetouchwebinar @onfrontpage @OnGoBee @onizhang @online_advrtsng @ONLINE_DOWNLOAD @online_JT @Online_Producer @online_shopper @onlineaction @OnlineAffairs @onlineamplify @onlineavatars @onlinebiz4u @OnlineBizss @onlineBRIDGE @OnlineByDesign @Onlinecasinos4u @onlinechurchof @onlineclickshop @OnlineFantastic @OnlineFilm @onlineguide1 @OnlineIsBetter @onlinelaurens @OnlineLegalNews @OnlineLegitJob @OnlineMarketer8 @OnlineMarktg @onlinemlm_magic @OnlineMoney_ @onlinenomad @onlineprbook @onlinepresse @onlinepro @onlinearts @OnlineResume @onlinesalsa @onlinescooters @Onlinesteve @onlinesuperstar @OnlineSupportMJ @OnlineToolMan @onlinetrainer4u @onlinevents @onlinewithfergy @onlineinexpert @onlineyournight @OnlyAng @OnlyGadgetNews @onlyinbelize @OnlyJokes @onlyneed5 @onlyopensource @onlyTRAINS @OnManiHandomaUn @OnnoHoogendoorn @onocom @Onomatophobic @OnTheMarkDesign @OnViagra @OnYourWeb @OnyxSix @oorion @ootwpizza @OpaVino @OPCGal @OpenBrands @OPENBY_ @OpenInno @openknow @OpenNetworker @openskyproject @OperaCarolina @Operation_VAF @operationcarbon @OperationFollow @OperationOF @OperationSLives @opinioes_best @opphoto @oppsconnect @OprahFan @oprotech @oprteamxbox @OpticSugarMedia @OPTIMALde @optimisation @OptimiseUK @OptimOffice @OptimumEntrep @optin_marketing @OptiOpportunity @OptsumAttendees @Oragenics @OrangeLeadsNews @orangemarketing @oranges43 @orangesprocket @Orbius @OrderFlowTrader @orderyourname @ordinarybee @ordinarycintya @Oregon_Coast @orengadesign @OrenTodoros @OrettaNorris @orezzero @Org9 @organic_beauty_ @Organic_PR @organicconnect @OrganicEats @organicfoodbar @OrganicGroov @organicguru @OrganicJOOS @OrganicMeds @organictatay @Organized1Chaos @OrganizerSandy @orgKrishnamurti @OrinVoice @orioloriol @orion_case @OrionPartners @Orkut_Com @orlandoelbert @OrlandSquare @OrmondocaC @OrmusGoddess @ornerier @OROSSI23 @Orrin_Woodward @orthostichy @osakasaul @osboneco @OscarBaron @oscarbehrens @OscarDavila @oscarfalcon @OscarLuppi @oscarmagar @oscartr @oseme22 @osemekang @osheaslasvegas @OScardSebel @Osnick @OSsarahlundy @ostaz4u @OSUscooterGRAD @oswaldoforty @otakubrewing @otbthink @OTCRPTR_AndreaS @OTCRPTR_AntDWal @OTCRPTR_DevMind @OTCRPTR_DuffStk @OTCRPTR_Emerald @OTCRPTR_FLYONTH @OTCRPTR_HotStoc @OTCRPTR_Nixon48 @OTCRPTR_RichStk @OTCRPTR_SavvySt @OTCRPTR_StockAl @OTCRPTR_StockGl @OTCStockPro @OTCstockTrader @OTCVault @OteroJC @othl1 @othmani_imadoo @OtimoLLC @otiscollier @Otto_R @ottugui @OuaisPapa @OUITStore @OUKristyn @Oumiro @ounascloset @our3day @ourbizdeal @OurFamilyWizard @ourladyofashes @ourmancanberra @ourmoney @OurNEWSCafe @ourparents @ourscotland @OurTownMagazine @OurTripVideos @ourvemmateam @Out_of_clay @outcropcom @outdoors_r_us @outdoorsblog @OUTEXphoto @OutgrowingQB @outilammi @Outlaw_Media @OutlawsTeam @outofblue9 @OutOfYourRut @outpost54 @OutRankAll @OutsideInThink @outsidervocals @OutSmarts @outsourcinguniv @OutTheBoat @OutToOwn @OVER_TON @OverDelivery @OverMoonJewel @Overstock @overstockbuyer @overthrownkings @overyy @OviedoFlorida @Ovind24 @ovrdrv @owcf @owenallen @OwenAnthonys @owendbanks @OwenGreaves @OwenOlo @owensddb @Owenshi @OwlsLounge @Own_Your_Future @OwnAsstLvngHome @OwnOtis @oxcom @OXIMAhomemade @OxsteinLabs @oxylus @oykusicakkanli @oyushche @ozaki0920 @ozdrivebuyz @ozestretch @ozimozi @OzITJobs @Ozwerk @OzyTribe @ozzipete @P_Belcher @P_V_Vacances @P00ki3sfknrude @P0TUS @P3t3rTl @PaavoKettunen @pablo1304 @pabloforavantt @PabloHernandezO @PabloPostigo @pabloskiff @pablosolano @PacCatchCOO @pacharrrin @PachinoPapes83 @PacificCove @pacificIT @pacificosunset @PacingPete @PackedBags @Paco_Carreno @PacSun @PaddedCellPro @PaddingtonPanda @paddocktalk @PaddoStacy @paddyosplaines @PadraigMcKeon @padschicago @padsha @PAEMCL415 @PageOneProfits @pagepropeller @PageRankSEO @pdraairm @PailKhe @paid_surveys1 @PaidMillionaire @PaidSurveysCDN @paige_oneill @paige661 @paigemccoysmith @paigetrist @pain_relief_33 @PainlessLiving @PaintballSkills @paintchip @paintermommy @PainterSydney @PaintingDenver @paintingsydney @PaintingWTwist @PajamaCEO @pakkoidea @Pakpandir @pakseri79 @Palidan @PalinBacker @PalindromeTweet @PalladioBeauty @palmendras @palmeralan @palmerreuther @paltex9 @Pam_Carroll @Pam_Ivey @Pam_Phillips @pam6cee @Pamajama99 @pambegnaud @pambrossman @pamcain @pdamma @pamelaanastasia @PamelaJMyers @PAMELAnotpam @PamelaWood @PamH53 @pamhett @pamkapur @pamlester @PamMktgNut @PamRagland @PamSlaterPrice @Pamyleeh @pan_ping @PANACEAPARTS @panderich @pandeypunit @PandoraBing @panegro @Panic_Relief @panicattackinfo @panicroom1 @PankajKedia @PankajMuthe @pankymathur @PanoramaRick @panser02 @pantiesdotcom @pantyOpanties @pantyOpantyO @paola_io @paolicelli @paolomajo @PaoloRicci @Papachote @papanoon @PaparazziDallas @paparazzo504 @papertigersoft @papodehomem @Pappadeaux @PappasitosTXMEX @Pappiart @PAProperties @paradisepure @parado888 @paragseo @paralisa2006 @paramendra @paranormalradio @Parasec @ParasolCreation @parent911 @parentcoaching @Parents_Talk @ParentsConnect @ParentsEduChild @ParentStream @parentwin22 @ParisConnect @PariseCatering @parishotel_sale @ParisJordan @parkbrees @ParkerMic @ParkinsonPD @parnellk63 @parnoaja @Parse3 @particles @Partnerpedia @party_pix @Partyaficionado @partyfavorgifts @partypmToronto @PartyRuegen @parvez20077 @Pascal_Gagnon

173

The Social Media Business Equation

@PascalSijen @PascoREOs @pascy @Pasmuz @Pass4sureIT @Passageyachts @passeos @passionate4life @passionexplorer @PassionGirlcom @passionration @Passive_Income_ @PassportIndiana @passportsfast @PassTheBar @pastafaris @Pastor_Pilao @PastorCortes @pastordemetrio @pastorrj09 @PastorYolanda @Pat_Lorna @PatAlexander @PatBluth @patches219 @patdoyle @patersonreos @PatFlynn @patgage @patgrahamblock @pathhelpdotcom @pathuston @pathwaypr @patingow @PatMeehanPA @PatNarciso @PatOBrienChevy @patowings @PatPriceInfo @PatriceMalloy @Patricia_7Moore @PatriciaHughes @PatriciaLabelle @PatriciaMartin @PatriciaMcCurdy @PatriciaPorn @PatriciaRossi @Patrick_Johner @Patrick_Parise @PatrickAbrar @PatrickAhler @PatrickAnna @PatrickBlessing @patrickdixon @PatrickDriessen @patrickghoward @PatrickMcTigue @PatrickQCC @patrickreyes @patricksingson @PatrickTiew @patrickwblack @PatriotCommons @PatriotConnect @PatriotJournal @PatriotQuotes @PatriotsFunClub @patrizio56 @PatSFitz @Patsiblogsquad @PatSikora @PatsyBailey @patthew @pattiebyron @pattigenko @pattijlarsen @PattiKeating @pattirahn @pattonservices @PatTravisChT @patty_herrera @pattyanniek @Pattycam @pattyfantasia @pattyfarmer @pattyonovak @PattySexy @PattyTownley @pattywoodley @patwan @patweber @patyta_ @PatZahn @pauaangel @Paul_Appleyard @Paul_Cole @Paul_Coomans @Paul_davis_4 @Paul_de_Jonghs @Paul_Gordelo @Paul_Holgorsen @paul_houle @Paul_J_L @Paul_Liburd @Paul_Majchrzak @Paul_Pleus @paul_steele @paul_wong @Paul4PureC @paula134 @PaulaBrett @PaulaBruno @paulafrye @paulalexgray @PaulAlford @PaulaMBHall @PaulandJess @PaulaRecruiter @paularojas @PaulatVBS @paulbarron @PaulBHegarty @paulboutin @PaulBParsons @PaulBritPhoto @paulbuijs @PaulBurdett @paulcastain @PaulCMartins @PaulColes @PaulConradSF @pauldav1d @PaulDawsonSr @Pauleichberger @PaulEntin @Paulette_Bethel @PaulFileman @paulfragermana @paulgerst @paulgoulding1 @paulhaynes @Paulien_H @PauliinaMakela @PaulineLange @paulineprice @Paulivar @pauljendrasiak @PaulKadillak @PaulKirchoff @PaulKlaszus @PaulLasaro @PaulMathiesen @paulmcarthur @PaulMcdowell @PaulMel @paulmerriwether @paulmess @paulmorphychess @PaulNJohnsonJr @PauloFava @paulostudio2002 @pauloverstreet @paulplantt @paulponna @PaulPorterShow @PaulPortugal @PaulRadkowski @PaulRahmat @PaulREdwardsJnr @paulrjdavich @PaulSchwend @PaulSegreto @paulshively @PaulSloane @paulsteinbrueck @Paultechman @paultharper @paulthemusician @paultillydesign @paulvharris @PaulWorswick @PaulyMortadella @paulzag @paumier1 @Paverlayer @pawmarks @Pawscorp @PayDayLoanHelp @PayerPlayerNow @payitfast @payitforwardz @PaylessInsider @payplayman @Payroll_Funding @paysco @pbadstibner @PBailey1073 @pbarbanes @PBCS_Uptown @pbelyeu @pbrannigan @pbsalestraining @pbwordpress @PC_Franchise @PC_Wargames @PCBHaitiConcert @pcburch @pchaney @pcharbonneau21 @PCHFoundation @pcianfrano @pcjholdings @PCLuxHomesTour @PCoisman @PComputerDoctor @pcoschallenge @pcowanatl @PCPassionistas @pcrampton @pcrisk @PCS_CLUB @PCSpeedGuy @pcvisitsoftware @PDahl @pdmaxwell @PDMMediaInfo @pdoncom @PDPowell @pdraper91 @pdsouza @pdwholesale1 @PDXfX @pdxschroeder @PeabodyOrlando @PeaceAndWisdom @Peacelily @PeaceNicole @PeaceQuotes @peachpittv @PeachSanchez @Peak_Potentials @PeakAccounting @peakenergy @PeakOilNews @PeakT @pearlms1974 @pearlrevolution @peasandbananas @peddlewin @pedrobelize @pedrocaramez @PedrodeVicente @pedroelrey @pedroheimlich @PedroMaia @pedroramirez @PeepliLiveFilm @peerform @pegahorn @PegasiEvents @PeggyMcColl @PeggyShirrel @PEGUEROSqro @peiert @peitarobinson @PekkaPuhakka @pelpina @PembiRocks @pempu @pen9u1n @PenangCity @PendragonUK @PenHandler @penmydream @PennBarryVP @Penny_Investors @pennycrosson @PennyHaywood @pennypinchers @pennypixie @pennyramacom @pennyrunners @pennystkplayers @PennyStockAce @PennyStockFever @Pentalog @PenteGroup @PENUNGGANGBADAI @people__string @PeopleAdvisor @PeopleClues @peoplemaps @peoplereport @peoplesalmanac @PeopleSearch125 @PeopleSmartz @PeopleString @pepe7 @pepecuesta @pepperlowell @PepperTheDog @pepsiYOSUMO @perceptionweb @PerfectBodyPlan @PerfectedLove @PerfectJulia @perfectlyv @PerfectPitchPR @PerfectSEOPages @Performable @PerformanceTips @performics @PerkettPR @PerlsOfWisdom @PerlStalker @permission_syd @pernillan @perrasc19 @PerrieMenoPudge @PerryaWilson @PerryBlock @perrytemps @perryvanbeek @PersianSlangs @Person1233 @PersonaAffairs @personalbrander @PersonalBrandPR @PersonalBrandUK @personaljaz @PersonhoodCA @PersonhoodFL @personified @PersuasionTips @perth140 @pervidel @PervyVageat @pesajian @petahpham @petartishev @PetDepot @pete_kistler @pete_montgomery @Pete_Warrior @petebray @peteevans @PeteHall @peteinoz @petekane @petekelly21 @PeteMc2001 @PeteOlsen @Peter_ebizQ @Peter_maas84 @peter511 @PeterAHolst @PeterArceo @PeterBeckers @peterclayton @petercoppola @petercutforth @peterfrancis @peterfreund @Peterg1234 @peterhartl @peterhough @peterjabraham @PeterLang @peterlocuratolo @peterlutz @peternity @peterparkerpics @PeterPek @peterramsden @PeterReitano @PeterScotts @petersrin @PetersServices @petersthoughts @PeterWestlund @peterwillo @peterwilm43 @peterwink @peterworsfold @petezdanis @petinsurance101 @PetiteAntoin @PetitePeople @petlover817 @petmopolitan @Petra_Berg @PetraJohansson @PetraKohlmann @Petre_Bogdan @petrumpaolo @Petrus88 @Pets_Blog @PetSmart @petsugarglider @petzru @pezholio @pfinane @pfminy @pfmonaco @PFWRIGHT @pg5150 @pgarzon @PGauthier_RI @PGCountyRealtor @pgiblett @pgiles1 @pgoss @pgpbcl @pgready @pgscoeby @pguptadelhi @PhaedraStock @phamstapher @phamthanhthao @Phans2 @phantom_kw @PharmaTwits @PhaseWare @phataya @Phatprovider @pheadrick @PheasantPhun @PHenry1775 @PheromoneKing @Phil_Lauterjung @Phil3ev @phil90x @philainsworth @PhilanthropyCFP @PhilBellamyInc @philbilbrough @PhilGerb @Philgloire @PhilHanCNN @philhiller @PhilipDonahue @philipjd_nv @philippedo @philippineLife @philippmuller @PhilipsOralCare @philipvanzyl @PhilJ @PHILJAC @PhilJKowalski @PhilJohncock @philColeman @phillcross @Phill_Durrant @Phillip_Beacon @phillipabiggs @phillipperry @PhillipRather @Phillips_mktgrp @PhillipsRouse @PhillipTanzilo @philly51 @PhillyLandShark @PhilMazo @philmutrie @PhilMyers1 @philrandall @PhilReinhardt @philrichards @philseneker @PhilSnelgrove @PhilStratton @PhilTerrett @PhilTing @philveksel @philwblackwell @phirz14 @phlattrascal @phlexi @phocusNgrind @PhoenixHart @phoenixnai @phoenixrei @Phoernicia @phoinix21 @PhonAppsReviews @PhoneBuddies @phonepowerpam @phones_cell @phonomenon @PhoQueen @photo_joe_va @photoalliance @photoandvector @photocopied @PhotogNews @photographix501 @photographywiz @PhotoLeoknee @PhotoLeonne @photomerchant @Photoshopinaday @PhotoshopSugar @photoskull @photovirginia @PhottixJournal @phrommin @PhuketGayResort @phuvidu @PhxEvents @PhxFamousDaves @phxgroup @phxmission @phyl6443 @Phyllis_Fruit @PhyllisDoyle @phylliskhare @phyllismufson @phyneballs @Physiotraining @Pia_Pinaar @piabo @piahogberg @plblogger1 @pic_pal @PiccolaDowling @picfresh @pickensplan @PicksForLife @PicosClark @piece2dot0 @pieceofgreen @piedpiper77 @piepier @piercedanielle @Pierferdinando @Pierian_Media @Pierre_Paperon @Pierrebellerose @PierreDenier @pierreysrevraz @piersoncci @pif43 @pigandpeacock @pigeonwisdom @piggiesandpaws @PiglooMegacorp @PiKaHsSo @pilarwish @pilot77 @pimplomat @PimpMyKicks @PimpMyWorld @pinarsan @PinBud @PineappleHero @pingpompom @PingPongHua @pinheirodasilva @Pinitos @pink_connect @PinkDeb @pinkempowerment @pinkginghamom @pinkgurlz @pinkluna84 @PinkPassportSoc @PinkPoundUK @PinkSlipMixerLV @PinkStinksUK @PinkTreeMediaCo @PinkyAlmada @pinnaclehills @Pinny @pinomauriello @pinotblush @pinoydeal @PinoyNetwork @pinoytutorial @pintara3 @piohefner @piotrbut @piotrkrzyzek @pipelineb2b @Pipes4Mike @PiratePlanet @pirhchy @pirulitu @piskopatski @PiSocialMedia @pistonandrotary @Pitch_Doctor @pitchedin @Pitts_Wines @pivotaltracker @PixelsPhotog @pixie_play @pixie1212 @pixie658 @pixiehornet @pixldinc @pixtale @pizzahut @PizzaMarktplace @PJA64X @pjaquinto @PJCwasHere @PJfletch @pjnoonan @pkahncpa @pkolenick @PlaceatPerrys @plagiarismstoday @plake777 @Planalytics @PlanetBritney @PlanetChantelle @planetnetwork @PlanetOfHealth @planetprotect @PlanetSelf @PlanetWaterLive @planMG @planning_prodj @PlanoOnline @plant_trees @plantwars @plantweb @platepledge1 @PlatesNapkins @PlatinumBill @PLATINUMHOTEL @PlatinumListing @plattchai125 @PlattCollege @Platypus11 @platzpirsch @Playadel_Carmen @playbigstocks @Playbingo365 @playderecordCLB @playfulgenius @playgrounddad @playrdotorg @playrecrds @Playsintraffic @playtongits @PlayzureDynazty @plazamayormed @plb8156 @pldsolutions @PleasureEllis @PleasureNews @Pleasuresdudes @pleiter @PlentyDiamond @plibb @PlinkingReality @plish @PlongeeAuQuebec @PLProTravellers @plrmaven

Acknowledgments

@PLRrights @plubbo @pluckyblond @pluckypea @PluggedInLawyer @PLUGGEDMAGAZINE @plugola @plumjava @pluralsight @pluser005 @plxtransformer @pm1992 @PMADesign @pmardian @pmol @pmsolutionsaust @PN_DCG @PocketHistory @PocketSmith @podcampaz @podcastdoors @PodCmpCleveland @podscms @PoeCommunicate @PoemVidz @PoesiasGospel @Poetrymoments @POGODABY @PogojoEmma @Pogonina @pogproperties @Point_PR @pointlessbanter @PointRoberts @poker_starting @PokerAdore @Pokerbets @PokerGremlin @pokerman80 @pokernight @PokerOnline4u @pokerpr @pokerpromo @PokerReview @PokerScholar @pokertastic @Pokerullz @pokiesonline @polcika @Polekatz @Policani @PolicySettle @Polignostix @politicalcrunch @PoliticalFools @PoliticalGFX @politicalhound @politicaljokers @PoliticalStupid @politicsforce @Politwitt @Pollin8theWeb @PollNOLA @POLOELEGANCI @pololuvsU2 @pom_love_usa @pom101 @pomahony2 @POMOCreate @PomodoroMutti @ponderyourpath @ponmayil @poochiesan24 @POOLBUSINESSE3 @POOLCENTER @POOLSOCIALPOLIT @poonamsagar @PoorRed @POPBASS @PopcornSodaFlic @PopCultureBuzz @PophamBeachME @poppendijn @popqwqmnmn @poptimal @PopularCulture_ @populartwit @PorchLightMA @porkbarrelbbq @porkchoptweets @porn_sex @PornForBibles @pornprom @PornSexDating @PortableFlack @PortaldCoaching @porterairlines @portiaballard @portiaperez @portnik @Porturtle @Posdijk @PoshByJones @POSHhotel @PoshNailSpa @posimperative @PositionKing @PositiphLOLA @positiveKristen @PositiveRich @positivetourism @positivetravel @post_free_ad @Postbrief @PostBuster @PostCheckOut @PosterPrinter @posterxxl @postitos @pot___head @potdebates @potusa @PoundersGrill @poundincome @poundpitz @POW49 @power4life @powerblog @powercooking @Powercouch @powerdee22 @PoweredBytheSun @powerfollow @PowerForex @PowerfulHER @PowerfulSystems @PowerfulTeam @PowerJab @PowerMarketers @Powermat @PowerPointPres @powerpoole @PowerRead @powersellerpro @PowerSellingMom @powershoppers @PowersSuccess @Powerstarxyz @powertwitter @powervsforce1 @PowerWomenMag @Powwownow @pozycjonerka @PozzieMusic @ppalme @pparris9 @pphilp @Ppl_B4_profit @pprobinson @pprothe @ppstrat @ppuppal @pqp_pqp @PR_Diva26 @PR_Guy_Vic @PR_ShopTalk @PR_Writer @pR0M0TRAiNS @PrabhakarSri @Prabhjot_Kaur @PracticalExpert @pradeephypnosis @PragueBob @prairiemama @pramitjnathan @PranaliVichare @PranaRX @pranmaz @praprisri @Prashant_0734 @praso2006 @PRAStaffingATL @prateek @prateekagarrwal @PrateekThapar @PRAtraining @pratyushagarwal @prav_k @prawfeed @Praxis_LA @PrayagBangalore @Prayer_Network @PrayForGod @PrayForJapan @PrayMaddyMcCann @prBote @PRBristolblog @PRbyKelly @prchicago @PRDivaRach @PreAtlas @PreChannel @preciseinternet @PrecisionTime @PreCruiseParty @Predictband @preetistore @preetizbac @prefdesign @prefixmag @preguntatodo @Preiya_Pri @Prelaunch_Zone @PremEjacDoc @PremeWritez @PreMiddleAge @PremierCG @Premiercruises @premiumformat @PremiumMarket @PremiumPassport @prepaidlegalopp @prepayasyougo @prescotttourism @PrescriptionSG @presidentsmith @PresleyHandW @PresqueIsleLib @Press8 @PressAbout @pressdr @pressnet @PressNewsRoom1 @pressreleases @PrestigeTax @Preston777 @PrestonEhrler @prestonpardy @PrestonShamblen @pretapourtea @PrettyFinay @Pretzelmaker @prezi @prezwebdesigns @PrfessorJen @PRFilms_Shahira @prgeek @PRGUY2 @PRguyonline @pricebeaters @PriceBiter @PriceTravel @Prietiitah @PrimaCare @primaryaffect @PrimaryGroupinc @PrimerMedia @primeview @primoseats @Prince_Majid @princess_misia @Princess_Tmo @princessbowie @princesslons @princesstimetoy @princesswendel @princetown09 @princevio @print_house @print_xpert @print24_de @printdaddy @PrintEquip4Less @PrintHub @printsbyapex @PrintxPressUtah @PriorityMGT @PrisciGomes @PriscyllaDuarte @Prismopaco @PrisonReformMvt @PriteshGupta @PRitzaDFW @PRIVADAVS @private_wealth_ @PrivateKVO @privatemembers @privateschools @PrivateTeacher @priya_banglore @priyankapamnani @PrizeDrawsUK @PRjeff @prkworld @PrlantaJewelry @prmd @PRMediaBlog @prnewsus @Pro_SharePoint @PROACT_ive @ProAdPlacers @problogg @processpayroll @ProColour @procopy @productent @productful @productionguy @ProductSampler @ProducTweet_01 @productweet_02 @Productweetity @ProfBrendi @ProferoSolution @profesionapunch @ProfessionIMojo @ProfessorGary @ProfilerPatB @ProfileZones @Profilwerkstatt @profiness @Profit_Master @profitable_blog @ProfitHere @ProfitHouse @ProfitMarketing @ProfitOnlineNow @ProfitRank @profits4uonline @profittool @profootballref @profyspace @programmingns @ProgramWithJan @ProGrowthTEAM @proimer @Project7 @projectguy @ProjectSocializ @projectvalhalla @projectzangezi @projektlotse @ProLifeBlogs @prolire @promenda @promena @promeneroy @PrometheusIV @PROMIS @ProMLMTrainer @Promo_Beast @promodan @Promofix @promolotto @Promote_YourBiz @promoteabook @PromoteLinkedIn @PROMOTER2010 @PromoteUGuru @Promotion_News @promotionstube @proorgfinder @prootime @ProperLongboard @property_domain @propertybookman @propertyhustler @PropertyMagnate @PropertyMatters @propertyontv @PropertyToSell @propertytribe @propgoluxury @prophetesstli @propinvestors @ProPlayersRealT @propmarketer @PropMaverick @proresearch @ProResume @ProsConsMovie @prosourceSEO @ProsperbyDesign @ProsperityMedia @ProsperityWhiz @prosperouswomen @prosperpreneurs @prospertxhome @ProSpirity @prosstarprofits @protectauto @ProtectRite @Protegebranding @proteus72 @protoplazm @providepeople @Provision3D @provokecreative @prozentegeber @Prozestra @PRPalPaul @PRPigeon @PRresearchSthlm @PRSA_MD @PRSAFinancial @prsnalcaretruth @PRSoapbox @PRspective @prstini @PRTGURU @PRTlovely @prtodd @PRTomShort @PRToTheTrade @PruComm @PrudenceCG @prumos @PRraw @psanjaymenon @PSAnney @psfnick @PsicotecJobs @PSMOnlineRadio @psogge @psol_sergipe @PSonlineBiz @Psoriasis1 @pspinw @PSRegina @psusallc @psywalkofstars @PsychicDentist @PsychicHolly @PsychicRegistry @Psycho_Ex_Movie @PsychodudeCom @Psychogym @PsychoPuckLady @Psyqe @ptcyclist @PTGrouponHartfd @ptmartinez @PTNPokerSponsor @ptsaldari @pub44 @public_funds @public_image @Public_News @PublicAnger @PublicDatabase @PublicGoodPR @PublicityGuru @PublicityHound @PublicityQueen @publicrecords4u @publicrelate @PublicSavings @publicwords @PubliGestion @PublishingGuru @publishover40 @PUBLISIDE @pubsterjosh @PuckGruenenwald @pueblocomputer @puffaddering @puffclean @pulido2010 @pullmarketer @pulsdJFK @pulse2dotcom @pulsedirect @pumpintt1 @PumpkinPelfrey @PunchMediaotca @punitastrologer @punkrockHR @puppetsholic @PurAman_Health @PurdueMensHoops @Pure_Hoodia @pure_ink @Pure_Truth @PureAveda @PureBarreNBMV @PureChuffed @PureDriven @puregroove_org @PureMagazineDFW @PuReMonKeY @PureNaturalDiva @PureshBeauty @PURIA_Spa @purplehayz @PurpleRosa @PurposeDirected @PurseDogTV @pursue_riches @Pursuitist @PushbackWines @pushboundaries @PushGapRadio @pushrealestate @PUSPEM_NGO @putitinyourears @PuttingEdge_QC @PuttingEdgeBar @puzzlepieced @pvesey @pvthotieschool @pweiderholm @pwilson @pwmcmahon @pwonders @Pyeman @PygmalionWeb @PYMConnect @PymeActiva @PYMLive @PYNcompany @pyracashbang @pyramidsonmars @pyrmontvillage @pzadearmasq @Q_Consulting @q3technologies @qaa4032 @qanetworkers @qapacity @qayang @QDI0 @qdME @QEDbaton @QI_Business @QianaaRathburn @QiGong_Healer @QinaBrand @qlcoach @qofsevens @qoswhit @qpheVe @qqyuan @qsullivan198 @quadir386 @QuadMedia @QuailHillEstate @QuakerQuotes @QualityHerbals @qualitylinks @Qualitytoys @QuaneshiaHolden @quaninte @QuantumAttract @QuantumKnight @quantumtouch @QuantumTouch_GS @quapet @Quaranj @QuarterJap @Quartz164 @Qubits_Toy @QueCEUs @QueenBeforTila @queenmarypat @QueenofJoy @QueenSchmooze @QueenTips @QuesaDYas @QuestarSoftware @questionswork @quetzel2012 @Queue61 @quickcomedy @quickenloans @QuickInbox @quicksparx @quickstartnl @QuickTellPro @quickw0man @quierounpiso @QuietAgent @Quiethits @QuillQuasar @Quimichen @quinceandquilt @Quinnandco @Quirpo @QuitSnoring @quitsville @QuitToGrowRich @QuizOfTheWeek @Quizzle @QuoteBooks @quotedb @quotejoy @quoteshash @QuotesInternet @QuoteStore @QuoteSuccess @qvassist @qwerty98311 @Qworky @R_Computers @R_I_C_A_R_D_O_F @r_riquelmeh @R_Wullie @r0derik @r2tweet @R3FitWorld @r3n3h3ln @r3trosteve @RA_Enterprise_ @RA_Gray @rabattfuchs @rabbitrich443 @racertodd @RaceShout @RACEspiloy @RaceTraks @rachadaswd @rachaeleyisrael @RachAllen @RachEden @Rachel_H128 @rachel_rcw @Rachel_V_Smith @Rachel1019 @RachelBagby @rachelflavin @rachelgurulong @RachelHolmes @RachelKellar @rachelkhanna @RachelLavern @racheloconnell @racheloreilly @RachelP728 @rachelpr @racheldr98 @RachelResnick @RachelWillisUK @RachePerlmutter @rachnajain @rachparker @RacingExperts @raczilla

@RadarEddie @radekstangel @radhyka @radiance_dream @Radio_8IX @Radioblogger @RadioDash @radiofamousdanz @RadioFreeFrisco @radiogagakk @radiomystic @radioneilly @radiopotatol @Radiospectives @radmilovitch @raduboncea @RaeganHill @RaelianMovement @raetedy @RaffleMansion @rafiqque @RAgainstSlavery @rageandpride @Rageblog @Raghavsharmaone @ragmanist @ragythomas @rahimaina @rahulrakesh @rahulsingh29 @rahumadas @rahweezyy @Rain_wheel @rainbow_phoenix @rainbownichole @RainbowUSA @RainCollection @Raindawg @raine_ok @rainee_rai @Rainer_Seiffert @RainerGS @RainierDigital @RainMakerResume @rainmakertom @RainNutrition09 @Rainwave @raj555 @RajaFranklin @Rajasekharan @Rajat_Sinnha @RajeevSamtani @Rajeshshen @RajinderYadav @rajivWORLD @rajk3657 @RajRajasri @rajshekhart @rakeshcoms1 @rakhtar @RalfDahler @ralfnoel @RallyGeek @RalphArcamone @RalphCanon @ralphclaxton @ralphdapromoter @RalphealJackson @RalphieReport @ralphjanisch @RalphKooi @ralphmuhler @RalphNapolitano @RalphOWalker @RalphPici @RALPHPROMOTER @RalphSerrano @ralphtalmont @RalphYoder @ram3366 @ramcnn @rameshng @Ramikantari @RamilDebo @RamirCamu @ramkrissh @Ramona_Werst @ramonap @Rams704 @Ramsestencil @ramseyric @ranaahmed124 @rancov @Randall_Wofford @randallevenson @RandallJon @RandDMagazine @RandiRummer @Random_AF @Random_Flyness @RandombyteCom @randomlost @Randomnacity @RandomPmoreFanS @Randowski @randrblog @Randy_Duermyer @Randy_Gage @Randy_Thompson @randybauch @RandyCodolski @randydrummond @randyeagar @randyfmyers @randyfritz @RandyInman @randylewiskemp @randysavagevo @RandySchrum @randyselzer @randyslabey @randysnotes @RandyViperRKO @RandyWhitesBBQ @randyyoung @ranganathanc08 @rangelie @rangelim @RaniiDiamonds @ranjitha_milo @rankingsite @RankinReyes @RankmarkGolf @RanShanTelecom @RaoulFOX5 @raovallab @RapidBI @RapidPropertySo @rapidsuccessnow @RapidWebDomains @rappingyogi @RapportIntl @Raquel16 @raquelbrandim @RaquelCortazar @raquelcortesmm @RaquelP1073 @RareCat @rarelydull @RareRevolution @rariryru @rarobinson @RascalTweets @RashadHouston @rashmi19kiran @rashton2004 @RasmusAuction @rasnas @raspberryswrl81 @Raspee @Rastataco @RatedGRomance @RATES_BY @rationalmd @rattanasamy @ratusafirar @raulbarattini @ravedelay @RaveenaMusic @ravengurl65 @ravennagolf @RavenOn @RavensandRubies @ravensorb @RavenSu @ravichandranbr @ravimohanv @ravingredhead @RaviTangri @rawbodybar @RawC @rawfooddietfan @RawJuiceGirl @rawrocksfood @raxadesign @raxlakhani @ray_dietrich @ray_harries @RayBriscard @Raych_M @raycool1 @RayDisplays @RayFenster @raygill1 @RayGoldberg @rayhansen @rayhigdon @raykwong @raylance @RayLinDairy @RayMcBerry @Raymondavich @raymondbae @RaymundoMonge @RayneRebecca @RayProsek @rayuotila1 @raywatts @RaywBriscard @RayzDesignz @RazChorev @razi00780 @razvan_popescu @rbacal @rbakercnn @rbarlowsadler @rbcook @rbfdds @rblackmanonline @rbludworth @rbuscemi @rc_pg @RCAM @rcandeias @rcarpenter51 @rcborer @RchBe @RChenette @RCHomes @rchristopher @rcl4rk @Rcmzinvestments @rcpatterson @rcthegreatblog @RCWilley @rcyoung87 @rd1776 @RD71 @RD77 @RDBConcepts @RDCushing @rdeclermont @rdelrio @RDeRouchey @rdfrench @rdrean @Rdusenbery @RdyBenGoss @Re_Animator @RE_Braintrust @Reaburn @reachbranding @reachconnection @ReachNathalie @ReachYourMax @ReadingWriter @readvocate @reagan_2 @reags @RealEstate @Real_Ent @Real_Eslate @real_estate_ad @real_time_llc @Real_WeightLoss @realartistship @RealBabyFood @realbrilliant @realchange2012 @realCoryWaters @realcuzcletus @RealDavidJohn @RealeFlix @RealEst8Tweets @RealEstate__ @realestate_book @RealEstate_Site @RealEstate_TV @RealEstate2050 @realestateasset @RealEstateBabbl @RealEstateCast @realestatehub01 @realestateisgr8 @realestatemke @RealEstateSwish @realestatevidyo @Realfunmaza @RealHomeLogic @RealisticBiz @realitydigital @RealJackCherry @RealJanF @RealJimmiStone @RealKymRobinson @reallybuffalo @reallyleila @ReallyShecky @ReallySocial @ReallyWho @RealMadridCR9 @RealMarketer @realmatrix @RealmNationSA @realmsdev @RealPropFinder @RealRindo @realSEM @realsource @RealtorAngieP @RealtorResidual @RealtorRyan @RealtorsForPets @RealTweetTank @realtyflipper @RealtyMarket @realtypartner09 @RealtyScholar @RealViralVideos @RealVoiceMedia @RealWaterNow @RealWaystoEarn @realworldweb @ReanaSousa @reapr @reasonapplied @REBATHSCV @rebaverrall @rebecaknowles @rebeccacheng @RebeccaEmin @rebeccaesparza @RebeccaforReal @RebeccaGWilson @RebeccaHabel @RebeccaMichaels @rebeccanoelle @rebeccaolkowski @RebeccaQuinn @RebeccaRuck @RebeccaSorrells @rebeccataylorpr @RebeccaThompson @rebeccawoodhead @rebeccawoods @rebecka7 @RebekahNale @RebekahRadice @rebelbrown @RebirthBB @Rebja @reBreastCancer @rebrivved @ReBuild_homes @ReBuildingYou @recblogs @recdirectory @recentissue2day @recessionprfmkt @RecessionRemedy @REChamp @rechargelife @recipconsult @recipescorner @RECLAIMEDTHREAD @ReclaimPD @recordingguru1 @recordrep @recoveringlazy @Recruit_Leaders @Recruit121_SAP @RecruiterDanB @RecruiterEarth @recruiterkaren @RecruiterKiel @recruiterlady @RecruiterMaster @RecruiterNinja @Recruiterpoet @Recruiterreqs @RecruiterRyan @recruithire @RecruitingBlogs @RecruitingDaily @RecruitingH2H @Recruitingsft @RecruitingXpert @recruitmentagen @RecruitmentFirm @RecruitmentProf @RecruitTrainer @Red_autumn @red_elvis @Red_Rose2 @red57wolf @redballer76 @Redbeard00 @redcarpetcrash @RedCarpetDesign @Redcarracing @RedClayDiaries @RedCop007 @RedCrossDallas @reddoch @reddomain @reddotleasing @RedeemingRiches @RedefChristmas @Redevice @Redfoxx12 @RedHouse_Films @RedKiteLLC @redlemonclub @redneckmommy @redooce @RedRosesPetrol @redsonia @RedStarKim @redstateleader @Redsyn @redtechmedia @Reduce_print_ @RedWineTaster @RedzillaMedia @reeddesigngroup @reedsmith @reelseo @ReemShafaki @reenchanter @ReenergizeLife @Reenit @reenjang @Reesuh @refereekayu2 @ReferralKey @ReferralTeams @reFido @refinanceguy @refinch @refinerymedia @refinnej @reftlauderdale @regan_george @ReganGlobal @Reganomic @regathwal @RegentGrand @reggierozay @reggupton @Regina_Realtor @reginabaker @reginaldcuffee @reginazaz @RegisGaspar @regoa01 @Regoog_dotcom @RegReady @RegretfulMorn @RegulusdeLeo @regususa @rehablist @rehablist13 @RehabResources @Rehearsaldinner @rehor @rei_educator @reitred @ReicheOma @reiconferences @reidigitalmedia @ReidMcCallHHI @Reigning1 @REILeadTracker @reincanada @reinhardmuller @reinsurancegirl @reintreeppl @ReinventionGuru @reiselinde_de @reishi_coffee @REITV @reiwebtools @ReiWorks @RejectedCards @rejectnation @Rejuvhair @ReL8table @relationcoach @RelationEcon @RelativelyFX @relaxsuite @ReleaseTEAMInc @relevance @RELEVANTmag @RelevantNewsNow @Releve_ @ReliableAssist @reliefcomm @religionlive @RelinaShirley @relizer @Reloaded_Egg @ReLoanBroker @reman_controls @Remarkable_10 @remarkmarketing @REMAXLegacy @REMcloud @RemcovanBuren @Remedy_Health @remesarpro @Remi_Vladuceanu @Remifemin @remiz @remodelingrx @RemoveBellyFat @remowill @RemRnB @RenaissanceBeer @renaldocreative @renaudedba @renbarau @Renbor @renchenza @rencosch @rendernodes @rendondesigns @Rene20091 @reneebrohard @reneecassard @ReneeDS @ReneeinTx @reneerawlings @ReneeShupe @Renegade_JD @RenegadeCoach @renems_ @ReneRuebner @renewabill @renewacycle @RenExecForums @RenHanami @RenierC @renitafarrall @rennabruce @rennatobarbosa @RenoQB @renoss @renroy @RentaBizTeam @RentalReview @rentcentralpa @rentwikiHQ @REOGeek @reomco @Rep_Giffords @repeatnone @replicachicago @RepMikeRogersAL @ReporterKT @ReporterLindsey @reprosites @RepublicanCar @republicofmath @ReputationDr @ReputationFixer @res_change @Resandy13 @RescoApps @ResearchReggie @ResellEbooks @ResidentLinks @resideo @ResidualHomeBiz @ResistTyranny @resiteonline @resofactor @ResortDelivery @ResortsBiz360 @Resource_mag @ResourceDallas @resourcefuljohn @resourcemedia @ResponseMine @responsiva @restaurantfunds @restorehair @restorewetlands @resuccess @Resultants @resultsfreak @resultsrev @resume_writers1 @ResumeBear @ResumeCart @ResumeChicks @ResumeExpert @resumeideas @ResumeMachine @ResumeReviewer @ResumeROI @resumeservice @ResumeStrategy @ResumeWoman @RetailHelper @retailindustry @Retire21 @retirecontent @RetiredTeacherD @RetireWithCarla @RetireWithOnly2 @RETradio @Retroloco @Retweet_Man @ReTweetAlater @reubenrr @ReubenYau @reuseit @Rev_Gene @Rev_Sidnei @rev2tweet101 @RevAlan @revbtgilligan @Revenews @RevenueAds @RevenueDoctor @revenuestreams @reverend_andy @revgibbs @review_ipad @reviewledger @ReviewProducts @reviewsguru @Reviewtter @Revision3 @revistaem @revistaverbo @ReviveComm @ReviveVending @revjohnkirst @RevMarkBrown @REVOLUTION_Jill @revolutionKing @RevolutionRacin @revpinheiro @RevRaceClub @revtrev

176

Acknowledgments

@RevTwtPays @RevYourHotel @Reward_Me @rewindmemories @REworkingparent @rexolio @RExpertWitness @ReyInsurance @reynbow101 @rezav @Rezeptideen @RF_I @RfactorGraffix @RFDAmerica @RFIPR @RFNovotny @rfugers @rfussa @rfvritter @RGarip @RGartman87 @rgerrick @rgiraldi @RGMCA @rgogos @RH2_0 @rhalbheer @RHC_Outpatient @rhcerff @RheaPerry @Rheba_B_Berte @rheinmainescort @rhetormusic @rhimedia @Rhino_Marketing @RhoadesShawn @rhodanmc @RhodesCollege @RhodesNews @rhodesone @rhondagessner @rhondamiller67 @rhondawaters @rhoughton @rhpranapati @rhw007 @Rhydemz @RhydianMusic @Rhythms_Fitness @ri_vacation @RiaFSB895 @RianneDekker @ribeiraotv @ribock @rica_yumi @RicaChristina @ricalo @ricardo_ideia @ricberbal @ricbrockmeier @RicCantrell @ricgllg @rich_bohemian @Rich_Gallagher @richaffiliates @richagent @Richanddebyoerg @richard_duggan @Richard_Flewitt @Richard_O @Richard_RN @Richard_Watts @richard515680 @Richardaa4life @RichardAlberg @RichardAlderson @richardarcand @RichardatDELL @richardbender @RichardC @richardcoppen @RichardDalke @richarddd_ @RichardDedor @RichardDParker @RichardEJordan2 @RichardHarmon @richardhartley @richardjbirch @richardjkirkham @RichardMaybury @richardmobbs1 @RichardPosey @RichardRansom3 @RichardSalgado @richardscenna @RichardsonCoC @richardspeaks @RichardSPearson @RichCurrie @richdarby @richdirtygirl @richgeasey @RichGerman @RichGranatelli @RichGuzman @RichHitchcock @RichHopkins @Richie_Rey @Richie799 @RichieNeedham @richiereveley2 @RichJaeger @RichMartin @RichMcKinney @richmondford @richms5 @richnthick @Richonlinetwtr @RichPAnderson @richschott @richsmithphoto @richtaylorllc @RichTrish @richwebnews @Rick_S @Rick_Aguiluz @Rick_Burnett @Rick_Frank @Rick_Howard @Rick_Paradigm @Rick_TAGR @Rickbischoff @rickbraddy @rickbrotherton @RickBurdo @RickCartwright @RickCollierOJ @RickCooper @rickdean06 @RickDiBiasio @RickDRoberts @RickGalan @RickGantley @RickGonz @rickhancock @RickHoening @RickM @rickosborne @RichPantera @RickRosemond @rickross10 @RickSchwartz @ricksorkin @Ricksreview @RickStoner @RickUpshaw @rickwiginton @RickWyatt @ricky_chotai @Ricky1782 @RickyWright2 @Riclargo @RicoFig @Ricoh_Photo_AU @RicohCamerasAus @ricoladrop @ricpratte @rictownsend @Rida_ZA @rIdentitynet @ridestory @ridgelyjohnson @ridgey28 @Riding4aCause @ridwan_mcfadden @ridwan2906 @Rien_Fch @rieskariesha @Rieszie @riezkasusan @rightbiz @RightCandidates @rightcommentary @rightforkdiner @rightgrrl75 @rightinvention @RightOnWisc @RightSideAustin @RightWingNews @Riico @riikkakrenn @rikkisixx @rikymag81 @rilescat @rimawaril @RimbaJati @rinaldiginting @rincevm @Rinconzuliano @rinehanel1981 @RingCentral @RingtoneRampage @rinteractive @RioCreative @RioDJaneiro @riol_xx @RioRasco @riotkat @RiotVineSXSW @ripedcherry @ripla @RIPmediagroup @RippDemUp @ripplegivers @ripvanwrinkles @RiseSmart @rishikhanna @rishikmajum @RiseSecurity @RisingWaters @RiskQuantALMJob @Rita_Long @ritabarber @ritman @RitterGroup @rituraj @ritzylady @Riussi @rivalmktg @RivenCactus @RiverBoatin @RIVERFLOW777 @RiverFork @Rivescpa @RizzoTees @rj_c @RJ_Medak @rjacquez @rjagosta @rjd728 @rjdjohnston @rjdoerflinger @rjenbarr @RJFortier @rjfrasca @rjhockin04 @RJMesenbourg @rjmortensen @RJNielson @rjonrobins @rjpennington @RJRussell @rjsellscheap @rjtweettraffic @rjwiginton @RK0407 @rkburns @RKfitnessUK @rlapp @RLavigne42 @rleger2 @rlepold @RLEschler @rleseberg @rlevans @rlew @rlilyengren @rlloren @RM_Marketing33 @rmassingham @rmcooke42 @RMHCNorthTexas @rmichaelnorman @rmilano @RMM_Online @rmolden @RMondavi_Winery @rmoore74 @rmoreno_ca @RMSorg @rmsylte @RnBE_HomeDesign @Rnite @RNorthfield @RNReport @rntrades @Ro_iBlog @RoachDotSteve @RoadrunnerNames @RoadWarriorsUSA @roam2me @RoamingSoldiers @RoanokeCatholic @rob_b72 @Rob_Gant @Rob_Moshe @Rob_Ross @Rob_Shrake @RobAdvertising @robandmark @robangeles @robanspach @robatherton @robb_ish @RobbBeltran @robbboyd @RobbCorbett @RobBeauchamp @robbertdehaan @robbnotes @RobBtG @robbunting @robbytweets @RobCCraig @robcersbrad @robcip @robcizek @RobCoats @RobCopp @RobCrumby @RobDennisH4H @RoberleighHaig @Robert_Rose @robert6969 @roberta_sa @robertanalesso @RobertBarry @robertbobert100 @RobertBucci @RobertCInnis @RobertEMitchell @RobertEReed @robertgrant @RobertHathhorn @robertjgardner @robertjrussell @RobertLTw @RobertMartz @robertmcrowe @robertnewham @roberto_mazzoni @robertomazzoni @robertphelps @RobertPickstone @robertronline @RobertSalceda @robertschafer @robertSchafnitz @robertshouses @RobertsHP @RobertSiciliano @RobertStockham @Robert Thompson3 @RobertWHughes @robertyoung11 @RobH3 @Robathrnett @Robin_Goel @robin_low @Robin4Homes @RobinAllen @robinana @RobinAndJudy @RobinatRibit @Robinbk @RobinDotNet @RobinettMktg @robinives @RobinKruk @RobinLynneLaFay @RobinMelina @RobinMPowers @robinngphoto @Robinovich @robinpedrero @Robinresumes @RobinSchooling @Robinshl23 @robinsonjohn @RobinTaylorRoth @robinthomas1 @robintramble @RobinWalker @RobinZygs @robjcameron @robkerry @RobKoster @RobLear @roblynam @robmapes @robmarreel @RobMcDougall @RobMcNealy @Robo_Stew @Robo6puck @robogolfer @RoboSteel @RobotoCaliento @robroggsiii @Roburmohr @RobSalzman @robsimons @RobSmithJr @robsonrmsk8s3t @robsonvicent @RobStitzer @robstrump @robswanson @robtillman @RobWakes @robwayharris @robweaverrepen @robwilley @RobWilmot @RobynConnolly @robynlandau @RobynsWorld @rocdomz @ROChabitat @RocheForw @RochelleCarr @RochelleVeturis @rocioesevich @Rock_Metal_Pub @rock_star00173 @rockalong @RockAndMetal @rockandrollmama @RockandSox @rockawaywriter @RockBottomGym @RockChristopher @RockClimbingMx @RockerChickWG @rockerlifecoach @rockersvsmods @RocketGroup @RocketPopScott @rockeltrobin2 @rockett @RocketTencom @RockFord_IL @RockFordSFSBO @RockfordLink @RockFordReal @RockiitRich @rockingjude @RockingtheRobin @rockinringtones @RockJamaica @RocklandUSA @ROCKMEETSBLUES @rockmore @RockPlanck @RockProtoStar @RockShirts @rocksolidmedia @rocksstar10 @Rockstar_Group @RockstarBuzz @rockstarmonies @rockybullwink @RockyII @RocSocialMedia @rod_Harper @rodalan @RodBeckstrom @rode_o @rodeocool @rodeoking @rodeomartina @Rodericklow @RodgerHyatt @RodHarlan @RodMarriott @RodneyGaylor @rodneyrasmussen @rodolfofrausto @rodrigoborgia @Rodriguez_Alej @RodSeip @rodtofoli @rodtrent @rodwhisnant @RoelsC @roforex @Rog42 @Roger_Allen @Roger_Tee @rogerbauer @RogerBezanis @rogerchristie @rogercp @rogerhamilton @RogerKafer @rogerleads @rogermather @RogersFord @RogerTan @rogerthatcash7 @rogervankampen @RogerZeng @Rohan_E_Squad @rohetherington @rohfun @rohitbapat23 @rohnmartino @rojas2com @rokensa @roland_moesl @rolandfricke @RolandRillander @RolfSimons @rolfthefinn @roliekan @rolosandoval @rolyvie @Romain_Bernard @romanbraun @romanbraun @romanceproes @romanofaria @RomanParadigm @RomanticCougars @romantico24de @romasdanks @romeo2584 @RomeoLanning @romerobv @romyraves @romyrivera @Ron @Ron_Duff @Ron_Jones @Ron_Maxim @Ron_Saballus @Ron_Wheeler @ron_z @RonaD @ronaldjackson @ronaldjacksonX @RonaldLewis @RonaldNevers @ronaldo2750 @ronaldskelton @ronaldzouein @ronanvance @ronattias @ronbrownmusic @rondabertram @rondurant @RonEdmondson @roneluys @RonForte @RonFortier @rongraham1 @ronhuxley @roniejauod @RonitDiamonds @ronjsauer @ronkarr @RonMakan @RonMarkberg @ronnc1 @ronmcdowell @ronmcgoo @RonneRock @RonnieLopez @RonProctor @RonRuggless @RonsTweetTank @RonUpshaw @ROOFINGSERVICE @RooftopJewell @roofwindowdave @roojwright @rookiepops @roomynaqvy @rooney33 @roonie_g @rooribbet @rootika @rootwoman123 @RoriStories @roritravel @rorworks @rory_vaden @rorymurray @rorystern @ros624 @ros4401 @rosaleeddison @rosamunde3 @RoscoeRussellYK @Rose_Mis @rose_realestate @RoseannHiggins @RoseASP @RoseBevan @RoseBusinessSol @RoseCityTattoo @roseclark @rosemaven @rosesanda6 @RosettaCareers @rosettathurman @rosewrite @roseydow2 @rosh @Rosiehorner @rosiestewart44 @RosinaWilson @RositaCortez @RoSoftDownload @Ross_Owen @rossbay @RossBoy @rossdecker @rossfrain @Rossio @RossMaguire @RossPretorius @rosstmw @rostarco @rotarybocawest @roth_conversion @rotiprata @Rotivation @rottenluck101 @Roughside @RousingAbout @Route22Toyota @Route53 @Route66Boston @Rouxlettmarktng @ROUXSTAR @rovies @rovingtweet @RowanBarnett @rowanjessica @rowdycity @rowdygrandma @RowdyOrbit @rowhite67 @roxanne2323 @Roxanne2u @RoxanneEmmerich @roxanneravenel @roxannesmolen @RoxieSprings @Roy8vies @RoyalAtlantisGp @RoyalDrama @royalecms @RoyalPoinciana @RoyAylmer @Roybuilt @RoyCampos @Roychavarcode @royderrick @RoyGBryant @roygene @royjwells @royljestr @RoyOsing @RozHannibal @rpatwebb @RPIGroup @rpliska @rpndc @RProject @rrhhol @rricart @rricker @RSACorp

177

@RSALISTSERVICES @rsazevedo @rseenal @rsgbiz @rsgrice @RSHotel @rsjewell @RSMcGr @rsmoot @rstbob @RSVPhere @rt_clik @rtaylor @rtaylor61 @rtbest @rtkrum @rtmjkwanbondcop @rtmoore77 @rtooms @RTtips4u @rtulp @RUASuccess @rubbermaid @RubbermaidTwo @Rubee100 @ruben86 @RubenCurryBD @rubenq @rubwaste57064 @ruby4love @rubyga49 @RubySlipperVA @rubywatch @RUcareers @Ruckdaschel2010 @rucsb @rude64 @rudezen @RudhirSharan @Rudi3CantFh52 @RudyCaceres @RudyFDF @rudys @Ruel_Antonio @Ruff_Ride @ruffinadvisory @RufRecords @ruhanirabin @RuiMartelo @RuiqiY @Ruivo @RulingCouncil @rumadison @runenthusiast @runlevelmedia @RunLove @runnerforchrist @running66miles @runningcouple @RunningPixel @RunSpired @rupertwhittam @rushabhrambhia @rusher81572 @RushThePug @russ_dean @RussCoach @russellmasters @RussellOrganics @RussellORourke @russellquotes @russellshih @russellsmartin @russelltripp @russian_rock @RussLoL @RussMack @rusty338 @rustybadge @rustyc77 @RustyCampbell @Ruth_Z @RuthBradford @ruthdfw @ruthhegarty @ruthless_phil94 @ruthmedia @ruthperryman @RuthSherman @ruv @rvandersar @RVLmakelaars @RVLuver @rvoegtli @RVRB @rvsbg @rwang0 @rwmovies @rwpcs @rwperkinsjr @rwphan @RWT711 @RWWRSS @rx4good @rxcareer @RxTaskForce @Ry_Curran @Ryan_Cornelius @Ryan_Dobbsy @ryan_gledhill @ryanbazeley @ryanbokros @ryanbovey @RyanCPeterson @RyanDehler @ryandeiss @RyanDerous @ryandmckinney @ryanhandinc @ryanleisure @RyanMakes @ryanmega @RyanOFlinn @RyanPaine @ryanpinnick @ryanpphelan @RyanPrillman @RyanRancatore @RyanRobbins @RyanRockstarr @RyanSammy @RyanSteinolfson @RyanStyleTM @RyanSuccess @RyanTheInvestor @RyanThompson @RyanV49er @ryanyouens @ryanzuk @rycak @RyderMedia @RyersonDMZ @RyokanYachiyo @rytaran @s_adinugroho @s_lehner @s_levaillant @S_NelsonBuckley @s_u_r_y_a_rockz @s_uccess @S0CIALCAPITAL @s2space @S4SRVTour @s6mkt4 @Sa_DiegoWeather @SaarMaxi @sabaidress @Sabaiweb @SAbestCPAs @SabineBraun @sabinelenz @SabineOsmanovic @sabita_anju @Sabrina_PHR @sabrina00a @sabrinacoffin @sabrinacrider @sabrinagibson @sabrinasolesbee @SabriRondinelli @SAbsalom @sacalvo @SacHarlows @sacrebleuwine @Sacredsecret @SacredSunbeam @sadhana8 @sadhanakh @SadieMHarris @sadodhifhhaihsh @SAdoreBoutique @sadoty @SaedAbuHmud @SafecountJenn @safeeyes @safeips @safekidsusa @saferdates @saferreefer @SafetDeals @Safetycares @safetysecurity @safetyweb @SafeVegasFeeds @saffsam @SaffyFox @safii76 @sagaragarwl @SageIsland @SageMcGreen @SagePhotoWorld @SageRecruiter @sagesalzer @SageTalk @saggal0 @SagraAustin @sahasuriani @sahbay @SAHMI7 @sahm411 @saidb @saiimarketing @saikerdes @SailingUpdates @saimonesays @SaintConsulting @SAINTEBEAUTE @saintlucian @Saints_News @Saints_NFL_ @SAINTSpeeps @sairbear @sajits @sajivalife @sakshisharda @salal1 @salad1948 @SaladCreationTX @Saladehistoria @SaladLove @Salaguinto @Salamfood @salarybuzz @Salazar0187 @SaleBusiness @sales_eu_org @sales2marketing @sales4art @SalesBlogcast @SalesCooke @SalesDNA @SalesFacts @SalesGravy @salesgrok @SalesGuruReview @salesinstitute @salesjobsearch @SalesLeeds @Salesologist @salespop @salesrecruiter @SalesRemedy @salessafari @SalesStrong @SaleStart @salestweet_ @salesvisionary @SalesWhisperer @Sally_K @sallycute17 @sallyhoney @sallyleonard @sallymarchand @sallyppeterson @SallyCHan @SallyStevensen @SallyWalker @Salmagio @salmanj10 @salmanofficial @SalonRepublic @SaltChalet @saltfish6768 @SaltyMaltese @saludwinenow @salvationtrips @Salventrex @SalventrexSales @sam_mason1979 @sam_sorenson @sam101 @sam7116 @samabomo @samadei @saman325 @Samantha_Austin @Samantha_ML @samantha_us @Samari @samatlounge @sametradesigns @samfjacobs @samhawkins1 @samhickmann @SamMoulton @sammutimer @SammyBlindell @samomidi @SamPalazzolo @samprince2 @samrag @SamSilverstein @SamsonBlinded @SamsungMobileUS @samsungnx10 @samsungsoul @Samsungtweets @SamTheButcher @SamTheTutor @samtittle @samtryagain @samualvags @Samuel_Smith @samyz @san_diego_seo @sanchezjb @sandanyi @sandembergp @sanderssays @SandeSaimond @Sandestin @sandflei @Sandhu1301 @sandiatravel @SanDiegoInjury @SanDiegoSauceCo @SanDiegoSoccer @SanDiegoSpine @sandimaki @sandios @sandividal @sandlerphilly @sandmjewelry @sandra_tolopas2 @sandra002533 @Sandrachick @SandraLopulalan @sandramp @SandraRodrigues @sandraschubert @sandrasims @Sandrawalts @SandraWilken @sandrinea @SANDROANDRINE @sandy_carter @Sandy_Schmidt @sandybasker @SandyBuller @SandyFarms @SandyHarper @SandyHowlett @SandyJordan @sandyleverone @SandyMorris @sandyspiderbite @sanix62 @sanjayakannath @SanjayCho @sanjoydalia @sanjuclicktweet @SanMarcoCoffee @SannyBieber @Sanoviv @santaguitarsolo @Santana1969 @Santi_Garcia @santidemierre @santilli @santosh0207 @sanuzis @sanyikaboyce @saodarafie @saoireobrien @SapereSolutions @sapiraaw @Sapphire_Dakini @SapphireBayCons @sapphiredrinks @saquinaakanni @sar_kirkby @sara6633 @SaraBeckford @SaraCrowe @SaraEyobHaile @sarah_4you @Sarah_Nicolas @Sarah_Prentice @sarah_rahman @sarah_starry @Sarah_x_Rose @sarah_x10 @SaraHamil @SarahatDell @SarahAtPSBJ @SarahBuchanan1 @SarahButtonedUp @SarahCaminker @SarahCares4U2 @SaraHMooney @SarahElles @sarahEmagee @SarahFulton @SarahGirl122 @SarahHathorn @Sarahhh91x @sarahjoaustin @sarahkalaj @sarahkilbourne @sarahlashua @SarahLCook @Sarahlevy @sarahmorgera @SarahNelson_ @sarahnewton @sarahsantacroce @SarahStaar @sarahstips @SarahTLV1 @SarahWhiteKC @sarahwitten @SaraJacksonValo @sarallenconsult @SaraLWood @SaraMazur @SaraMcQ @SaraMeaney @SaraMish @saraohman @sarasocialmedia @sarasotadream @sarawanders @sarelimarketing @SaresE @sarinsuares @Sarita_Moreno @SaritaGandhi @sarjalis @Sarosresearch @SashaGaya @SashaXarrian @sasikrishna @sass @SASSYKITKITTY @SassyNetworker @sassyword @satchmofest @sathishisaac @satori_zen @SatoriCoffee @SatoriNation @satoru_yukie @SatoshiSato @SatoyaJohnson @satpal192 @SatsugaiCat @saucyglo @Saul2884 @saulerick @SaunWashington @saurabparakh @SAVAAHH @savageink @SavagelySocial @SavannahxLee @savasavasava @save_2_years @Save_the_Nation @save4closureSD @SaveDraft @SaveMeDebra @savenhawk @SaveOurPlanet @savethatstuff @SavetheDateing @Savetherehearts @SaveUrCredit @savingdinner @SavingEveryday @savingRXdollars @SavingsTKuljis @SavingYourMoney @savor @SavorTheSuccess @savoysignal @Savvy_MoM @savvybizowner @SavvyBoomers @savvyendeavor @SavvyExplorer @savvyinbiz @savvypromoter @SavvySocialist @savvysocialmed @SavvySpeculator @savvystudent @SavvyWithJenna @savweightloss @Sawbuck @SaWht @SawyerTMS @SaxonHenry @sayiamgreen @SayingsOnLove @SayItWitYaBrest @SaySocialMedia @sayvings @sazbean @SB_Entrepreneur @sba_daily @sbarnes0215 @sbarton1220 @sbass10080 @sbblex @sbbuzz @SBCarmenSchmidt @sbeasla @SBellPR @sbenavid @SBGGlobalMobile @sbgraceLLc @sbiby @sblackburn @SBMediaGroupInc @sboatella @sboulios @SBPacks @sbriannaparker @SBSConsultingF @SBToday @sburda @sburges2 @sbwalsh @SBWeddings1 @SBWorkforce @sc72_ @Scabr @scandhock @Scanyours @scare_the_cat @ScareMeNot @scarfacejo @ScarletNetworks @ScarlettaMedia @scarlettmadi @scartertn @scarylawyer @scbalazs @SceneStealrEric @scentsbytiffany @schapsis @Schauerte_NRW @SCHEFFXP @schilly1 @Schizo456 @schmitt_it @SchnacksJewelry @schoe22 @schoenfeldj @ScholarBuyChris @ScholarBuys @ScholarBuysAdam @ScholarBuysJess @ScholarBuysMike @Scholarjack @ScholarshipsDB @SchorrThing @SchroederBrown @Schubert_B2B @schufa_loeschen @schumannwebs @schumpert @SchutteDolt @SchwansManTony @schwaps @Schwarts @schwarzesgold @schweizerbank @schwerdtfeger @sci_twiterista @SciacCard @SciFiFunk @SciTechDC @sclbits @SCMEC @ScoMo @Scone @sconsult @ScoopTheDirt @scoopville @Scootek @ScooterWrecker @score114 @SCOREChicago @scoremoresales @scoresfm @scorewithTwtr2 @scorpiontheater @ScotDuke @scotfazell @Scotlandhols @ScotMcKay @Scott__Miller @Scott_Allan1 @scott_case @Scott_Fain @scott_hughes691 @scott_jaworski @Scott_Lord @Scott_Manesis @scott_shapiro @scott_ulrich @Scott4Software @scott6509 @ScottAllen @scottamv @scottarvin @scottbabcock @ScottBravell @scottciborowski @scottdblog @scottdeaks @ScottDeYager @scotters @ScottFishman @ScottGiorgini @scottgow @scotthaley @scottica @ScottishLassKel @scottjmanley @ScottJSchaefer @scottkoegler @ScottMarkman @scottmckain @ScottMeldrum @scottmonaco @ScottMonty @ScottNoir @scottothomas @scottpdavis @scottrossow @ScottScanlon @scottswhertly @ScottSimson @scottstank @ScottTheFirst @ScottWasham @ScottWilliams @scottybee_ @ScottyScanlon @ScottyStevens @ScottyWalks @scoty2htycolati @scoutadeal2 @scoutadealDOD @scrapbookDiva76 @scrappergirl106 @Scratch2Cash3 @scratchepad @Scream13 @ScreaminCoupons @screen_capture @ScreenDoorTX @ScreenTeamShow @screweduptexan @scribblrgirls @Scribulz @scripped @ScriptingGuys

Acknowledgments

@ScriptureGuide @scriptwritert4 @scrubbuzz @scrubzbody @scruffybarn @Scrumpyboy @scubadivergirls @ScubaInCanada @sculpterra @Scumlabs @sd22rivers @SD6Degrees @sdas86 @sdcalifornia14 @sdchcc @sddagg @sdeclomesnil @sdentrepreneur @sdesic @sdevon @SDFlashSoccer @SDFunctionalMed @SDGalerie @SDGalloway @sdh2oman @sdmts @sdot @sdphotoes @sdpix @sdpride @sdtaxcpa @sdubagunta @SDuinhouwer @Se7enMagazine @Seabellies @SeaDreamYC @sean_furey @Sean_Kinney @SeanBBrown @seanbmarketing @seanbossie @seancarlson1920 @SeanCooperSmith @SeanDonahoe @seanearleyrocks @SeanEGarland @SeanENelson @SeanieSS @seanlyons78 @SeanMalarkey @SeanMc_Carthy @SeanMcColgan @SEANMCGINTYcom @SeanMcPheat @seanrnicholson @seansmallman @seansviewdotcom @SeanToole @SeanVanity @SeanVera @seanwhittaker @Seaport_Village @SeaPortAir @Search_Profits @search_trend @searchandsocial @searchcircus @searchengine0 @searchguru @searchkeywords1 @SearchMojo @SearchPeopleDir @SearchReadyInc @SearchReminder @SearchStimulus @searchsuccess @SearchtoEmploy @SearchTrends @SearsBlueCrewHA @SeasonsGreet1 @seattle_paul @SeattleAdTalk @Seattlestaged @seattlewinegal @SeattleWorksOut @SeaYu @Sebastene @SebastianD @SebastienPage @Sebbe_Munich @sebdavila @sebyfromsherby @seckmanbusiness @secondflush_de @Secret_4Success @secretaffairs @secretdaniela @SecretiveArmy @secretnetworker @SecretsOnLinee @secrettweet @SECSportsMan @SECSportsWire @SecureDBA @SecurityProf @securitystuff @sedgewick @sedonahotel @see_stan_run @seeallnews @SeebCon @SeeboldMarCom @seecrab @seedingideas @seegullmedia @SeekingMinds @SeeKrisRun @seemediet @SeePigeonForge @SeeTheRealYou @seetravrun @SeeYOUonTheBUS @segedoo @seizethedealdfw @sejadahmerah @sekeljic @SelaMissirian @selamo @selbyb @SelenaBoby @self_improve @Self_JohnGSelf @self_seeking @SelfBuildMentor @selfdefense @SelfHelpGoddess @SelfHelpIdeas @selfpublishingx @selfshotsssss @sellelectron @sellhomefinally @sellingcraft @SellingHouse @SellingOmaha @SellingRaleigh @SellingWoman @SellitonBixbe @sellnextdoor @sellshorttoday @sellsmarts @sellurcellular @sellwithphil @SEM_SEO_PPC @sem_watch @semanio @semenz @SeminOzmorali @SEMJunkie @semmerson @semomarketplace @SempreAvanti @SEMSEO1 @sen3016 @Senate_GOPs @SenatorBurr @Sender_1 @SenderOK @sendoutcardz @seneeseale @SengWeiland @SeniorBiz @SeniorManager @SeniorTweet @senobarak @SenorCollege @SensaWeightLoss @SensibleSpender @sensorpro @sensual_touch @SensuaVitality @Sentimently @SEO_Amigo @seo_bd @seo_freelancer @SEO_Kat @SEO_Mastery @SEO_Pirate @SEO_Pittsburgh @seo_plans @SEO_Services4U @SEO_SPECIALIST @SEO_Tool @SEO_tricks @seo_tv @seo4vertical @seoadvice @SEOAlicia @seoaranyak @SEObat @SEObookmarking @SEObySEM @seocom @seodiger @seoelektro @seoexpertmaster @seoformat @SEOGeneration @seogezwitscher @seogod73 @seogr @seohotsolutions @seoinc @seoinlasvegas @SEOisEasy @SEOiswhatido @SeoLair @SEOMarketingPro @seomaster @SEOMastermind @SEOnewz @seonow @seoppcsmo @seoproffesional @SEOProfiteer @seoprofits @SeoProNZ @seopros2 @SEOPunch @seoredhead @seorocks @SEORockstars @SEOroddy @SeoroII @seosam1 @SeoServicesBD @SEOsnoop @SeoSoftwareAmaz @seospecialists @seosport @SEOSpy @SEOSubmission @SEOsummary @seotopper @seotraining @SEOTurboCharger @seoul_shannen @SeoulLady @seovalencia @SEOwatcher @SEOxpert @SEPItweets @Septdk @SeptemberMay @septicvault @Serchen @Serenahills @serenasocial @serendipitySEO @serenityva @sergioenelsur @Sergiotrumpet @serichards @seriouslywalker @seriously_steph @SeriousMLM @seror @Sertifi @servantek @serve77 @serverdir @service51 @ServicedSociety @serviceplease20 @servicezoom @Servijer_Ar_Vro @ServoSell @seshn @sessionsfan @SethBackus @sethjoseph @setiawanh @setiawati1972 @setla @Setsights @Setsuko_412 @SettleDebt610 @SetUpMyBrand @seucoach @SeungMLee @sevacruro @sevcance @SevenChildren @Sevenhalos @SevenLunches @SewellFord @SewWithPassion @Sex_IYC @sex4flat @sexfollowdotcom @SEXGame_prOpa @SEXIBOSSLADY @sexijessical2 @sexxnz @SeXy_ER_NuRsE @SexyCelebz @SexyHolly12 @SexyMessy21 @sexynbol @sexypast @SexyRob @sexysthinker @SexyWorkingMom @sexyyetpolite @sexyzanny @seyahchoumeh @SeymourKitty @sfaithlovesden @SFDoug @SFLFoodandWine @SFOX14 @sfriedman126 @sfsam22 @sfsfdog @SFUalumni @SG_Ramon @sgfoley @sghardin @sgierick @sglider12 @shadonna @ShadowTalks @shadwatson @ShafMatthews @shahalong @shaik99 @ShainaChristine @Shainsha2010 @shakibrown @ShallieBey @shally @ShalondaGordon @Shama @ShamelessShamus @shamir @shane_dillon @Shane_W @ShaneBryan @shanegibson @ShanelleLeigh09 @shanerhyne @ShaneRussel @shangshang333 @ShannaBriyant @shannagordon @shannan0 @shannaohmes @shannon_filing @shannonawhite @shannoncherry @shannonevanssm @ShannonEvansSM @ShannonOKeeffe @ShannonShubert @ShannonSwenson @Shannonyelland @shannonpop @shantaydavies @Shanteeeeeeee @ShantelleG @Shanti_nz @shantidjs @ShapingYouth @Shaputalica @SharafTravel @sharayray @sharecommons @SharelOmer @ShareMee @ShareMyDeal @SharePointWhiz @sharepro @shares4u @ShareTheDreams @ShareTheGeek @ShareThis @ShareTompkins @Sharetops @sharinasmith @ShariniJaji @sharisax @SharittaAllen @SharkBaitSales @SharkGirl1220 @SharleneStevens @sharlyn_lauby @sharmaineSainta @Sharon_Chan @Sharon_Higbee @Sharon_Phoenix @sharonarose @sharonbarel @SharonDexter @sharongadbois @SharonGaskin @SharonKnecht @SharonKolker @sharonmarkovsky @SharonMcP @sharonmeyers @sharonreinhard @SharpendtraIn @SharpeTailor @sharpkwon @SharonThornton @Sharshelafem @SharynAbbott @sharynread @shasherslife @shashib @Shasick @StatterboxVox @ShaunaCausey @ShaunaGallagher @shaunamclean @ShaunErk @ShaunHailes @shaunjamison @Shave_Dallas @shavereview @shawanyi @ShawHomesTulsa @Shawn_Leonard @ShawnaArmstrong @ShawnaCoronado @ShawnaCulp @shawnaseigel @shawnavercher @ShawnCMason @ShawnKCastille @shawnkhorassani @shawnmcpike @shawnrobinson @shawnrorick @shawnshahani @shawnweston @shaxx @shay2132 @shayr22 @shayzvia @shazelectronics @shazcreations @SHDickson @SHDixon @ShearCreativity @shearerrima @SHEATHER703 @SheBlogsNetwork @shecky76 @sheelectric @SHEEmusic @sheenaindhul @SheetalJaitly @shegeek @Sheidamohebbi @SheilaAtwood @SheilaBerg @SheilaBlackford @sheilacolon1 @sheilamba @SheilaStarkey @shelbilavender @shelbybowman8 @shelbyhomes @shelbyhumes @shelbyleland @sheldon1creates @shelbyhome4judge @shellcat13 @ShelleyCall @ShelleyErnst @shelleyrae @ShelliNoca @shellisxena @shelly_adams @shellybean123 @ShellyLodes @shellyroche @ShellyWolfe @SheltonCharl @ShelÍMay @shelzolkewich @Shennee_Rutt @SheratonDallas @SheratonMoscow @SHerdegen @Sheree2055 @Shereine @sheridansmithf @Sherriff_Rick @SherriGoddard @sherikayehoff @SheriLWatkins @sheriNOLA @SheriTingle @SherleyGrace @SherlindaNews @sherlyn99 @ShermanCSI @ShermanVisa @sherri_g @SherriGarrity @sherrilynne @sherrisheerr @sherroddine @sherry326 @Sherry9779 @sherryfetzer @sherryj @sherrykirksy @sherryrodden @shersteve @sheryl_craft @sherylmandel @shesaid_dallas @ShesSoSocial @SheTeamTweets @shetech @shibleylondon @shibuya246 @shiegie @ShiftAgeTrends @shikigal @ShilpaJadhavSEO @shilpanicodemus @shilpiarts @shimusicworld @ShiningClover @shinng @shino_katsuragi @shinyzhu @shionline @shiratoken @Shirestone @shirlnick @shirlandc69 @ShirleMitchell @ShirleySchlag @shirleyshair @Shizo_Shirley @shizuka131 @shkebino01 @shmelanie @shobi23 @shockprices @ShoeBoxFiends @ShoesCoUK @shoesdotcom @ShoestringGal @ShoeTweeter @sholasmansion @sholist @Shon_Toni @shonajesta @ShoniquaShandai @shooberdoober @Shookspeare @ShootersOnly @shopably @shopathome @shopclicks @shopexperts @ShopLOFT @shopmobbing @ShopOUAF @ShopperDolly @ShopperSaving @shopping_cheap @shopping_frenzy @shopping_ok @shoppingfocal @shoppingmobile @shoppoligist @ShopSanctuary @ShopSaveBest @ShopSavvyMama @shopsareshine @shopsindex_com @shoppindex @shore10 @ShoreFire @short_men @ShortcutsOnline @shortfilmfest @shortform_tv @SHORTME_EU @ShortNews_Auto @shortsalebabe @shortsalecourse @ShortSaleGuy1 @Shortsalejane @shortsalekid @shosized @shoutwit @showcaseclosets @showcasesuccess @ShowerThinker @Showingbook @showmetheodds @showmetheoddspr @ShowmoneyDotNet @ShowtymeJazzDuo @showupyourself @shreddel @Shreechirps @shresthayash @shreyam @shrinkingjeans @shu5kanou @shustir @ShutterBugGeek @shw72388 @Shyanneksom @ShylaGarder86 @ShylaKleppen86 @ShyneBeats @shynichols @Si_Clark @silvery @siamkittie @siarkv @sibylleito @SicilianMentor @Sick_Tweets @SicolaMartin @Siddeley @Siddharth_IN @sidereelKendra @sidhai @sidnieioliveira @sidneyeve @sidneyferresi @sidraqasim @SidWiseman @SIEGEINDUSTRIES @SierraSci @SiftGroups @Sifumusic @Sigbj0rn @sight2seize @SigisRam @SignalGroup

179

The Social Media Business Equation

@SignatureAd @Signazon @signevent @signsnowdallas @sigsiu_net @sijj786 @silencespeaker @Silentium @SilentLeoinMTY @silgerd @Siliconhil @SiliconValleyDJ @SiliconVllyNews @SiljeValseth @SilkCharm @SilkRoad2010 @SillySticker @Silver_Queen @silverarcade @SilverbackCM @silvergreenssb @silverguru1 @silverimagelimo @silvermax2 @silveroaklimo @silverpeanut @SilverRaeFox @silversafecoin @Silversea @Silversmyth @SilverViiyy @silverzeal @silvia_delgado @silviacontar @silviagm_ @SilviaOrtizNin @SilviaSchwibi @silviodopanico @silviovailante @simanda @simasays @simchabe @simeonm @Simon_D_Young @Simon_Ry @SimonBayliss_ @simone_says @SimoneGuild @Simonephillips @simonevroom @SimonFord @simonfoster1 @simonhamer @simonjulian @simonkuo @Simonl33 @simonleung @simonmainwaring @simonpreacher @SimonRosenberg @simontoddcom @SimonWetherell @simonwhite @simple_heal @simple_truths @SimpleActs @SimpleFit101 @SimpleHomeOrg @simplelb @SimpleMillion @simplemlm2 @SimpleNetSecure @simplespace @simplestartcon @simplicityinc @SimplyBAHIA @simplybcreative @simplycast @simplygifts @SimplyGreenLife @simplyplates @Simpsonology @SimranSamtani @SIMUSA @Sinareet @SinbadsSF @sinclair_music @singlecitadine @singlefathers @singlemomcoach @singlemomoftwin @sinifian @sinith99 @sinkra @SinTecInc @siobhancoyle @SiODonovan @sipland @sir_gerold @siraf_2 @siraju @Sirblamkhan @siremusicgroup @siriusbmusic @siriusdecisions @Sirjohn_writer @SirJohnEvent3 @SirLinkedAlot @sirpokey @sirtwat @SirWebby @Sisdetec @SiSELpro @SisterActBiz @sisti @SitAndGoPro @SiteAHolics @sitemidas @sitepromotor @SiteSays @SitesDesign @SitewireAgency @Siteworx @sithburns @Sixpaww @sixsevenx @Sixth_Sense_Mkt @SizzlingSuccess @SJackCreative @sjchalk @sjknutson @sjl @SJMMtogether @SJohnson85 @sjpheikkinen @sjsturkie @sjwku @skalovers @skap5 @skarritt @skashliwal @skbrewer1 @SkeeterHansen @SkeeTVvp @sketchfanatic @SkiCoupons @skilletblack @skillscentral @SkillSource @SkillStorm @SkinCareDoc @SkinCareTweets @skingl1 @SkinnyArtist @SkinSpaMed @SKINTASTIC @Skintus @skip7547 @SkipAnderson @SKIPPROGRAM @SkipStein @skiptomlou @skirtmuse @skittles_fanz @skquinn @Skretz @skribente @SKSofCalifornia @skump @skweon @SkyBlew @skydeer @skydowning @skyebardallas @SkyeKing @SKYENICOLAS @SkyeYork @SkyHighFlyer1 @skyhithere @Skyito @skyjefans @SkylabGlobal @Skylar_Johnson @skylinemanager @SkynUK @SkySocial @sla360 @SlabGA @Sladed @sladesundar @SlamStreet @slamtheworld @SlapApp @Slapman4u @SlavaRybalka @SlayterCreative @slcmyers @slcupcakes @sleepandsnoring @sleepbamboo @SleepSeller @slevaillant @slickpic @SlideRocket @slideshare @slideshowguy @SLIDETVNEWS @slideworld @sliggitay @slimacaiformen @slimbeanscoffee @SlingshotERP @slkbrooke @SLMConsulting @sloaninnovation @slocricchio @SlopeViews @SlowCookerMate @slowittedbanker @slump_diverted @slv35 @slvideo @Slycaj @slyfoot3 @SlyFoxOne @sm2extensions @SM3ND3Z @SmackPR @smaknews @small_talks @smallbits @SmallBizBee @smallbizchat @smallbizIQ @SmallBizLady @Smallcapalert @Smallcapweekly @smallcitymusic @smallfri @Smalltalkwitht @Smart_Bride @Smart_Business @smartbandwidth @smartbarterusa @smartbloggerz @SmartBoyDesigns @SmartCookieMktg @SmartDad @smarthomeguide @smartonlinetwit @SmartPropertiez @SmartStorming @smarttradepro @SmartVAforU @smartwebs @SmartWoman @SmartWomenClub @smartwomentrav @SmartyWireless @smasotti @smasuch @smaxbrown @SMBConsultant @smbirddog @SMCCoLUmBus @SMCDallas @smcnulty @SMCSac @SMczarina @SMDudes @SMediaSource @Smehogolik @SMEMarketingTip @SMEPR @smerky216 @SMH_SocialMedia @smichm @Smile_n_Shine @SmileBooks @smileegirl @SmileeToLife @SmilenErin @SmilesHappen @smileyharly @smileyhealth @Smileysredbarn @SmilingMarketer @Smilinsteve @sMillys @smirchi @Smirnoff_There @smith_blarney @Smith_miniMBA2 @Smith_Tanya @SmithsonAnders @Smithy_001 @smitty_one_each @smiyao @SMKSensei @SMM_UK @smm360 @smm41263 @SMMadagency @smmcamp @smmguide @SMMindset @SMMmagazine @SMMonster @SMMProductions @SMMTweets @SMOBangalore @smoblogger @SMOCafe @smoke77777 @SmokeyMiller @SmokingWomen @SmokinHotPR @smoochydate2 @smoothsale @smorkinlabbit_ @SMOsocialmedia @smozee @SMP4you @SMPlans @SMSDallas @smt504 @smtrafficschool @SMU_HegiCareer @SMX_London @smykos @snackfanjapan @snagajob @snailmailnotes @snapon3 @SnapOutOfItShow @snappysalads @snbaird @sneakart @sneha_rg @Snikiddy @snipercatcher @snipermusic @SnippetGarden @SNKT @sno_buny @snoopyrufus @snorbrown @snovianty @snowbird122 @snowboardcast @Snowbrrd @snowgator69 @Snowisle @SNReach @SNSanalytics @snstouch @snuckertook @snunitliss @Snuzzy @SO_pr @SoakUpLiving @soapbox @SoapySoapy @sobreimoveis @sobseries @Soc_Media_Beast @soc08 @socalgirl @SoCalWriterGuy @soccer_football @SOCFX @sochristine @social_analysis @social_buttrfly @Social_Divas @Social_Dynamics @Social_Gal @Social_Manny @social_media @Social_Media_ @Social_MediaB2B @social_news @Social_Success @Social_USA @social2b @SocialBizNow @SocialBizTips @SocialBuzzOC @SocialCashGuy @SocialChadder @SocialClassroom @socialcloudnow @socialcpr @SocialDave @SocialDojo @socialemon @socialexpertnow @socialfans @SocialFire @SocialFlyr @SocialGreg @SocialGround @SocialGrow @SocialGuide @SocialInc @socialize4Money @SocializedWeb @SocializeUAE @socialJacqui @socialjana @socialkaren @SocialKeith @SociallySavvy4U @SociallySweet @SocialMarketin1 @SocialMassMktg @socialmbossuk @socialmedia_buz @socialmedia_mgr @socialmedia_Mk @Socialmedia_NZ @socialmedia_U @socialmedia0615 @socialmedia283 @socialmedia2u @socialmedia4bus @socialmedia78 @socialmedia815 @socialmediabiz @socialmediabros @SocialMediaBuch @SocialMediaBust @SocialMediaCRE @SocialMediaD @socialmediadeb @SocialMediaDel @SocialMediaDJ @socialmediadmd @SocialMediaEat @SocialMediaFan8 @SocialMediaGo @SocialMedialnEd @SOCIALMEDIAINFO @socialmediainmd @socialmediainst @SocialMediaJew @SocialMediaJob_ @SocialMediaMax @SocialMediaMaze @socialmediamind @socialmediamn @SocialMediaMum @Socialmediapath @SOCIALMEDIAPRO1 @SocialMediaSol @SocialMediaSt @SocialMediate @socialmediatek @SocialMediaWonk @SocialMktgDiva @socialmouths @socialMPH @socialmrkting @SocialMtgExpert @socialmushroom @SocialNapa @socialnate @socialnetandyou @SocialNetDaily @socialnetmarket @SocialNetNanny @SocialNetworkIt @SocialNetworkTV @SocialNetworkUs @socialnews09 @socialoomph @socialpage @SocialPMChick @socialpr @socialpsuccess @SocialPRMarket @SocialPro @SocialPsyche @socialradius @socialram @socialROI @SocialSammy @SocialSavvyGeek @SocialSideMedia @SocialSmarter @SocialStylist @SocialSundayNL @SocialTalkLive @socialtips @socialtoddler @SocialToolKit @socialtweeting @SocialVenture @SocialVisor @SocialWants @socialware @SocialWebMktg @socialwebnet @SOCIALWEBPR @SocialwebT @SocialWendy @socialwendypr @socialworkplace @socialxblog @Society @SocietyBakery @sociotope @SOCJacki @socks2739 @Socks4HappyPPL @SOCLoriandMark @SocMandthePea @socme2 @socmed_superman @SocMediabrain @SocmediaRckStr @SocMediaReviews @SocMediaTravel @SocMedRetweeter @socnetnews @socrecruitau @Soda_Hurts @Soffici @SofiaKeck @sofiazmf @sofiemoulin @SofitelDC @SofitelPhilly @SoFlaCommercial @soflatechlawyer @soFNcute @SoFreysh @softapps @SoftBeddingSets @softinet @softspotbywozzy @Softsquatch @Softwareex @Software4Free @SoftwareForFree @softwurkz @sogeshirts @SoGoEarn @SOGRnetwork @sohealthy4u @sohlfl @SOHLTC @SohlUSA @sohoaccessories @SOHOBusiness @SOHP_com @sokairavi @Sokos6 @sokule @sokule1 @Solamar @solar_power_kit @SolarAcademyInt @solardude1 @SolarEnergyNews @solarfeeds @Solargroupies @SolarGurus @SolarIdeas @solarisdesigns @SolarisStudios @solarmoneysaver @solarpv @SolarPanelHelp @SolarPowerNow @SolarSecurity @SolaSalonStudio @SoldOnEbay @Sole_Pro @SolfegeRadio @solismarchela @SOLive_RBatzer @SollevaGroup @solofo @sologan @solomons_homes @SolomonSaleh @solomonsucceeds @SolTecElec @solution2peace @solution416 @somaJohn @SOMD_Waterfront @Some1Has2Sayit @SoMeCentral @SomeChum @somediaintegcon @Someguynamedpat @SomeLifeBlog @SomersetMtg @soSeMtg @somistvan @somodii @sompongh @SONARconnects @Songpeople @Songster2000 @SoniaHolland @sonicallstar @sonja4health @SonjaandLibrary @Sonny1974 @SonnyAhuja @SonnyDayDreamer @sonnyfe @sonnyg @SonnyJohns @SonnyTuesday @SonOfGoom @Sonos_DMU @SonyaDomanski @sonyaga @soocee @sooncm @SoothingSkin @SoovoxSocialIQ @SooWhoopcom @sooz100359 @SophiaCR @sophiarael @sophie_charity @SophieBifield @sophieheng @SophomoricTumor @SoravJain @sorayapa @sorenbreiting @sorensson @sorgsorg @soriuq @sortprice @sos_haiti @soshle @SoSoJo

Acknowledgments

@sosusereva @sotaventure @sotiris1 @SotomayorScotus @SoTravelNow @Souihli @soulbmx @soulcaretv @soulfoodnetwork @soulfulbeauty @soulfulll_k @SoulHeartPart @soulmagnet75 @soulpossum @soulspiritual @soumyapr @SoundbiteCoach @soundtastykid3 @SouperSalad @souplantation @sourabhgoho @sourcedbykelly @sourcer21 @SourcerKelly @Southeasternr @southeasttouris @Southern_Living @SouthernGhosts @SouthernGifts @southernskiesag @SouthlakeChiro1 @southsidekustom @SouthWestFord @southwestliz @SouthwestMedia @sovbiz @Sovereign28 @soverland @SOWeiterbildung @soxgal @SOXGUY @soxiflue @spaatwillowbend @SpaBooker @SpaceSnark @SpaceyTracy2 @spamitis @SpammingReport @SpanishNow @spanktar @SpankyBrown @SparBernstein @spark_pc @sparkie5150 @SparklicAcid @sparklife @sparklingonline @sparklingruby @sparklyscotty @sparkypowell @sparticatv @SPARTICUSIAN @spassas @Spbwealth @spdesigns1 @SpeakerNinja @SpeakerSharyn @speakersnetwork @speakingbadger @speakingexpert @Speakingroses @SpeakingTech @SPEAKMANENT @SpecHosting @SpecialCupid @specialdesigns @Specisoft @Spectrumfcu @spectrumgraphix @SpeedCameraPOI @SpeedCoaching @speedhot @SpeedLearnNow @speedmarx @speedupyourlife @speimusic @speljamr @spencer_hunt @SpencerClick @SpencerHorn @SpencerMontgom @Spencersa @Spencerswife @spencerw3 @SpenceSmith @spes123 @SPFsocial @Spherion @sphoward @spidaman @spidercam @SpidermanGuru @spidersandmilk @SpiderWriters @Spiewak @Spike72AFA @spikehumer @SpilledInkRepU @spillspace @Spin_Thicket @spin1success @SpineBBMag @spinecor @Spinecor_brace @spininternet @Spiotter @spiraluptoday @spiritedal @SpiritEssences @Spiritfriends @spiritledrecov @spiritniche @SpiritOfAutism @SpiritualCarter @SpitCreekRanch @splgroup @Spluchster @spmu @spohlit @spoilerSource @Sponsume @Spoonfulofchoco @spoortsdood @sporebuster1 @spornaso @sport1912 @SportConference @SportinaHotels @sportinggoods1 @sportnewsdude @Sports4398 @sportsbetcappin @sportsbetspro @sportsosphere @SportSpotter @SportsPower @sportsviews @sportz123dotnet @Sportzlonl @SpotOn3D @SpottedWombat @SpouseCentrals @SpreadingIdeas @SpreadingJam @Spredfast @SpringAqua @SpringfieldEdge @springfwd @SpringhouseEduc @SpringsSEO @sprintertour @sproutqueen @spryd @Sptzllama @Spunky_PR @spurdave @spurinteractive @spwelch @SPwrite @SpychResearch @spyphoneguy @spyrosm @spyshopguy @sqltech2 @squarebeans @squaredcloud @SquareToesKern @Squeezeltln @squidoo_u_2 @Squinkman @srabe @sramana @srBurtonCook @srdill @sreede @srikar_techdrag @srimudigere @SriniMetta @SrinivasNarne @srirams @srivanihyd @srodriguezd @Srschierling @SRStran @SRVP @ss_telecombum @ssaikia @sschwend @SSDTEAM @sseagal @ssentamu @ssilvestrone @SSInc_STL @SSMVlogs @ssossen @SSP080594 @SStirling @Ssussanin @sswindale @ST_Louis_Rams @st_weiss @St0pSmokingNow @staceysoleil @staceywalker @Staci32 @staciacavalcante @StacidOCDate @staciedale @StaceinAtlanta @StacieShepp @staciestaub @stacigauny @stacihtims @StaciPerry @stacy_blackman @stacy_laurence4 @stacycrosby @stacyharp @stackinney @stacyknows @StacyMossHR @staenman @staffingsavvy @Staged_2_Design @stagingdiva @STALJO @Stalwartcom @StalyonMusic @stample @Stan_Lang @StandardofTrust @Standing_Stones @StandingFirmCM @StandOutMan @standupcomedy @StandUpComedy7 @StanfordFCU @stanfossum @StanGill @stangwizdak @StanHjerleid @Stanimiroff @stanlee @StanLenssen @StanleyGale @stanleysuen @stanlouw @stansmith2 @stantonmjones @Star9905 @Staralicious @Starbucker @starchycarb123 @starctchr @starexp @starkcb @StarlightAff @starpulp @starstreet @StarStruk @startaheart @StarTargets @StartASmallBiz @StartingPt @StartNewBiz @startupacademy @startupbiztalk @startupcoach @StartupGuru @StartupKey @startupprincess @StartupPro @Startuprecroot @StartUpsCA @STARTUPSMAP @StartupWeek_ly @startwithmoxie @StarwoodBuzz @starZdal @StateInsurance1 @Statelman @stateofelation @statesman @statu_boy @status_il @StaybridgeDFWN @stayclassyCHI @StayTunedReport @stayyoungernow @StBartsPremium @stbonaventure @stbsmith @StChristine @STCSTREET @StealingKitty @SteamRollerEQ @steamrollerinc @steamykitchen @steelemodels @SteelStudios @Stef_Cormont @Stefan_Berg @Stefan_Fischer @stefanal27 @stefanbell @stefanbraus @stefanedwards72 @stefaneyram @stefanholt @Stefanie_Bauer @StefanieFB @stefanilnin @stefanomizzella @stefantopfer @stefbonnet @steffenmoller @steffenson @StefMoore @StefSchumann @stegibson @SteinbrecherInc @Steinhude @steitiyeh @stella_design @Stella_Hernandz @stellaokc @StellarStrategy @stellarvisions @StellasBlossoms @stelzner @stemcellshealth @steph_begley @Steph_Nuvo @StephaneSandron @stephaniec2c @stephaniecombs @StephanieDeneke @StephanieFrank @StephanieJHale @StephanieMater @StephanieMDavis @StephanieNickel @StephaniePeck @stephanieshott @stephanieswann @StephanieWatson @StephanyPuno @StephCalakan @StephDHayes @Stephen_ATN @Stephen_Bray @stephen_dan @StephenBienko @stephbsanders @StephenClinton @stephencoles @StephenCourt @stephencurtin @stephendaviscxo @stephendebruyn @StephenDinehart @stephenkruiser @stephenleesings @stephenlynch @stephenodonnell @StephenRPohlit @stephensmith3 @StephenWelton @StephenWLarson @stephfox @stephgreenkc @Stephie_Lewis @stephleggett @StephSammons @StephSouthwick @StepIntoChina @StereoStone @SterlingFive @SterlingMail @SternalPR @StetsonU @steube @steve_dodd @steve_hartkopf @steve_kindred @Steve_MLM_Jones @Steve_SEO_UK @Steve_Wakefield @steve_ward @steve1johnson @SteveAkinsSEO @stevealfaronet @steveant @steveatrma @steveauthentic @steveb2u @SteveBauer @SteveBreitman @SteveBrossman @stevebuelow @stevecowan @stevedarnell @stevefarber @SteveFrerich @stevegasser @steveglissman @SteveGrim @SteveGTaylor @SteveHandy @SteveHMills @SteveHofstetter @steveholt27 @SteveInOhio @Stevejankowski @SteveKayser @stevekleber @SteveKoss @Stevelemons @Stevelev17 @SteveLevine1 @SteveLorenzo @SteveMacDonald @SteveManning @SteveMeehan5 @stevemordue @stevemullen @steven_fletcher @Steven_Shaw @StevenALowe @stevenaquaffect @stevenbrubaker @StevenBrun @StevenDownward @STEVENETWORK @StevenFudd @stevengiles @stevengmiller @stevengoforth @stevenhealey @StevenHudson @SteveniBiz @StevenLSnyder @stevenmills70 @stevenpdennis @stevenpmeadows @StevenRobello @stevenroddy @StevenRothberg @stevensanchez3 @StevenSchlagel @stevenseagul @stevenwagstaff @StevenZoernack @steveohscereal @Steveology @stevepohlit @steveriege @SteveRosenbaum @SteveRothaus @SteveSaimon @stevesipress @SteveSmith_Cake @SteveSmorgon @stevesoma @SteveStelzner @stevethegoose @stevetheseeker @SteveTN @stevetuf @SteveTylock @steveuk007 @SteveVale @SteveWoda @stevez33 @stevie11 @steviedove @SteveSays @steview @stewartbuzz @StewartWilson @StewySongs @StGeorgeCreativ @sthBodyJewelry @Stiberg @sticiviews @stiennon @Stigmare @stillatulsagirl @StillettoChick @stillgoingon @stillsafe @StillSoftVoice @stillsoul @stimulusaccess @StinkingRoseLA @stinman @stiridebine @stirlingbond @STISingles @StitcherDeb @stitchkingdom @StKonrath @STLChildrens @StLmate @StLNetworkGuru @StLouisWebTech @stlsmr @StMaartenDivers @StMarysU @stmnetwork @stoansteirer @Stoccado @stockaplus @StockGoodies @stockinvestor2 @stockmarketing @stocknetwork @stockphotog @stockplays @StocksDiva @StockSolution @Stocksox @StockStrategies @StockTalkRadio @StocktonBOGO @StockTweeters @StockyardsTexas @StokerAllure @StolenDogs @StoneCS @StoneleighHotel @stonepimp @stoneteam1 @stoneWoodOutlet @Stonyfield @StopBitingNails @stopsigntweets @stopsnoringtips @StopTheHike @stopthepolitics @Storage_News @StorageMonkeys @StorageNeighbor @storebrowser @Storenvy @storeprofits @Stormil8 @storylinePR @StoryofMyLife @StoryWorldwide @StowasserFranz @str8photography @str8biotch @stradablog @StraightSimon @strandstoelen @strange_surpris @stratlk @Strategic_Web @StrategicAdvice @StrategicGen @strategicsense @strategywebd @StratLearner @stratovaari @Stratspecialist @strawberry_luv @StreamedMovies @streamingepisod @streamingmarv @StreamiumTweets @streamlabel @StreamlineFS @streetadsmedia2 @streetforce1 @StreetKingEnt @Streetmachine @StreetReeves @STREETwear_ @stremcha @StressFreeBill @StressFreeCook @stressless @strick @StrikeBowling @Strikerphil @strongcitytech @stronghuman @StrongmanTweets @stroupsam @StructuredMindz @strulowitz @stuartchap @StuartDMT @stuartfeigley @stuartflatt @stuartlang @stuartlockley @StuartMilton @stuarttan @stuartwitts @StuartZadel @stubsy315 @Stuck_Together @StudentLifeOC @StudentMindPwr @students4money @studio_automate @studio525 @StudiodiMare @studiomoviegril @Studios92_ @StudyDroid @StudyingAbroad @studyingskills @stuffmagazine @stulrix @StuMcMullin @StuMSmith @stuntmenmovie @stupid_fish @StureNyberg @sturg58 @StuSmaab @StuWeinstock @stweetdeals @stweetSHAUNA @STXherry @style_house @styledo @styleontherun

The Social Media Business Equation

@styleshark @stylishcurves @stylishlyme @stylishtalk @StyriaEventscom @suarezmoises @sub5mango @subashs @subbujois @sublimebakery @subliminalvideo @submit_articles @submitexpress @SubmitWizard @subq @SubsFrisco @Suburban_Farmer @suburbanmama @suburbansurvive @SuburbanWines @suburbanwino @suburbview @SubZeroService @Success__Secret @Success_4_All @success_brenda @Success_Search @Success_with_BP @successadvisor @successbiz @SuccessBooks @SuccessCoachNJ @SuccessExpo @SuccessFit @successforum @successfulmlm @successify @Successmate @successnation @successtab @successstrategy @SuccessTutor @successwalls @SuccessWithMike @succoach @SucksDiary @SuckyPoems @sudharsanece @sudiptaroy @sudoCoder @Sue_Koch @sue_oshea @sueandsteve @SueAwesome @sueballmann @sueblaney @suecartwright @suegresham @SueInge @sueissilly @suekearney @Suellen_Hughes @SueMarks @suemassey83 @suendercafe @SueOppies @SuePapadoulis @SueRileyRealty @SueScaletta @suevanfleet @sueyoungmedia @suffrena @Sugar_Smash @SugarDee @SugarfootRock @SugarJones @sugeshg @SugestFollow @SuggestionBox @sugoiasiangirl @suhel_khan @SujataChadha @SujataKohli @sumal @sumaya @summer_goodwin @summersidePEI @summitlifecoach @SummittBusiness @sun_and_Beach_ @SundanceSuccess @SunDiety @sundognet @Sung_H_Lee @SunilJaiswal @SunitaRaheja @SunLifeGuys @SunMergers @SunnyMegatron @SunnyRainer @SunnyThoughts @sunpech @SunRemuServices @SunriseFiction @sunryyse_tw @SunsetMotorsLA @sunshail @sunshineserious @SunStudioLA @sunti_wide @Sunwarrior @SupAcademy @Suparnamalhotra @super_mango @SuperAffiliateC @SuperAffiliateI @SUPERbau @superbowlsmash @SupercoolAgency @superdupershark @superearners @SuperEB @SuperFairyQueen @SuperGirl @SuperHeroPS @superhomebiz @SuperiorAZ @superiorpayday @superkiing @Superkoala_FR @Superlearning @SupermanLovesU @supermom_in_ny @supermoms @superonlineman @SuperParentMom @SuperShopperorg @Superyax @SupJoseph @suplementa @SupplyChainBlog @SupporterHAITI @SupportShidonii @SupportUSForces @supremeluxe @Supt_surcease @SurajOpenBook @SurfAds @surfcanyon @Surfcityhurley @Surfettes @surffit @SurfGirlBrit @surfingchef @surfingmaniac @surfjar @SurfRecession @SurfSportsCoach @surfster99 @surfvoucher @SurgeryUSA @SurgiSil @surrealchicago @SurRylgroup @survey4u @surveysam @SurveysRock @Surya_Sage @susan_boyle_com @Susan_Cox @Susan_Eller @Susan_Hopper @susan_neonlily @Susan_Nicol @Susan_OHara @susan300tweets @SusanBonfiglio @SusanBoylesCat @SusanCareerTrek @SusanCosmos @SusanCritelli @susandore @susanemeadmh @SusanFinco @susangilmore @susangiurleo @susanhaimet @susanhanshaw @susanjarema @SusanKovalesky @SusanMazza @susannegriffing @susannewcomer @SusanOdev @SusanPreston @susanroane @SusanSargood @susansoaps @susantellem @susanwilson39 @susaye @susby @Sushi_Zushi @sushilpunia @sushisurfer @susiemac @susiecheng @susiecheng @SusieKline @susiequilter @susiescarth @susihendarti @sustainableweb @SustainSites @susybb @Sutclip1957 @SuuperG @SuuzWestgeest @SuzanaPR @Suzanasoares @Suzanna60 @Suzanne_Lavigne @SuzanneHI10 @suzannekattau @suzannepeters @SuzanneShaffer @suzanschmitt @suzi_fairbairn @SuzieCheel @suzieholmes @SuziMorris @suzipphillips @suzipomerantz @suzmccormick @SuzooMukherjee @suzukiofwichita @suzyspaatz @suzyturn @svartling @svb @svcprodirect @SvenJohnston @svennyg @svenschweizer @svitasek @Swag_Web_Design @SwagTips101 @swallow_town @SwamiCity @SwamiScotty @SwampSchool @swampy52 @SwamBlog @SwankyPaper @swapalease @swarnavarb @swarnaw @swarrman @swarup @SWAT_Institute @swaygrl @SWBizCom @swbuyers @swedal @SwedishGirlLisa @swee06840 @sweet_chris23 @sweet_mallows @sweetdebbie101 @sweeters14 @SweetEsKitchen @SweetestBids @sweethoneybee6 @SweetLeafTV @SweetMarketing @sweetnsexy210 @SweetRetreatHC @sweetsfoods @SweetSoaps @SweetSue @sweetwatersavin @swentz @swervinErv @Sweta6 @swhitegrass @swierm @SwiftIncome @Swiggs @SwirlIWine @swissbusiness @swisschasy @SwissTourism @switchyourhouse @SWITTERmrossi @swjetski_rental @SWJS @swmcon @swonderlin @swopper_news @SWSF @SWTulsa @SXM_Intern @syafiqrahman @Sybil_B @SyedmRaza @sylifamukdas @sylvamc @Sylvia_Cheong @sylviabrowder @SylviaBuetow @SylviaPerreault @sylviavillagran @SylvieDahl @SylvieGuiziou @sylwilson @Symfonic @SympoOBGYN @synapseone @synaurabusiness @SyncCreation @syndicatescoop @SYNERGYCLUBS @synergyofmind @SynergySG @Syracusejobs @SysCommUK @SysCorp @syseda @systemwidgets @sytasa @sytru @Sze_Lee @sztorinethu @t_asia @T_Central @T_Harv_Eker @t_retoevents @T_RoyJackson @t_xu @t0dds @tl8u @TInyPrinc3ss @T2_BackAlley @T2TNetworkCom @T3CHN0L0GIC @t5blog @TaaDaaGina @TAB_ZThree @tabat @Table4Five2 @TablesFurniture @taboohairsalon @TAC_NISO @TachelleDaniels @Tacklesaver @Taco_Bueno @TacticalContact @TaenGZaaZy @tagnest_au @TAGoldMine @tagrr @TAH99 @tahoeblu @TiagaCompany @taikosolutions @TaipanCoin @tairby @tairoy @tajujoseph @takapitcha @takatezu @take26media0 @Take2seconds @takeaction2 @takeastand @TakeMeNational @takemoneyfree @TakeThe_Plunge @TakeTheNextStep @takingchargenow @takisrs @taksu33 @Talenpalet1 @TalentArrow @TalentAsia @TalentCulture @TalentFishInc @TalentHook @TalentTalks @talenttribes @TaliGillette @talk_business @talk2brazil @TalKamal @TalkativePR @TalkDebbie @TalkDisney @Talkin_Sport @TalkShowNews @TalkStaff_Gary @TallWithTracy @TallChicknVegas @tallshipp @Talya @tamagawl @TamalanehH @tamara_cobbin @tamaradull @TamaraFulcher @tamcdonald @tamebay @TamelaJaeger @tamhajerry @TamiAtVCConnex @tamihonesty @TamiSchiller @Tammie_Nielsen @TammyAndFriends @TammyBurnell @TammyLandau @tammymoore @TammySievers @tammymuy @tammmywjones @TampaEFL @tampico @Tampogonow @tamrataylor @tamuken @Tanamaree @tanay46 @TAndersonAZ @Tangara @tangerinesalons @taniawil @tankbiz @tankforyou @TannersDad @TantricMaster @tantwy @tanyamarie13 @TanyaRoseS @TanyaSahota @taosays @tapaslunchco @tappetalk @tapsearcher @Tara__S @tara_camp @Tara_Nelson @Tara_SpeakSay @taracarbo @TARAdactyl @TaraHFO @TaraHolling @TaraKachaturoff @TaraLangey @Taramichener @tarantellamedia @tarapos @tarasgetz @tarasview @taraturkl @tarekmohamed @targetedprofits @TargetLatino @TargetRecruiter @TargetStars @TARHhhhh @tarrell69 @tarrikjackson @tarshajacksonva @TART_Bakery @tarunguptal989 @TarynP @TarzanRusso @TaserPartyGirl @Tashaeva @TashadyHodaro @tashmanna @TashDiary @Tasi_Lima @TaskRabbit @TaskStreetTeam @TasteAddison @TasteandTintle @tasteforcooking @TasteForLife @tasteNZ @tasteofaz @tastetvnetwork @tatagra @TatianaGonzalez @tatopu @tatterscoops @TattooLifestyle @TattooRebel @Tattoos2 @Tauhidahl @TauhidChappell @tauhidul @Taurus3DLogos @tavanloc @tavomi15 @Taw9eel @tax_me_less @taxgirl @taxhelprightnow @taxhelpukcom @TaxPro2HelpYou @taxresolution @taxreturnuk @taxtherapy @Taxthink @taxtweeter @TaydeAburto @tayfilms @Taylor_K @Taylor_Robins @tayloredassess @taylorfyhrie @Taylorjordin @TaylorLauren @taylormadeideas @TaylorMntr @TaylorRMarshall @TayoRockson @tayuda @TazSolutions @tbctainment @TBilich @TBMMinc @tbouchey @tboyum @tbranchsolution @tbusbey @tc_furnace @TC247_Networks @tcaoitTW @Tcat @tchinformer @TCLMarshals @TCMortgage @tcmtweet @tcotchat @TCS_biz @TCSKINNER @tcstamara @TCTaxTeaParty @TCsuzuk247 @TD_TestBot @tdanford @tdcinhawaii @tdgobux @tdisanta @TdotHuskies @tdowns1964 @tdwusavalues @TeaBreakCrumbs @teachalotgirl @Teachersgrammar @teachinghands @TeachMeGP @teamejordan @teachmetech @Teachtofreedom @TeacupGardener @Teafft @tealac @Tealow @Team_Grandma @Team2Infinity @TeamAverageJoe @TeamBeadlesIndo @teambuild @teamfactor @teamFFriends_ @TeamKay @teamkreate @TeamMarketing @TeamMerkaba @Teamplayer02 @teamplayer14 @teamplayers @TeamSurgical @teamtobinhomes @TeamWBC @TeamworkRadio @TeamworkTimG @Teapartier2010 @teapartysigns @teapriestess @TEApublican @Tears_ofCrimson @teastal @tecdat3 @Tech_Bit @TechArmy @TechChunks @techclubcpr @TechCoach @TechEEZ @TechFrog @TechGeek54 @techglance @techintwenty @TechLemmings @techmashup @techmedicus2 @technewsmiw @TechnicaGroep @TechniCOWL @Technisource @technocrom @TechnoEvanGuy @TechnologyFeed @technomania @TechnoPaganism @technograph @TechnoScotty @Technomics1 @techpinas @TechPRMaven @techrecruiterva @techroid @techsavvychic @TechShali @techydude46 @TechyTommy @TechZader @TechZoomIn @TECMidwest @tecnoinfo_br @ted_mcgrath @tedbradford2 @tedcoine @TeddyTester @TeddyTowncrier @TedInJest @TEDJohnMark @tedkinzer @tedmurphy @TedNguyen @TedRobertson @TedRubin @tedsv @TEDxB @TEENchirp @TeenDomainer @teendotvn @teenfabulous @Tegart @tegernsee_tv @tehnoskomputi @tehostamo @TeitoKlein @tejas74 @tejima @tejones @TEK2_CARDS

Acknowledgments

@tekany @TekBz @TEKELPOLO @TEKGROUP @tekkieblog @teknews @telamony @Tele_Watch @TeleCollege @TelecomRush @TelecomSpe @telekton @teletrack @teliaco @TellaFriend @Tellem @tellmethursday @teltub_daily @temacafe1000 @temazo @TembuaLanguage @TemerityMag @temhideki @TemperedMC @TemplateCascade @templehayes @tenaciousartist @tencredit @tenfacesofshe @tengreenones @TenPercentLegal @tentop10 @TenutaVitanza @TeoGelato @TeppoT @TequilaRack @TeraRecipes @tercerowines @terencechung @terencedwards @Teresa_MrsB @teresaberry @TeresaCleveland @teresacuervo @TeresaFBarrett @TeresaLynn9 @TeresasFengShui @TeresaSimons @teresawhite @teri_sawers @teridusold @TeriGatarz @teriguill @terilg @terimorris @teripayne @TerjeSkakstad @term_papers @terner6 @Terraellen @Terrance247 @TerranceCharles @TerranceDJones @terrasantapr @TerraSD @TerrellSandefur @TerrenceYoung @terriclay @TerriDolan @TerriKosecki @Terrillific @terrimcculloch @terripark @Terry_Allison @terry_levine @Terry_Long @TerryAlmond @terrycoker @terryjbrown @TerryJett @TerryLawFirm @terryloving @terrymarkle @terrymslobodian @terrypetrovick @terryptb @terrystarkey1 @TerryUnrau @TerryVoth @TerryWygal @terunghijau @TeruoArtistry @tess0318 @Tessazan @TesslerPT @teteroces @tetka @tetsumo @Tetsuya_K @tevaloa @tevami @texanrose @Texaplex @Texas_News @Texas4god @TexasBarBooks @texasdefensive @TexasGarabedian @TexasGrand @texashealth_jen @Texasholly @TexasJackFlash @TexasLegendsNBA @TexasLending @texasmag @TexasPhotoBooth @texasranchscape @TexasRV @TexasTavern @TexasTech @TexasTripper @TexasWineTweets @texeyes @Texfoot @Text4Cocktails @textinsicht @textlicious @textopportunity @textprovider @texttogift @texttur @TezOsman @Tfawcett1310 @tfdu @TferThomas @tfhall @TFInternational @TGarzaPhotog @tginnett @tgmason @th_watches @ThaiiisR @ThaiVest @ThaLoveOfMoney @Thames21 @thamusicmaster @thankuthursday @ThanMerrill @TharaldsonHosp @ThaRealMisfit @That_DanRyan @ThatDamnKwash @ThatEricAlper @ThatFeelsNICE2 @thathurtabit @thatMLMbeat @thatreallybites @thatsbusiness @thatspeaker @thattalldude @thatwoman_is @ThaVM @ThBusinessCoach @thdon @THE_MVP @The_Amplifetes @the_antitweet @the_ASPEARS @The_CLA_Group @The_Crums @The_Dallas_Man @the_dubsters @the_ferg @the_great_i_am @the_jamielynn @The_Jerri_Ann @the_kid1130 @the_killer65 @The_Life_Coach @the_mane_scene @the_netwerk @the_nose @The_Proposal @the_Rich_Kidd @the_RT_guy @The_Seeder @The_Social_CEO @The_Thunderbolt @the_vinci @the_wallpapers @the33news @the3rdgoal @TheAaronBowley @TheAbramson @theabundantgift @TheaClay @TheActingCenter @TheAdolphus @theahaguy @theairportvalet @theajayieffect @thealphafemme @theantijared @theAOMC @TheArrivalGuide @TheAssistant4u @theaterprogram @TheatreIV @TheAveStylist @TheB0yW0nder @thebabyelmoshow @thebachelorguy @thebandwagonfw @thebarblogger @thebarista159 @TheBasookaBoys @TheBBWPersonals @thebeachshow @TheBeanCast @thebeaverhousen @thebetterlife @TheBibleGuy @TheBigfella @TheBigKlosowski @thebikenut @thebitbit @THEBLASTINGCAP @theblogstudio @TheBodTEAShop @thebodyknows @TheBoffinTeam @thebookchannel @theboxlounge @TheBreastCancer @TheBritishTexan @TheBruzzBuzz @TheBuddhaWay @TheBumpMeister @thebutterlife @TheBuzzinator @Thecamecenter @thecandlelady @TheCatCo @thechannelc @thechimachine @TheChrisDockery @TheChrisWalters @thecircuit_ @theclickbankcde @TheClineGroup @TheCoffeeKlatch @TheComedyShop @TheCommonGolfer @TheCommonHoster @TheCompEdge @TheCompWizard @TheConceptWhiz @TheConcupiscent @TheCoolestCool @thecopypro @TheCosmonaut @TheCostMagazine @thecrazymonkey @TheCrazyOleMan @TheCreditReport @TheCrexent @TheCRMGuy @thecrowies @TheCupcakeBlog @thecurelist @TheCVClinic @thecwordagency @TheDailyBlonde @TheDailyWoman @TheDanaReport @TheDapAffect @TheDaringWoman @thedarrenhughes @TheDateSafeTeam @TheDawsonMethod @thediaperbaker @TheDietAdvisors @TheDigitalDoctr @TheDigiWAVE @THEDJPHAZE @thedogmeister @thedomesticdiva @thedoodlemoodle @thedoomsday @TheDoorClubs @theDoOverGuy @TheDougAnderson @thedroidguy @TheDrop @thedropshipper @TheDuffyAgency @TheDukeofEarle @TheECI @TheEGOExpert @TheEllipseCow @theeMailguide @TheEndReview @TheExpert @TheFactRemains @thefatigue @TheFeinsteins @TheFifthDriver @TheFirstCup @TheFirstTeeLR @TheFishCatcher @theflagsofdawn @thefloorbroker @THEFLYLADY @thefolllower @thefollowking @thefoodwarrior @thefootballnut @theForexArticle @thefoundationau @TheFreeGazette @TheFrownies @thefrugalchef @TheFullNoise @TheFundingGuru @thefutureisred @TheGadgetHound @TheGadgetStack @TheGaming411 @TheGazzMan @thegiftlady @TheGLDC @thegoddelusion @TheGoldenhearts @TheGoodOnes_srl @TheGoToSite @thegrammardoc @thegrandcinema @TheGreatDanaJ @thegreenchick @TheGreenHome @TheGreenOTCHB @TheGreenPM @thegreenslam @thegregbell @TheGscape @TheGuruGirls @TheGutes @TheGymCoach @thehalloffamers @TheHandymanPro @thehannaclarke @thehappypainter @TheHealthJunky @theheartofArt @TheHenry @thehilltweets @TheHippieDiva @TheHoCal @TheHolmesGroup @TheHomeBizWoman @TheHRExpert_Sam @thehrgoddess @TheHRmaven @thehrphenomenal @thehrstore @thehulkster @TheHWFactor @theilife @theimpactzone @theIMStrategy @TheInspirista @TheIntelligentW @theintelligiser @TheInterviewPro @TheInterzone @theiphonereview @TheJanF @TheJayJones @thejeffkaller @TheJEMKelly @TheJeffWagner @thejimjams @TheJimmyHart @thejobmatch @theJogarGroup @thejoule @TheJoyntChicago @thejuicywoman @TheKansan_News @TheKarleeStar @TheKayWay @thekells @thekevincouch @TheKeydotcom @TheKidsDoctor @thekillertweets @thekindlekraze @thekindlestop @TheKingsGinger @thekjacrew @TheKrabb @thelamestdotcom @thelaptopgeek @TheLastGoodYear @thelastshow @TheLatestDeal @TheLauraJackson @TheLazyMan @TheLeaderLab @TheLeadShop @Thelegendress @TheLemonadeBoy @TheLesbianMafia @thelifedesigner @TheLifeinChrist @TheLifeofPower @TheLinkedinGuy @TheLittleGuy @theLIUtenant @thelivingwork @TheLmaBaker @TheLmaDreyer @thelocaltourist @TheLouRecruiter @theloyaltyfirm @thelundrgrengang @TheLundy @TheLVTweetUP @TheMadeBed @TheMaidenVoyage @TheMark1000 @TheMarketaire @TheMartaReport @themartinidiva @TheMarvelman1 @TheMattDuggan @themattymiller @TheMDBrand @themediamatters @themediamogul @themeetmarket @themelib @Themelis_Cuiper @themestyles @TheMierz @TheMisfitsRep @TheMissionSpec @TheMitchellz @TheMoeYouKnow @TheMomiverse @TheMommaGuide @TheMoneyDealer @TheMontereyCo @themoversreview @themoviepool @theMRC @TheMsAnonymous @TheMuscats @THEMUSTANG @Themwap @thenakedpilot @TheNameEngine @thenameshopnyc @TheNeelGroup @TheNegotiator @TheNetConnector @thenetshop @TheNewsChick @TheNextFollower @theoaksatboca @theoddnumbers @TheoHanden @theoilMD @TheOldFarmHouse @TheOmahaBeef @TheOnion_ @theonlinebizman @TheOnlineMLM8 @Theonlygoodguy @TheOnlyMocha @TheOperaInsider @theopportunity @TheOregonianBoo @TheORing360Live @TheOysters @TheParentHive @ThePastime @ThePetPip @ThePetPortal @thepetsplace2 @thephillife @thephotoargus @thepianomarket @thepizzaexpert @theplanetd @ThePMCoach @thepokerusablog @ThePondJumper @thepowerbrasil @ThePresentCo @ThePrettyBxtch @thePRguycom @ThePriceGroup @thePrintDaddy @theprintlounge @theprjkt @TheProfit @TheProfitShare @thepropertybiz @THEpropertyDiva @TheProphetBar @ThePRwriter @ThePWshowXXX @TheQuoteWhore @TheQwoffBoys @therabreath @TherapyDogGabe @TherapyOnline @therealamyzents @TheRealJFella @therealkatia @TheRealMenice @therealmfb @TheRealUmar @TheReOwl @theredrecruiter @theredstapler @TheReelCritics @theresabaiocco @TheresaBClarke @theresadowning @TheresaDurrant @TheresaGreen101 @theresajohnson @theresajones @TheresaLargusa @ThereseMiu @theresumechick @TheResumeMama @theresumewriter @thereyougothen @TheRichardScott @therichman001 @TheRightJobs @TheRiseToTheTop @TheRoomMovie @TheRoxor @theroxy @therriensecure @TheRudeTypist @TheRudyReport @TheSantaYnezInn @thestarigroup @thesavingqueen @TheSavvyDoc @thesavvyseller @theschoolbag @thescoop1 @thescottbishop @TheSeanTucker @thesearchagents @TheSearchGuru @thesecretbrasil @theSeobaba @TheSEOGenie @TheShanAlwis @theshearsfamily @TheShyMuse @thesidestrip @thesilverbarn @TheSkinSociety @Thesmallvoice @thesmmguru @thesocialbiddy @TheSocialCHRO @TheSocialCMO @TheSocialOlive @thesocialpro @TheSocialSquad @thesocialtour @TheSocMediaPro @thesolarcoach @TheSolardiva @theSongLine @thesoulchick @thespecific @TheStarFactory @thestinkingrose @TheStockScout @TheStockTwitter @thestreetsiknow @thesuccesszone @TheSurfBeagle @Theta_Miracles

183

The Social Media Business Equation

@TheTASCGroup @theteachingbox @thetearooms @theteeshirts @TheTerzaFactor @TheThirdStage @TheThreePeaks @thetich @thetico4ll @thetigerdouble @TheTimeTamer @TheTinyJEWELBox @thetoiletpaper @TheTonyChan @TheTrafalgar @TheTravelEditor @thetravelsecret @thetweet_tank @TheTweet_tanks @thetweetcheckr @thetweetiegirl @thetweettanklen @TheTweetTankone @thetwinkieaward @TheUltraBeast @TheUMS @TheUNPAclub @TheUWC @TheValentyne @TheValOlsonCos @TheVCF @theVETRecruiter @thevikings @theVIPERroom @TheWanjiru @TheWarriorSage @TheWatersAgency @TheWealthyCop @thewebchef @TheWebRockstar @TheWebSqueeze @TheWebWarrior @theweddingproje @thewhalehunters @TheWhistlingElk @TheWineWhore @thewiredserf @TheWisdomCrowds @TheWizardofO @TheWomensMuseum @thewritersroad @thewritingcode @thextremebiz @TheYaffeGroup @TheYandR_Lady @theyne @theyoungdread @TheYoungTurks @TheZenBull @TheZuckerTeam @ThierrySmeekes @thijssie @Things2sell @thingstotweet @THINK_write @thinkbigKC @ThinkBigLabs @ThinkBigNow @thinkbsg @ThinkBusiness @ThinkCausality @ThinkingCoach @ThinkInNewAreas @thinkproductive @ThinkPyxl @thinkreferrals @thinktosucceed @thinkvaulter @ThinkWithSatish @thinkyourmoney @thirddoor @ThirdSectorLab @thirstyfishinfo @Thirteen11 @ThirtyOne_Gifts @ThisDayInRock @thisgoodriddle @thisisbigfish @ThisisDrewMeyer @thisisjustin @thisismattball @thisistokyo @ThisIsW @ThisnThatBlog @THmelar @thomannlTZ @Thomas_Weil @Thomas0985 @thomas3762 @ThomasAllenlV @thomascarroll @thomascjensen @thomascook @ThomasGordonONE @thomasjames201 @ThomasKastor @ThomasKish @ThomasMarzano @ThomasMcEvoy @ThomasNutrition @thomasrieke @thomasrobinson1 @ThomasShea @ThomasShort2334 @ThomasTimely @thomaswigington @thomericardo @ThommiOdom @ThomRainer @ThomScott @thomswartwood @thorbengeyer @thorstnbrck @Thotpot @thoughtLEADERS @ThoughtPartner @thoward @thpeppermntleaf @thprwil @Three_Ten @Threedot @ThreeGirlsMedia @ThreeSixtyPhoto @threestonefire @ThriftyNWMom @ThriftyVault @thrillbuys @thrillophilia @ThriveDavie @thtlighting @thubten @THull @ThumpNetwork @ThunderandBlood @thuypro @Thwapr @Tia_Mateo @TiaDobi @TiasOWNshow @TiciaEvans @tickethaters @Ticketmaster @TicketOS @TickleLipoNow @TickStream @TickTocKs @TickYes @ticopost @TiDoma @TiEcon @tiefmesser @tiegsj @Tiemorch @Tientjesnet @TifaLockhart @tifanny_g @tifastrife17 @TiffaniBear @TiffanieTillman @tiffanycarlen @TiffanyDoughty @TiffanyEckhardt @TiffanyHo @TiffanyLacy @thiffanyodutoye @tifffanyandco @tifftaylorx @TigerEye_MLM @TigerFanatics @tigernow @tigerwoodsman @TigerYung @Tigger668 @tiggertagger @tiggio @TiheiMauriora @tijuanaHavenhil @tikanew @TikejaOnline @tikilis @tilakhira @tildensky @tilphotoNorway @Tim_Long @tim_malone @tim_woods @tim8155 @tim9house @timacummins @timandjulie @timastevens @TimAtkinson_ @timbay @TimBesecker @Timbofoster @TimBonds @TimBransford @timbruner @timcarter @TimClowers @TimDanyo @TimDarnellAC @TimDebronsky @Time2Design @time2evolvit @Time2LivYRvison @timeapplication @TimeBridge @timecoaching @TimeforLifeVA @TimeOutMom @timepicks @timesharebuyer @TimeshareExit @TimeToGetYours @TimeToGoVirtual @timewarnerc4ble @timfrick @timhastings @timheeney @TimJensen @timjonesdenver @TimLovitt @TimMoore @TimmyBx @TimmyRex @TimmySabre @TimoJappinen @timonlinementor @TimoRonkainen @timothyBlack @TimothyBurke @TimothyCaron @TimothyEnalls @timotis @TimProvise @TimRandle @TimRedmond @TimSackett @timsander @Timsociety @TimsStrategy @TimSteamboat @timsthomas @timtaxde @TimTyus @TimWoda @tina_w_hudson @tina_yip @Tinabobina808 @TinaBradfordPR @TinaCook @TinaGonda @tinakouts @TinaLouise16 @TinaMc @tinamills @tinammichaud @TinaPFoster @tinastullracing @TinHangLiu @Tinu @TinyDancer500 @tinyprint @Tips4BecomeRich @tips4smo @tipshowtomake @TIQ1 @Tirgumit @tiroaconsulting @Tis_Himslf @tishyb @TitaSGarcia @Tiwankiw @TiXiTBox @TizJustCool @TizJustStupid @TJBillings @tjbuffoonery @TJCarter02 @TJeffersonQuote @tjholthaus @tjhuckabee @TJMcCue @tjnowakl @TJNTIY @tjones0 @tjowensl @tjsitback @tjuan @TKarlMiller @tkellenaers @TKFwriter @tkinder @tkireilis @tkmoss @tkolsto @tkpleslie @tkripas @tkung @tkusano @TLBaker1 @TLCxHOME @tlindorfer @tlmaurer @TLOTL @tlpeery @TLS_Marketing @TLWH @tmaduri @tmantra @TMarieHilton @TMatlack @tmattis67 @tmblairla @tmcbeliever @TMCdynamicsGP @tmchappy @tmclain @tmcprdctns @tmctyping @TMGmedia @TMHComputer @tmjhelp @tmmJill @tmmywllms @tmonhollon @tmopperman @tmoreira @tmpfeiffer @tmpollard @tmraider @TMRDirect @TMS_Apps @tmsilvers @tnash77 @tnbasant @TNbase @tnchocolatier @tnmg4u @tnooz @TNR01 @Tobaccokills @tobefreeman @tobey4 @tobiasblake @ToBKingsley @Toby_Metcalf @toby_zeta @tobyparkins @ToccaraLuv @tod_bods @Today_Coupon @todayisdifferen @todaysgiveaways @todaysgolfdeal @todd_herman @Todd_Rutledge @Todd_Staples @toddafoster @toddbesser @ToddBrink @ToddGellman @ToddGilmore @toddhuff123 @ToddMGreene @toddmintz @ToddMuffley @ToddPLamb @ToddPosey @toddschlomer @toddschnick @ToddTilley @toddvo @ToddZebert @ToDoInDallas @ToDoInDFW @Toewie @togetherdating @togetherwf @Togzee @ToJuchem @TokiTover @Tolis_Potiomkin @Toltecjohn @TOLuxurySuites @Tom_Brumpton_PR @Tom_Duke @Tom_Foxy @Tom_John @tom_mcleod @Tom_Messett @tom_proost @tom_siwik @Tom_Strebbot @Tom_Zegan_ @tom4cam @tomaadv @tomagotchi @tomallinder @TomAntion @tomaslau @tombed @tomblanco @tombolt @tombrooks1211 @TomBuford @tomcanning @tomchand @TOMCOGroup @TomConvers @TomDickson @TomDoherty @TomDuong @TomEHenderson @TomEllisAB @tomesimpson @tomeuCabrer @tomfeyer @TomFlowerPro @tomhalle @tomhaney @TomHangs @TomHaupt @TomHCAnderson @tomhodbod @TomHumbarger @tominsky @tomkeating @tomleblanc0124 @TomMalesic @TomMangone @TomMartin @tommur @tommycummings @tommyismyname @TommyKovatch @tommylinsley @tommythomas1523 @tommytrc @TommyWierper @tommyworld @TomOdell @tomotake1873 @TomOwens149 @Tomplay @tomremington @tomretterbusch @TomRoyce @TomSalataLaw @tomschaepper @tomsebastiani @TomsRiverHomes @TomStrignano @TomSwift @tomthielman @tomtravel2 @TomTuohy @tomturnbull @tomupton33 @TomVeo @tomwer_usa2day @tonerdiva @TonerForAutism @toneyfitzgerald @ToniBahn @tonibirdsong @tonicascio @tonichanakas @tonifad @ToniHoffmann @tonipalone @ToniShrader @TonkaPR @Tonny3 @tonton_mtl @Tony_Dao @tony_deol @Tony_van_Kessel @Tony_Verde @tonyadam57 @TonyAlverio @TonyaStaab @TonyAtDQ @tonybeach @TonyBurroughs @tonyburrus @tonyChackeres @tonydbaker @TonyDiCostanzo @tonydisanza @tonyeldridge @tonygates44 @TonyLazz @tonylogue @tonylongo @TonyMacKGD @TonyMarino @tonymorganlive @TonymZito @tonynwright @tonypchicago @tonypisano @tonyrgee @tonyriggins @TonyRobbinsFans @tonysfi @tonyshan @TonyStorti @tonyuk42 @TonyValkov @tonyvirtual @TonyZito5_37 @tools_seo @toon_c @tooncap @TooNiceStocks @toonkerssemaker @Toonmix @toothfairycall @top_body @Top_Lanches @Top100PSStores @top20reos @top500listpromo @TopAchievers @topbananas @TopBibleVerses @TopCameraReview @topcashcow @TopCashGifting @topcasinos4u @topchoise @TopDogNews @TopDollar1000 @TopEmailMarket @topfloorstudio @topgrowthstock @TopGunMLM @TopHitPerfume @TopLinked @TopMarketingTip @topmastermind @TOPpercent @TopProperties @toprecruiters @topsalesmaker @TopSec1 @topsecrets4u @topseoservices @TopStarDiamond @TopTravelAsia @TopTweeterTools @TopUserRetweets @Torch762 @torchingigloos @ToriJarvis @ToriJohnson @ToriMacLean @tornadotorino @tornow @Toronto_PR_Guy @TorontoCityNews @TorontoTruth @TorPix @TorresAcid @torsten_panzer @TorstenNeumann @torvijs @toryradio @ToshikaR @ToshioShoko @toshreekant @toskana @tostina @tosyali @Total_Meaghan @Total_Rewards @Total_Telecom @Totalinvest @totallychadders @TotalRealEstate @totaltennis @TotalViperNet @totc @ToThink @totruck @TouchingWood @touchitcreative @touchkarma @touchscreenfad @touchygirl @Tourismstudents @TourismTrends @TouristCroatia @touristtracker @TourLafayetteLA @Tournantinc @tours4fun @torscotland @towelfolding @TownMeDallas @toxic1 @toxic_stores @Toy_Joy @toyinosunlaja @ToyotaLew @ToysbUs @ToysRUs @toytips @tp1977 @tpandika @TPEntrepreneur @tpettis @tpholmes @TPinkCouture @TPO_Hisself @TPOs_BlogList @TPOs_Daily_Love @TPOs_Favorites @TPPCtv @tpr2 @tr1sh @traackr @Trace_Cohen @TraceTV @Tracey_D @TraceyBruns @TraceyCJones @TraceyDelCamp @TraceyMMOwen @traceynile @tracie914 @TraciGregory @traciking @tracitoguchi @TrackDaddyProd @trackur @tracmaroney @tracy_tp @Tracy_White_ @tracyandmatt

Acknowledgments

@TracyBN @TracyBrinkmann @tracyclancy @tracydecicco @tracydiziere @TracyGazzard @tracyhiner @TracyLiebmann @tracyphaup @TracySayWhat @TracyStar @TracyWashington @traddr @TradeMavenPT @TradepalAustin @TradepalBoston @TradepalCLT @TradepalDallas @TradepalIndy @TradepalPhoenix @TradePlumbing @tradercatl @Traderjoe @TradersLog @TraderVisions @TradeShowIdea @TradesLive @tradespot_forex @tradingrichmom @TradUR @traffexone @Traffic_Binge @Traffic_Machine @traffic_queen @traffic2u4free @TrafficGenius @Trafficman60 @TrafficMastery @trafficmillsl @Trafficologist @trafficology @TrafficOnDemand @trafficoweb @TrafficPhill @traffictoolbelt @TrafficVault @trailrunnerz @Train4Employers @traindom @TrainerZack @TrainingCKaren @TrainingLoopy @trainingspuls @TrainWithMark @transContext @TRANSFORM_LIFE @transfx @transparenceweb @TransWorkflow @trappersherwood @travel_life @travel_lover @travel_notebook @traveladvicegal @travelblggr @travelbully @TravelCharme @TravelChatForum @traveldeals_usa @TravelDealsNet @traveldudes @TravelFollowers @TravelGator @TravelGoddess4u @travelgrdnsbuzz @TravelGuide_TV @Travelin_Papers @Travelingsingle @TravelingwSusan @Travelinsingle @travelisay @TravelLaneCo @travelmedia @travelnmood @travelonly_Greg @TravelOnPennies @TravelorShops @travelpodcast @traveln @TravelsInfo @travelsitel @traveltipsguy @traveltomaui @TravelToursNow @Traveltron3000 @TravelV @travelwithdayo @travelwithlisa @travelworldnow @travid @TravisASwain @travisfitzwater @TravisGreenlee @TravisHeinrich @TravisMoffitt @travisro @TravisSharp @TravisWallerCRS @TRAVSocialMedia @Traz38 @TrazgodKing @TRDonnelly @treasurecoachl @Treat_ADHD @TrebbauKoop @trebonasomreb @TreceDallas @treedup @treegiving @treehousei @TRENDadvisor @TrendAndBrand @TrendingCasts @trendsinfo @trendsmagparis @TrendTown @TrendTweeter @trentab @trentcox @tresahardt @TresCoach @TresRiosResort @tressalynne @TrevArmstrong @TreverMcGhee @TrevizoHarrin @TrevNetMedia @TrevorCoxen @trevordierdorff @TrevorSwampy @trevoryoung @TrevR @treydalton @treypennington @trgtricities @trialbyjury @TriBabbitt @tribeofnoise @TribeTuesday @Triboda @tribuffalo @Triciachat @triciakl0 @TriciaLJohnson @trickscorner @TricksnTips @trickytriskuts @Tricolor_FC @tricos_sascha @triercompany @TrieuNguyen @trifamenz @TrigamServices @TrillionStars @TrilogyPayment @TrimBellyOver40 @triMirror @Trina_Willard @TrinaClaiborne @TrinaKaMarie @TrinaWardell @TrinaWell @TRINI_ZUELEAN @Trinityhall @TrinityIns @trinityriver @trinsicnews @TriOdysseyGPS @TRIOmedia @TripDawg @TripDucky @triplemast @triplib @tripology @triponicom @trisamaliarnid @trish_forex @trish0400 @TrishaGary @TrishAJohnson @TrishBeach @TrishDonmall @trishlawrence @TrishsVoice @trishwalsh66 @triskinity @TriStaff @Tristan_Latge @tristanginnett @TristanrIC @TristaRodeo @TristateVW @TriTecLes @TRIUMPHLVHILTON @TriumphTitle @Trivani4Life @Triviable @TrivWorks @TRMeson @TRNUSA @TrollyNick @trompyx @TropicalDelight @tropicalgourmet @TropicalMBA @tropicalstormEA @tropigal @troxellsr @troyajohnson @TroyErickson @troyjensen @troylanderson @troynice @TroyPattee @TroyScheerTMG @trpixman @trpurcell @trsjobs @Truckdrivernews @TruckerDesiree @truckersteve @truckersutopia @TruckingSpace @truckingsuccess @TrueBY Kutylo @true_Simona @truebluepatriot @TrueLifeOfBrian @TrueLoveAfter40 @truenaturetrust @truenegative @TrueNorthCustom @TrueShare @TrueSocialMedia @trueUvoice @trugeml @TrulySocial @trumpglobal @TrumpMLMNetwork @trumpnetwrkbill @Trumpthat @Trumpuplinelst @truquality @truresidence @Trushphoto @TrustBranding @TrustedCoaching @trustednerd @trustedreferral @truststartshere @truth4girls @truthabs @TruthBellyFat @TruthMission @truthplane @TRW_CreditGroup @tryantiaging @Trybarefoot @TryBPO @tryin2getfollow @tryingthebiz @tryoneofakind @TrySofter @TrystIndonesia @TSC_Tweets @TSCB @tscochrane @tseamon @TSHaero @tshiunghan @tsieck @tsieger @TSINonprofit @TSONetwork @TSportsLegends @tsquest @TStanowski @TsunamiMNetwork @tsureto @TSXstockpicks @tszymanski @tt904 @ttalola @TTaunya @TTNTeam @ttrenz @TubacGolfResort @tubefilter @tubevideo @TubeYouVideo @tubgoddess @TuesdayTip @Tuffour @Tuffylynn @TugaK @tuija @TulaHotYoga @TulioRatto @tunes2901 @tunespill @TuneTalks @Tunetheradio @tungvnpt @Tuni @Tunis @tunisieweb @tunneltrilogie @TupperwareLady @turbol40 @turbobux @turbomarketing @turbomoneygener @TurboSMM @TurboTextAds @Turfetc @TurkishCoffeeUS @turkmadden @turnagingback @TurnKeyCoach @turnqCEO @TurnSocial @TurtleBayResort @tuscanblog @tushar @TUSIC @tutelage @TutorTina @Tutuca @TuvelComms @TVAspen @tvincome @tvpnr @TVSerials @tvshowcentre @TW_Design @Twl1tterDynamics @twl1tterschool @twae @Twaitter @twalaxy @twalkin @twalkr @TwaveITweeter @twaveltwita @twdpm @tweaknotes @Tweal_Estate @Tweash @tweasier @tweegoo @tweeneedajob @tweeple_adder @tweepmarketing @tweepmktg @tweepstats @Tweet_Center @tweet_flirt @tweet_my_biz @tweet_n_win @tweet_programs @Tweet_Twenius @Tweet4thecause @tweetadderdeals @tweetakademie @TweetAnnounce @tweetaprize @TweetasticBro @TweetAuto @TweetAutomator @tweetbird2 @TweetBizConsult @tweetboobdude @tweetcaroline @tweetcashing @tweetcashtools @tweetclean @TweetCoachNow @TweetComet @tweetcotton @tweetdal @TweetDeck @tweetdistrict @tweetdynamite @TweetEchos @tweetemplates @Tweeter2Help @tweeterdiva @tweetermeetings @tweetersforum @TweeterSteele @TweetExploders @tweetfestme @tweetformoolah @TweetHealthTips @Tweetin4Dummies @tweetinabe @tweetindollars @Tweeting_Angel @TweetingCHURCH @tweetingdeals @TweetingTools @tweetinspiratif @TweetItRight @tweetjosht @tweetjunky @tweetlaunch @Tweetlistix @tweetmaker @TweetmanGary @Tweetmatix @tweetmktng @Tweetmoneymoney @tweetmony @tweetmyjobs @TweetNoke @tweetomatic_de @TweetOnTheRun @TWEEToption @TweetOrTrick @tweetpaste @tweetpiggy @tweetproblems @TweetrafficEZ @tweetrandomizer @tweetreasures @TweetRiches @tweetrqueen @Tweets2Cash @tweets4living @tweetsandtwits @tweetsarmy @tweetsas @tweetsbotl @TweetsByUs @tweetsdollars @tweetsdrama @tweetsformoney3 @TweetsGoneMadUS @tweetsguru @tweetsmagic @TweetSmarter @tweetSponso @tweetsteve4cash @tweetsurge @TweetTankGold @tweetTankMktg @TweetTankpro @TweetTex @tweetthatpoll @tweetthisjob @TweetToKnow @Tweettwins @tweetuniversal @tweetupdirectry @tweetusoon @tweetusright @TweetVerve @tweetVIPmedia @tweetwarpspeed @TweetWeapon @tweetwithbob @Tweetz_traffic @TweetZAK @TweetZda @twentyfoursix @twetl01man @twetouch @twettank2gether @twetterfollow22 @Twexperimental @Twexponential @Tweye @twfaster @twhitaker1974 @TWhiteCreations @Twi_Star @twi5 @twibackerSticker @twideoguide @Twience @Twifoo @twiglgy @twiiterguide @Twikimter @Twilight_Tweetz @TwilightContest @TwilightDesk @twilightsernet @twillydy @twilmott @twimarketing @Twincitysam @TwinklesJewels @Twinnovate @TwinPeaksTravel @twistedlime @Twit_Expert @Twit_Jam @Twit2000Barrier @twitatonui @twitB4U @twitbefriend @TwitBizDay @TwitCashExpert @Twitching Puppie @twitduir2000 @twiteconomy @TwiterHero @twiteristic @twiterpro4me @twitersecret @twitfanta @twitfools @twitgoldmine003 @twithawk @Twithearl @twithope @twitingly @TwitJobsLondon @TwitjobsUK @TwitJumpGuest @twitlinker @TwitMlmTools @TwitMuscle @Twitr_Addict @twitreferral @TwitRestaurants @twitrfuel @TwitROLGolfers @twitRocket @twitrpros @Twitsphere @twitstat @twitt_erfolg_de @twitt_erlytix @Twitt_inator @twittablestuff @TwittaBling @twittank @twittcoach @TwittConv @Twittegy @TwitterFollower @twittforprofit @twittin4job @twitting_lawyer @TwittInsider @TwittInsights @twittinvestor @twittloans @TwittMasterGold @twittme_mobi @Twittoing @twittprofit @twittsifu @twitttolllower @twitty7x @twittycash @twiturmarketing @twitwebtester @Twix_Fits @Twixcel01 @twizzersays @TWJCOHA @twletsmakemoney @twmel @twocupsconnect @twodigitworld @twollow @twoofusorg @TwooTools @TwoRowsGrille @TWOwomenANDaHOE @twpq @TYMR_Insights @TwtGuy @TWTRCON @twtrmoneyl @TwtrPro @TwtrReviews @TwtSecrets @twtultimatebody @Twunique @twuttevaer @twyingout @tx_vacation @TXBirder @txconflictcoach @txdistancerider @txdivadoll @TXEric @txGarage @TXGrandpa @TxJogger12 @TXLoneStarStaff @txmama @TXMortgages @txmusicchannel @TXRealtorl @txroadshow @TXStopShopTheStng @TxTough @TxtSpecs @Txtworks @TyBennett @tydomain @TyDowning @tyhychi @tyler6914 @tylerbel @TylerDurbin @tylerforsberg @TylerFyke @tylergray @TylerLClark @tylersmiller_ @tyoguritno @typeamom @typelabs @typepad @typingbug @TyroneAmerine @tyrstag @tysalliance @tzabaoth @U_Laugh @U_M_A_H @U_together_moon @u2cjb @u4wealth @UAMSlibrary @uber_apparatus @ubercool @ubergio @Uberoom @UBF_ @ubiquitousrat @UBuyUSA @uc2i @ucminfo @UCSDExtFarnan @UCYIMD1 @udaypalsingh @UdcBadiaPol @UEvents @ufginfo @ufgmandura

185

The Social Media Business Equation

@UGDT @uggbootshop @uggsonline @ugotmojo @ugraesser @ugurarcan @UHartfordNews @uhavebeenserved @uiandme @UIdahoNews @UISCareerCenter @uitysan @uk_landlord @UK_Medical_Jobs @UK_SEO @ukelia @Ukenings @UKJobTweets @uklandforsale @UKPostbox @UKprecision @ukpremier @ulcma @UlrikeGerloff @ultimateAleks @ultimategadgets @ultoday @ultranex @ultras03 @umairkundi @umarnasir @umarvadas @Umattan @UmbertoTassoni @umbz @UMHB @Umma_Do_Breeze @UMUTULASER @Un_reality @UnaMamaConHijas @UnattendedMin0r @unbounce @UncleBobCW @UncleBobsTitle @UncleRick @UncleVicDeals @uncomman @undauctions @UnderAssault @Underbundle @Undercover @UndergradReview @undergroundmk @UndertheDave @UnderTheSunShop @undinecoaching @UndiscoveredStx @undo0720 @UNDRGROUNDHERO @unemployedsucks @unfairconcealin @unfollowtuesday @unhatched @UniBulMrcntSvcs @unified360 @Unikatemarkt @unilyzer @UniqueArticles @UniqueSynergy @UniqueVitamins @Unisfair @Unisys_Careers @unitedcb @UnitedTraining @unitedwaydaneco @UnitedWayNola @unitweeter @UniversalAcct @UniversityVisit @unkleEL @unkn0wnq @unlimited1044 @UnlimitedUsage @UNLOCKmagazine @UNLVtickets @Unreal_G @UnrealCafe @unseenrajasthan @Unsinkable3 @UnsolvedArtifax @UnsolvedMurders @unstickingcoach @UntilimInCharge @Unuruu @unwindbeverage @UofCincyAlumni @UofHartford @UOWHO @uphoria @upicks @upiqcom @UpMo @UPNEPA @uponabranch @uponrequest_oc @UPS_FAIL @UpsideUp @upstartbootcamp @Upstatemamma @upthevortex @UptownLaserSkin @uqie @urban_mode @Urban_Springs @urbanapartments @UrbanDecorSue @UrbanElementIN @Urbanidad @urbanprojectz @urbansmiler @urbanverve @urbiztopranked @urbnlatinoradio @UrFamilyLivin @urgent_tweets @URHealthy2 @urizeldman @urjobcouldbnext @Urlar @URManEnough1 @urmomeatsglass @ursanju @UrviMehta @urwealthwizard @usa_wealth @usACTIONnews @USAirlinePilots @usamaverick @USANAwealth @USAShopper @USATweetMeets @usbargains @uscapa @USchirodirect @uschles @USCRUDEOIL @usdmnet @usedequipments @usefultools @UsefulWebApps @useglobalreach @USfestival @USHAREIMG @UshaSliva @ushealthcrisis @Usidus @USJ778 @usmale55 @usmanzk @usnavyseals @USNMcKinney @usopenofsurf @USOpportunities @USPassenger @ustaymotivated @UStrafficschool @USvisaEasy @utah_analytics @utahaccounting @utahREpro @utahwsoccer @UTAJETS @utamavirod @utcampusdeals @UTCoverage @UTDBananaKiller @UTDiTella @utegoebels @UteWKing @uthomas68 @utoh @UtopiaComm @Utopical @Utrecht_Art @utterhip @uuimages @Uurte @uVizz @uwelang @UWOrat @uxmag @v_shakthi @VIOLETTE @VA_IT_Jobs @va_mommy @VA_Office @va4hire @vabisin @vacation4 @VacationHmQueen @VacationInfo @vacationkids @vacationnetwork @vacationtribe @VacenTaylor @VAConnections @VacTimeshareRen @vadesktop @VADuff @VAerin @Vagabondangler @vagabondvistas @VAGirlFriday @Vaiebhav @VAinParadise @ValBloomberg @Valee_Bieber @ValeGRRR @valentineblog @valentinedolce @valentinesstore @valeomarketing @valericcione @Valerie2u @ValerieFM80 @valeriemerrill @valerienichols @ValerieSimon @valgoodman @valiantmedia @valkhot @vallarda @valleriastracha @ValleryGraham @valmg @ValPopescu @ValuePagesGroup @valukao2 @Valuu_xD @ValveInteract @VAmatchmaker @Vambry @vampirezoey @vamsri @VanajaGhose @vanbarreto @vanbergeijk @VandaLynnHughes @vandenboomen @vandexter @VandiverGroup @Vanessa_Green @vanessasanger @vanetworking @vangole @Vanguard_M_G_T @vanialex @VanillalceKid @vannjeffreys @vanSpriing @VanstageBiz @VantageIT1Jobs @VantagePointCRM @VanWestCoastBC @Vanygirl @vanyyy @VaproTweets @varchassri @VArenovations @varinder_seo @various5 @varjuluceno @VarsityBuys @varsitytutors @varunsundar @vascosoares1 @VASERPro @vashtihorvat @Vasilius @vasimpleservice @VAsolutionsNOW @Vassist @VastgoedDirect @VastInIncome @VaszaryGabor @VaultComm @VaultCSR @vavangue @vayvi @vb2ae @vbehzadi @VBoynton @vbsondemand @VCI_helps @vcordo @vcubeusa @vddingman @VDmitruk @vdub01 @vedo @veeh1 @veg3l1 @VegaLawyer @Veganmainstream @VegasBiLL @vegasblender @VegasCLEARguy @VegasHouseSale @VegasNewsFlash @Vegaspromo @VegasStilettos @vegasventures @VegetarianInfo @VeggieGrill @vegtv @vejalagos @VeJason @VeloraStudios @Veloview @VELTINSarena @velvetskirt @vemmakids @vemmasa_verve @Vendegvaro @VendorSourcing @VenueGen @venusvision @verdandisquidoo @Vered @Veredusatl @VeretaLee @VergeConsulting @verhaall40 @Veribatim @Veritas_Design @verkauffoerdern @verkoren @VerndaleTweets @VernonDavis @vernongirl @VernonMack @veronica_duran @VeronicaHay @VeronicaTanBK @VeronikMartinz @Veroniqque @Versatron @Versicherungsde @versustv @Vertizy @VerveCards @VerveHealthyNRG @Very1967 @VeryCherryCoCo @vest31 @vestival @VeteranWarrior @vetsurvivor @vexxyjenna @vfsdark @vfthjournals @VGalFriday @vgardening @VHenry @VHTrabosh @Vhutchisoncoach @viable4u @viaddress @Viadeo @Viakeywest @viaMelissa @vianovagroup @vibesandstuff @Vibracoes @VibrantSpirit @vibsters @vic_cholet @vicbarrera @vicentesaraiva @vices @viciousvst @Vicki_in_Greece @vicki_s_young @vickicaruana @Vickie_Sayce @Vickie_Smith @vickiebadams @vickietolbert @VickiHiggins1 @vickijjasper @vickis36 @vickisalemi @vickiscannon @VickiSouthard @VickiZerbee @VickyHennegan @VickyLaney @vickylyn @viclibos @vicmangino @vicnuge @VicoRockMedia @victor_chan @victor_cheng @Victor_Go_Ham @VictorAntonio @victoreegadgets @victoreme @VictorGanan @victoria_stone1 @victorianetc @victoriarealtor @victoriashortt @victorliew @VictorOcampo @victorpagan @victorvigil @Victory_Credit @victorynjc @VictoryTavern @vidcom @Video20Q @VideoArmy @videocop @VideoEmail75 @VideoGuruToon @videohustling @VideoMafia @videoministry @videonacho @videophonervp @videoryan @VideoSales9 @videosocialcode @videoturf @vidmagmedia @vidmarketing1 @vidpr @VidPromotion @vidyasdesai @viensa @vieodesign @vietnamesegirls @vietnammobi @ViewsportNetwork @ViewTV @viikassood @VijayThangaraja @vikasjee @vikaskumar @vikassen @vikingkat @ViktoriaFoxx @ViktorLantos @Vilallonga @villageous @VillageShopping @VillainOrHero @VillaO_Dallas @VillTweet @vimel @Vimentis @VinayPaturu @Vince_Craine @VinceAllen @vincebaker @VinceBerthelot @vincedeon @VinceMayfield @Vincent_Ang @VincentAdams @VincentColes @VincentL @VincentMuir @VincentParker @vincentsmit @vincentvandam @vincentvhelle @vincentwhite @vindia @vineetsblog @vinestockUSA @viniciusbidarte @vinmegar @VinnieVasquez @VonThoth @Vino Thorsen @vinsalm @VinSolutions @VintageBelt @VintageBelts @ViolaEllsworth @VioletCaren @Vioroso @VIPazzi @VipeCanada @VIPlifestyle @viprealtydfw @vipregan @vipromoters @vipselling @vipspams @VipSports @viptalent @vipulananda @VIPVirtualSols @VIPwealthclub @viralclix @viraler_effekt @viralfirefly @viralhive @viralmarketing9 @viralmarketmom @viralspirals @viraltubedotnet @VirendraSEO @Virgin_Islands @virginiagaga @virginiog @Virideth @virtnews @virtualblessing @VirtualCloud_ @virtualewit @virtualiano @virtuallinda @VirtuallyAmaz @virtualyideal1 @virtuallyready @VirtualMarketer @VirtualOfficeB @virtualpm @VirtualSocial @virtualtea @virtuouswoman25 @vishalgarora @vishalgondal @visiatotravel @Vision_21 @Vision4Standard @VisionarySpirit @VisionTech_2015 @VisionTwits @visionwebnet @visit_dallas @VisitGalena @VisitGalenaOrg @VisitGBI @visitmytown @visitpuretravel @visomusic @VistageKC @VistaGoHomestay @visualartsaggie @VisualElite @VisualMap @VisualMediaPro @visualphone @vitalityrocket @vitalnutrients @VitalOxide @vitaltweets @vitalyvt @Vitta360Global @VivaViaNomads @VivekavonRosen @vivianb53 @vivianemacedo @vivianltk @VividEpiphany @VividMarketing @vivienneho @VivitaGirl @vivvos @vixwrld @viziondanz @VizzTone @VJLasorsa @VJVazquez @vknipper @VKovalenko @vladikus999 @VladimrC @vladonpoker @vlavlavla @vlddilv @vlemx @vlogtedio @vmarketingguru @vmcmurray @VmealsBoston @VMPCC @vmsajan @vnetpulse @VOAGNO @vocetweets @Vodbay @voice_Boks @voiceoftexas @voilalalal @VoipComputer @VoipConference @VoIPStartsHere @vojago @volcom_sa @VolkerRupprecht @Vollkin @vollmerpr @VolntrMilwaukee @volodiakamenniy @voltrezman @Volumehive @volvoshine @volnauff @VonGenFCG @vonkakus @VonReventlow @Voorsteegh @vorigelevens @Voslin @Vote4Wallace @VoteGlobalPolls @VoteMattSchultz @votenet @votescotttaylor @VoxOptima @VProcunier @vpsean @vpvertti @VR4SmallBiz @vredeals @vrental @VRIDETV @vrojas70 @vrsocialmedia @vrwd @vscribe @vsells @vshimoyama @vshivone @vsNEWS @VsTheDailyLine @VSWoodPsyD @vtorresmx @VTravelTours @vtwit4u @vvinsuranceguru @VWworld @vyouz @ViralMarketing @vyuh_in @VZWChandler @W_C_marketing @W_Debauchez @W_Paul_Williams @W_Rutledge @w0rdpress @w2e @w2Fund @w2scott @W2WIT @w3buck @waahootravel @waalston @Wacoboard @wadebroder @wadeburgess @wadever @WaferTango @wagandt @wagerking @wah4life @wahagain

Acknowledgments

@wahbi63 @wahgypsy @WahMagzine @wahoocandyman @wakeup2life @wakooz @Wakooz_RSS @Wakooz_RSSfeeds @waku_waku @walaaumedia @Waldo_Bar_None @waldowaldman @Wales_Online @walidmrealtor @WalkerTaft @WalkerWork @walkies1 @Walking1974 @walkscotland @WalkwithSally @wallglamour @WallopOnDemand @Wallpapers_Cool @WallSt_Surfers @WallStGames @wallstickersau @wallstpick @WallStreetGrand @WalMartFreedomC @walshcollege @walshypop2010 @walter_fischer @WalterAacf @WalterGordy @walterkb79 @WalterRose @waltonsearch @Wandafay @WanderingWilbo @wanderlustmktg @Wandia_Info @wantandblog @Wanting2Succeed @wanttogetfree @waqas6 @Warcraft_Guides @WarcraftMastery @WardBurksPD @warkmalsh @WarnerCarter @warosesr @warrencass @WarrenMason @WarrenPeas @WarrenTan @WarrenWhitlock @warriorlight @wasisg @waspdesign @Wasteawaygroup @waterdesign @WaterwayRealty @WatkinsLadybeth @WattersCreek @WattsKidsNews @WaveScript @WavesGratitude @waxing_lounge @waybackengine @Wayne_Belair @Wayne_D_Brown @Wayne_Faye @Wayne_Walker @wayne1120 @wayne1169 @wayne1hutchins @WayneBreitbarth @WayneHurlbert @WayneMansfield @WayneMarr @waynermb @waynevaughn @WayoftheWizard @wayrustic @WBaranowski @wbaustin @WBHBoston @wbidiwale @wbill1 @wbrnet @wbryuocc1684 @WCCOBreaking @wclements @WComGroup @wcs2 @wcweeks @wcwellness @WDCB @wdccdisney @WdenTonkelaar @wds7 @WDT_Schubert @WDYC @We_bestseller @We_Recommend_ @weakwolves @wealth_builder7 @Wealth2050 @WealthBuilderNY @wealthbuilding @wealthbychoice @wealthcreation9 @WealthEvite @WealthForTeens @WealthForYou @wealthtoday @WealthyAfiliate @wealthysmurf326 @WealthyState @wearesocial @WeAreTheTopTeam @WeatherPlanet @WeaverContent @WeaversWay @web_host_info @web_news @web_preneurs @web_wacko @web2_smm @web20_marketing @web2client @Web2Greg @web2guru @web2rule @web2summit @Web4pointO @WebAdMetrics @WebAdvantage @webalicious @webanatics @WebBadgerBrock @webbizceo @webbizmarketing @WebBusinesses @WebBuyz @WebcastCity @webchurchgbg @WebConnect411 @webcurl @webdefenders @WebDesign_info @WebDesign6 @webdesignfan @webdesignleads @WebDesignPeoria @WebDivaAshley @WebDonuts @WebErika @webermedia @WebExperiment @webfaststart @WebForceOne @WebFugitive @webgabs @WebGeekPH @WebGossip @WebGridAds @webheadservice @WebHealthClinic @WebHealthMag @WebHost697 @webhostdir @webi5 @Webinetry @WebinetryJA @webinfomktg @webist @Webjutsu @weblaunches @WeBlogtheWorld @WebMallOnline @WebMarketing123 @webmarketingmav @webmasterananya @webmasterfr @webmastergeek @webmastersc @webmastery @webmediaexpert @WebmetricsSpain @webmktinggroup @WebMktrsSpk @webnextstep @WebNoos @webomac @weboptimiser @weborglodge @WebPaz @webpos @webpresencewiz @webprofitz @WebPRpro @webrecruit @WebrecruitJobs @webresident @webs_craic @websatan @websavvymoms @WebScheduling @WebsElevators @websitedevel @websitegratuit @websiteinfo4U @Websites4Result @websitesdotcom @websitessoft @websmith1 @websnacker @websocialmediaM @WebSolarStore @websolutions1 @WebStatements @WebStrategyShop @websuccessdiva @WebSuccessGurus @websuccessideas @webtechblog @webtickle @Webtique @webtrafficnet @webtrepreneur @WebTVWire @webtweetwizard @webvideocoach @WebVideoMax @WebVideoVenture @webws @webyogi @Webzie @WECAl @WeCanDoItFRW @weddingflorist @weddingsbytracy @weddingz @WedgeLee @wedirectllc @wednesdayadams1 @weedott @WeejeeMedia @WeekDate @weeklyroast @weeklystandard @WeeklyWebinar @Weezawear @WeGayFriends @wehype @WeightCoach4U @WeightForAge @WeightLoss1st @WeightLoss86 @WeightLossFit @weightlosshelpr @WeightlossKing2 @WeightOffDude @weightprograms @WeightWatchers @WeightWatchers_ @weimin2008 @weiran_li @weirdchina @weirdchina2 @weirdnews @WeirdNewsForU @weirdralph @weissallison @WeiYoongLim @weknowmore @welchdavid @welinamia @welintonlori @welittler @wellbeinglive @wellface @wellness_guide @wellness4all @wellnessbill @wellnessblast @wellnessdestiny @wellnessexpo @WellnessNut @WellnessSpa24 @Wellsleypark @welltalkradio @WellWire @welovejbyeah_x @WeLoveSoapsTV @wenbryant @wendell_1980 @WendiMooreAgncy @Wendistry @wendroffcpa @wendy_moore @wendycwilliams @wendyflanagan @wendygelberg @WendyLFlynn @wendymarx @WendyMaynard @WendyMeuret @WendyMLMSinger @Wendytaylor01 @wendyweiss @WeNetProfit @WenHud @wentzeldk @WePostMedia @WeppoCom @WEPromote @weRaustin @weRhouston @Werkadoo @WernerKamphuis @WesBo @weseebusiness @wesellnmail @wesjohnson8 @weskriesel @WesleyHendriks @westeross @WestHorse @westkirbysailin @westonwoodward @WestSoundTech @WestVil @Westwindsa @WetFeet_Career @wettgiggles @wewantitall @WeyLessNow @WezPyke @WFAAalexa @wfaaizzy @wfaashelly @wfmkt @WFP @WFTVShows @wgaultier @wgcommunities @wgooden @wgpasunny1100 @wh_education @wh_health @WH2OLE @whackonly @Whale2020 @Whaleoil @WhatamanJackson @whatawebsite @whatchawearing @WhatIsOnNet @whatloversdo @whatma @WhatOdor @WhatsHappN @WhatsHappnRVA @WhatsHappnVA @whatshedoinnow @whatskochin @whatsthepoint_ @whattoknow @whatwecallarose @WHBsolutions @whchaminda @wheatgrassplace @wheatlands @wheelchairsteve @wheelchiro @wheelcipher @whentoyzattack @wheredallas @Whereisannabel @whereivebeen @whereNewOrleans @whereRyou @WHHG_InMotion @whichforex @whichwich @WhichWichDFW @WhichWichHou @WhistlerGroup @WhistleTweets @whitehatmedia @whitehausny @WHITEMAJOR @WhiteWallsArt @whitgorham @whitneypannell @WhitRecruiter @whitsundays @WhittleHomSecu @Whodeeni @whoisandywarner @whoisjob @WhoIsRickBerg @WhoIsWaterman @whojin @WholeFoods @WholeFoodsDFW @wholesaleautos1 @Wholesalebrands @WholesaleJohn @wholesalemaster @wholesaler @wholeself @whomq @WhoopDays @whoopsitweeted @whorunsgov @whosbackstage @whosChrisHughes @whosty @WhosYourAnnie @WhoYaWearin2day @whoyouhatin @WhyGeorge @WhyProperty @WhyReese @whySquidoo @whywetweet @Wi_FiMAN @wickedjava @WickedSunny @WiderScreenings @wifeycha @Wig_Superstore @wigoutnow @WigSuperstore @wiil101 @wiifanatic @wiinpon @wikiHow @WiLawAnjel @Wild_Chloe @wildcatloren @WildcatWire @wildeidea @wilderinbound @wildhipichld @wildinspire @wildlifeaid @WildlySuccesful @WildMountain @WildPeekDesign @wildskye @WildwatersLodge @WildWebWomen @wildwestbob @WilElliott @WileyVCH @wilhelser @wiliamkill @Will_Hanson @will_ran @WillBerthiaume @willbobby @Willdobbs @willemrt @WillEnglishIV @willfrancis @william_lee @williamarruda @WilliamAston @WilliamBforLess @WilliamBrant @WilliamCoquerel @williamEd1975 @WilliamLark @WilliamLohse @williamoo06 @williampbarnes @WilliamRamirez6 @williamroe @williamscott1 @WilliamsKim @WilliamWomack @williebaronet @willierandle @WillieStylez @williger @WillisClark @willisteam @williwyss @WilKumy @willofnature @willowyspirit @WillPao @WillPaysTheBill @WillRogersUSA @willstaney @willylim @WillyWonksUF @wilmallan @wilmer2004 @WilsonBooo @wilywenches @wilwomanderman @Win_Control @win_together @Win2012GOP @Windbaron @windlegends @Windova @windowshop_mt @WindowsHowToDo @WindPowerSystem @windsorarms @WindsorHills4u @WindsorHillsClb @windycitysocial @Wine_Connection @WINE_DINE @wine594 @wineauctioneer @winedinners @WineDiverGirl @Winedustry @WineInside @WineMcGee @wineOmoms @WineOnTheVine @wineportfolio @winerecipes @WineReview @WinesCom @WineSouthAfrica @winetrends @WineTwits @WineWithTheGuys @winnevents @Winning_MLM @winninghelix @winnitcouk @WinnWins @winsoar @Winst_Inc @winstontaylorUK @WintersOnline @winwithsue @Wipro @WireACake @wiredmessenger @wiredmoms @wireheadlance @wireless_phones @WirelessButler @winjetzthier @wisdom @wisebread @WiseDreams @wisematize @Wisepreneur1 @WiseQuotes_ca @Wisestepp @wisewomanwoods @Wish2Earn @wishes2u @wishnie @wishopen @witqld @wits29usa @wittlake @wizardgold @wizardofwords @wizardssecret @WizardSurf @WizardUbiz @Wize_Print_AZ @wjaegel @wjasynthesis @WjyMPk @wlockhart @wlstreet @WLVideoMessages @WM_Recordings @wmcommunities @wmdean @WmJHartman @WMMadv @wmwinc @wnabcreative @Wntz @woaikjkong @Wolak_Interiors @wolfepk1 @wolfie3556 @Wolfram2112 @WolfwoodXLV @womanbehappier @Womanifesting @Womanocracy @WomansDay @WomansWealthA @women_power @Women_Worldwide @womenbizlisting @WomenGunOwners @WomeninCrimeInk @WomenProNetwork @womenrepublic @WomensCampaign @WomensLingerie @womensproducts @womentorz @womenwhowine @WominBiz @WOMWorldNokia

The Social Media Business Equation

@WonderfulCA @WonderNBeAmazed @Wonderwordy @WonderWy @WoNoJo @WoodAtterWolf @WoodenBearCabin @Woodenhawk @Woodfloorpro @woodkatm @Woodland_Ridge @woodlandslawyer @woodswine @woodworkingsite @woofcp @woofette30 @woohoo56 @wookiemunch @wordchick @WordFrame @WordFromWISt @wordmartini @WordofChrist @wordondernemer @wordpress_on_ms @WordpressPlug @WordPressWizard @WordRock @Words101 @WordsBySusan @wordsdonewrite @wordsideas @WordStream @Wordstrumpet @wordupworld @wordwrangler @wordywoman @work8homesucces @workathomejoe @workathometips @WorkCoachCafe @WorkDayRadio @workfmhomeDiva @workforceremix @workforvacation @workfromhome4u @workhomexpert @WorkInColour @workingnature @workingvirtuall @workinseo @worklawyer @workmind @workNOLA @works_from_home @WorkTubeCV @workwithdave @workwithorlando @WorkWithSusanna @workwithted @World_of_DMCs @WorldAccToWelch @worldatlasman @worldbeats1 @WorldBlicx @WorldBlotter @Worldclass52 @worldcrisisbook @worldcruiser09 @Worldhotels @worldimart @WorldinMotion @WorldNewsNet @worldnibber @worldofmarble @WorldofTea @worldpokerforum @WorldProNews @WorldStuffer @WorldSymbols @worldup @WorldUtopia @WorldVisa313 @WORLDWIDEELITE @worldwidescam @WormScoop @Worob @wouldee5150 @woutervannierop @wowawebdesign @WOWbroadcasting @woweeone @wowtvmobile @Wp_Indeed @wp7dev @wpbc @wpdealshare @wphash @wpinasecond @wpinternational @wpmuorg @wpramik @wpside @wpsmash @WPstaff @wrecycleit @wreichard @wrestlingandy @wright1foru @wrightreverend1 @WRiskManager @Write_GetPaid @WriteAdvantage @writebuy @writefly @WriteNowOP @writer_sheri @writer2go @writerauthorart @WriterChanelle @WriterChick47 @WriteResearch @WritersBlog @WritersRelief @writingfriend @WritingonLife @writtenbeat @wrldinformation @wrox @wrross1 @wrzscene @WS49Texan @WSBTalkRadio @WSE123 @wsh5 @wsidom @wsinetpower @wsionlinebiz @WSIWebScience @WSPA_Germany @wswarm @WtLossDoctor @WTNonline @wtoppert @wturnhout @Wulffy @Wulfmansworld @Wuxflux @wvanderbloemen @wvierra @WVIW @wvrknight @wvtwinklestar @wvwater @wwcasey @wwediting @wwmpc @WWMPC_CEO @wwrcoach @www_cinri_com @wwwabidin @wwwIMtoolbox @wwWomenNetwork @wwwPoet @wwwwinwithsueco @wyattbrand @wycombeweb @WyoMom @wysebrasil @wyvernaxe @wzzm13 @X10Rommel @x11r5 @XanderBrown @xanderkitty @XanderPLT @xanpearson @XavierMann @xaviermir @XavierNelson @xavlur @xavmonty @xBeckkks @xbitbird @xbitech @XBox360Free @xboxfreepoints @xCassandraClark @xcastorx @XcelAccounting @xcheater @xcheyanx @xclusiveflyers @xebwilson @xeduarda @Xeesm @xEmmaGibneyx @XenonAsh @XeroError @xerrex3 @XerRexDgrey @XERXESSS @xFranco @xgineer @xiam007 @xiaojing_chen @ximenarojas @XkikaXfran @xkinetic @Xlead @xlnation @xlntcommunicate @xMellyJayne @xmizanx87 @XO7Brainiac @xobione @xobni @Xocailchocolate @xodpod @XOJAPAN @xowiipro @XowiiTopteam @XPACS_CEO_Scott @xpatcost @xpressabhi @Xpressomarketin @XpressURNess @xQmail @XRobinson @xscenemidgetx2 @xspond @xtofke @Xtreme_Bieber @xtrememarketer @xtremepicks_com @XtremePowerPC @XuanYA @xurxovidal @xuxamonangereal @xxBeckinessxx @XxEmOShOrTyXx @xxIpay123 @xxrhodamyrnaxx @xxThalyxx @xxxlingerie @ya2sabe @yabar @YabberDigital @Yabogat @YachtsByAce @Yahoo_Fanz @YahooAdBuzzCA @YahooJobs @yahuauctions @YahyaHenry @yalechk @Yalitze @YamahaCommAudio @yamdelacruz @YaminiBhatt @YanceyG @yancyscot @Yangutu @yanisa5 @YannickvdBos @YanRozovsky @yanuzzi @Yapparent @Yapparently @yapstream @yardbird1964 @yardlighting @YasirKhan @YasminAishah @yasminbendror @yasniMe @yayson2masde10 @Yasser_Vidal @yassi2009 @yawarecords @YayForFollowing @yayokay @YazTay @ybillingslea @ycdwyl @ycika01 @ycng @YCTtx @yeahem @YearOfAffiliate @yellowdogPG @yellowsuits @YellowtailFP @yisusreynaldo @ykmrsw @Ylice @ylingz @yllib @ymangum @ymyconav @YNHMedia @yoBarney @YODspica @YODspica_Best @Yoep_com @yoga_mama @YogaArmy @YogaBistro @yogaheals @YogaNewsNow @YogaUpdates @yogeshgk @YohRach @yoichi0222 @yoitsadrian @yokuya @yolishemp @yoMansFeTisH @yomeocomunico @yominpostelnik @YongminJung @YoPopsDigzMe @YORanchSteaks @yorel95 @YosephCT @yoshuadaely @yosie23 @youarefiredboss @youarefoxy @YouAreMobile @youbring2 @YouEarn6Figures @youlooklikeshhh @youlsa @Young_and_Busty @youngandbrave @YoungAVONLady @YoungJBrooks @YoungLatinoNtwk @youngmankang @youngmax4 @youngmel @YoungYouCorp @YouniqueBiz @younmetweet @younyh @your_loans @Your_Say @Your8tweeT @YourAnxietyBlog @yourbadcredit @yourchapter11 @YourChessCoach @yourcrystalball @yourdailytask @YourDreamJob @YourEmployment @YourEzineCoach @YourFreeATM @yourgop @YourHeritage @YourHomeTeamAdv @yourjobmyoffice @YourLifeHappens @YourLittleAcre @yourLuxuryLANE2 @yourmentor08 @YourNeedToRead @yournetbiz42 @YourNetBizCafe @YouRockRadio @YourOrganicLife @YourPort @YourProfileNow @yoursalescopy @YourShoeStore @yourskinandmore @YourTechAdviser @YourtePrestige @YourVitaminLady @YourWaves @yourway2theweb @YourWebGuide @YourWriting @YourWritingDept @youthgrouptee @YouTractorCom @youtubeadvert @YoutubeGeeks @YoutubeHits @youtuberealest8 @Youvebeentagged @Yoyisdays @yoymer @YoYoYear2010 @YRSkudder @YRTMedia @ysabelvel @YSI @YTeutsch @ytomei @yukisek @yumichen @yumiliciouscup @YUNG_RICK @yungmemphis @YuriAll @yurself @yusep_aja @yuurn @yvettegr @yvonnecastr0 @YvonneKuypers @Yvonneloveslife @YvonneLyon @YvonneSanders @YvonneWolo @yweic @zaah @zablud @ZabreDVD @zacearly @Zach_Anderson @Zach_ary @ZacharyMeiu @ZacharySkinner @zachbow @zachhornsby @ZachSlobin @zack_miller @zackcovell @zackfreedman @ZackLuby @zaellen @zaffi @ZAGrrl @ZahidaKhan @zaibatsu @ZaibatsuPlanet @zaifmand @zainyk @zakaraya @Zakta @Zalisrg @ZamTravel @ZamZuuShopping @zaniaguy @zapalaAS @zappatier @Zartazan @zaruhablog @zarvo @zayuk @ZaZaDallas @ZaZaGallery @zazo @ZazZyu @zbeckman @zbegra @zbellak @zbest_global @ZBizforSEO @zbizinc @zbleumoon @zBusinessCoach @Zda144 @Zda145 @Zda146 @ZDa151 @ZDdesign @ze_machyne @ZE2Media @Zea_Restaurants @zeannjian @zebeauty @zebracross @zebrawear @zebrun @zebu75 @zecashtank @ZechParker @zedbiz @Zee_Hussain @zeebat @zeepha @ZeeVisram @ZeezleEarth @Zeitarbeit_Info @zeitgeist69 @Zelia @zemarketing @zenaweist @zenbeats @zenbitch @ZenDoc @ZenfulDance @zengal @zenofmba @zenorocha @ZENSUSHI @ZenTechMaster @zerenzitch @zer0friction @zeroDOTin @ZeroNineRacing @ZeroToRiches @zeus8894 @zhabuk @zhengjingjing96 @ZhuZhuHamsters @Ziing_dot_com @zijamoringa @zijisdemakelaar @Zimmermitch @zimpeterw @zininweb @ZINplicity @Zipab @ZipGiveSudbury @zippycart @ziptheusa @zirahnliz @ZKhan144 @ZnaTrainer @zoenewcombe @zoenfriends @ZoesDFW @zoeyshea @ZOMAGAZINE @ZombieRiot @ZombieStuff @zonabidesign @zonefraud @zonerdck @zonki @zonlyone @Zoom_1 @ZOOM7events @ZoomerangCJ @Zoomphed @zoomphotograph @zoomtechtv @ZoomTrendz @zoomzio @zoozli @zoranewyork @ZOS84 @ZoyaBurda @zritter @zudhy @zulemagvg @zulkar004 @ZurvitaShelley @zutroi @ZvonkoPavic @Zwinkycharacter @zyakaira @zyonhosting @Zystal @zytechx @ZZ0 @zzcrawfish @zzpboekhouder @ZZPnetwerk @zzpwerk

INDEX

21st Century Dental case
  study, 50–53
80/20 rule, 116–117

A

Aase, Lee, 19–22
The Adolphus Hotel case
  study, 84–87
advertising
  as dialogue, 5
  using social media for, 80
Amazon.com, reading
  reviews on, 15
Anheuser-Busch case study,
  27–30
audience, entertaining,
  121–123
Austin, Karen, 112–114
Avayou, Ruthy, 59

B

Beauty Cakes Cupcakes case
  study, 57–60
Black, Jay, 30

bloggers, recruitment by
  Sears, 108–114
Bodycology case study, 35–39
branding, using social media
  for, 80
Branson, Richard, 91
Burns, Colin, 25–26
business, asking for, 129. *See
  also* Social Media
  Business Equation
business needs
  21st Century Dental, 50
  The Adolphus Hotel, 84
  Anheuser-Busch, 27
  Beauty Cakes Cupcakes, 57
  Bodycology, 31
  CWW (Cable & Wireless
    Worldwide), 54
  The Fresh Diet, 99
  GM (General Motors), 93
  In the Know, 71
  James Wood Motors, 23
  Lane Bryant, 40
  Mayer Orsburn, Eve, 35
  Mayo Clinic, 18
  Pink Elephant, 104

Sears Blue Blogger Group, 108
Starwood Hotels and Resorts, 61
SU2C (Stand Up To Cancer), 88
The Women's Museum, 67

business results
21st Century Dental, 50–53
The Adolphus Hotel, 85–88
Anheuser-Busch, 28–30
Beauty Cakes Cupcakes, 57–60
Bodycology, 31–34
CWW (Cable & Wireless Worldwide), 54–56
The Fresh Diet, 99–103
GM (General Motors), 93–98
In the Know, 71–75
James Wood Motors, 23–26
Lane Bryant, 40–44
Mayer Orsburn, Eve, 35–39
Mayo Clinic, 18–22
Pink Elephant, 104–107
Sears Blue Blogger Group, 110–114
Starwood Hotels and Resorts, 63–66
SU2C (Stand Up To Cancer), 90–92
The Women's Museum, 67–70

C

Cable & Wireless Worldwide (CWW) case study, 54–56
Cabral, Fatima, 107
Cain, Kris, 112
call to action (CTA), 31–34

case studies
21st Century Dental, 50–53
The Adolphus Hotel, 84–87
Anheuser-Busch, 27–30
Beauty Cakes Cupcakes, 57–60
Bodycology, 35–39
CWW (Cable & Wireless Worldwide), 54
Eve Mayer Orsburn, 35–39
The Fresh Diet, 99–103
GM (General Motors), 93–98
In The Know, 71–75
James Wood Motors, 23–26
Lane Bryant, 40–44
Mayo Clinic, 18–22
Pink Elephant, 104–107
Sears Blue Blogger Group, 108–114
Starwood Hotels and Resorts, 61–66
SU2C (Stand Up To Cancer), 88–92
The Women's Museum, 67–70

CEOs (chief executive officers), interacting with, 130
CES (Consumer Electronics Show), 111–114
Clay, Kelly, 112
comments
as kernels of information, 79
reading about one's organization, 14–15
communication
art of, 123
human need to, 15–16, 124
impact of social media on, 7
via technology, 123
complaints, paying attention to, 79

consistency, importance of, 121
Consumer Electronics Show (CES), 111–114
conversation, one-on-one, 4. *See also* interaction; listening; talking
criticism, listening to, 16
CTA (call to action), 31–34
Curry, Haley, 69–70
customer service
leveraging social media for, 79–80
providing, 126–128
CWW (Cable & Wireless Worldwide) case study, 54–56

D
Davis, David, 85–86
Duchman, Zalmi, 99–100
Dunn, Jay, 41–42

E
Edwards, Andru, 112
entertaining audiences, 121–123
executive coaches, working with, 47–48

F
Facebook
The Adolphus Hotel, 86–87
Beauty Cakes Cupcakes, 60
The Fresh Diet, 102–103
Mayo Clinic, 21
SMD (Social Media Delivered), 37
Starwood Hotels and Resorts, 65
strength of, 6

feedback, paying attention to, 126
The Fresh Diet case study, 99–103

G
Gilbert, Jim, 102–103
GM (General Motors) case study, 93–98
goal fulfillment, using social media for, 81–83
groups, focusing on prospects in, 48–49
growth, monitoring, 80–81

H
Hatfield, Jenna, 112
Henderson, Fritz, 94, 96–97
Henige, Mary, 95
Huddle Productions, 28–30

I
In the Know case study, 71–75
industry trends, listening to, 13–14
information technology infrastructure library (ITIL), 104
Inside Curve network, 40–41
interaction
asking questions, 125
benefits of, 127–128
encouraging, 125
importance of, 123–128
See also conversation; listening; talking
Internet, strength of, 6
issues, solving, 80
ITIL (information technology infrastructure library), 104

J–K

James Wood Motors case study, 23–26
Knox, Jim, 28

L

Lane Bryant case study, 40–44
Learmonth, Michael, 44
LinkedIn
The Fresh Diet, 101–102
In the Know, 71–75
Mayer Orsburn, Eve, 35–37
listening
to comments about one's organization, 14–15
to comments about products, 15–16
to comments about services, 15–16
to criticism, 16
importance of, 12–13, 16–17
to industry trends, 13–14
See also conversation; interaction; talking

M

marketing, using social media for, 80–81
Mashable.com, 4
Mayer Orsburn, Eve case study, 35–39
Mayo Clinic case study, 18–22
McDaniel, Chad, 74
media, traditional forms of, 6–7
M.E.R. (McDaniel Executive Recruiters), 71

O

opposites attract, significance of, 48–49
organizations
21st Century Dental, 50
The Adolphus Hotel, 84
Anheuser-Busch, 27
Beauty Cakes Cupcakes, 57
Bodycology, 31
CWW (Cable & Wireless Worldwide), 54
The Fresh Diet, 99
GM (General Motors), 93
In the Know, 71
James Wood Motors, 23
Lane Bryant, 40
listening to comments about, 14–15
Mayer Orsburn, Eve, 35
Mayo Clinic, 18
Pink Elephant, 104
Sears Blue Blogger Group, 108
Starwood Hotels and Resorts, 61
SU2C (Stand Up To Cancer), 88
The Women's Museum, 67

P

party analogy, 17
personal relationships, essence of, 116–117. See also relationships
Pink Elephant case study, 104–107
PR (public relations), using social media for, 80–81
problems, solving, 80
products, listening to comments about, 15–16
promotions, using social media for, 80

Q

Qualman, Erik, 6

R

radio, strength of, 5
Ratcliffe, David, 104–107
relationships
asking for help in, 129
building, 120
See also personal relationships
return on investment (ROI),
achieving, 118
reviews
paying attention to, 79
reading on Amazon.com, 15
ROI (return on investment)
achieving, 118
measuring in social media,
133–137
Rozgonyi, Barbara, 112

S

sales, using social media for,
80
Schwartz, Yosef, 100, 103
Sci-Fi Channel, switch to
SyFy, 14
Scott, Craig, 86
Sears Blue Blogger Group
case study, 108–114
services, listening to com-
ments about, 15–16
SMD (Social Media
Delivered) Orsburn case
study, 35–39

social media

in communication, 8–9
converting to business, 116–117
in customer service, 8–9
deliverables, 8–9
growth of, 4–5
impact on communication, 7
leveraging for customer service, 79–80
in marketing, 8–9
measuring ROI in, 133–137
necessity of, 10
overview, 3–4
as a party, 17
setting goals to measure ROI,
133–135
strength of, 5–6
tracking goals for ROI,
134–136
uses of, 78
using for business, 47
using for company goal fulfillment, 81–83
using for marketing, 80–81
using for personal reasons, 47
Social Media Business
Equation
converting to business,
128–130
defined, 118
diagram, 119
effectiveness, 117–119
entertaining, 121–123
informing, 119–121
interacting, 123–128
See also business

social media solutions
21st Century Dental, 50
The Adolphus Hotel, 84
Anheuser-Busch, 27
Beauty Cakes Cupcakes, 57
Bodycology, 31
CWW (Cable & Wireless
  Worldwide), 54
The Fresh Diet, 99
GM (General Motors), 93
In the Know, 71
James Wood Motors, 23
Lane Bryant, 40
Mayer Orsburn, Eve, 35
Mayo Clinic, 18
Pink Elephant, 104
Sears Blue Blogger Group,
  108–114
Starwood Hotels and Resorts,
  61–63
SU2C (Stand Up To Cancer),
  88
The Women's Museum, 67
**social media vehicles, limit-
  ing, 136–137**
**South Beach Bed & Breakfast
  example, 134–136**
**specials, using social media
  for, 80**
**Starwood Hotels and Resorts
  case study, 61–66**
Stonestreet, Eric, 91
**SU2C (Stand Up To Cancer)
  case study, 88–92**

T

talking
at people, 3–5
with people, 3–5
See also conversation; interaction; listening

television, strength of, 6
Tierney, Maura, 91
**trends, paying attention to,
  79**
Twitter
21st Century Dental, 52–53
The Adolphus Hotel, 86–87
Beauty Cakes Cupcakes, 60
The Fresh Diet, 102–103
GM (General Motors), 95–96
James Wood Motors, 24
Mayo Clinic, 21
SMD (Social Media
  Delivered), 37
Starwood Hotels and Resorts,
  65
The Women's Museum,
  69–70

V

Virgin America, 88–92

W

Wallace, Ed, 94
websites
21st Century Dental, 50
The Adolphus Hotel, 84
Anheuser-Busch, 27
Beauty Cakes Cupcakes, 57
Bodycology, 31
Cain, Kris, 112
Clay, Kelly, 112
CWW (Cable & Wireless
  Worldwide), 54
Edwards, Andru, 112
The Fresh Diet, 99
GM (General Motors), 93, 97
Hatfield, Jenna, 112
In the Know, 71, 75
James Wood Motors, 23

Lane Bryant, 40
Mayer Orsburn, Eve, 35
Mayo Clinic, 18, 22
Pink Elephant, 104
Rozgonyi, Barbara, 112
Sears Blue Blogger Group, 108
SMD (Social Media
    Delivered), 37
Starwood Hotels and Resorts,
    61
SU2C (Stand Up To Cancer),
    88
The Women's Museum, 67,
    70

Williams, Amanda, 24–25
**The Women's Museum case
    study, 67–70**
Wood, James, 26

Y

Yates, Chris, 28
**Yelp, James Wood Motors
    case study, 25**
YouTube
    Mayo Clinic case study, 20
    statistics, 6